Teen Titans

DEATHTRAP

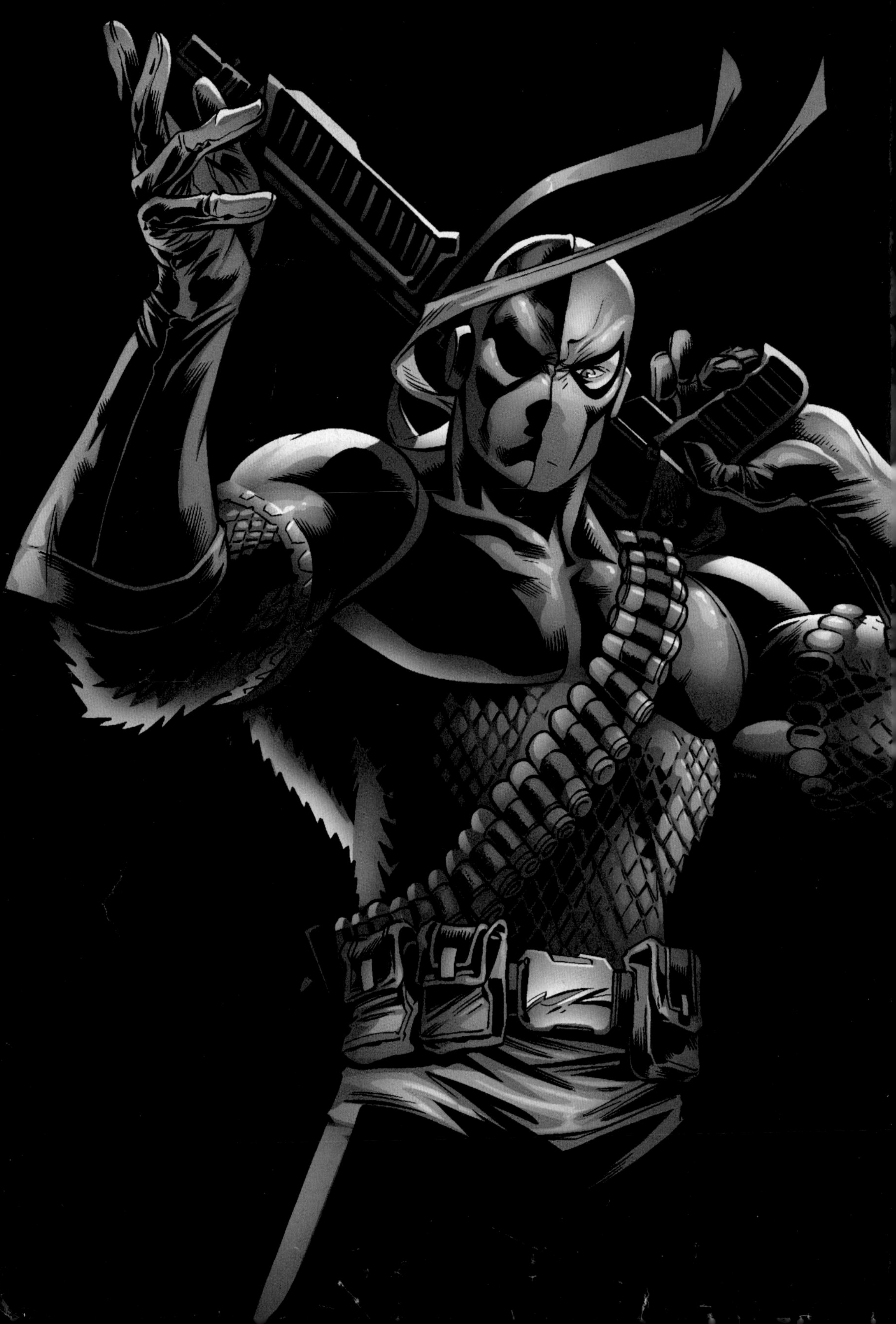

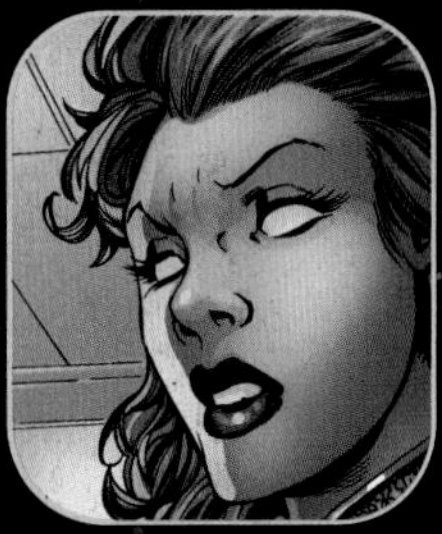

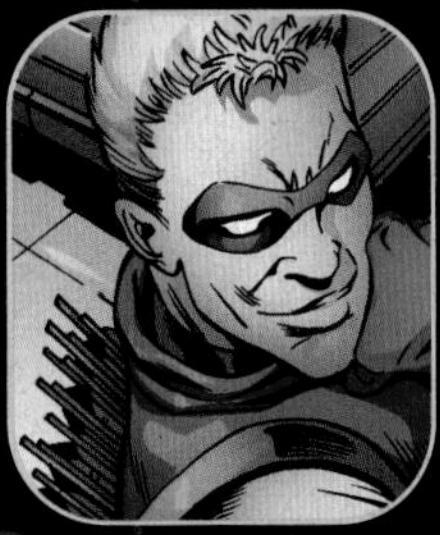

Teen Titans

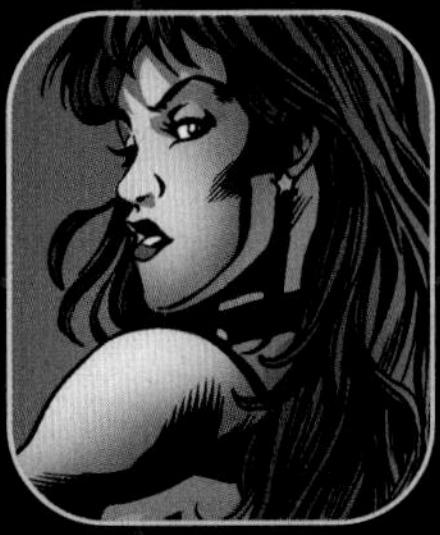

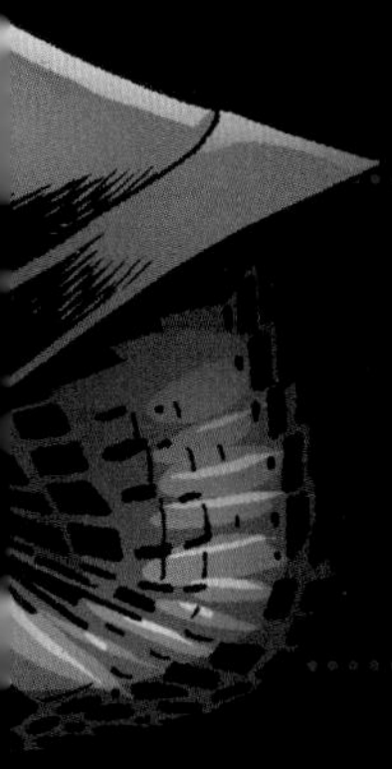

DEATHTRAP

Sean McKeever
Marv Wolfman
Writers

Fernando Dagnino
Rick Leonardi
Angel Unzueta
Tom Lyle
Joe Bennett
Pencillers

Raul Fernandez
John Stanisci
Wayne Faucher
Scott Hanna
Jack Jadson
Belardino Brabo
Inkers

Rod Reis
David Baron
Edgar Delgado
Hi-Fi Design
Colorist

Rob Clark Jr.
Steve Wands
Sal Cipriano
Letterers

Vigilante created by
Marv Wolfman
& George Pérez

Dan DiDio SVP-Executive Editor

Brian Cunningham Michael Siglain Editors-original series

Rex Ogle Harvey Richards Assistant Editors-original series

Georg Brewer VP-Design & DC Direct Creative

Bob Harras Group Editor-Collected Editions

Bob Joy Editor

Robbin Brosterman Design Director-Books

DC COMICS

Paul Levitz President & Publisher

Richard Bruning SVP-Creative Director

Patrick Caldon EVP-Finance & Operations

Amy Genkins SVP-Business & Legal Affairs

Jim Lee Editorial Director-WildStorm

Gregory Noveck SVP-Creative Affairs

Steve Rotterdam SVP-Sales & Marketing

Cheryl Rubin SVP-Brand Management

Cover art by **Eddy Barrows** and **Ruy José** with **Rod Reis**

TEEN TITANS: DEATHTRAP
Published by DC Comics. Cover, text and compilation
Copyright © 2009 DC Comics. All Rights Reserved.

DC Comics, 1700 Broadway, New York, NY 10019
A Warner Bros. Entertainment Company
Printed by World Color Press, Inc.
St-Romuald, QC, Canada. 11/04/2009
First Printing.
ISBN: 978-1-4012-2509-4

SUSTAINABLE
FORESTRY
INITIATIVE

Certified Fiber
Sourcing
www.sfiprogram.org

Fiber used in this product line meets the sourcing requirements
of the SFI program. www.sfiprogram.org PWC-SFICOC-260

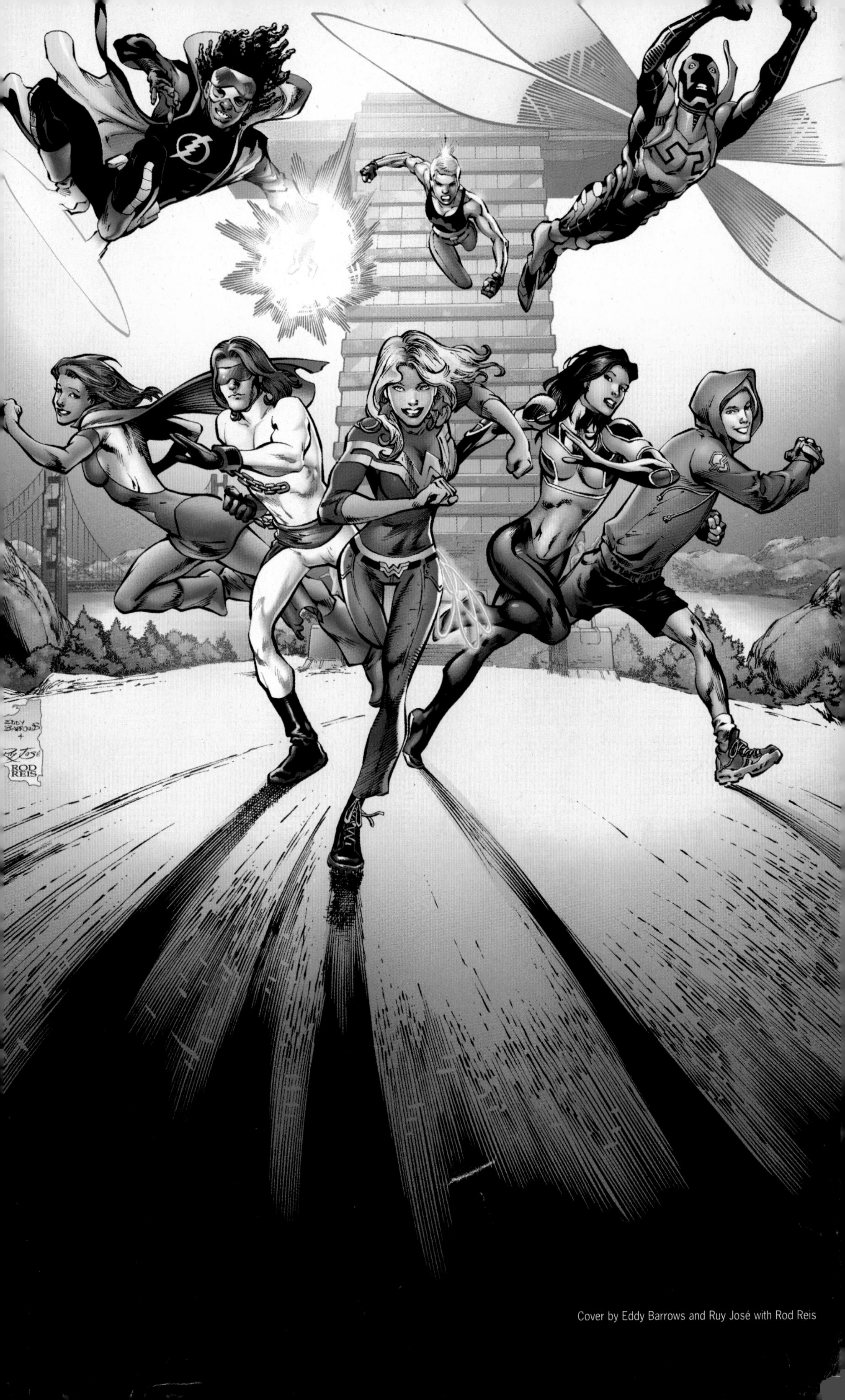
EDDY BARROWS
+
Ruy José
ROD REIS

Cover by Eddy Barrows and Ruy José with Rod Reis

Deathtrap Prelude: Home Invasion

Sean McKeever
Original Story

Fernando Dagnino
Pencils

Raul Fernandez
Inks

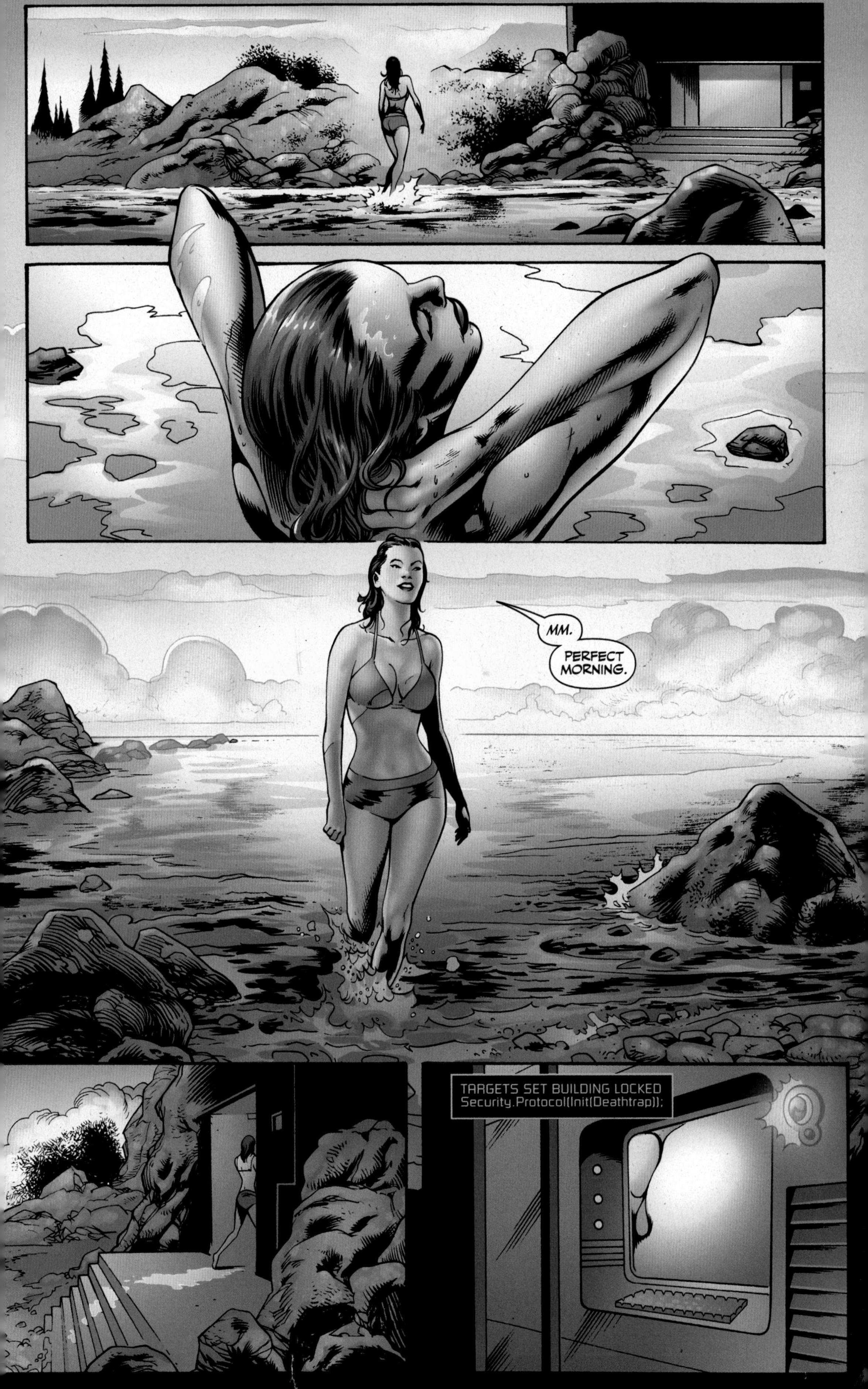
MM.
PERFECT MORNING.
TARGETS SET BUILDING LOCKED
Security.Protocol(Init(Deathtrap));

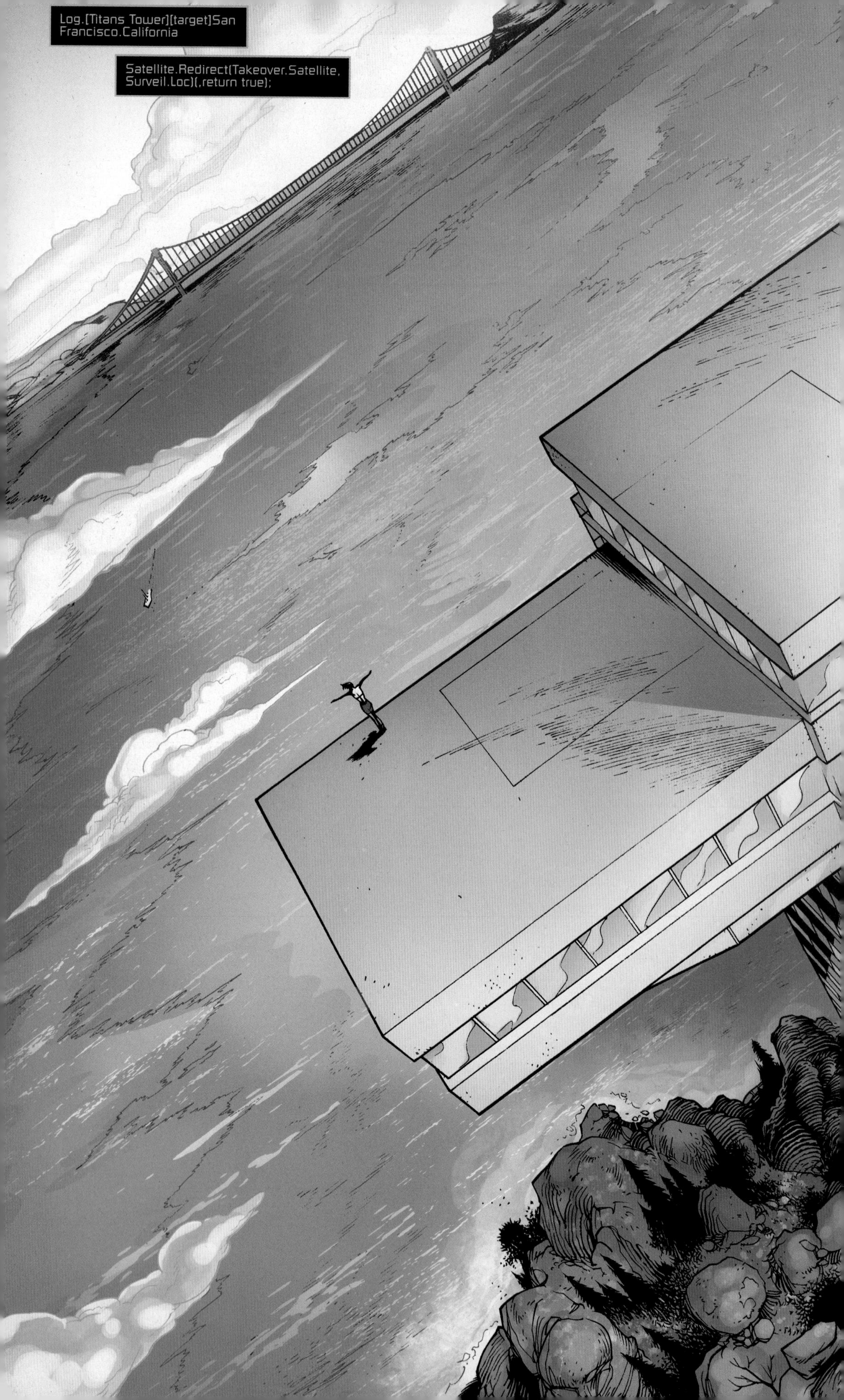
Log.[Titans Tower][target]San Francisco.California
Satellite.Redirect(Takeover.Satellite, Surveil.Loc)(,return true);

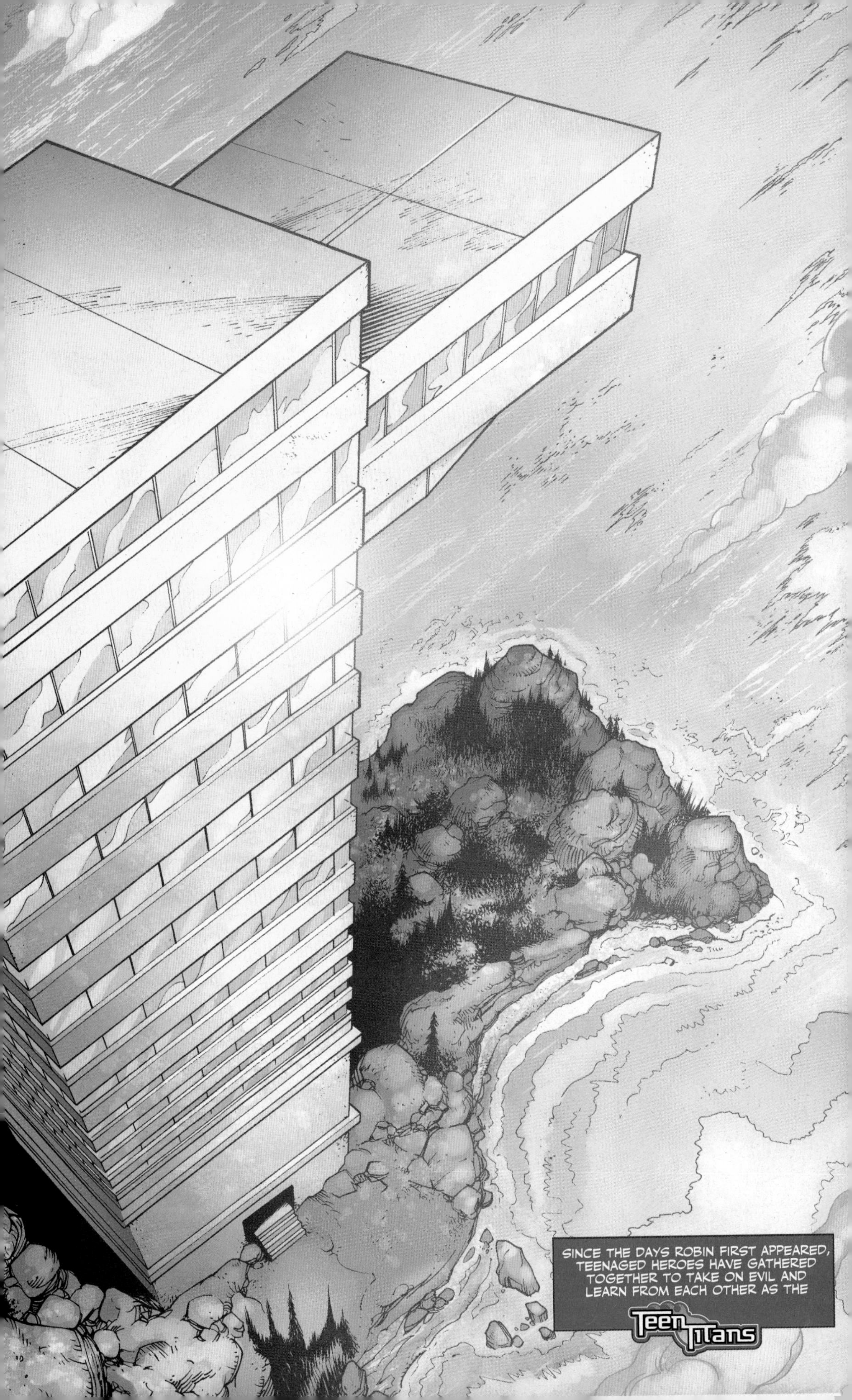
SINCE THE DAYS ROBIN FIRST APPEARED, TEENAGED HEROES HAVE GATHERED TOGETHER TO TAKE ON EVIL AND LEARN FROM EACH OTHER AS THE
Teen Titans

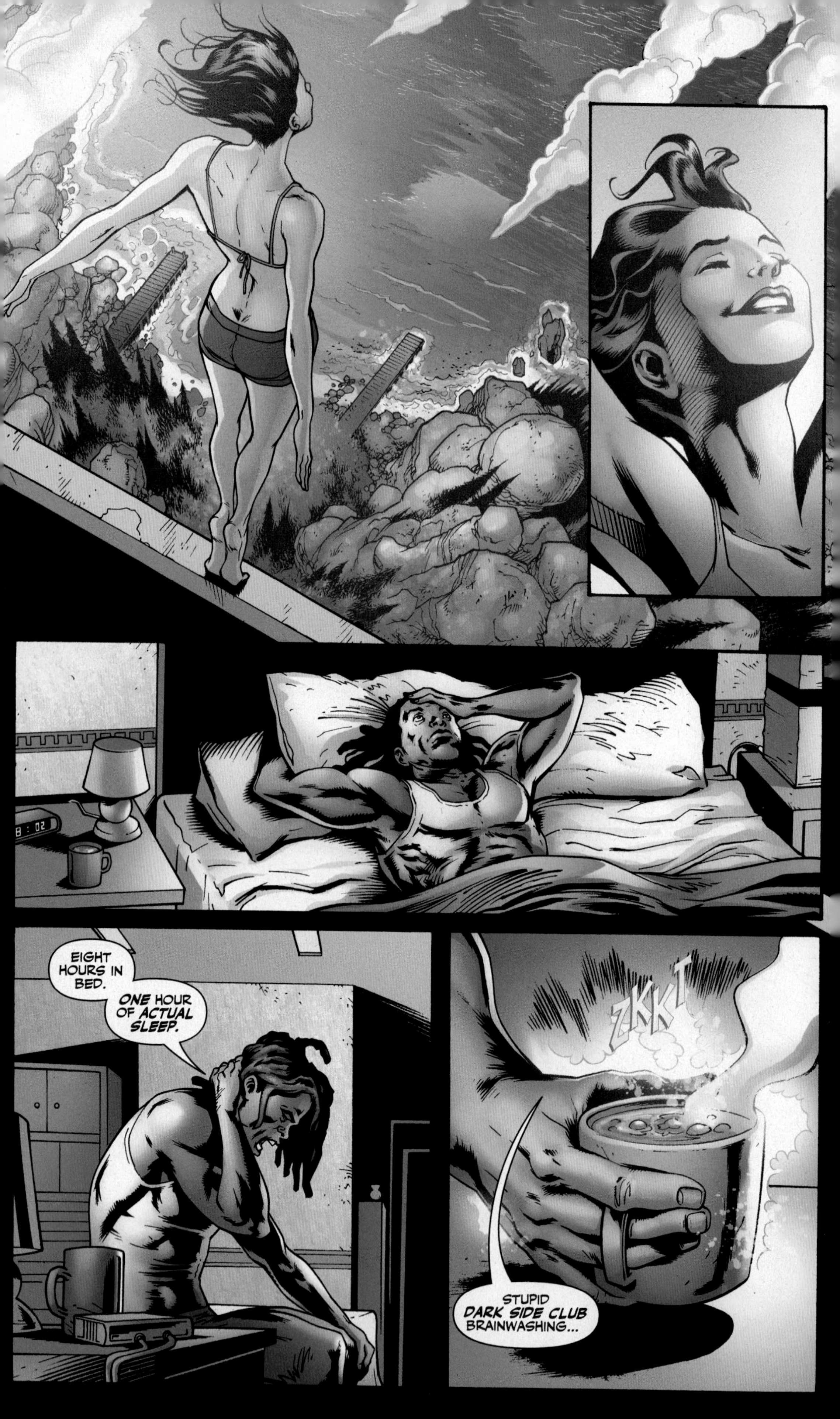
EIGHT HOURS IN BED.
ONE HOUR OF ACTUAL SLEEP.
ZKKT
STUPID DARK SIDE CLUB BRAINWASHING...

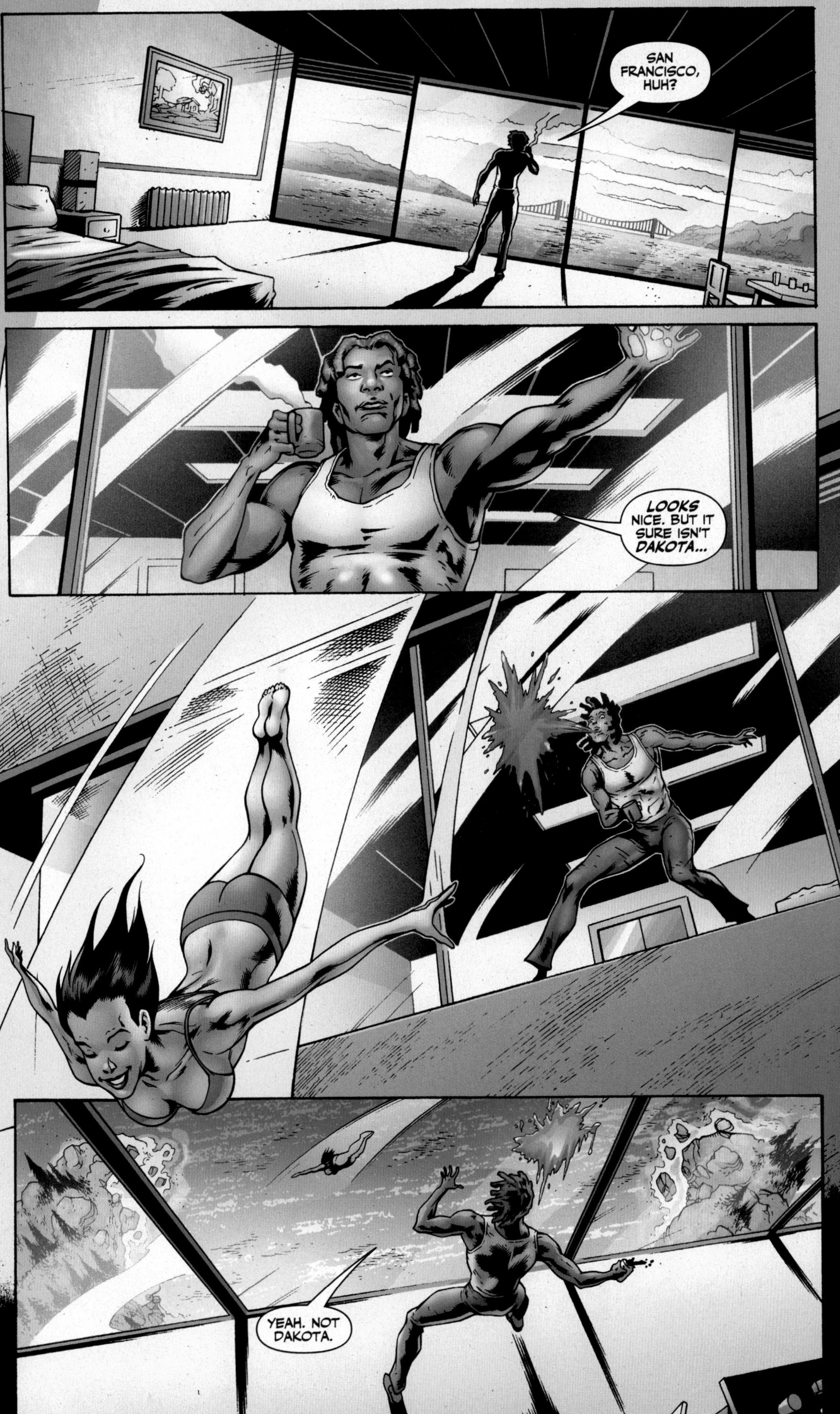
SAN FRANCISCO, HUH?
LOOKS NICE. BUT IT SURE ISN'T DAKOTA...
YEAH. NOT DAKOTA.

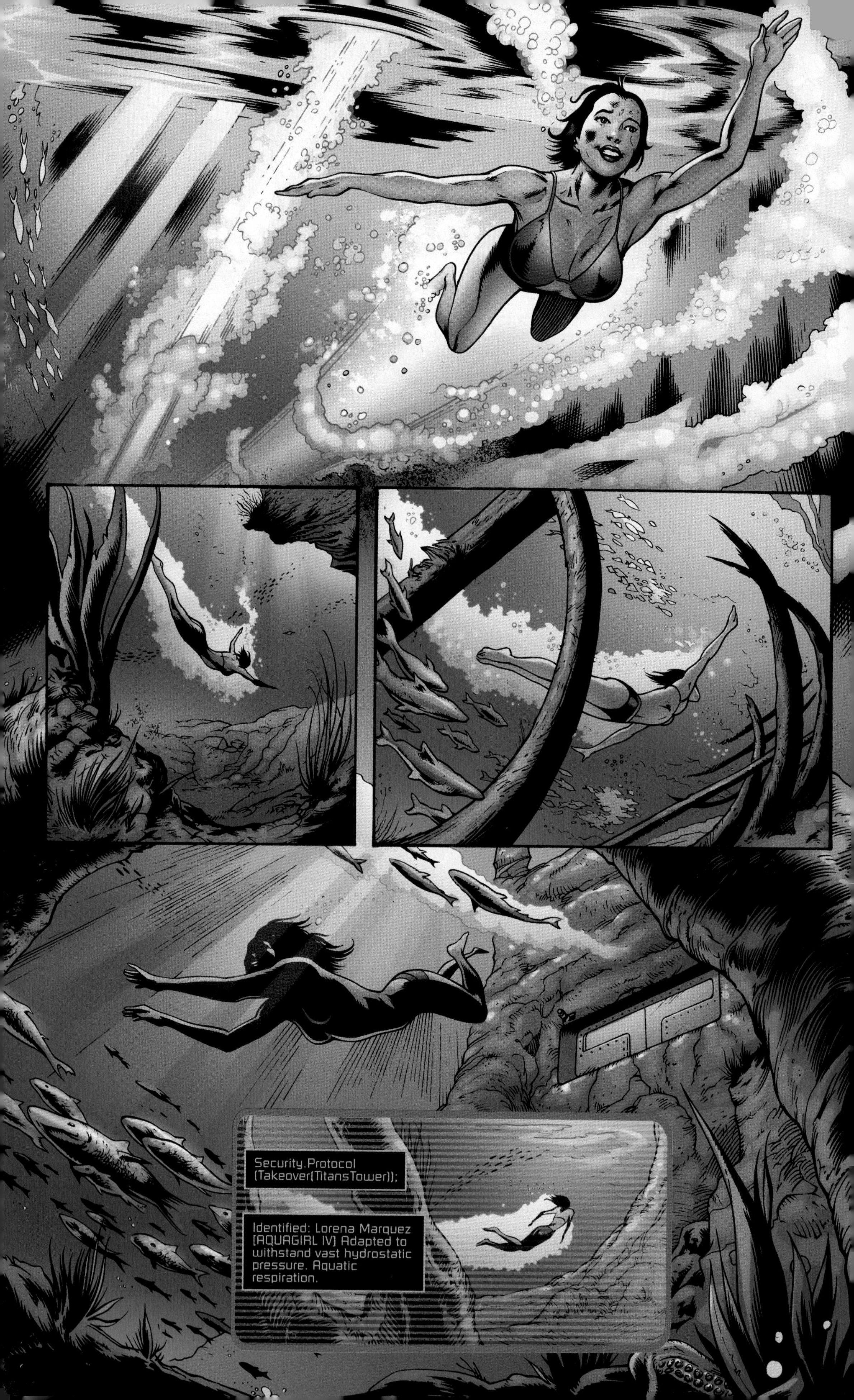
Security.Protocol
(Takeover(TitansTower));
Identified: Lorena Marquez
[AQUAGIRL IV] Adapted to
withstand vast hydrostatic
pressure. Aquatic
respiration.

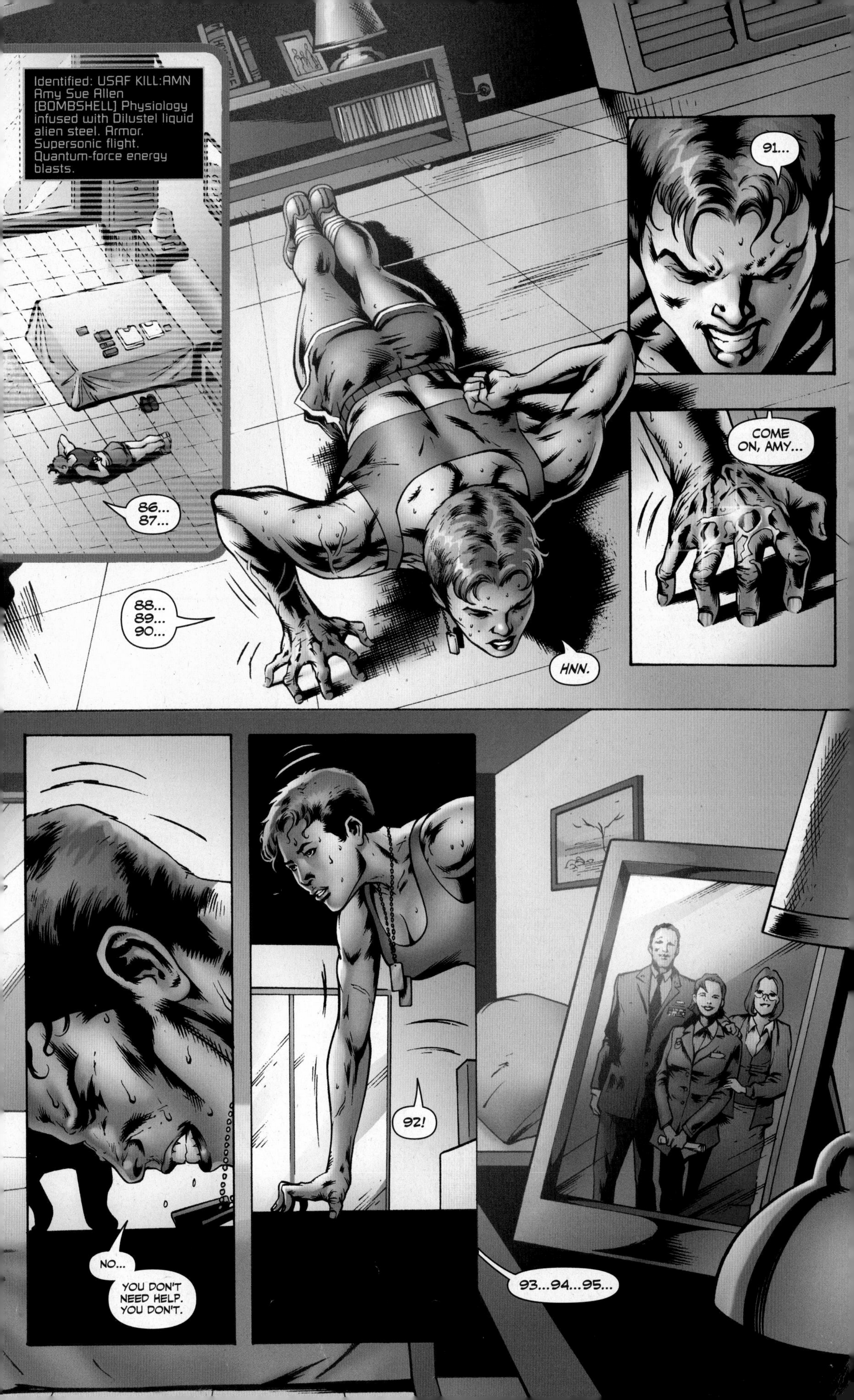
Identified: USAF KILL:AMN Amy Sue Allen [BOMBSHELL] Physiology infused with Dilustel liquid alien steel. Armor. Supersonic flight. Quantum-force energy blasts.
86... 87...
88... 89... 90...
HNN.
91...
COME ON, AMY...
NO...
YOU DON'T NEED HELP. YOU DON'T.
92!
93...94...95...

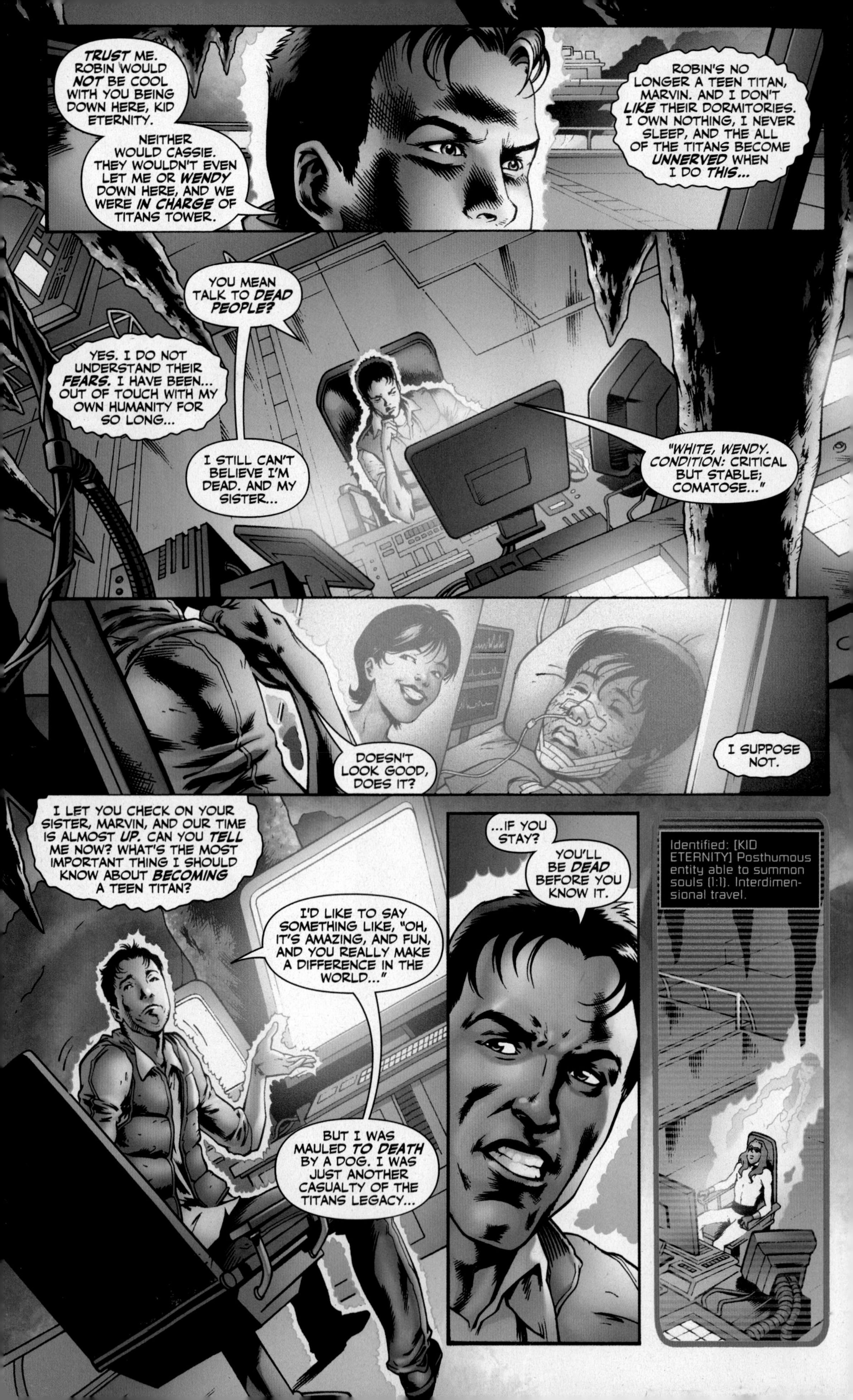
TRUST ME. ROBIN WOULD NOT BE COOL WITH YOU BEING DOWN HERE, KID ETERNITY.
NEITHER WOULD CASSIE. THEY WOULDN'T EVEN LET ME OR WENDY DOWN HERE, AND WE WERE IN CHARGE OF TITANS TOWER.
ROBIN'S NO LONGER A TEEN TITAN, MARVIN. AND I DON'T LIKE THEIR DORMITORIES. I OWN NOTHING, I NEVER SLEEP, AND THE ALL OF THE TITANS BECOME UNNERVED WHEN I DO THIS...
YOU MEAN TALK TO DEAD PEOPLE?
YES. I DO NOT UNDERSTAND THEIR FEARS. I HAVE BEEN... OUT OF TOUCH WITH MY OWN HUMANITY FOR SO LONG...
I STILL CAN'T BELIEVE I'M DEAD. AND MY SISTER...
"WHITE, WENDY. CONDITION: CRITICAL BUT STABLE; COMATOSE..."
DOESN'T LOOK GOOD, DOES IT?
I SUPPOSE NOT.
I LET YOU CHECK ON YOUR SISTER, MARVIN, AND OUR TIME IS ALMOST UP. CAN YOU TELL ME NOW? WHAT'S THE MOST IMPORTANT THING I SHOULD KNOW ABOUT BECOMING A TEEN TITAN?
I'D LIKE TO SAY SOMETHING LIKE, "OH, IT'S AMAZING, AND FUN, AND YOU REALLY MAKE A DIFFERENCE IN THE WORLD..."
BUT I WAS MAULED TO DEATH BY A DOG. I WAS JUST ANOTHER CASUALTY OF THE TITANS LEGACY...
...IF YOU STAY?
YOU'LL BE DEAD BEFORE YOU KNOW IT.
Identified: [KID ETERNITY] Posthumous entity able to summon souls (1:1). Interdimensional travel.

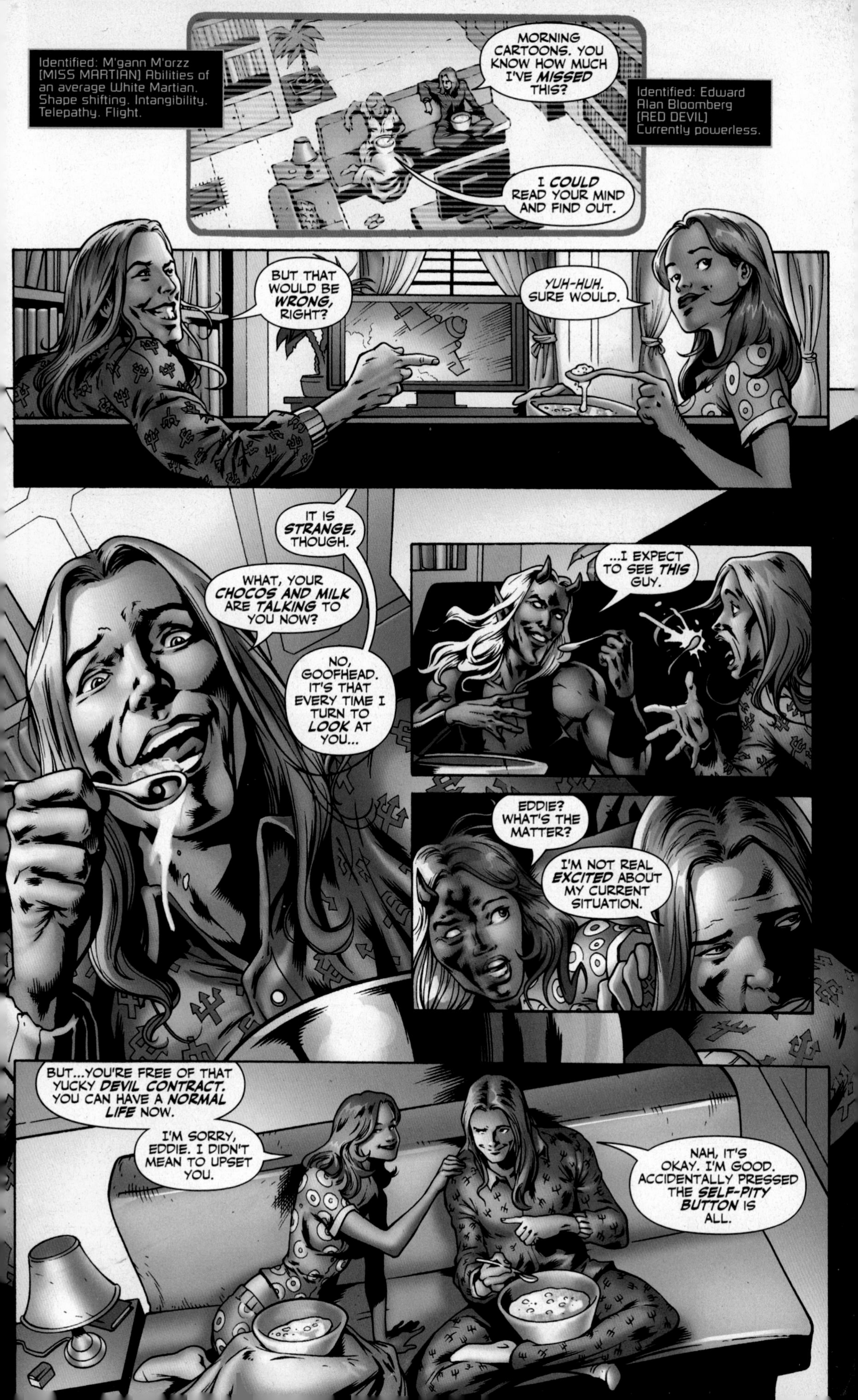

Identified: M'gann M'orzz [MISS MARTIAN] Abilities of an average White Martian. Shape shifting. Intangibility. Telepathy. Flight.
MORNING CARTOONS. YOU KNOW HOW MUCH I'VE MISSED THIS?
Identified: Edward Alan Bloomberg [RED DEVIL] Currently powerless.
I COULD READ YOUR MIND AND FIND OUT.
BUT THAT WOULD BE WRONG, RIGHT?
YUH-HUH. SURE WOULD.
IT IS STRANGE, THOUGH.
WHAT, YOUR CHOCOS AND MILK ARE TALKING TO YOU NOW?
NO, GOOFHEAD. IT'S THAT EVERY TIME I TURN TO LOOK AT YOU...
...I EXPECT TO SEE THIS GUY.
EDDIE? WHAT'S THE MATTER?
I'M NOT REAL EXCITED ABOUT MY CURRENT SITUATION.
BUT...YOU'RE FREE OF THAT YUCKY DEVIL CONTRACT. YOU CAN HAVE A NORMAL LIFE NOW.
I'M SORRY, EDDIE. I DIDN'T MEAN TO UPSET YOU.
NAH, IT'S OKAY. I'M GOOD. ACCIDENTALLY PRESSED THE SELF-PITY BUTTON IS ALL.

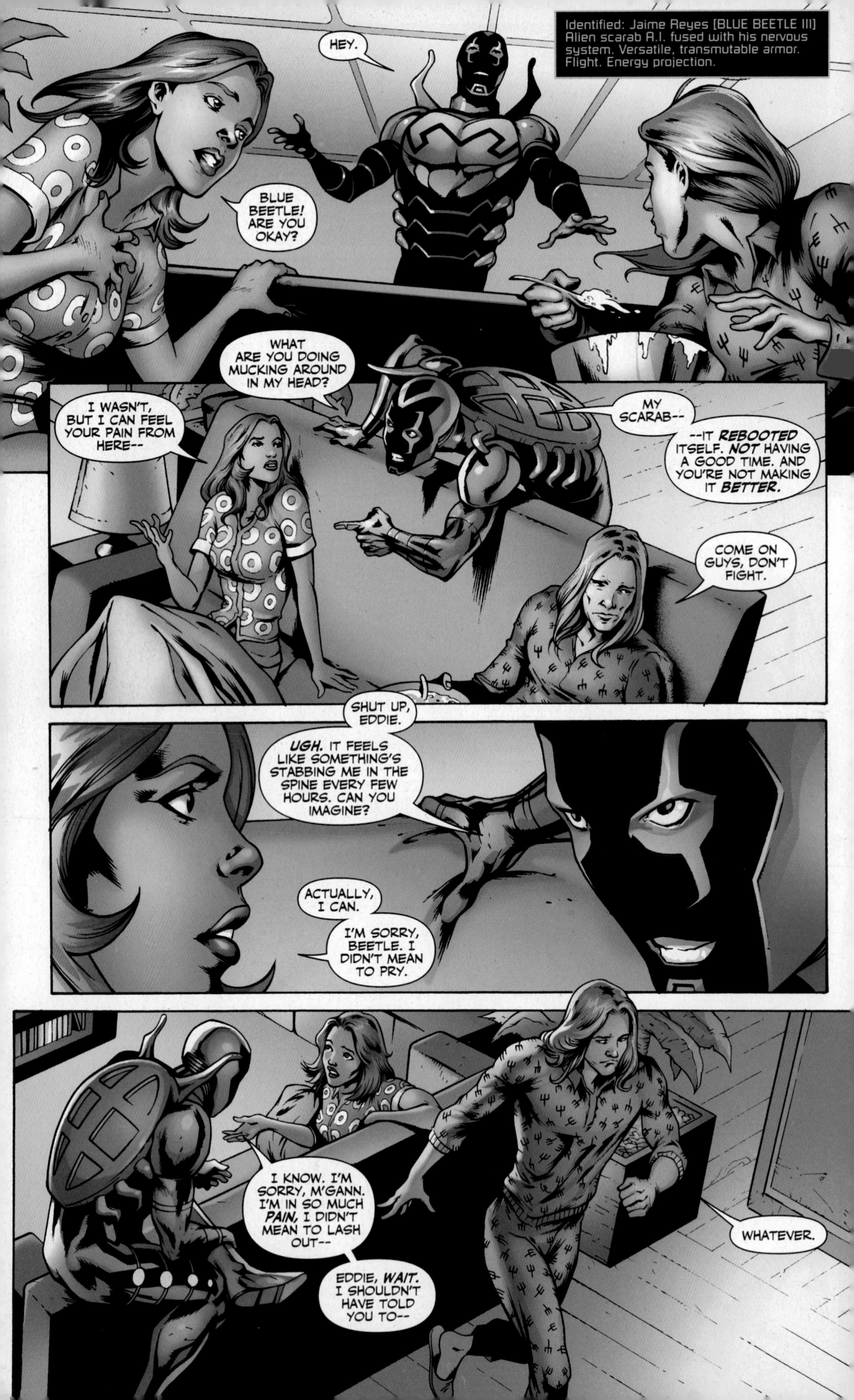
Identified: Jaime Reyes [BLUE BEETLE III] Alien scarab A.I. fused with his nervous system. Versatile, transmutable armor. Flight. Energy projection.
HEY.
BLUE BEETLE! ARE YOU OKAY?
WHAT ARE YOU DOING MUCKING AROUND IN MY HEAD?
I WASN'T, BUT I CAN FEEL YOUR PAIN FROM HERE--
MY SCARAB--
--IT REBOOTED ITSELF. NOT HAVING A GOOD TIME. AND YOU'RE NOT MAKING IT BETTER.
COME ON GUYS, DON'T FIGHT.
SHUT UP, EDDIE.
UGH. IT FEELS LIKE SOMETHING'S STABBING ME IN THE SPINE EVERY FEW HOURS. CAN YOU IMAGINE?
ACTUALLY, I CAN.
I'M SORRY, BEETLE. I DIDN'T MEAN TO PRY.
I KNOW. I'M SORRY, M'GANN. I'M IN SO MUCH PAIN, I DIDN'T MEAN TO LASH OUT--
EDDIE, WAIT. I SHOULDN'T HAVE TOLD YOU TO--
WHATEVER.

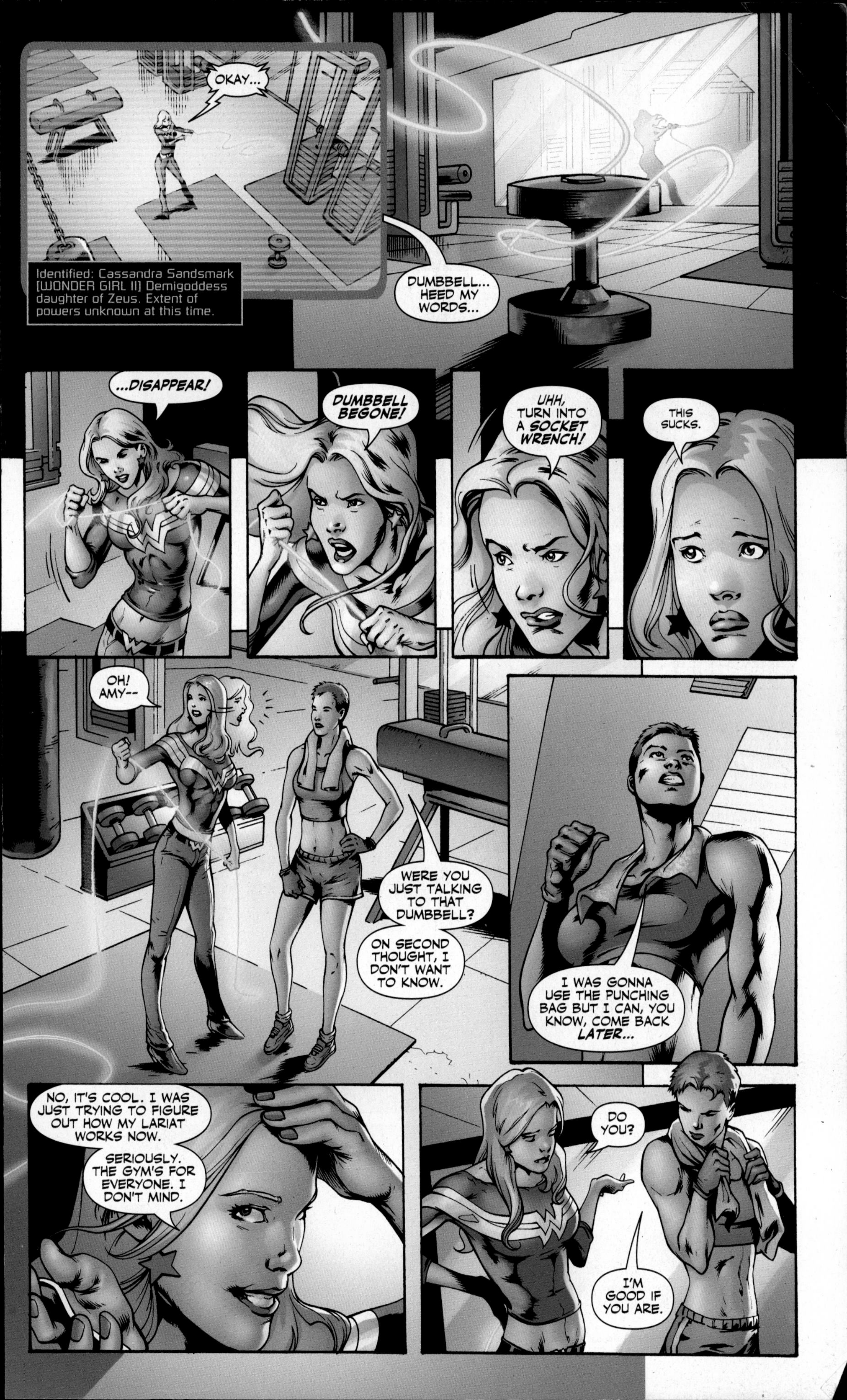
OKAY...
Identified: Cassandra Sandsmark [WONDER GIRL II] Demigoddess daughter of Zeus. Extent of powers unknown at this time.
DUMBBELL... HEED MY WORDS...
...DISAPPEAR!
DUMBBELL BEGONE!
UHH, TURN INTO A SOCKET WRENCH!
THIS SUCKS.
OH! AMY--
WERE YOU JUST TALKING TO THAT DUMBBELL?
ON SECOND THOUGHT, I DON'T WANT TO KNOW.
I WAS GONNA USE THE PUNCHING BAG BUT I CAN, YOU KNOW, COME BACK LATER...
NO, IT'S COOL. I WAS JUST TRYING TO FIGURE OUT HOW MY LARIAT WORKS NOW.
SERIOUSLY. THE GYM'S FOR EVERYONE. I DON'T MIND.
DO YOU?
I'M GOOD IF YOU ARE.

```
Init(Security);
```

```
Security.Protocol
(Takeover(Satellite));
```

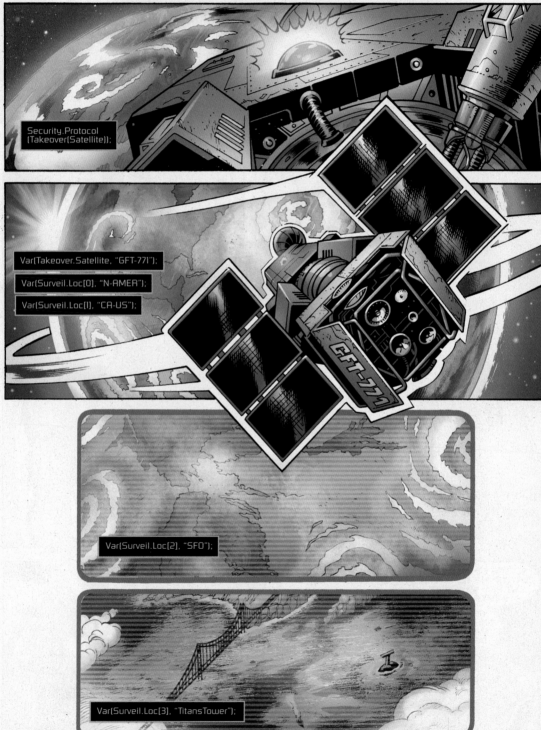

```
Var(Takeover.Satellite, "GFT-771");

Var(Surveil.Loc[0], "N-AMER");

Var(Surveil.Loc[1], "CA-US");
```

```
Var(Surveil.Loc[2], "SFO");
```

```
Var(Surveil.Loc[3], "TitansTower");
```

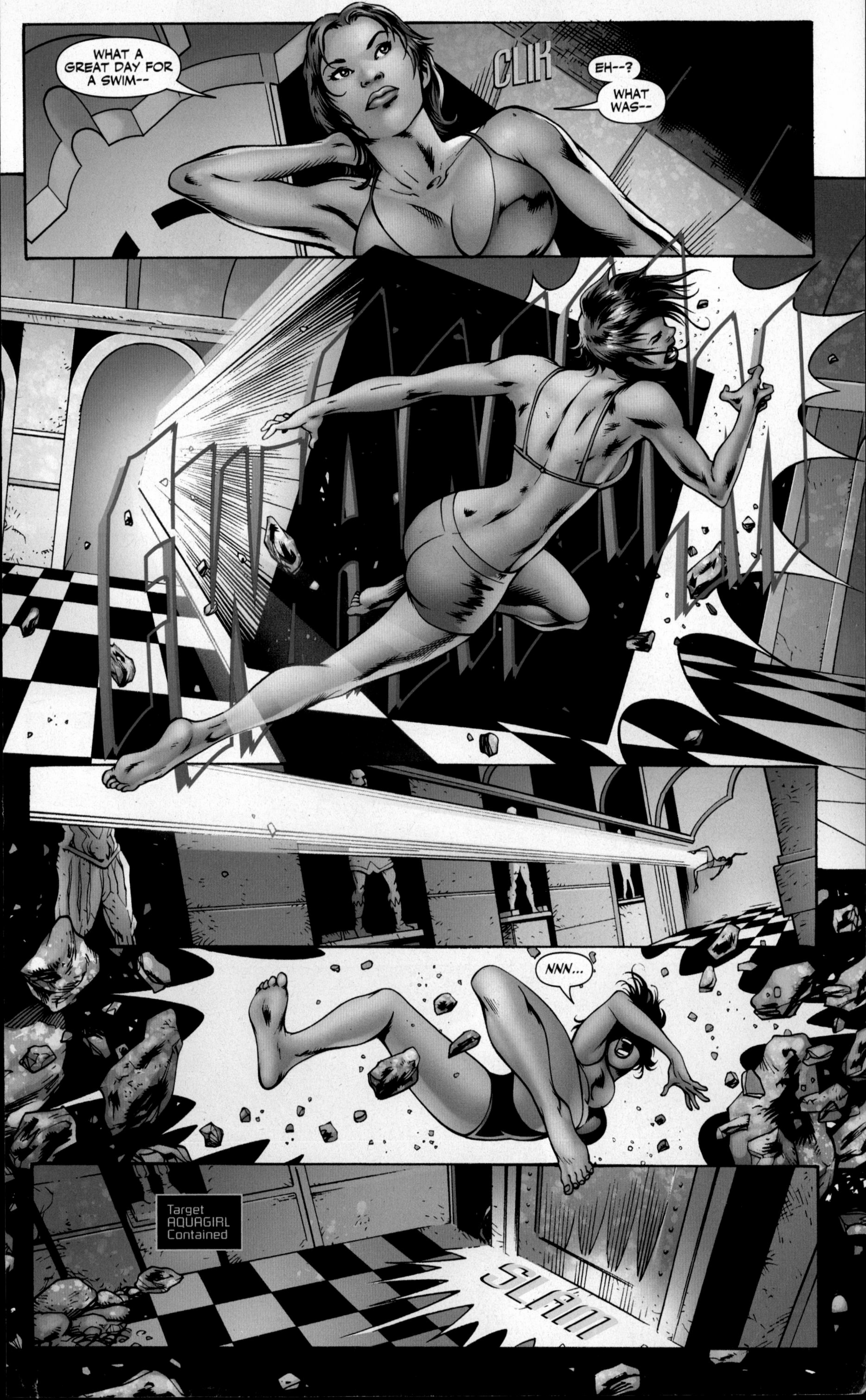
WHAT A GREAT DAY FOR A SWIM--
CLIK
EH--? WHAT WAS--
NNN...
Target AQUAGIRL Contained
SLAM

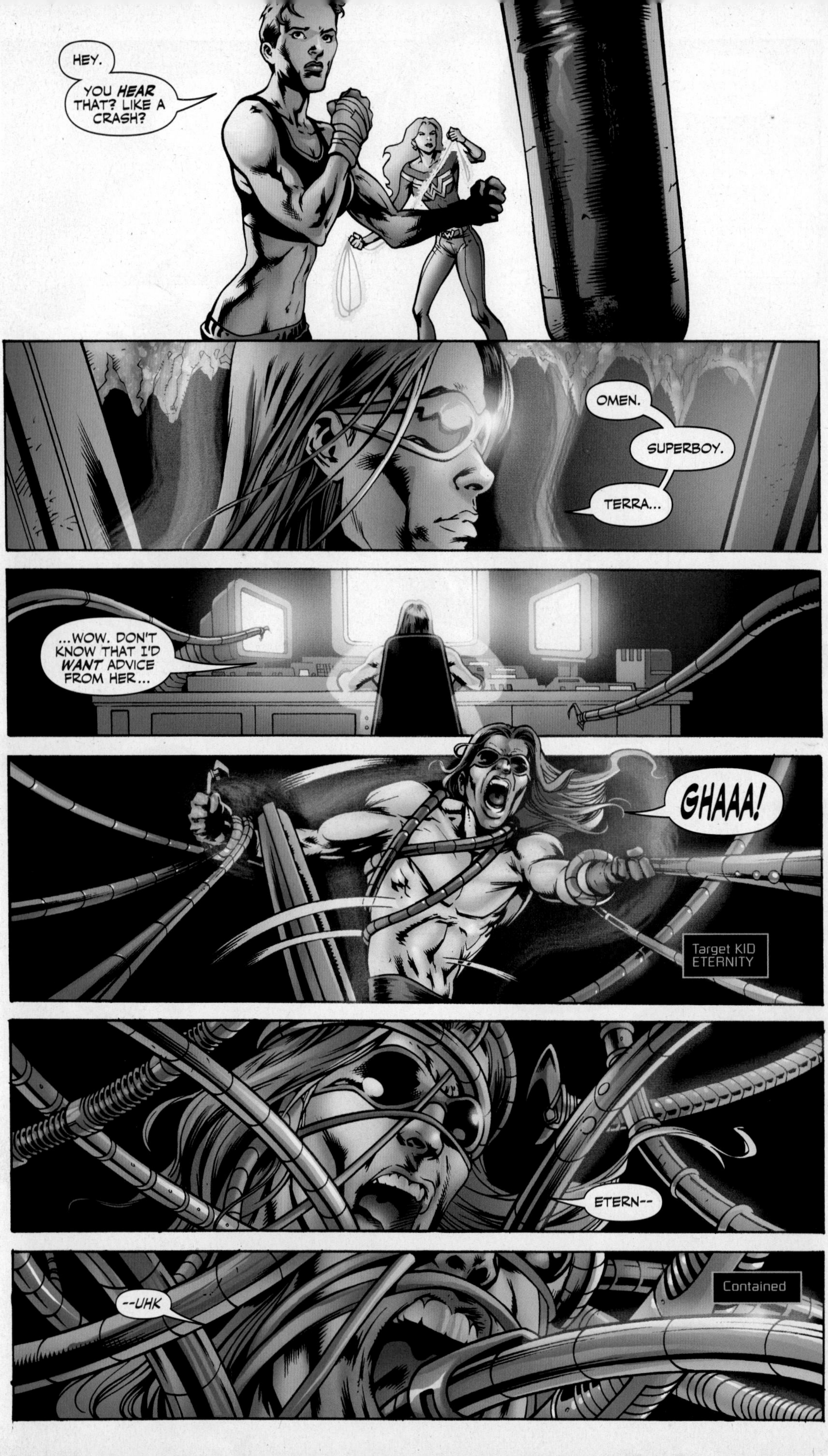
HEY.
YOU HEAR THAT? LIKE A CRASH?
OMEN.
SUPERBOY.
TERRA...
...WOW. DON'T KNOW THAT I'D WANT ADVICE FROM HER...
GHAAA!
Target KID ETERNITY
ETERN--
Contained
--UHK

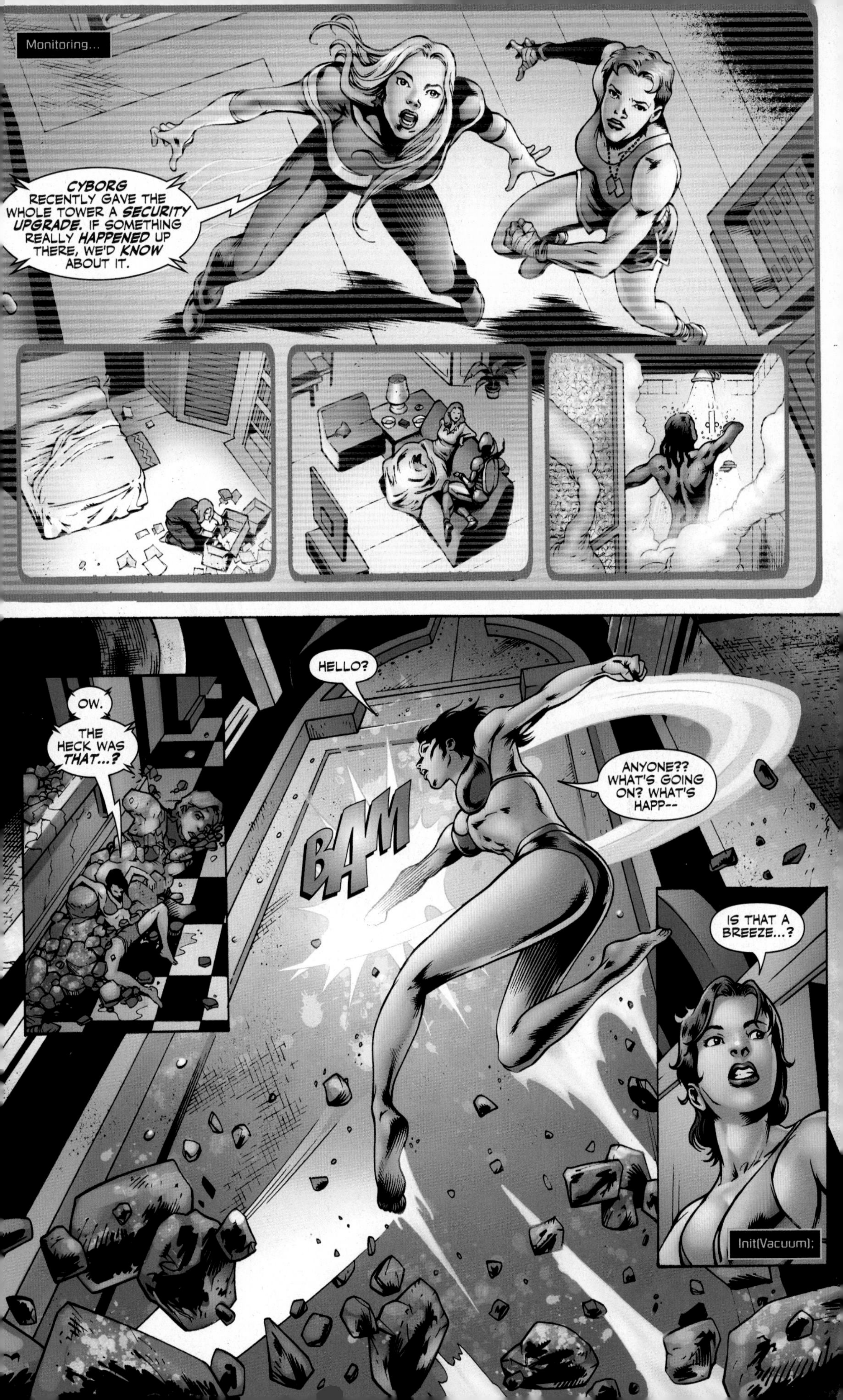
Monitoring...
CYBORG RECENTLY GAVE THE WHOLE TOWER A SECURITY UPGRADE. IF SOMETHING REALLY HAPPENED UP THERE, WE'D KNOW ABOUT IT.
HELLO?
OW.
THE HECK WAS THAT...?
ANYONE?? WHAT'S GOING ON? WHAT'S HAPP--
BAM
IS THAT A BREEZE...?
Init(Vacuum);

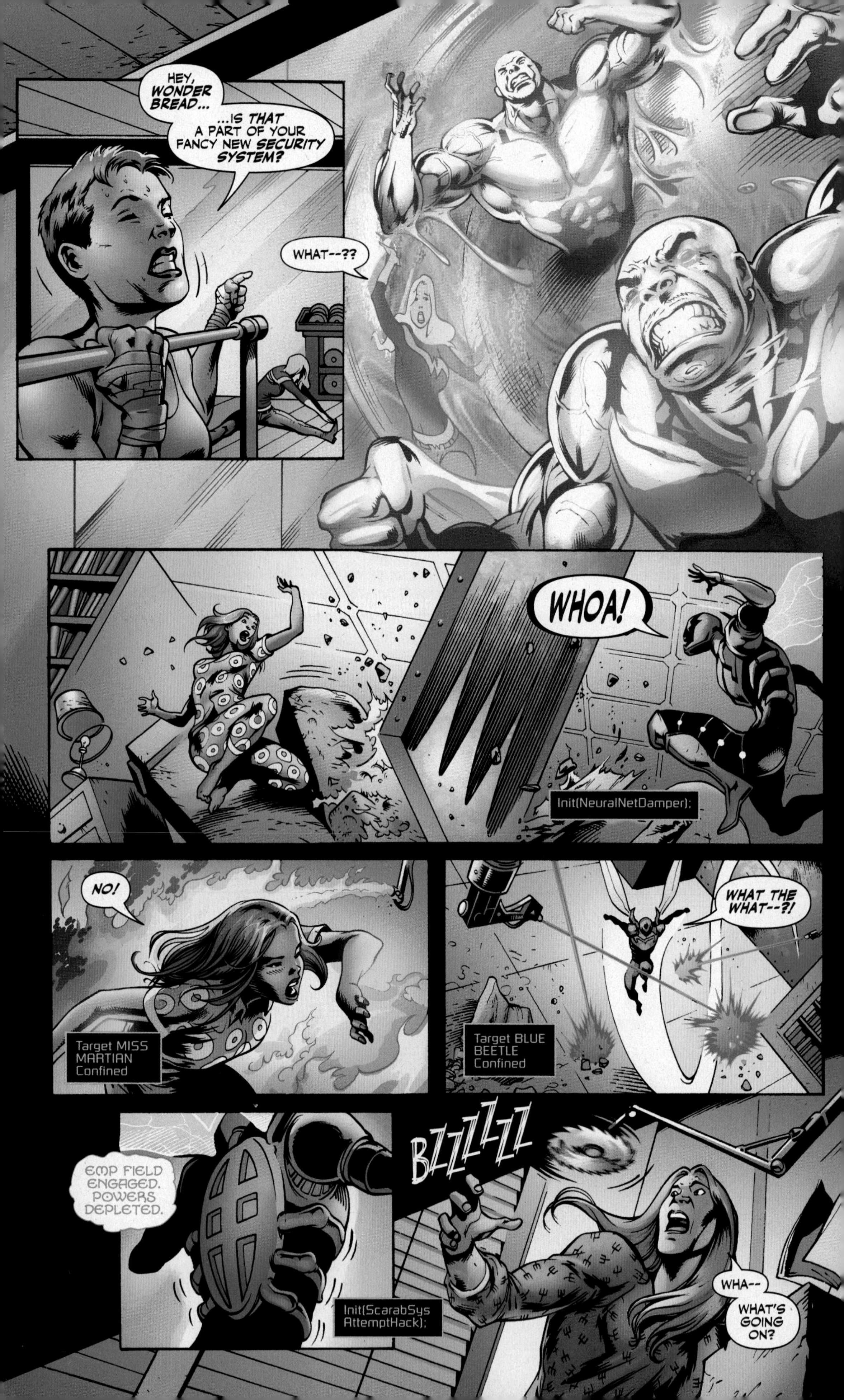
HEY, WONDER BREAD...
...IS THAT A PART OF YOUR FANCY NEW SECURITY SYSTEM?
WHAT--??
WHOA!
Init(NeuralNetDamper);
NO!
Target MISS MARTIAN Confined
WHAT THE WHAT--?!
Target BLUE BEETLE Confined
EMP FIELD ENGAGED. POWERS DEPLETED.
BZZZZZZ
Init(ScarabSys AttemptHack);
WHA--
WHAT'S GOING ON?

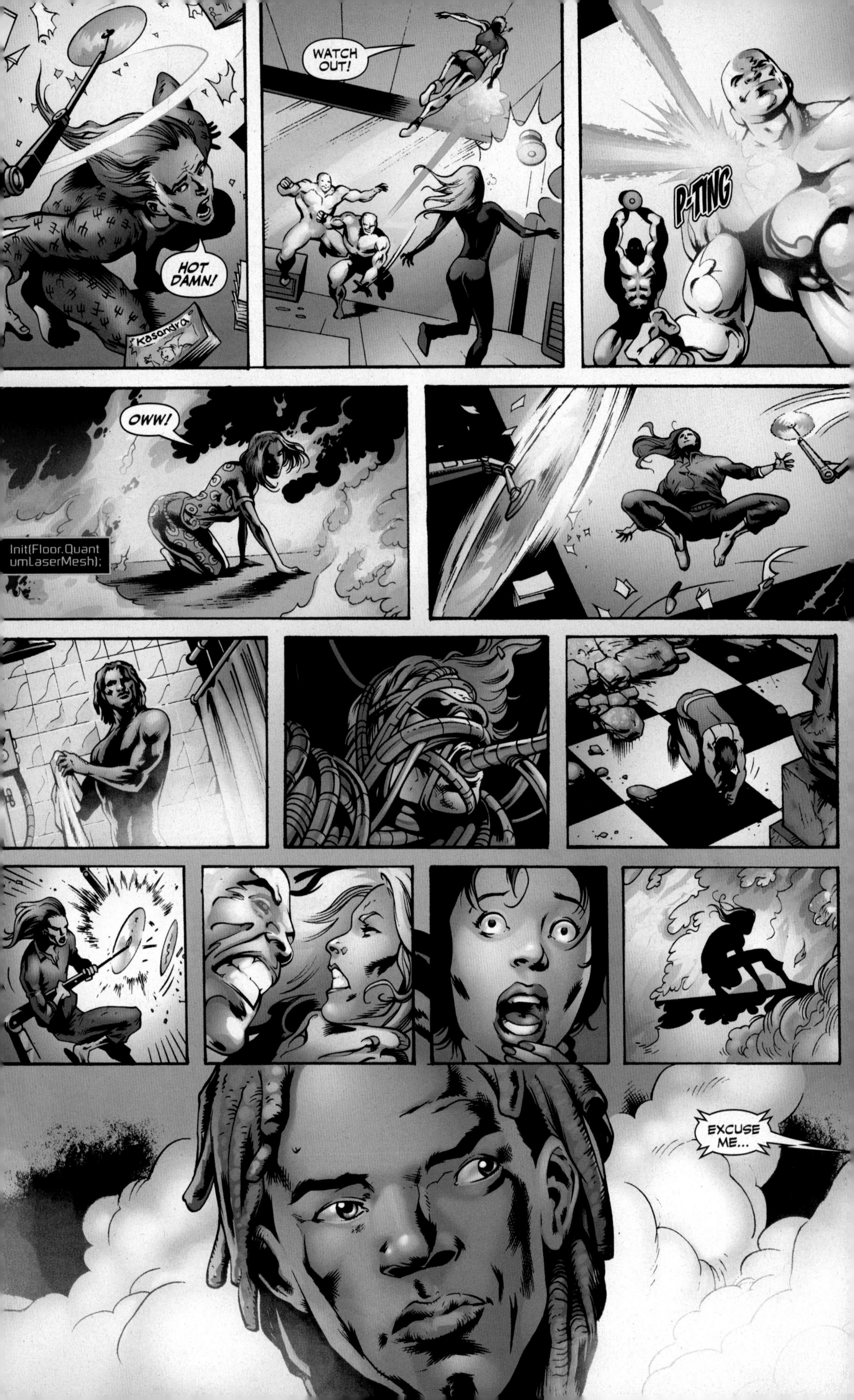
HOT DAMN!
Kasandra
WATCH OUT!
P-TING
OWW!
Init(Floor.QuantumLaserMesh);
EXCUSE ME...

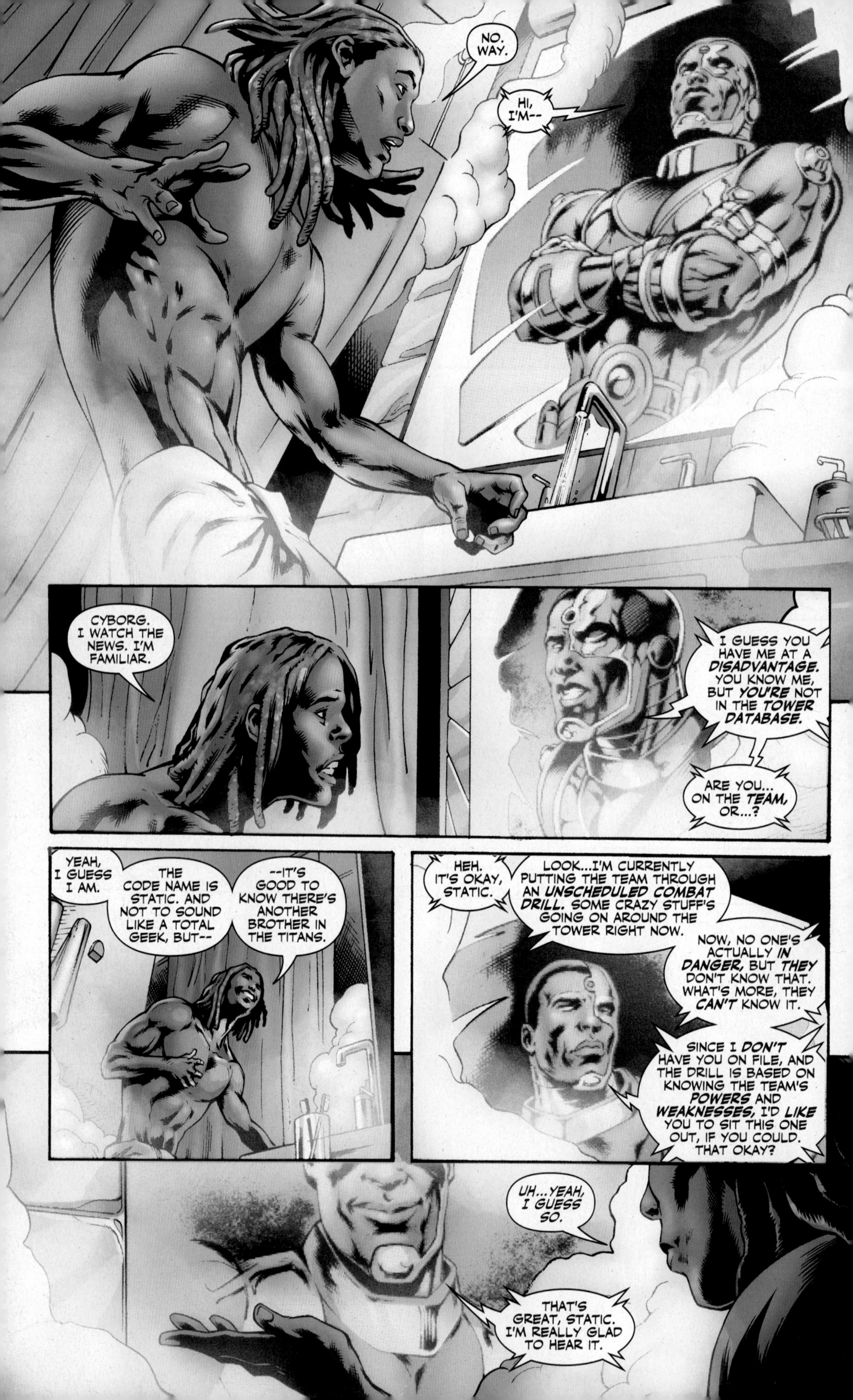
NO. WAY.
HI, I'M--
CYBORG. I WATCH THE NEWS. I'M FAMILIAR.
I GUESS YOU HAVE ME AT A DISADVANTAGE. YOU KNOW ME, BUT YOU'RE NOT IN THE TOWER DATABASE.
ARE YOU... ON THE TEAM, OR...?
YEAH, I GUESS I AM.
THE CODE NAME IS STATIC. AND NOT TO SOUND LIKE A TOTAL GEEK, BUT--
--IT'S GOOD TO KNOW THERE'S ANOTHER BROTHER IN THE TITANS.
HEH. IT'S OKAY, STATIC.
LOOK...I'M CURRENTLY PUTTING THE TEAM THROUGH AN UNSCHEDULED COMBAT DRILL. SOME CRAZY STUFF'S GOING ON AROUND THE TOWER RIGHT NOW.
NOW, NO ONE'S ACTUALLY IN DANGER, BUT THEY DON'T KNOW THAT. WHAT'S MORE, THEY CAN'T KNOW IT.
SINCE I DON'T HAVE YOU ON FILE, AND THE DRILL IS BASED ON KNOWING THE TEAM'S POWERS AND WEAKNESSES, I'D LIKE YOU TO SIT THIS ONE OUT, IF YOU COULD. THAT OKAY?
UH...YEAH, I GUESS SO.
THAT'S GREAT, STATIC. I'M REALLY GLAD TO HEAR IT.

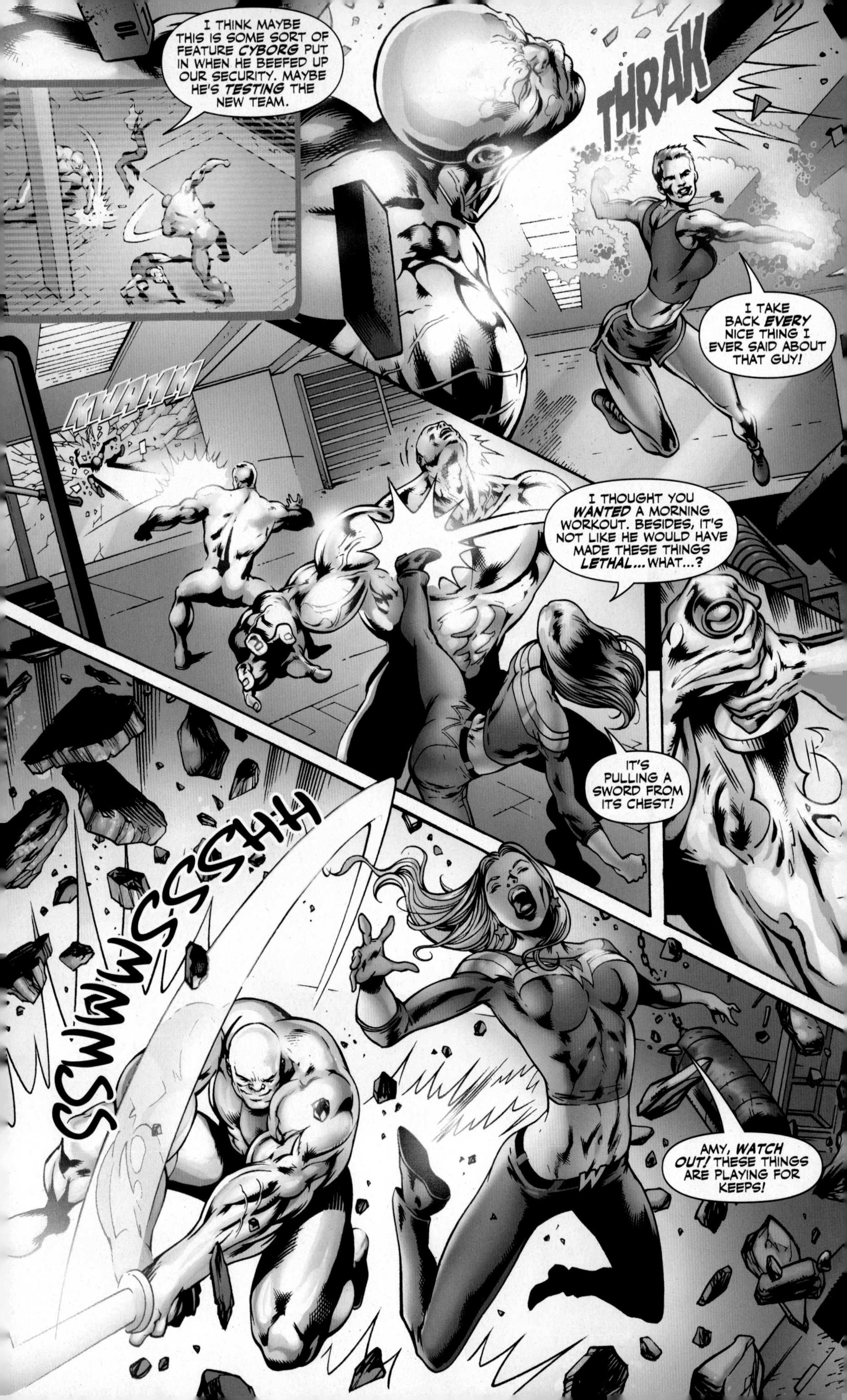

I THINK MAYBE THIS IS SOME SORT OF FEATURE CYBORG PUT IN WHEN HE BEEFED UP OUR SECURITY. MAYBE HE'S TESTING THE NEW TEAM.
THRAK
I TAKE BACK EVERY NICE THING I EVER SAID ABOUT THAT GUY!
KWAMM
I THOUGHT YOU WANTED A MORNING WORKOUT. BESIDES, IT'S NOT LIKE HE WOULD HAVE MADE THESE THINGS LETHAL... WHAT...?
IT'S PULLING A SWORD FROM ITS CHEST!
SSWWWSSSHH
AMY, WATCH OUT! THESE THINGS ARE PLAYING FOR KEEPS!

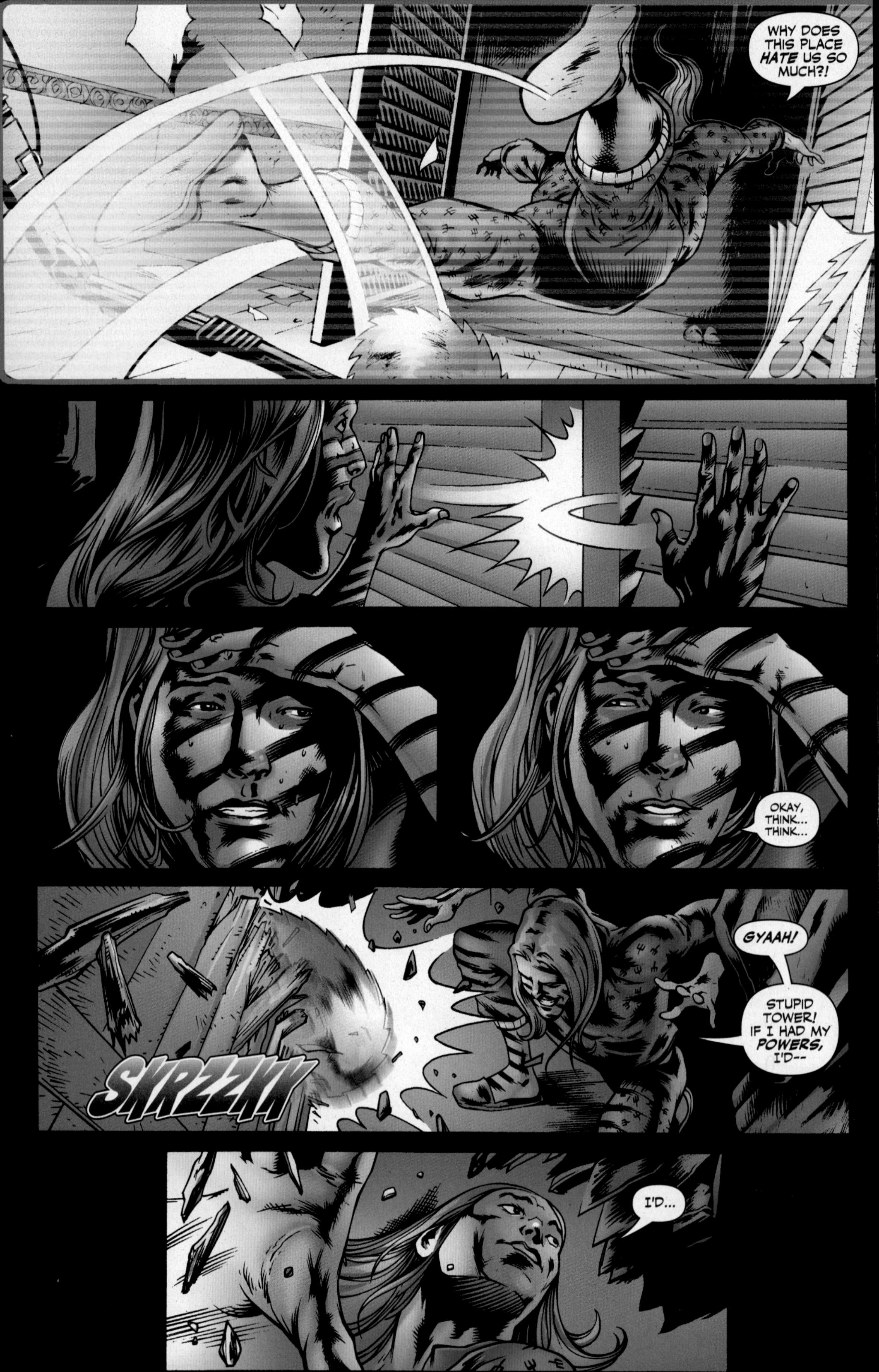
WHY DOES THIS PLACE HATE US SO MUCH?!
OKAY, THINK... THINK...
GYAAH!
STUPID TOWER! IF I HAD MY POWERS, I'D--
SKRZZAKK
I'D...

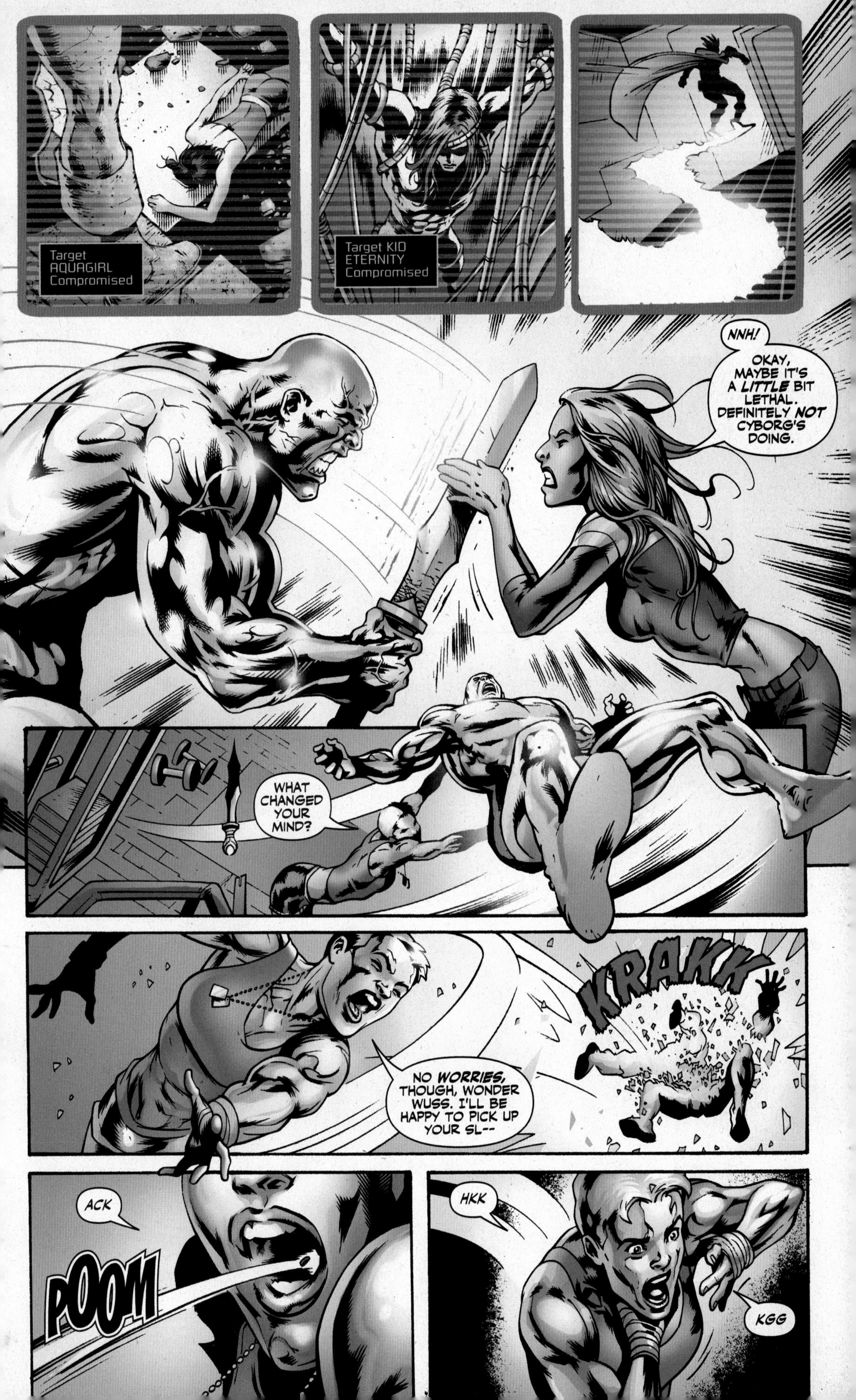
Target AQUAGIRL Compromised
Target KID ETERNITY Compromised
NNH!
OKAY, MAYBE IT'S A *LITTLE* BIT LETHAL. DEFINITELY *NOT* CYBORG'S DOING.
WHAT CHANGED YOUR MIND?
NO *WORRIES,* THOUGH, WONDER WUSS. I'LL BE HAPPY TO PICK UP YOUR SL--
KRAKK
ACK
POOM
HKK
KGG

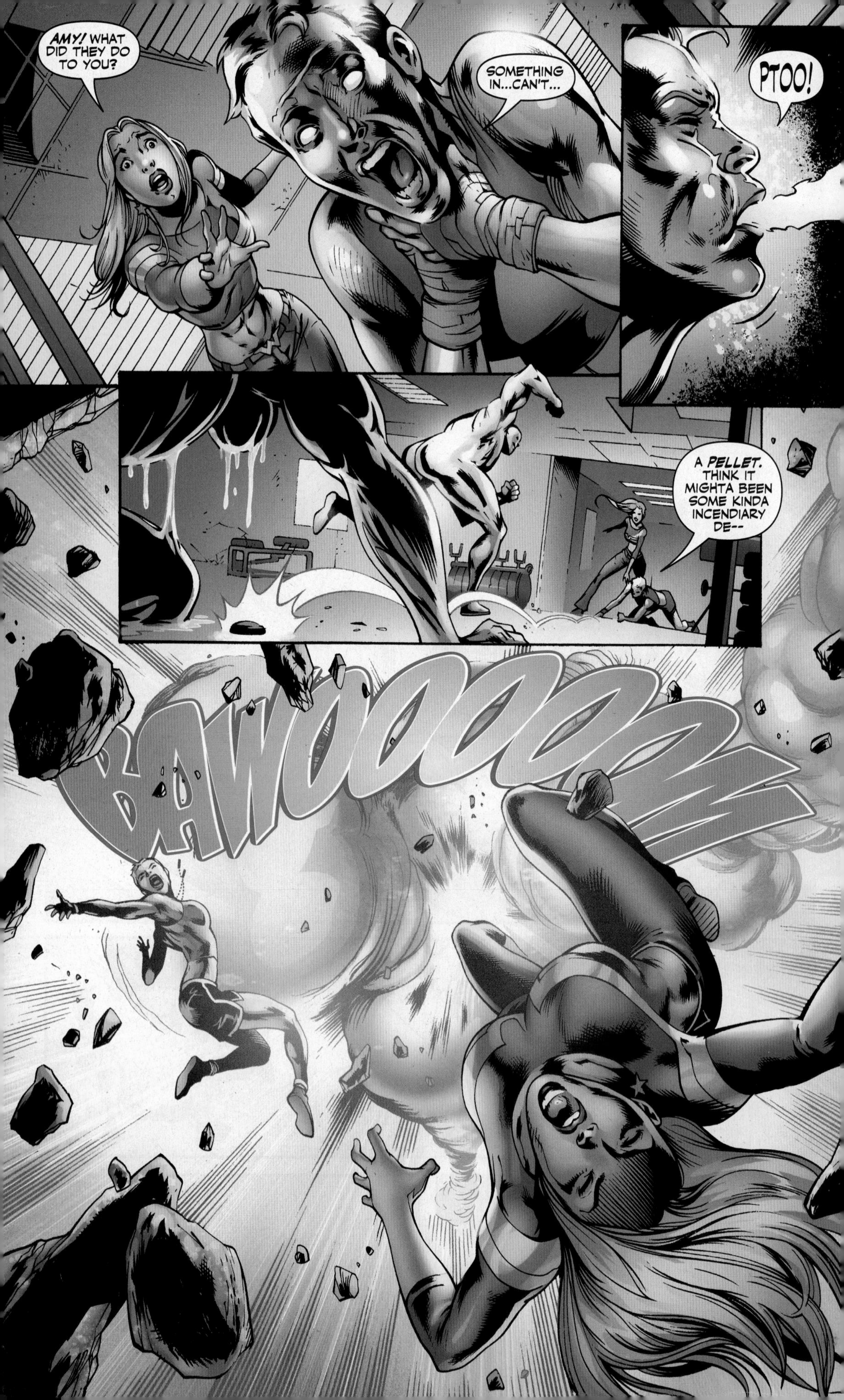
AMY! WHAT DID THEY DO TO YOU?
SOMETHING IN...CAN'T...
PTOO!
A PELLET. THINK IT MIGHTA BEEN SOME KINDA INCENDIARY DE--
BAWOOOOM

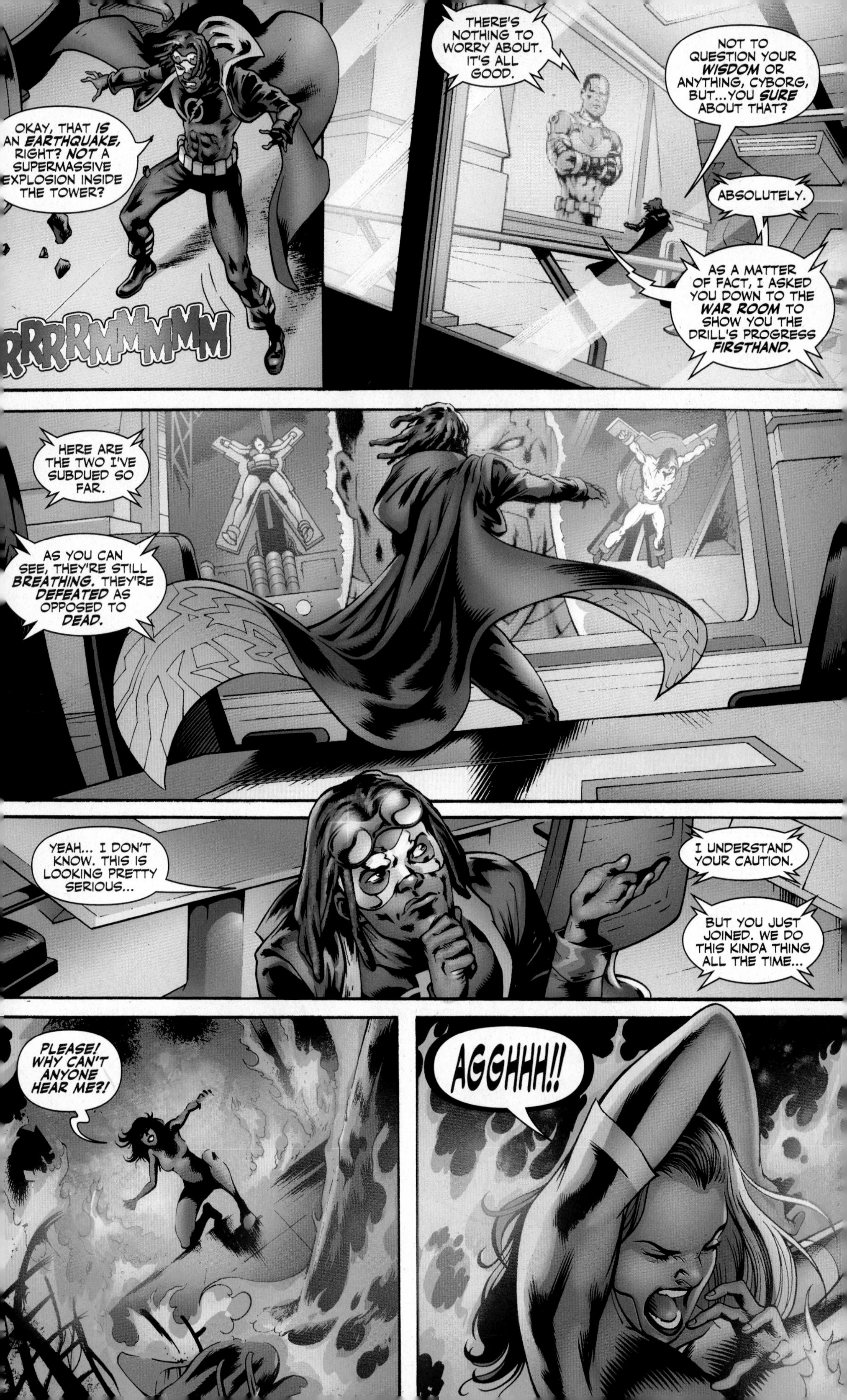
OKAY, THAT IS AN EARTHQUAKE, RIGHT? NOT A SUPERMASSIVE EXPLOSION INSIDE THE TOWER?
RRRRMMMMMM
THERE'S NOTHING TO WORRY ABOUT. IT'S ALL GOOD.
NOT TO QUESTION YOUR WISDOM OR ANYTHING, CYBORG, BUT...YOU SURE ABOUT THAT?
ABSOLUTELY.
AS A MATTER OF FACT, I ASKED YOU DOWN TO THE WAR ROOM TO SHOW YOU THE DRILL'S PROGRESS FIRSTHAND.
HERE ARE THE TWO I'VE SUBDUED SO FAR.
AS YOU CAN SEE, THEY'RE STILL BREATHING. THEY'RE DEFEATED AS OPPOSED TO DEAD.
YEAH... I DON'T KNOW. THIS IS LOOKING PRETTY SERIOUS...
I UNDERSTAND YOUR CAUTION.
BUT YOU JUST JOINED. WE DO THIS KINDA THING ALL THE TIME...
PLEASE! WHY CAN'T ANYONE HEAR ME?!
AGGHHH!!

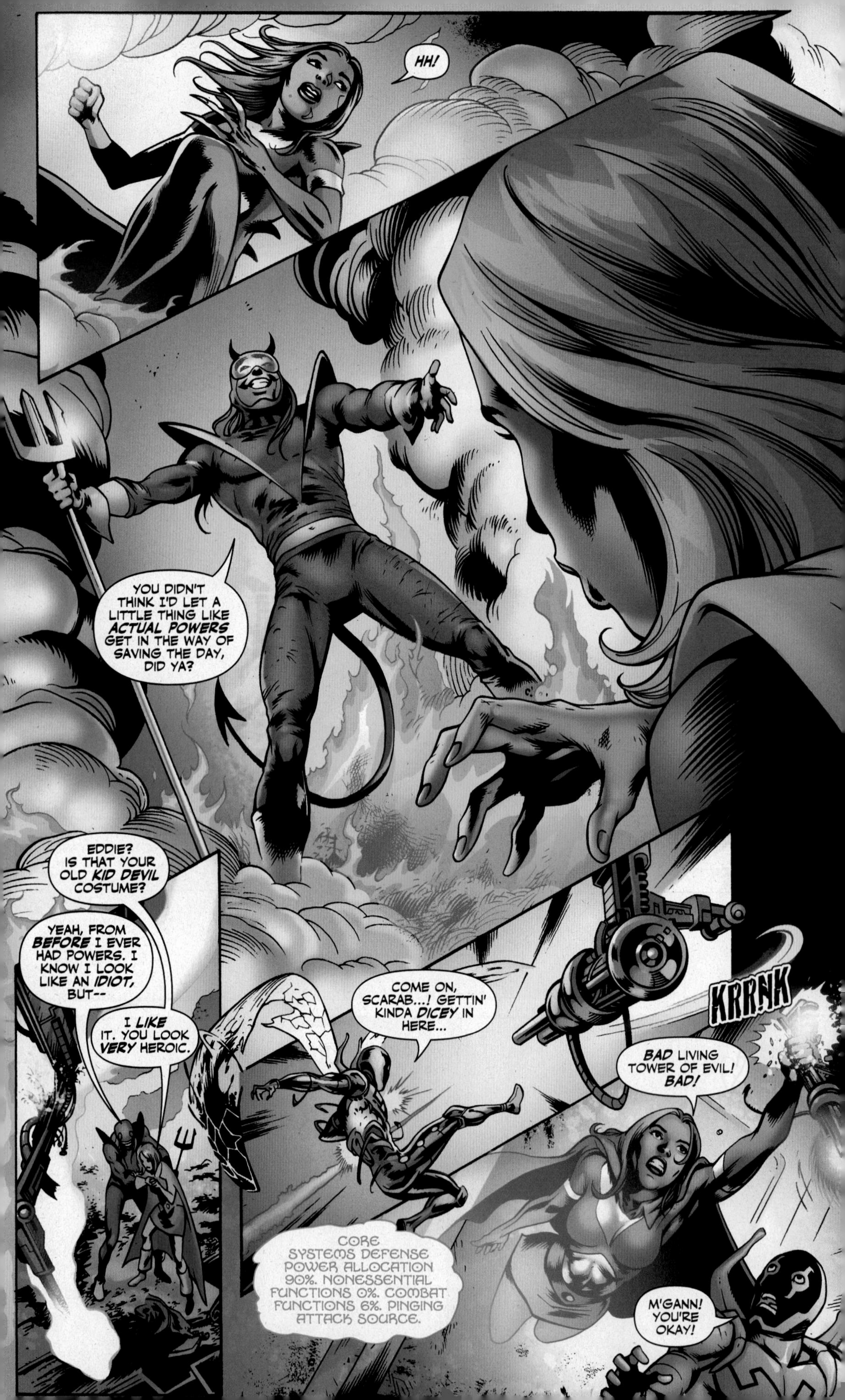
HH!
YOU DIDN'T THINK I'D LET A LITTLE THING LIKE ACTUAL POWERS GET IN THE WAY OF SAVING THE DAY, DID YA?
EDDIE? IS THAT YOUR OLD KID DEVIL COSTUME?
YEAH, FROM BEFORE I EVER HAD POWERS. I KNOW I LOOK LIKE AN IDIOT, BUT--
I LIKE IT. YOU LOOK VERY HEROIC.
COME ON, SCARAB...! GETTIN' KINDA DICEY IN HERE...
KRRNK
BAD LIVING TOWER OF EVIL! BAD!
CORE SYSTEMS DEFENSE POWER ALLOCATION 90%. NONESSENTIAL FUNCTIONS 0%. COMBAT FUNCTIONS 6%. PINGING ATTACK SOURCE.
M'GANN! YOU'RE OKAY!

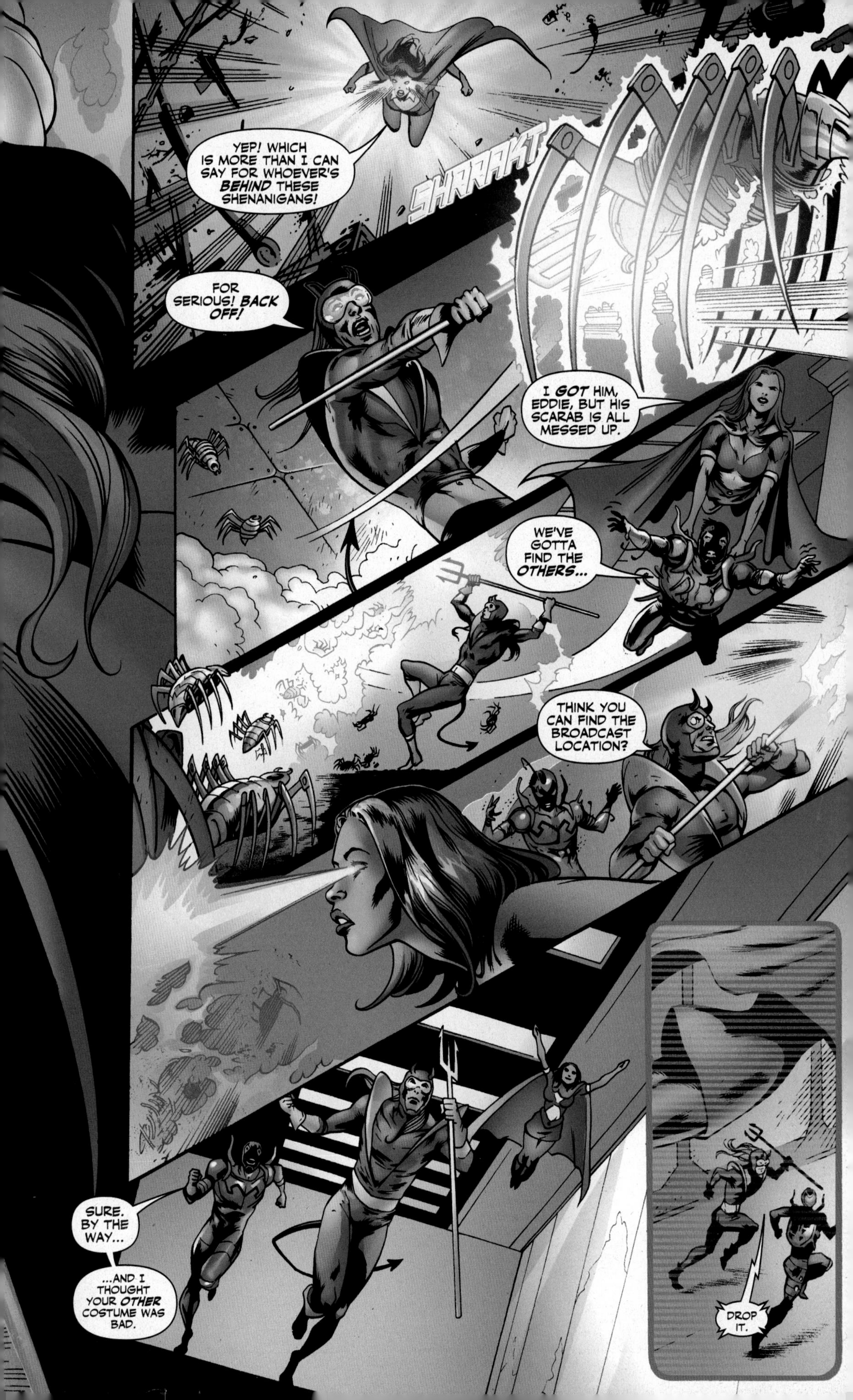
YEP! WHICH IS MORE THAN I CAN SAY FOR WHOEVER'S *BEHIND* THESE SHENANIGANS!
SHRRAKT
FOR SERIOUS! *BACK OFF!*
I *GOT* HIM, EDDIE, BUT HIS SCARAB IS ALL MESSED UP.
WE'VE GOTTA FIND THE *OTHERS...*
THINK YOU CAN FIND THE BROADCAST LOCATION?
SURE. BY THE WAY...
...AND I THOUGHT YOUR *OTHER* COSTUME WAS BAD.
DROP IT.

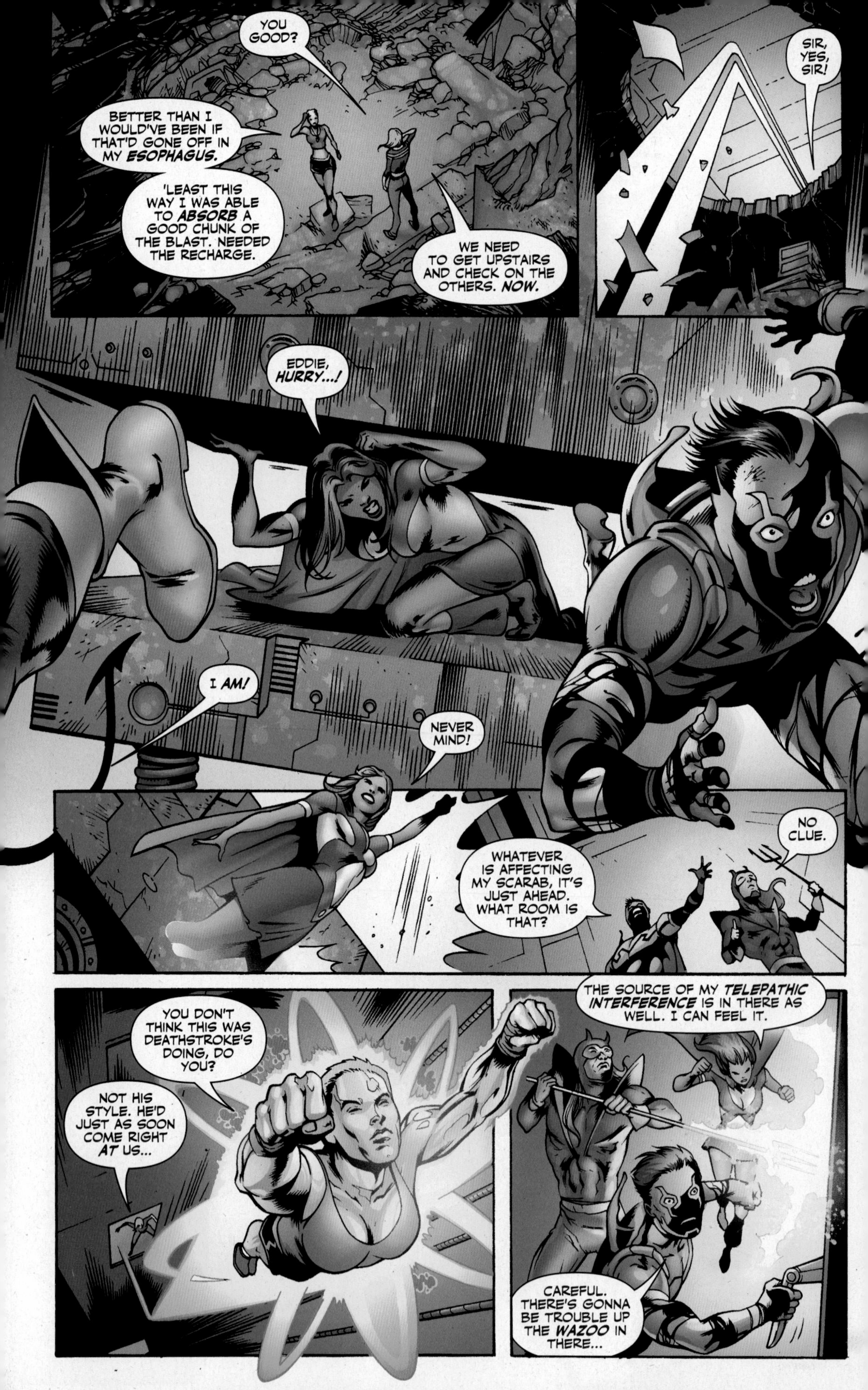
YOU GOOD?
BETTER THAN I WOULD'VE BEEN IF THAT'D GONE OFF IN MY ESOPHAGUS.
'LEAST THIS WAY I WAS ABLE TO ABSORB A GOOD CHUNK OF THE BLAST. NEEDED THE RECHARGE.
WE NEED TO GET UPSTAIRS AND CHECK ON THE OTHERS. NOW.
SIR, YES, SIR!
EDDIE, HURRY...!
I AM!
NEVER MIND!
WHATEVER IS AFFECTING MY SCARAB, IT'S JUST AHEAD. WHAT ROOM IS THAT?
NO CLUE.
YOU DON'T THINK THIS WAS DEATHSTROKE'S DOING, DO YOU?
NOT HIS STYLE. HE'D JUST AS SOON COME RIGHT AT US...
THE SOURCE OF MY TELEPATHIC INTERFERENCE IS IN THERE AS WELL. I CAN FEEL IT.
CAREFUL. THERE'S GONNA BE TROUBLE UP THE WAZOO IN THERE...

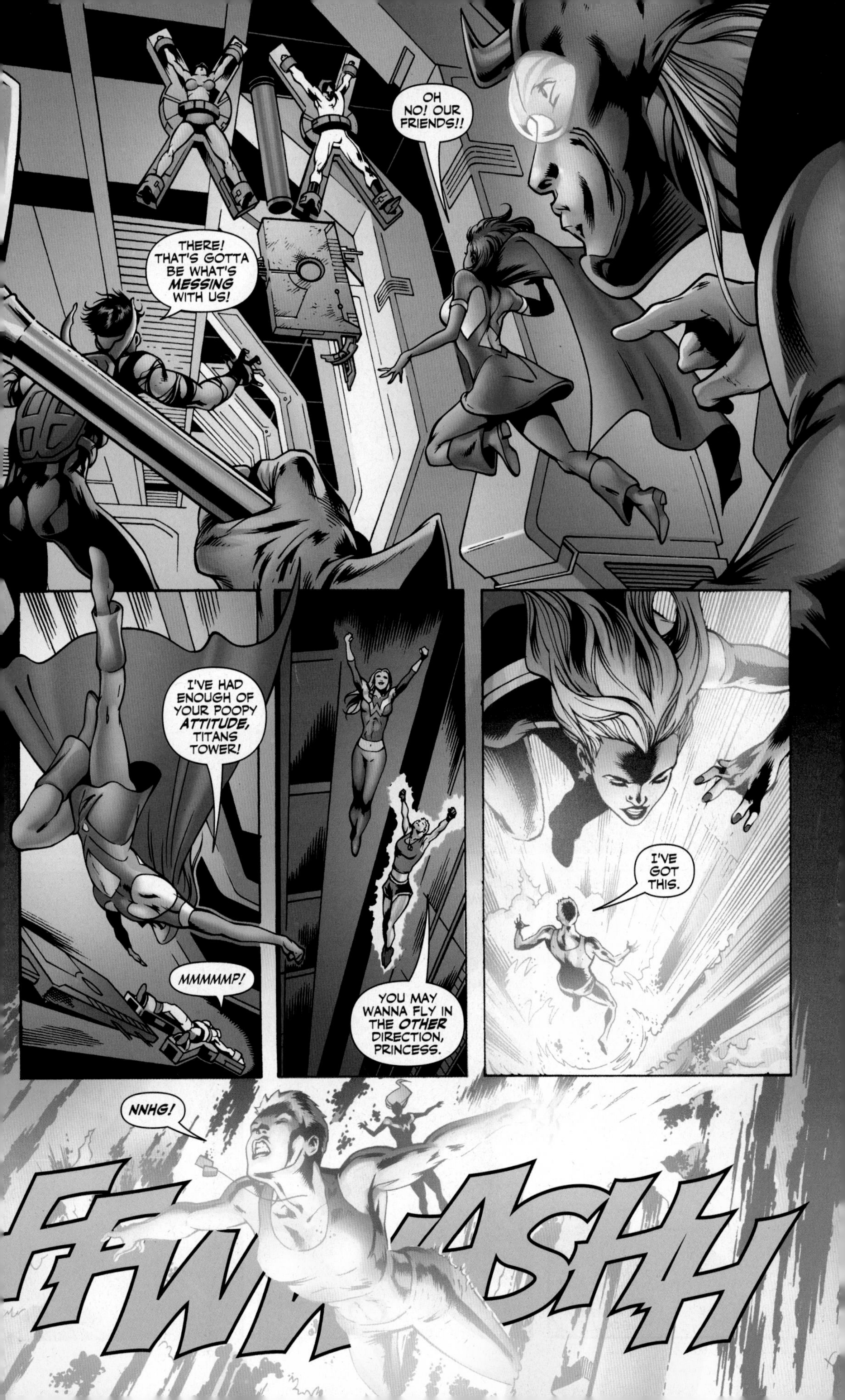
OH NO! OUR FRIENDS!!
THERE! THAT'S GOTTA BE WHAT'S *MESSING* WITH US!
I'VE HAD ENOUGH OF YOUR POOPY *ATTITUDE,* TITANS TOWER!
MMMMMP!
YOU MAY WANNA FLY IN THE *OTHER* DIRECTION, PRINCESS.
I'VE GOT THIS.
NNHG!
FWASH

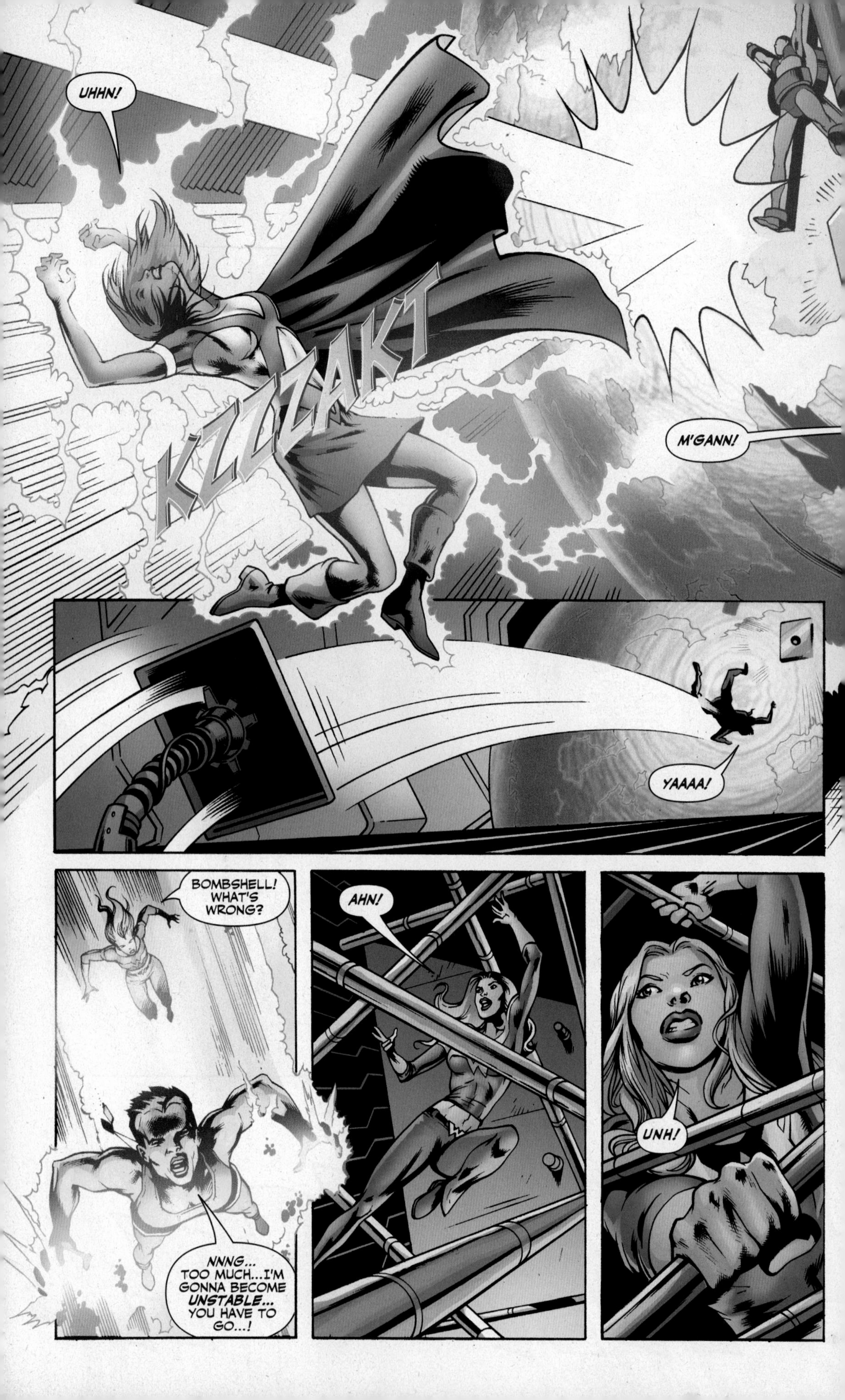
UHHN!
KZZZAKT
M'GANN!
YAAAA!
BOMBSHELL! WHAT'S WRONG?
NNNG... TOO MUCH...I'M GONNA BECOME UNSTABLE... YOU HAVE TO GO...!
AHN!
UNH!

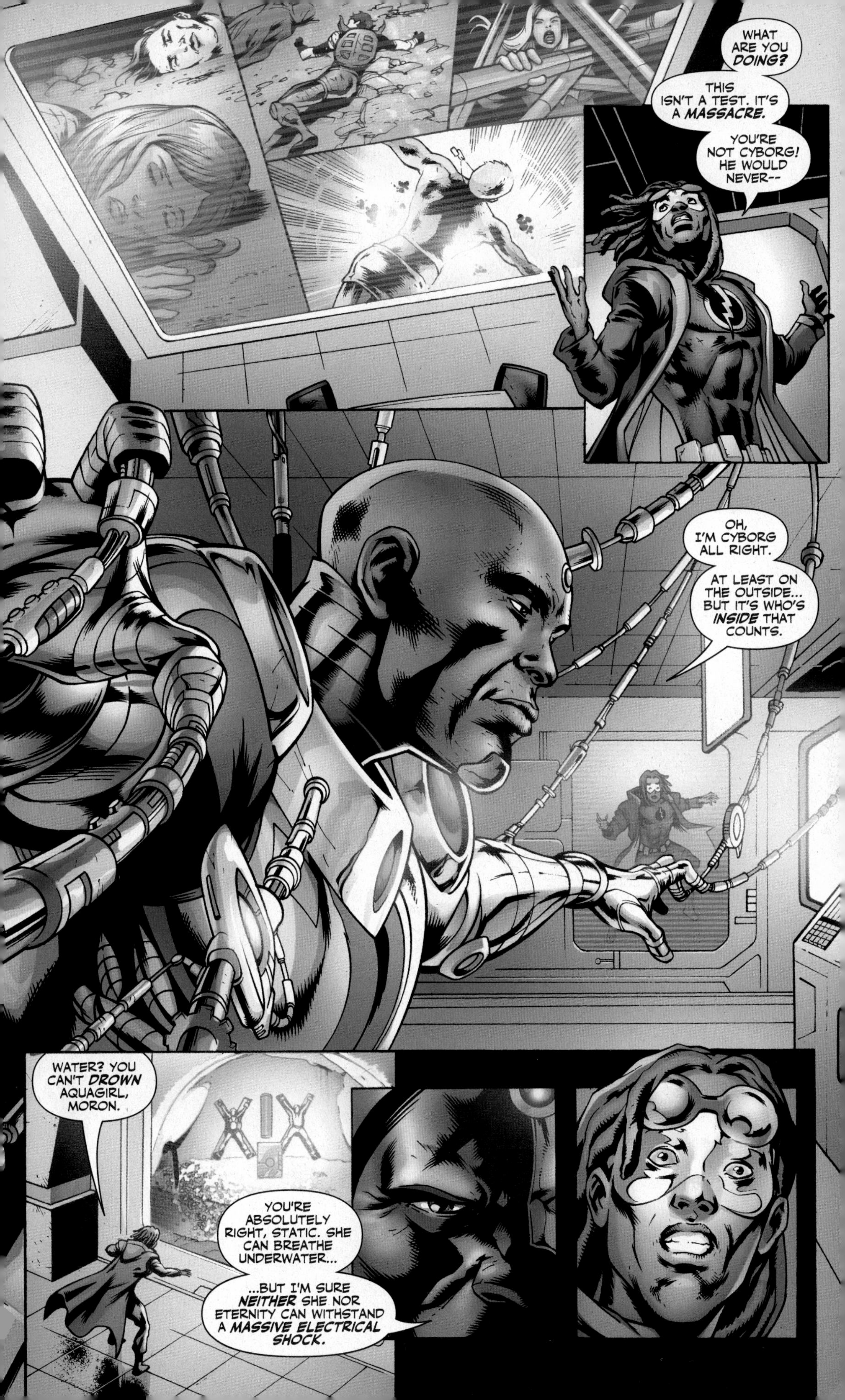
WHAT ARE YOU *DOING?*
THIS ISN'T A TEST. IT'S A *MASSACRE.*
YOU'RE NOT CYBORG! HE WOULD NEVER--
OH, I'M CYBORG ALL RIGHT.
AT LEAST ON THE OUTSIDE... BUT IT'S WHO'S *INSIDE* THAT COUNTS.
WATER? YOU CAN'T *DROWN* AQUAGIRL, MORON.
XIX
YOU'RE ABSOLUTELY RIGHT, STATIC. SHE CAN BREATHE UNDERWATER...
...BUT I'M SURE *NEITHER* SHE NOR ETERNITY CAN WITHSTAND A *MASSIVE ELECTRICAL SHOCK.*

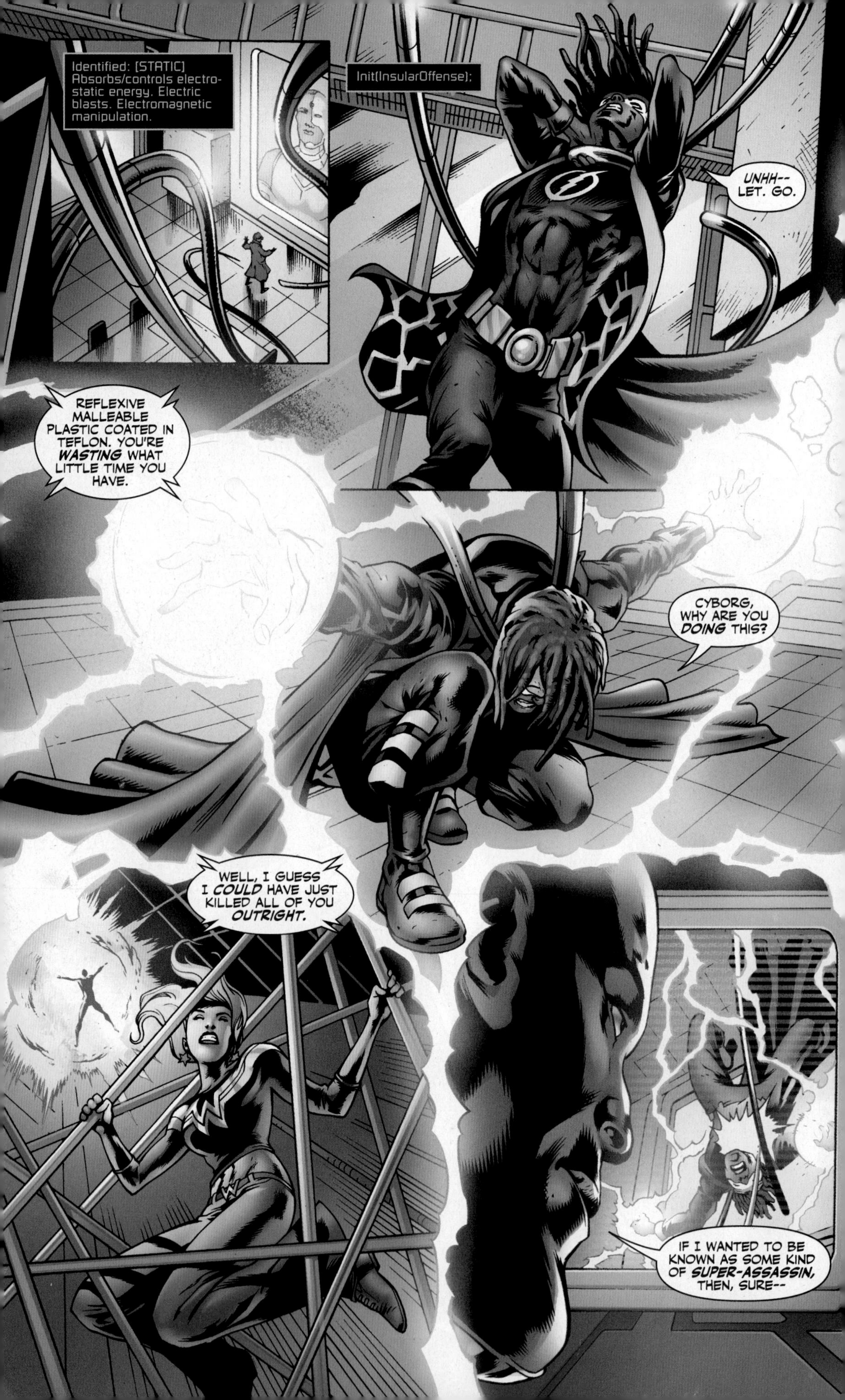
Identified: [STATIC] Absorbs/controls electro-static energy. Electric blasts. Electromagnetic manipulation.
Init(InsularOffense);
UNHH-- LET. GO.
REFLEXIVE MALLEABLE PLASTIC COATED IN TEFLON. YOU'RE WASTING WHAT LITTLE TIME YOU HAVE.
CYBORG, WHY ARE YOU DOING THIS?
WELL, I GUESS I COULD HAVE JUST KILLED ALL OF YOU OUTRIGHT.
IF I WANTED TO BE KNOWN AS SOME KIND OF SUPER-ASSASSIN, THEN, SURE--

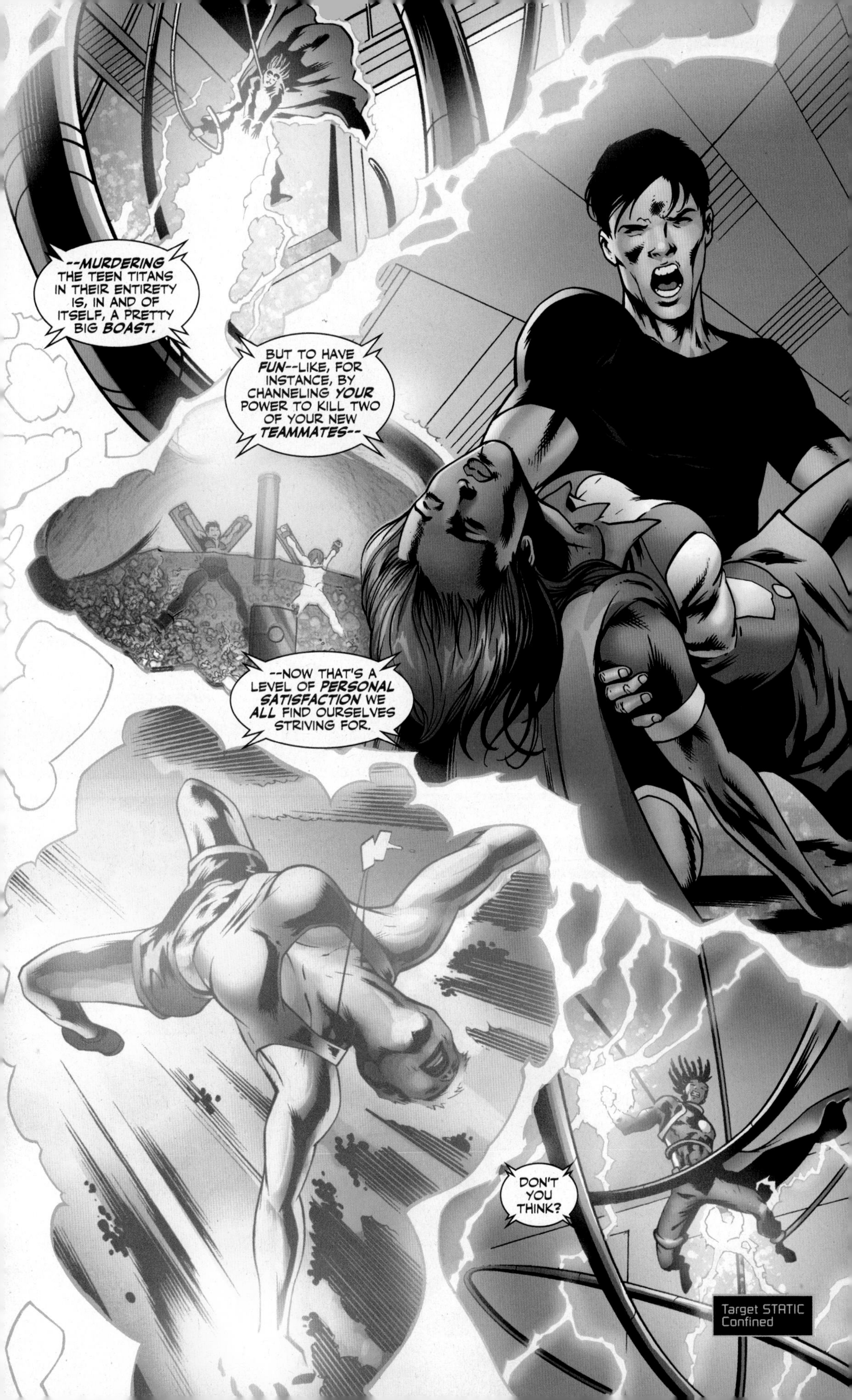
--MURDERING THE TEEN TITANS IN THEIR ENTIRETY IS, IN AND OF ITSELF, A PRETTY BIG BOAST.
BUT TO HAVE FUN--LIKE, FOR INSTANCE, BY CHANNELING YOUR POWER TO KILL TWO OF YOUR NEW TEAMMATES--
--NOW THAT'S A LEVEL OF PERSONAL SATISFACTION WE ALL FIND OURSELVES STRIVING FOR.
DON'T YOU THINK?
Target STATIC Confined

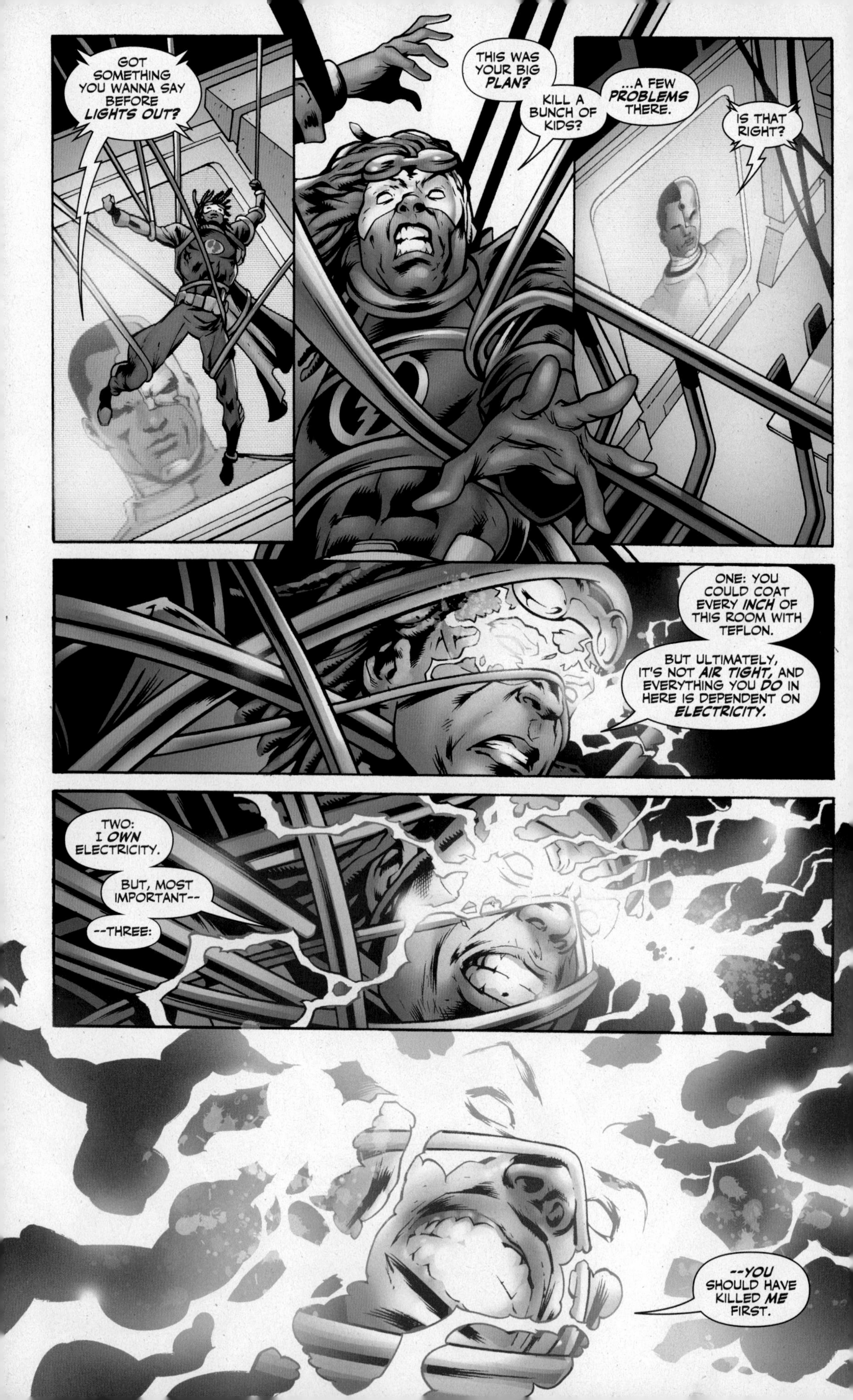
GOT SOMETHING YOU WANNA SAY BEFORE LIGHTS OUT?
THIS WAS YOUR BIG PLAN?
KILL A BUNCH OF KIDS?
...A FEW PROBLEMS THERE.
IS THAT RIGHT?
ONE: YOU COULD COAT EVERY INCH OF THIS ROOM WITH TEFLON.
BUT ULTIMATELY, IT'S NOT AIR TIGHT, AND EVERYTHING YOU DO IN HERE IS DEPENDENT ON ELECTRICITY.
TWO: I OWN ELECTRICITY.
BUT, MOST IMPORTANT--
--THREE:
--YOU SHOULD HAVE KILLED ME FIRST.

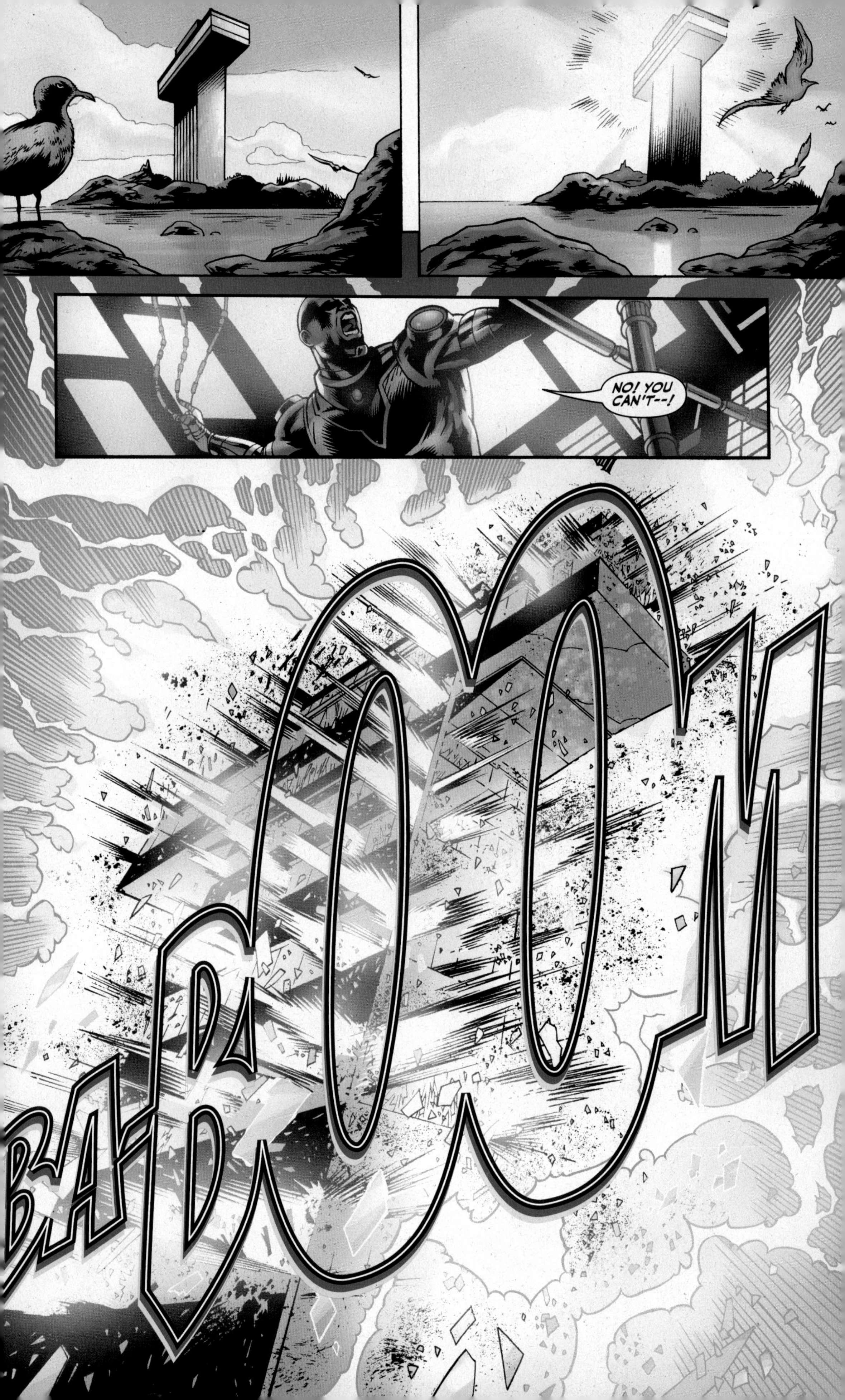
NO! YOU CAN'T--!
BADOOM

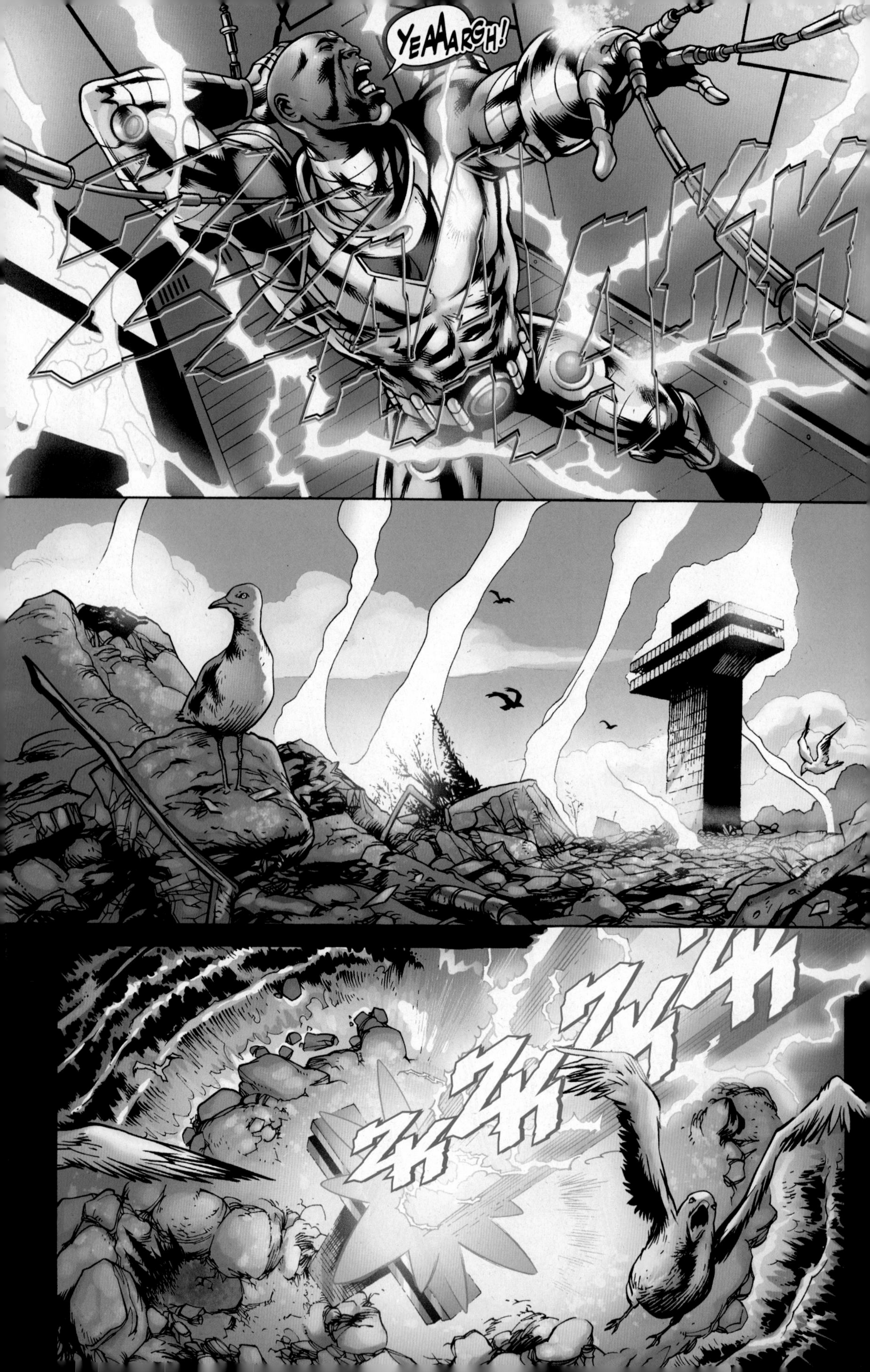
YEAAARGH!

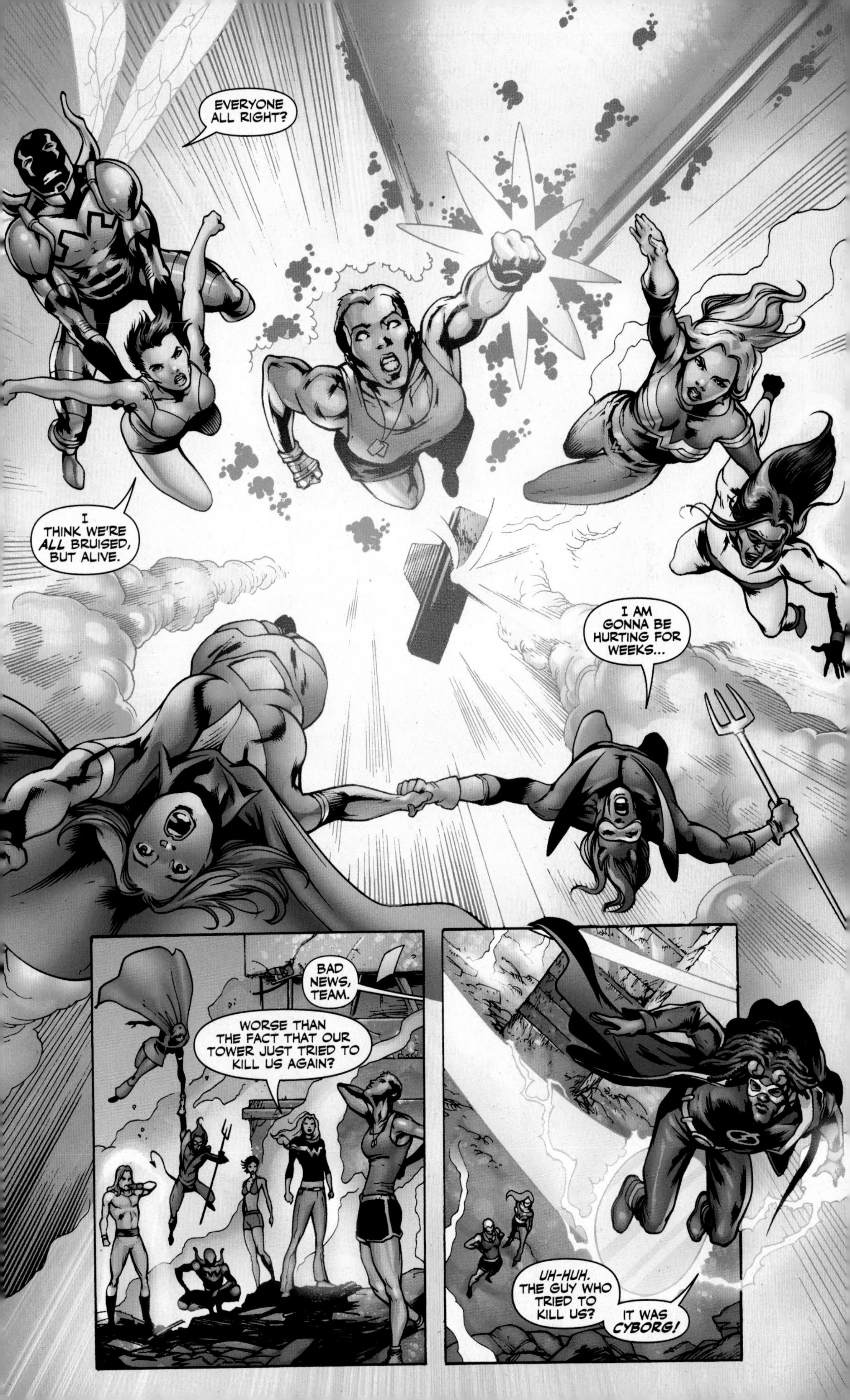
EVERYONE ALL RIGHT?
I THINK WE'RE *ALL* BRUISED, BUT ALIVE.
I AM GONNA BE HURTING FOR WEEKS...
BAD NEWS, TEAM.
WORSE THAN THE FACT THAT OUR TOWER JUST TRIED TO KILL US AGAIN?
UH-HUH. THE GUY WHO TRIED TO KILL US?
IT WAS *CYBORG!*

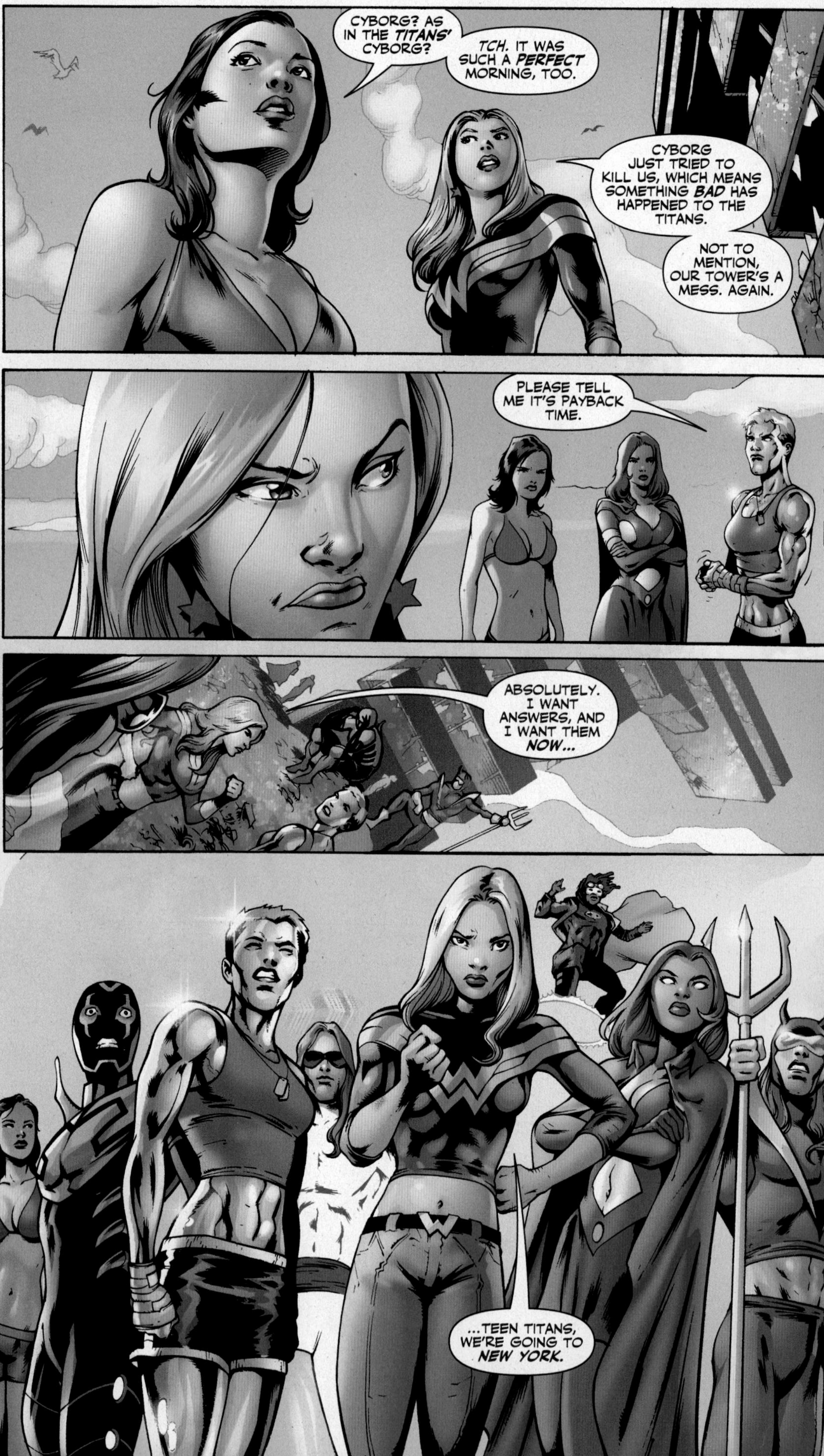
CYBORG? AS IN THE TITANS' CYBORG?
TCH. IT WAS SUCH A PERFECT MORNING, TOO.
CYBORG JUST TRIED TO KILL US, WHICH MEANS SOMETHING BAD HAS HAPPENED TO THE TITANS.
NOT TO MENTION, OUR TOWER'S A MESS. AGAIN.
PLEASE TELL ME IT'S PAYBACK TIME.
ABSOLUTELY. I WANT ANSWERS, AND I WANT THEM NOW...
...TEEN TITANS, WE'RE GOING TO NEW YORK.

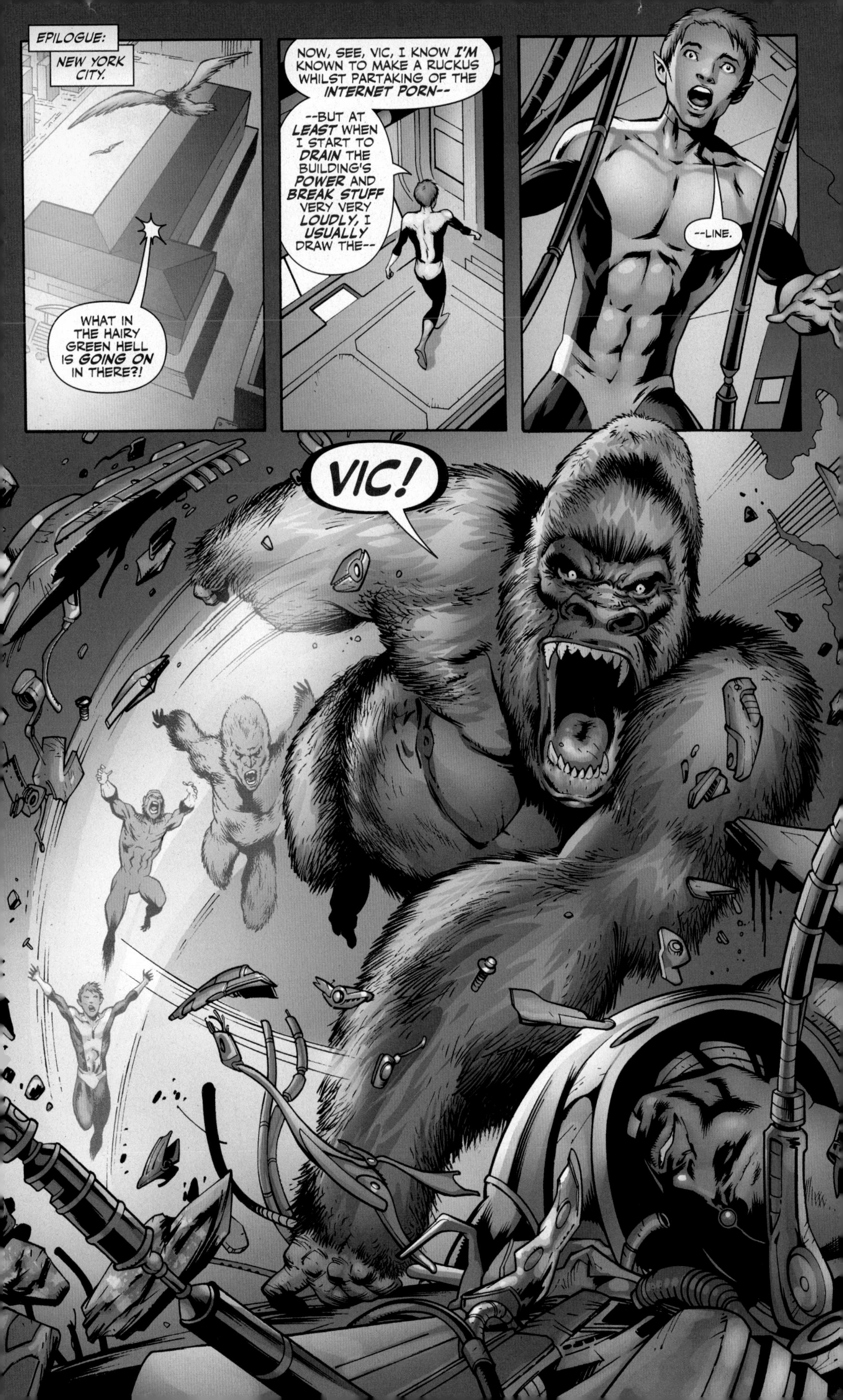
EPILOGUE:
NEW YORK CITY.
WHAT IN THE HAIRY GREEN HELL IS GOING ON IN THERE?!
NOW, SEE, VIC, I KNOW I'M KNOWN TO MAKE A RUCKUS WHILST PARTAKING OF THE INTERNET PORN--
--BUT AT LEAST WHEN I START TO DRAIN THE BUILDING'S POWER AND BREAK STUFF VERY VERY LOUDLY, I USUALLY DRAW THE--
--LINE.
VIC!

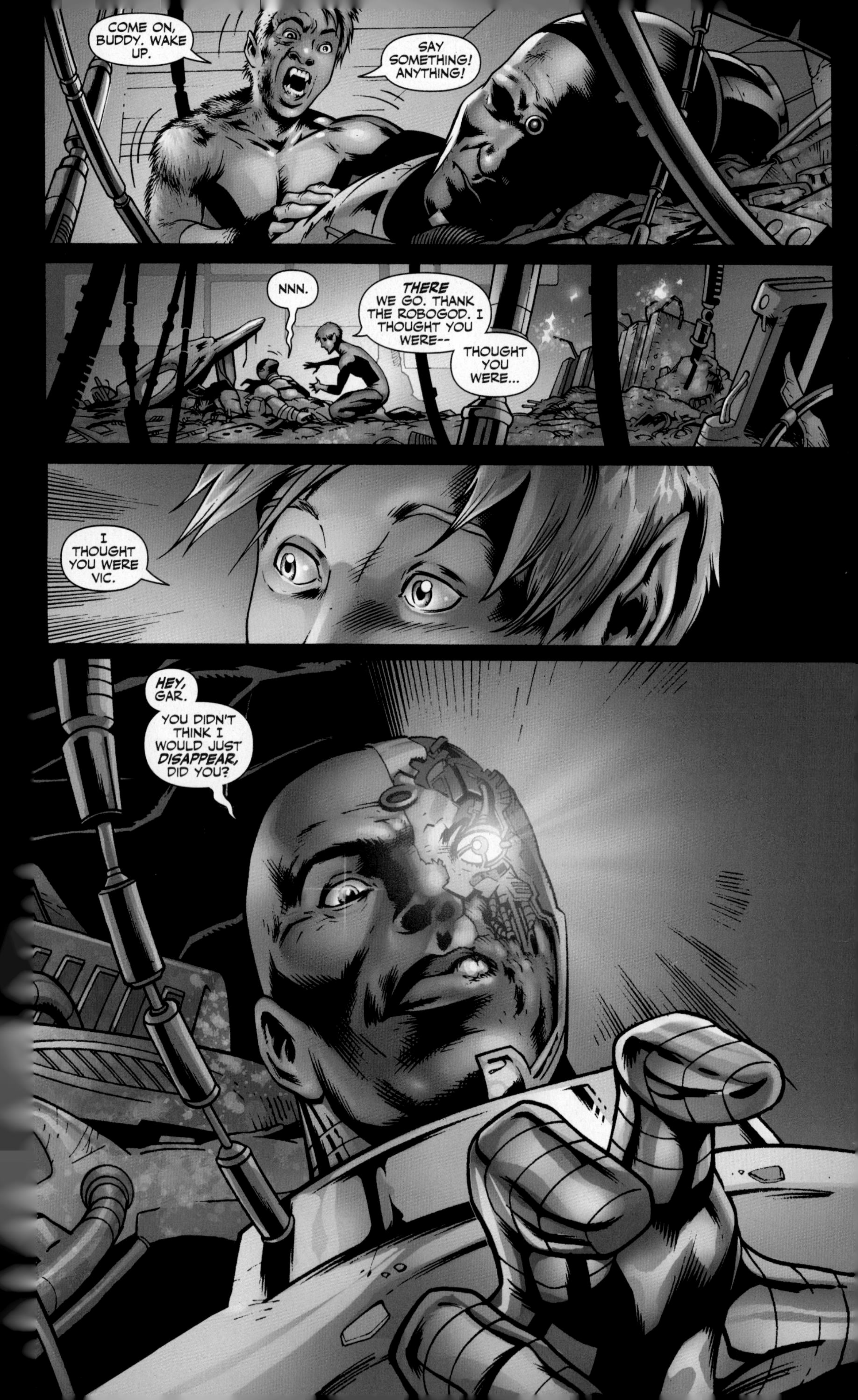
COME ON, BUDDY. WAKE UP.
SAY SOMETHING! ANYTHING!
NNN.
THERE WE GO. THANK THE ROBOGOD. I THOUGHT YOU WERE--
THOUGHT YOU WERE...
I THOUGHT YOU WERE VIC.
HEY, GAR.
YOU DIDN'T THINK I WOULD JUST DISAPPEAR, DID YOU?

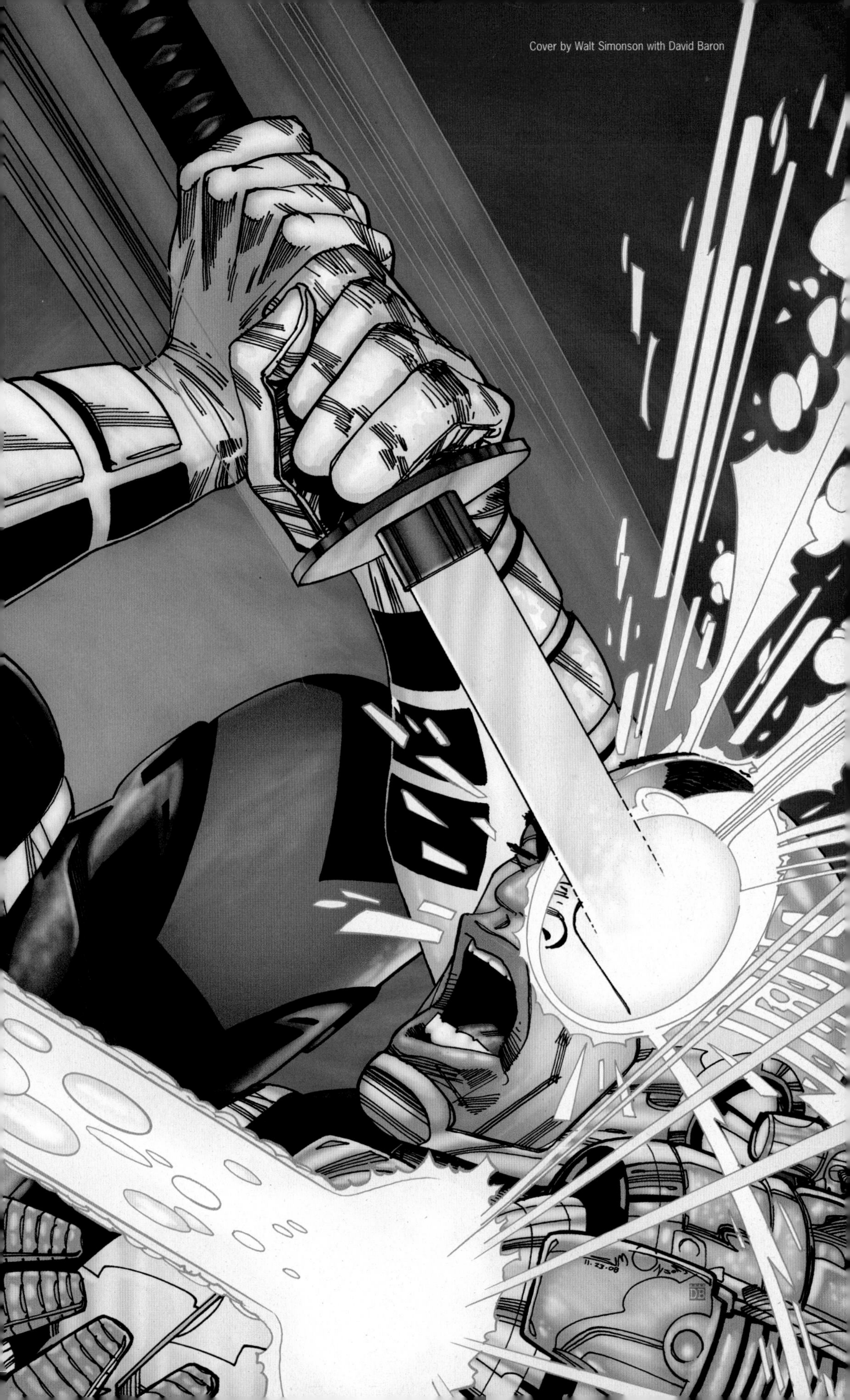

Cover by Walt Simonson with David Baron

Deathtrap Prelude: Part Two

Marv Wolfman
Writer

Rick Leonardi
Pencils

John Stanisci
Inks

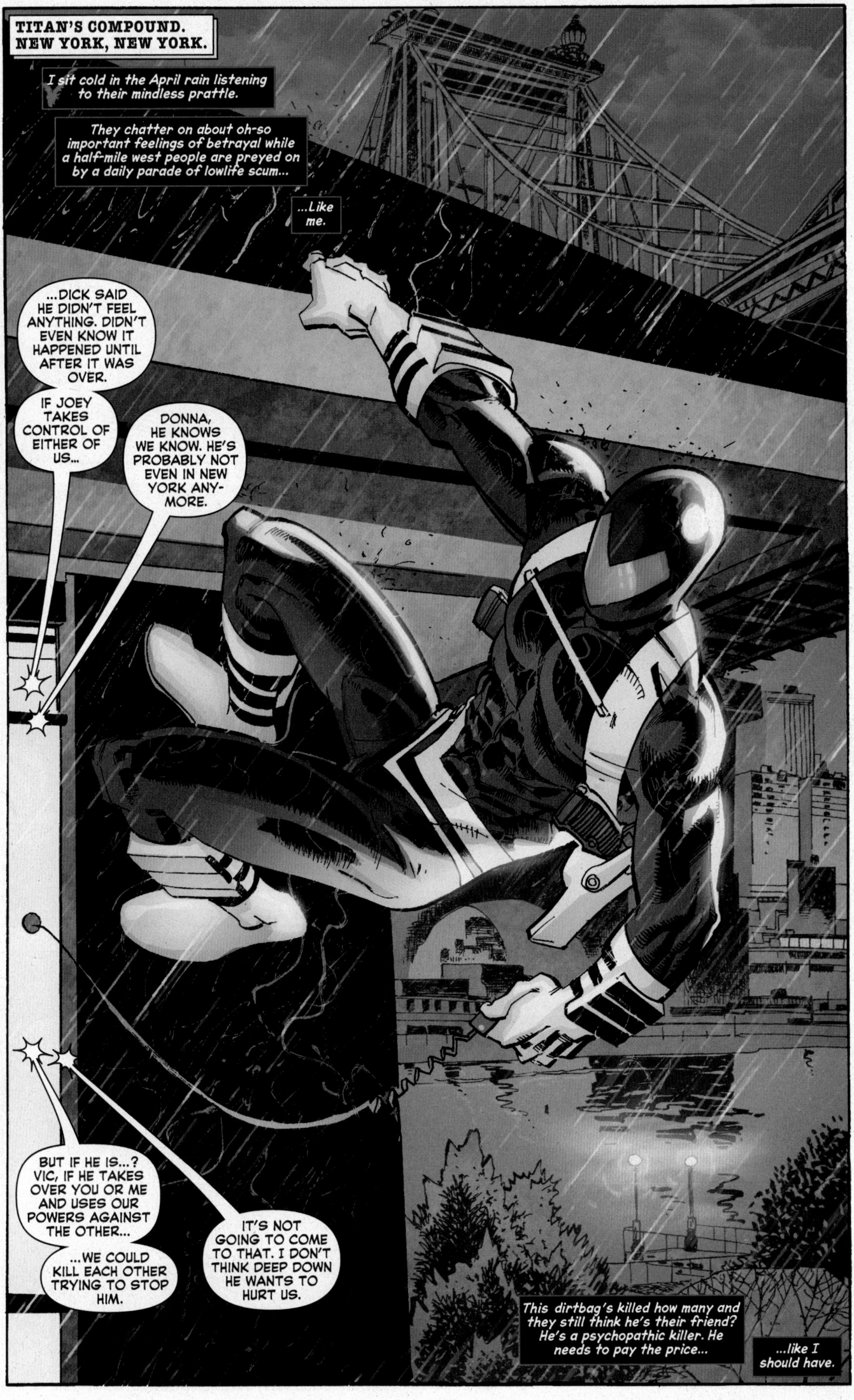
TITAN'S COMPOUND. NEW YORK, NEW YORK.
I sit cold in the April rain listening to their mindless prattle.
They chatter on about oh-so important feelings of betrayal while a half-mile west people are preyed on by a daily parade of lowlife scum...
...Like me.
...DICK SAID HE DIDN'T FEEL ANYTHING. DIDN'T EVEN KNOW IT HAPPENED UNTIL AFTER IT WAS OVER.
IF JOEY TAKES CONTROL OF EITHER OF US...
DONNA, HE KNOWS WE KNOW. HE'S PROBABLY NOT EVEN IN NEW YORK ANY-MORE.
BUT IF HE IS...? VIC, IF HE TAKES OVER YOU OR ME AND USES OUR POWERS AGAINST THE OTHER...
...WE COULD KILL EACH OTHER TRYING TO STOP HIM.
IT'S NOT GOING TO COME TO THAT. I DON'T THINK DEEP DOWN HE WANTS TO HURT US.
This dirtbag's killed how many and they still think he's their friend? He's a psychopathic killer. He needs to pay the price...
...like I should have.

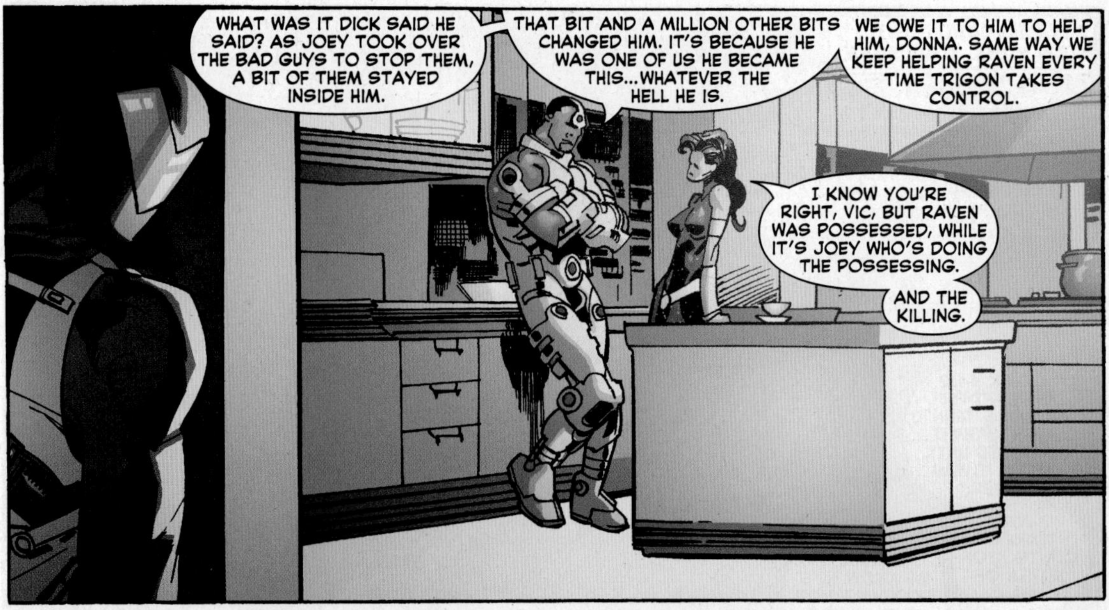
WHAT WAS IT DICK SAID HE SAID? AS JOEY TOOK OVER THE BAD GUYS TO STOP THEM, A BIT OF THEM STAYED INSIDE HIM.
THAT BIT AND A MILLION OTHER BITS CHANGED HIM. IT'S BECAUSE HE WAS ONE OF US HE BECAME THIS...WHATEVER THE HELL HE IS.
WE OWE IT TO HIM TO HELP HIM, DONNA. SAME WAY WE KEEP HELPING RAVEN EVERY TIME TRIGON TAKES CONTROL.
I KNOW YOU'RE RIGHT, VIC, BUT RAVEN WAS POSSESSED, WHILE IT'S JOEY WHO'S DOING THE POSSESSING.
AND THE KILLING.

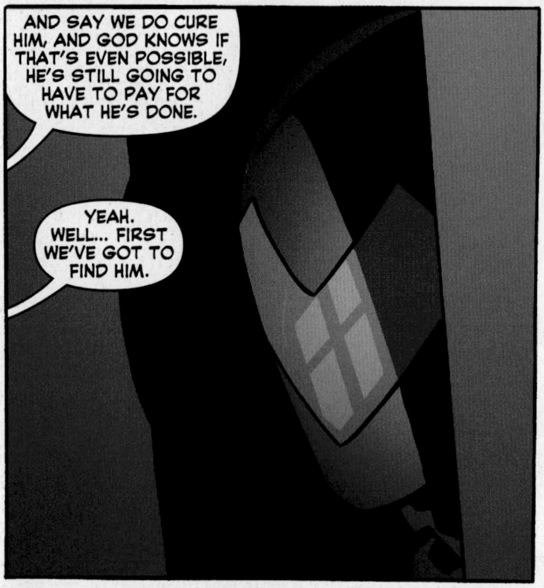
AND SAY WE DO CURE HIM, AND GOD KNOWS IF THAT'S EVEN POSSIBLE, HE'S STILL GOING TO HAVE TO PAY FOR WHAT HE'S DONE.
YEAH. WELL... FIRST WE'VE GOT TO FIND HIM.

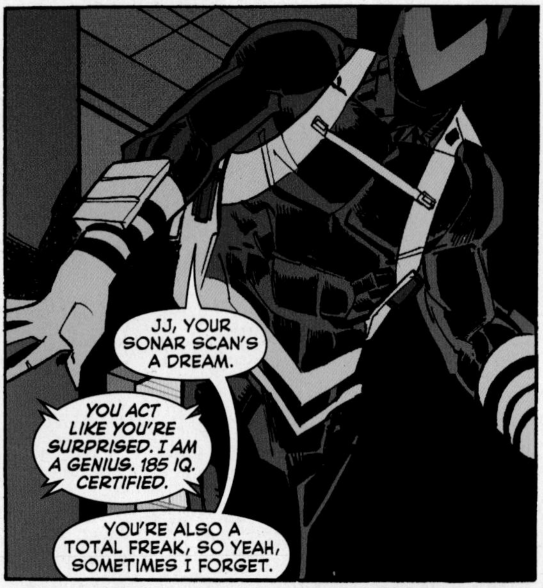
JJ, YOUR SONAR SCAN'S A DREAM.
YOU ACT LIKE YOU'RE SURPRISED. I AM A GENIUS. 185 IQ. CERTIFIED.
YOU'RE ALSO A TOTAL FREAK, SO YEAH, SOMETIMES I FORGET.

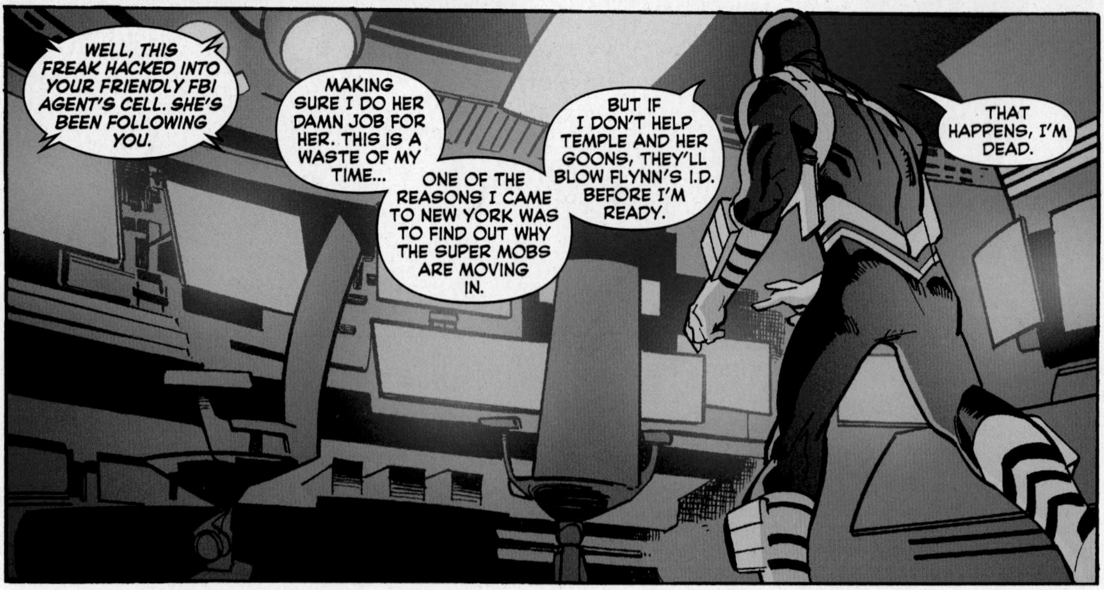
WELL, THIS FREAK HACKED INTO YOUR FRIENDLY FBI AGENT'S CELL. SHE'S BEEN FOLLOWING YOU.
MAKING SURE I DO HER DAMN JOB FOR HER. THIS IS A WASTE OF MY TIME...
ONE OF THE REASONS I CAME TO NEW YORK WAS TO FIND OUT WHY THE SUPER MOBS ARE MOVING IN.
BUT IF I DON'T HELP TEMPLE AND HER GOONS, THEY'LL BLOW FLYNN'S I.D. BEFORE I'M READY.
THAT HAPPENS, I'M DEAD.

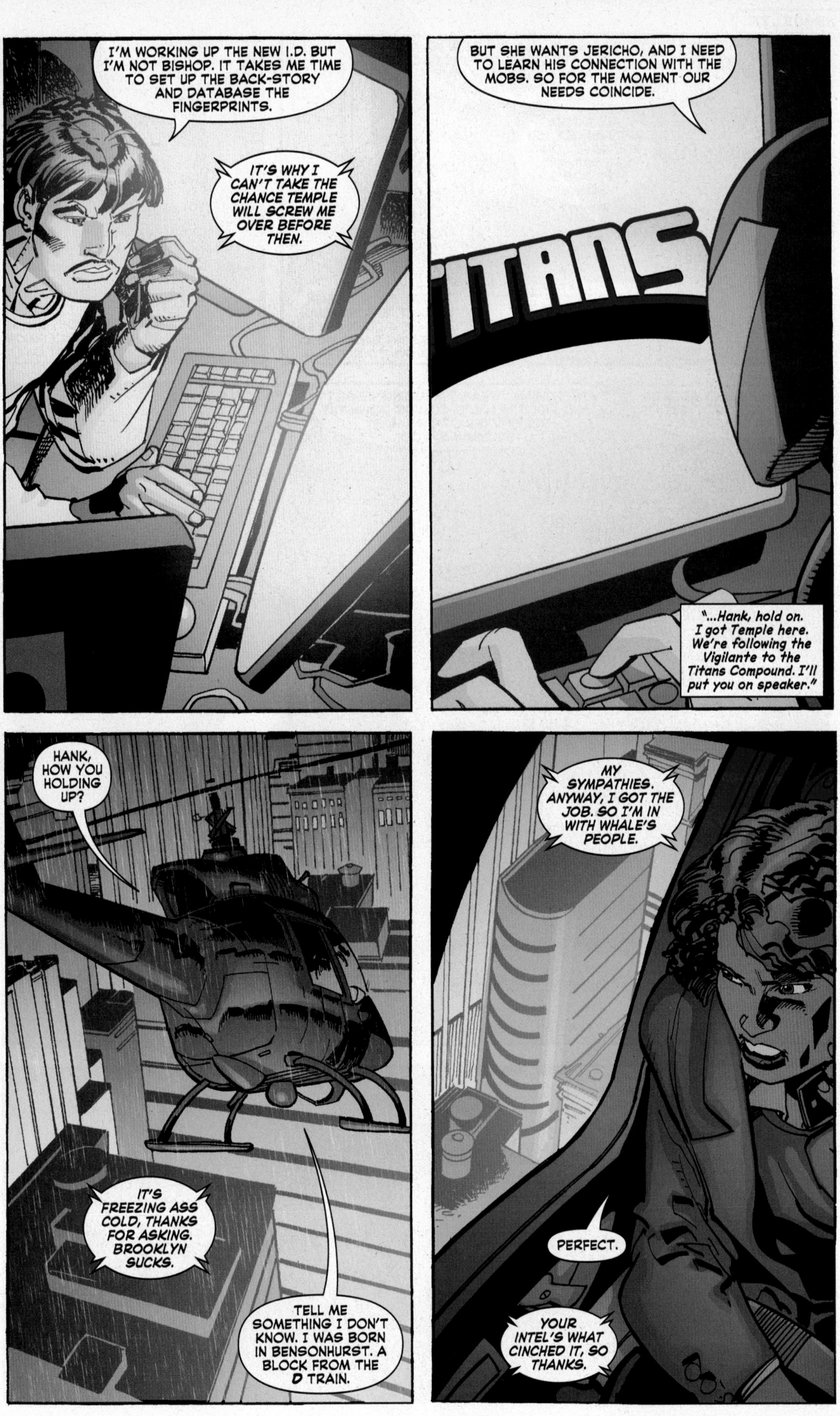

I'M WORKING UP THE NEW I.D. BUT I'M NOT BISHOP. IT TAKES ME TIME TO SET UP THE BACK-STORY AND DATABASE THE FINGERPRINTS.
IT'S WHY I CAN'T TAKE THE CHANCE TEMPLE WILL SCREW ME OVER BEFORE THEN.
BUT SHE WANTS JERICHO, AND I NEED TO LEARN HIS CONNECTION WITH THE MOBS. SO FOR THE MOMENT OUR NEEDS COINCIDE.
TITANS
"...Hank, hold on. I got Temple here. We're following the Vigilante to the Titans Compound. I'll put you on speaker."
HANK, HOW YOU HOLDING UP?
IT'S FREEZING ASS COLD, THANKS FOR ASKING. BROOKLYN SUCKS.
TELL ME SOMETHING I DON'T KNOW. I WAS BORN IN BENSONHURST. A BLOCK FROM THE D TRAIN.
MY SYMPATHIES. ANYWAY, I GOT THE JOB. SO I'M IN WITH WHALE'S PEOPLE.
PERFECT.
YOUR INTEL'S WHAT CINCHED IT, SO THANKS.

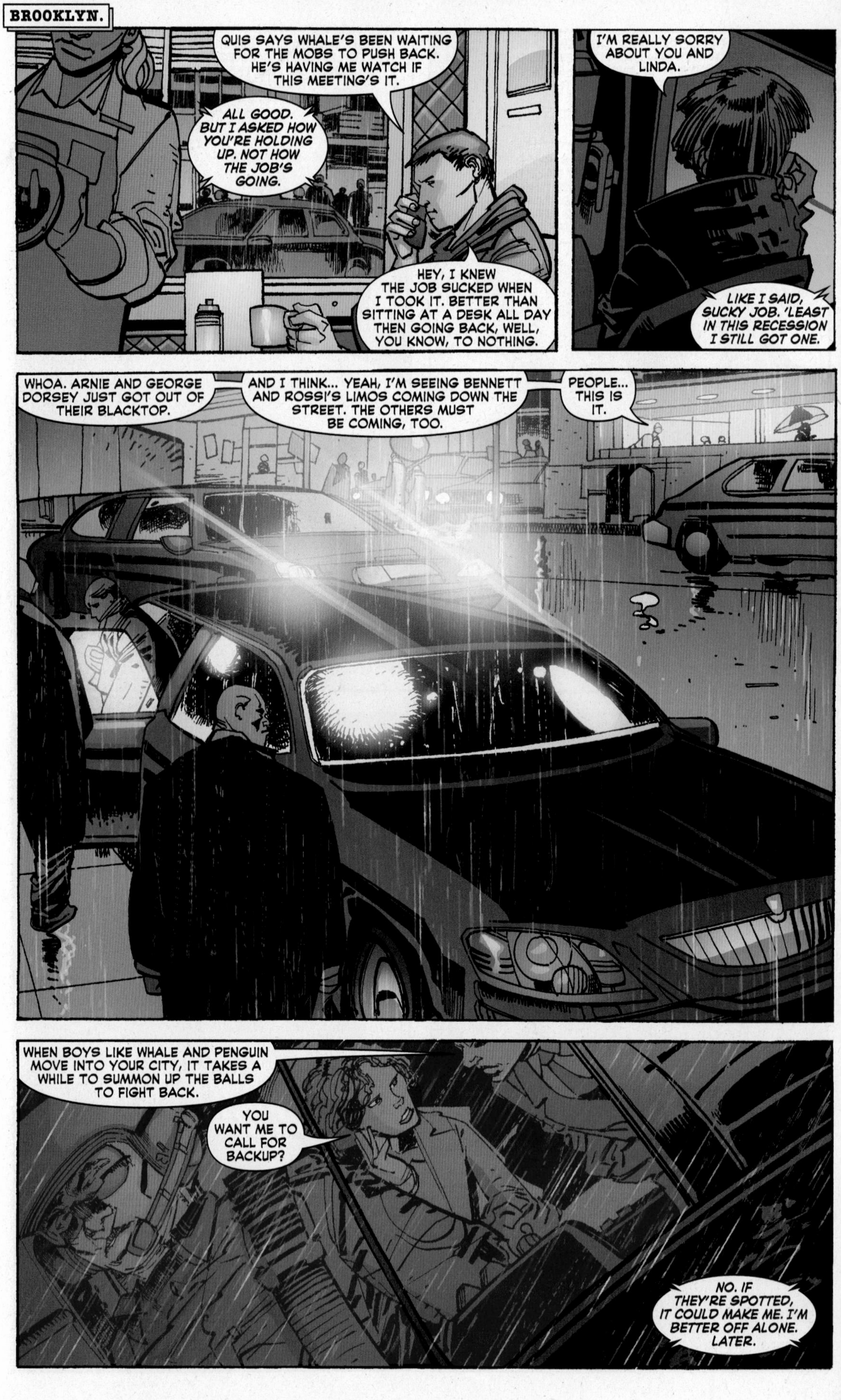
BROOKLYN.
QUIS SAYS WHALE'S BEEN WAITING FOR THE MOBS TO PUSH BACK. HE'S HAVING ME WATCH IF THIS MEETING'S IT.
ALL GOOD. BUT I ASKED HOW YOU'RE HOLDING UP. NOT HOW THE JOB'S GOING.
HEY, I KNEW THE JOB SUCKED WHEN I TOOK IT. BETTER THAN SITTING AT A DESK ALL DAY THEN GOING BACK, WELL, YOU KNOW, TO NOTHING.
I'M REALLY SORRY ABOUT YOU AND LINDA.
LIKE I SAID, SUCKY JOB. 'LEAST IN THIS RECESSION I STILL GOT ONE.
WHOA. ARNIE AND GEORGE DORSEY JUST GOT OUT OF THEIR BLACKTOP.
AND I THINK... YEAH, I'M SEEING BENNETT AND ROSSI'S LIMOS COMING DOWN THE STREET. THE OTHERS MUST BE COMING, TOO.
PEOPLE... THIS IS IT.
WHEN BOYS LIKE WHALE AND PENGUIN MOVE INTO YOUR CITY, IT TAKES A WHILE TO SUMMON UP THE BALLS TO FIGHT BACK.
YOU WANT ME TO CALL FOR BACKUP?
NO. IF THEY'RE SPOTTED, IT COULD MAKE ME. I'M BETTER OFF ALONE. LATER.

ARNIE. GEORGE. I DIDN'T GET THE CHANCE TO CALL. BUT WHAT HAPPENED TO JACKY, IT STILL SADDENS ME.

YEAH. EVERYONE HERE'S ALL BROKEN UP, ALFREDO. I KNOW.

WHOEVER GUNNED JACKY DOWN'S GONNA DIE, DON'T YOU WORRY.

GEORGE... WE DIDN'T COME HERE TO TALK FAMILY, DID WE, SOLOMON?

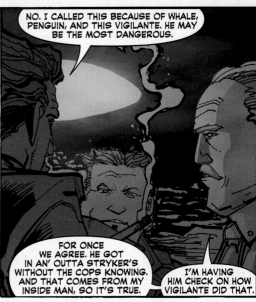

NO. I CALLED THIS BECAUSE OF WHALE, PENGUIN, AND THIS VIGILANTE. HE MAY BE THE MOST DANGEROUS.

FOR ONCE WE AGREE. HE GOT IN AN' OUTTA STRYKER'S WITHOUT THE COPS KNOWING. AND THAT COMES FROM MY INSIDE MAN, SO IT'S TRUE.

I'M HAVING HIM CHECK ON HOW VIGILANTE DID THAT.

MY GUY THINKS HE'S AN FBI MOLE AND HE'S HIDING IN ONE OF OUR GANGS. IF THAT'S TRUE, IT COULD EXPLAIN STRYKER'S.

THIS CITY'S ALREADY GOT ENOUGH MASKS. AND NONE OF THEM ARE GOING AFTER WHALE AND PENGUIN.

WHICH IS WHY THIS. SINCE THIS VIGILANTE IS HIDING UNDER OUR NOSES...

...WHY DON'T WE GIVE HIM SOMETHING HE CAN SMELL.

WE SET HIM UP AND SEND HIM AGAINST WHALE AND THE PENGUIN.

AND IF THEY KILL EACH OTHER, WHO THE HELL CARES?

PRECISELY.

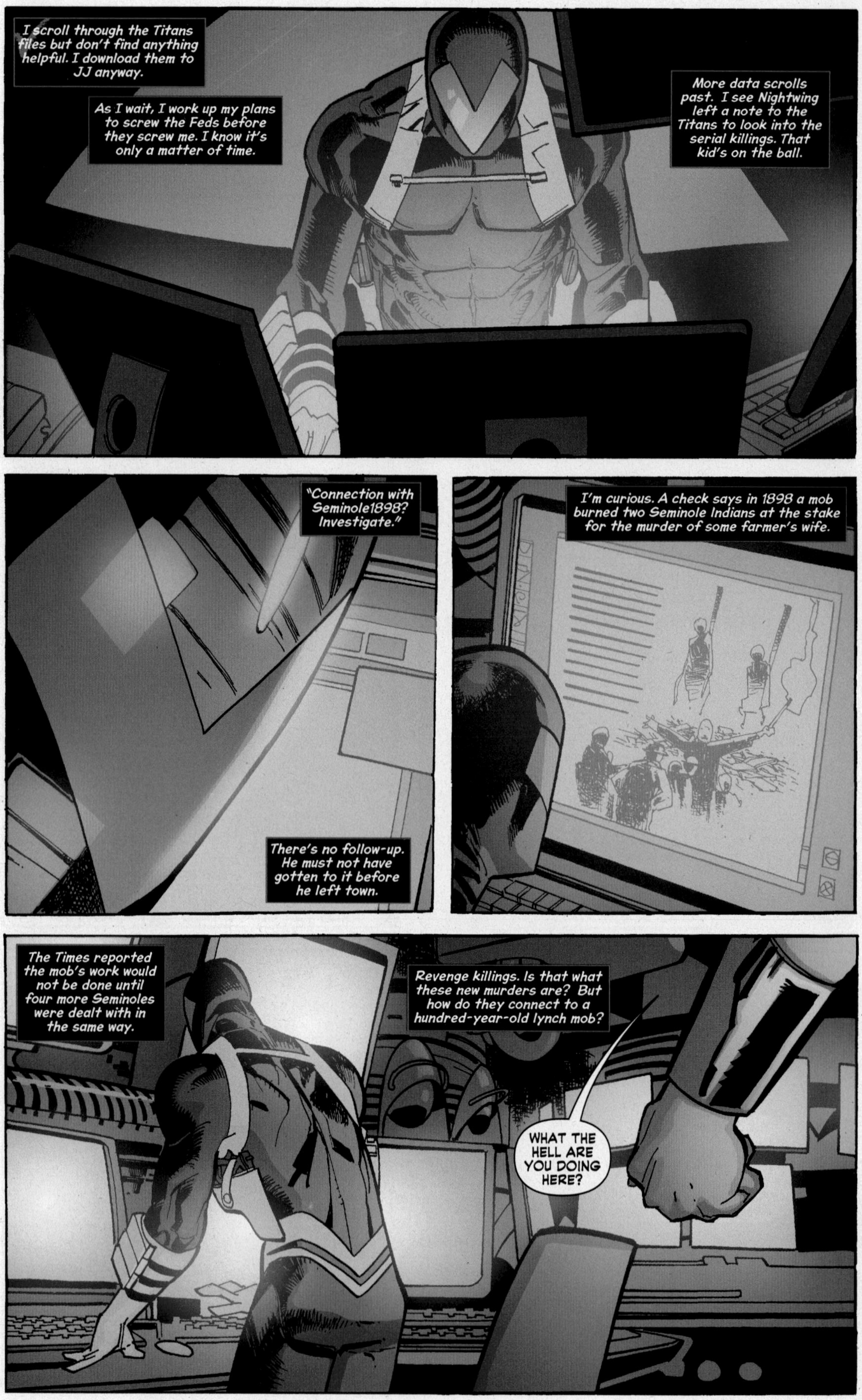
I scroll through the Titans files but don't find anything helpful. I download them to JJ anyway.
As I wait, I work up my plans to screw the Feds before they screw me. I know it's only a matter of time.
More data scrolls past. I see Nightwing left a note to the Titans to look into the serial killings. That kid's on the ball.
"Connection with Seminole1898? Investigate."
There's no follow-up. He must not have gotten to it before he left town.
I'm curious. A check says in 1898 a mob burned two Seminole Indians at the stake for the murder of some farmer's wife.
The Times reported the mob's work would not be done until four more Seminoles were dealt with in the same way.
Revenge killings. Is that what these new murders are? But how do they connect to a hundred-year-old lynch mob?
WHAT THE HELL ARE YOU DOING HERE?

TALK TO ME!
Talking messes up concentration. I say nothing but I'm wondering if Jericho is inside her.
If so, I try to stay out of reach. With her super-strength he could rip me apart without thinking.
I KNOW WHO YOU ARE. AND I KNOW YOU'RE WANTED FOR MURDER.
I WON'T LET YOU GET AWAY.
She's trying to stop me, not kil me. She's not Jericho. I can't kill her.
It would've been easier the other way.

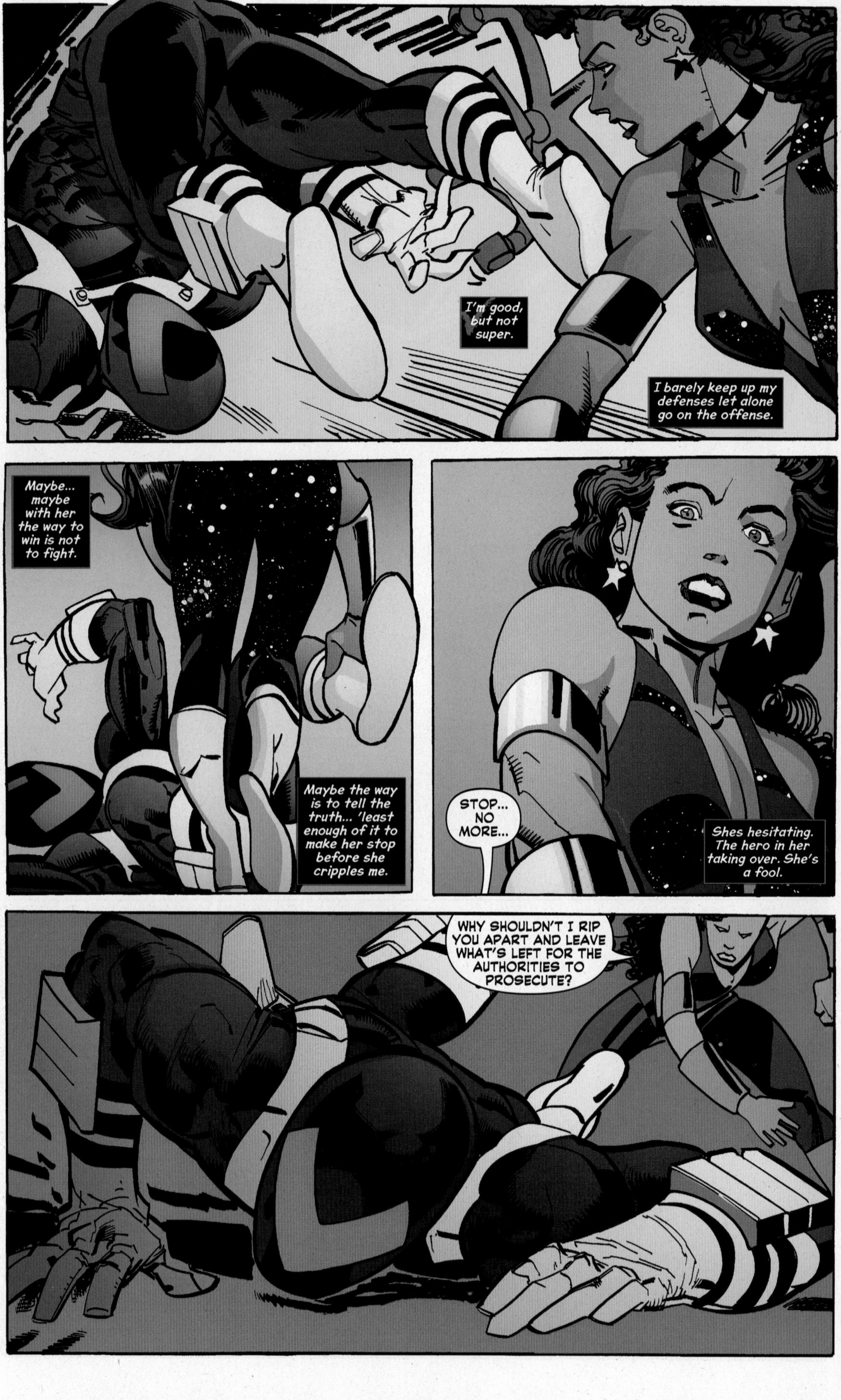

I'm good, but not super.
I barely keep up my defenses let alone go on the offense.
Maybe... maybe with her the way to win is not to fight.
Maybe the way is to tell the truth... 'least enough of it to make her stop before she cripples me.
STOP... NO MORE...
Shes hesitating. The hero in her taking over. She's a fool.
WHY SHOULDN'T I RIP YOU APART AND LEAVE WHAT'S LEFT FOR THE AUTHORITIES TO PROSECUTE?

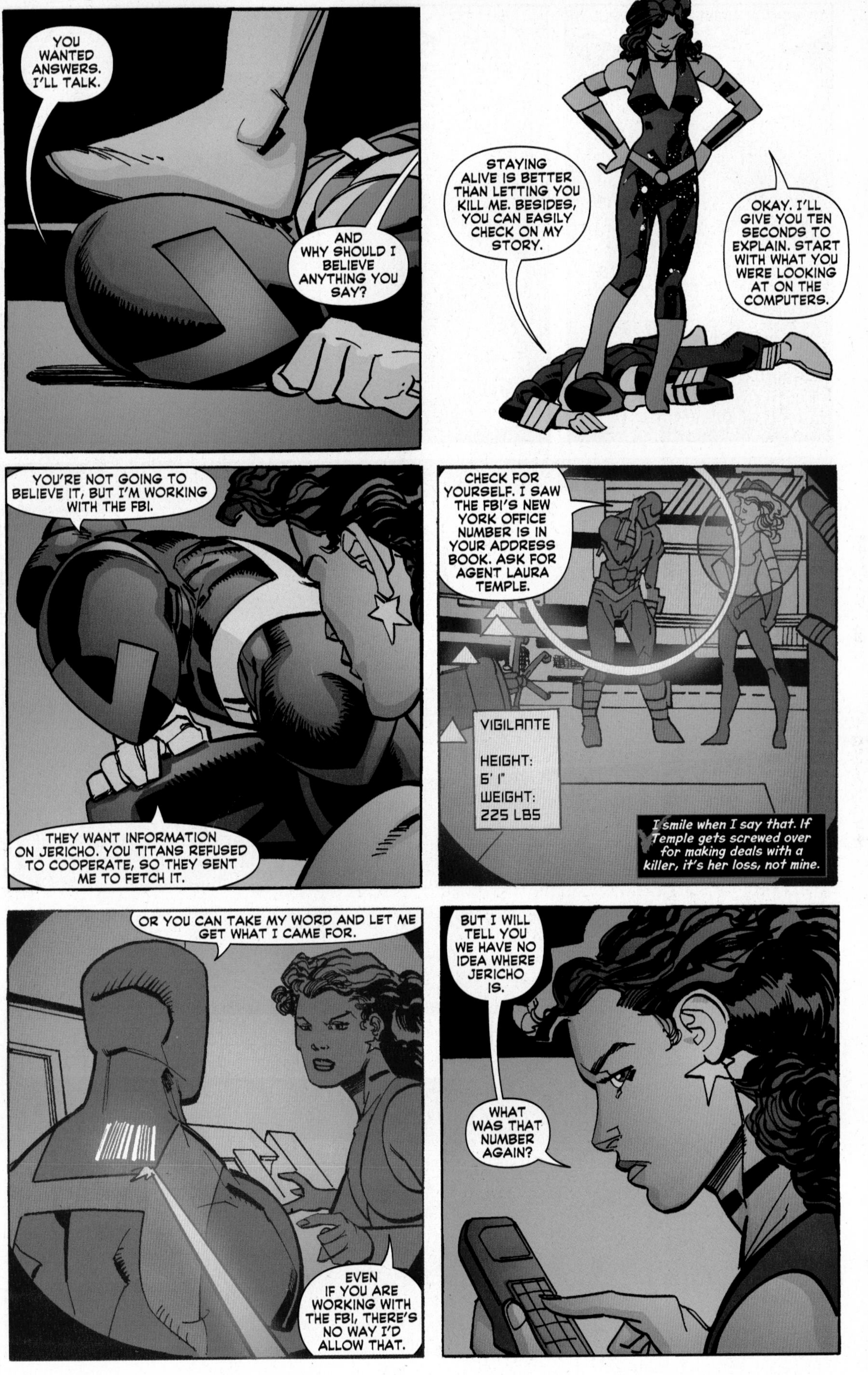
YOU WANTED ANSWERS. I'LL TALK.
AND WHY SHOULD I BELIEVE ANYTHING YOU SAY?
STAYING ALIVE IS BETTER THAN LETTING YOU KILL ME. BESIDES, YOU CAN EASILY CHECK ON MY STORY.
OKAY. I'LL GIVE YOU TEN SECONDS TO EXPLAIN. START WITH WHAT YOU WERE LOOKING AT ON THE COMPUTERS.
YOU'RE NOT GOING TO BELIEVE IT, BUT I'M WORKING WITH THE FBI.
THEY WANT INFORMATION ON JERICHO. YOU TITANS REFUSED TO COOPERATE, SO THEY SENT ME TO FETCH IT.
CHECK FOR YOURSELF. I SAW THE FBI'S NEW YORK OFFICE NUMBER IS IN YOUR ADDRESS BOOK. ASK FOR AGENT LAURA TEMPLE.
VIGILANTE
HEIGHT: 6' 1"
WEIGHT: 225 LBS
I smile when I say that. If Temple gets screwed over for making deals with a killer, it's her loss, not mine.
OR YOU CAN TAKE MY WORD AND LET ME GET WHAT I CAME FOR.
EVEN IF YOU ARE WORKING WITH THE FBI, THERE'S NO WAY I'D ALLOW THAT.
BUT I WILL TELL YOU WE HAVE NO IDEA WHERE JERICHO IS.
WHAT WAS THAT NUMBER AGAIN?

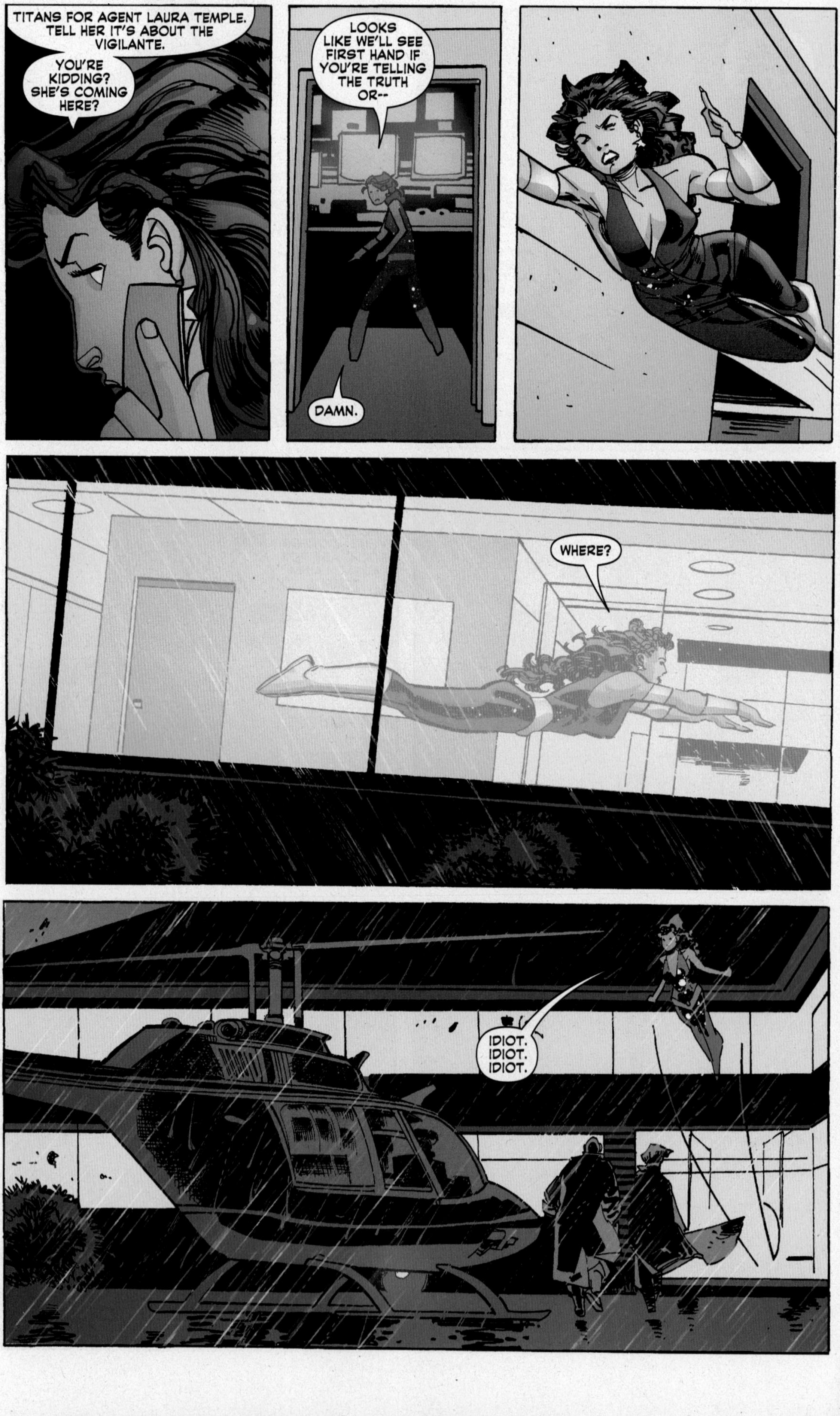
TITANS FOR AGENT LAURA TEMPLE. TELL HER IT'S ABOUT THE VIGILANTE.
YOU'RE KIDDING? SHE'S COMING HERE?
LOOKS LIKE WE'LL SEE FIRST HAND IF YOU'RE TELLING THE TRUTH OR--
DAMN.
WHERE?
IDIOT. IDIOT. IDIOT.

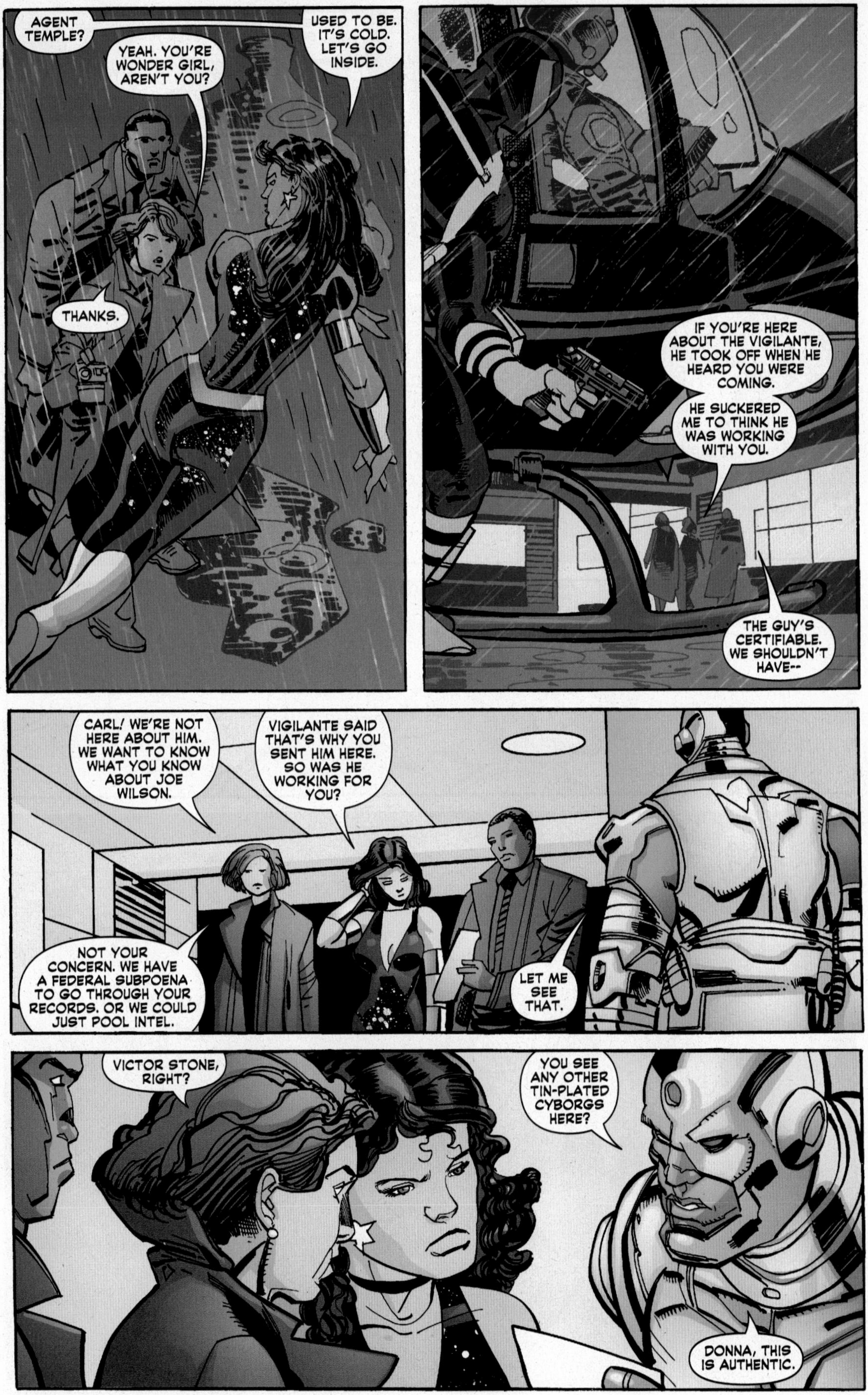
AGENT TEMPLE?
YEAH. YOU'RE WONDER GIRL, AREN'T YOU?
USED TO BE. IT'S COLD. LET'S GO INSIDE.
THANKS.
IF YOU'RE HERE ABOUT THE VIGILANTE, HE TOOK OFF WHEN HE HEARD YOU WERE COMING.
HE SUCKERED ME TO THINK HE WAS WORKING WITH YOU.
THE GUY'S CERTIFIABLE. WE SHOULDN'T HAVE--
CARL! WE'RE NOT HERE ABOUT HIM. WE WANT TO KNOW WHAT YOU KNOW ABOUT JOE WILSON.
VIGILANTE SAID THAT'S WHY YOU SENT HIM HERE. SO WAS HE WORKING FOR YOU?
NOT YOUR CONCERN. WE HAVE A FEDERAL SUBPOENA TO GO THROUGH YOUR RECORDS. OR WE COULD JUST POOL INTEL.
LET ME SEE THAT.
VICTOR STONE, RIGHT?
YOU SEE ANY OTHER TIN-PLATED CYBORGS HERE?
DONNA, THIS IS AUTHENTIC.

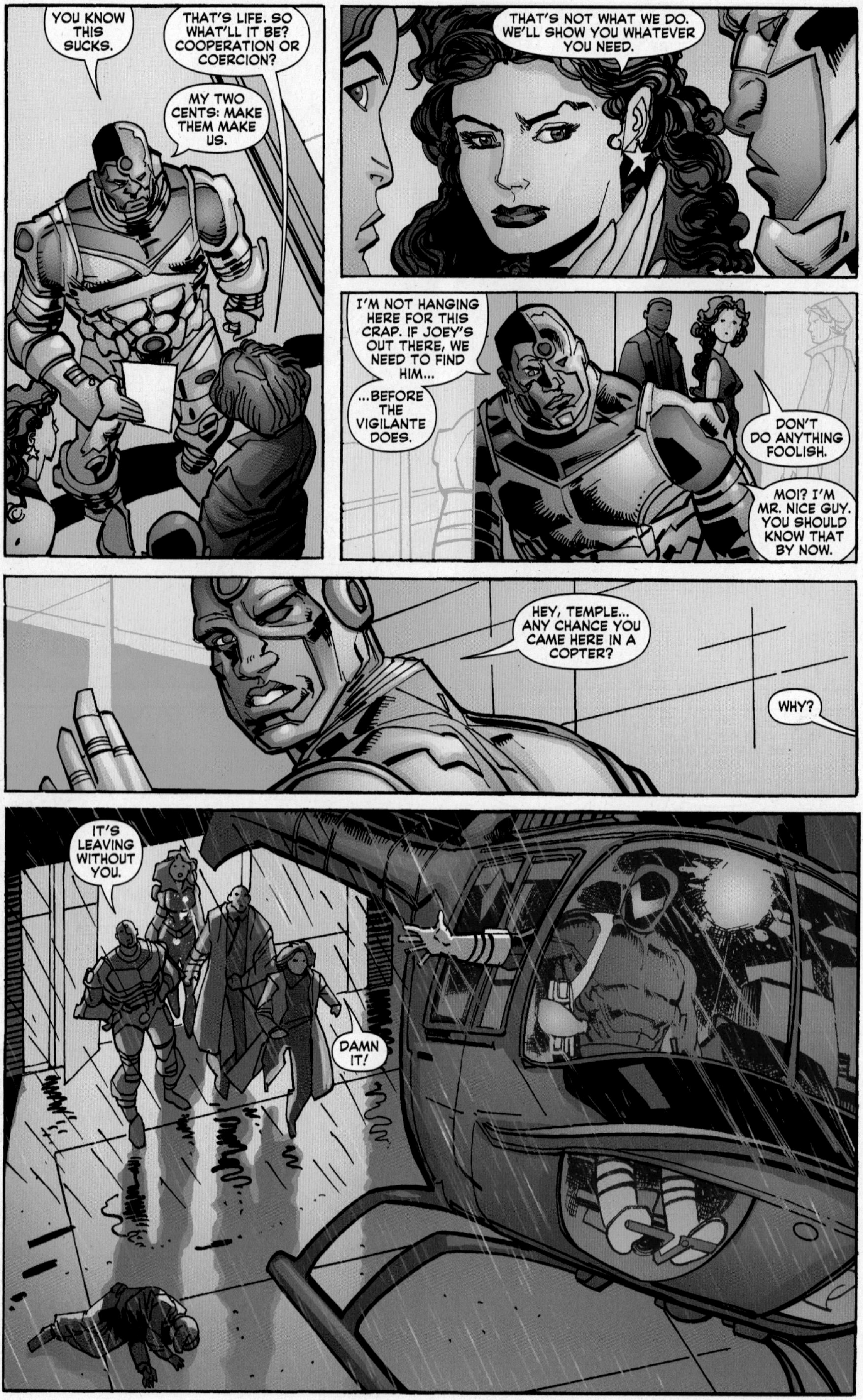
YOU KNOW THIS SUCKS.
THAT'S LIFE. SO WHAT'LL IT BE? COOPERATION OR COERCION?
MY TWO CENTS: MAKE THEM MAKE US.
THAT'S NOT WHAT WE DO. WE'LL SHOW YOU WHATEVER YOU NEED.
I'M NOT HANGING HERE FOR THIS CRAP. IF JOEY'S OUT THERE, WE NEED TO FIND HIM...
...BEFORE THE VIGILANTE DOES.
DON'T DO ANYTHING FOOLISH.
MOI? I'M MR. NICE GUY. YOU SHOULD KNOW THAT BY NOW.
HEY, TEMPLE... ANY CHANCE YOU CAME HERE IN A COPTER?
WHY?
IT'S LEAVING WITHOUT YOU.
DAMN IT!

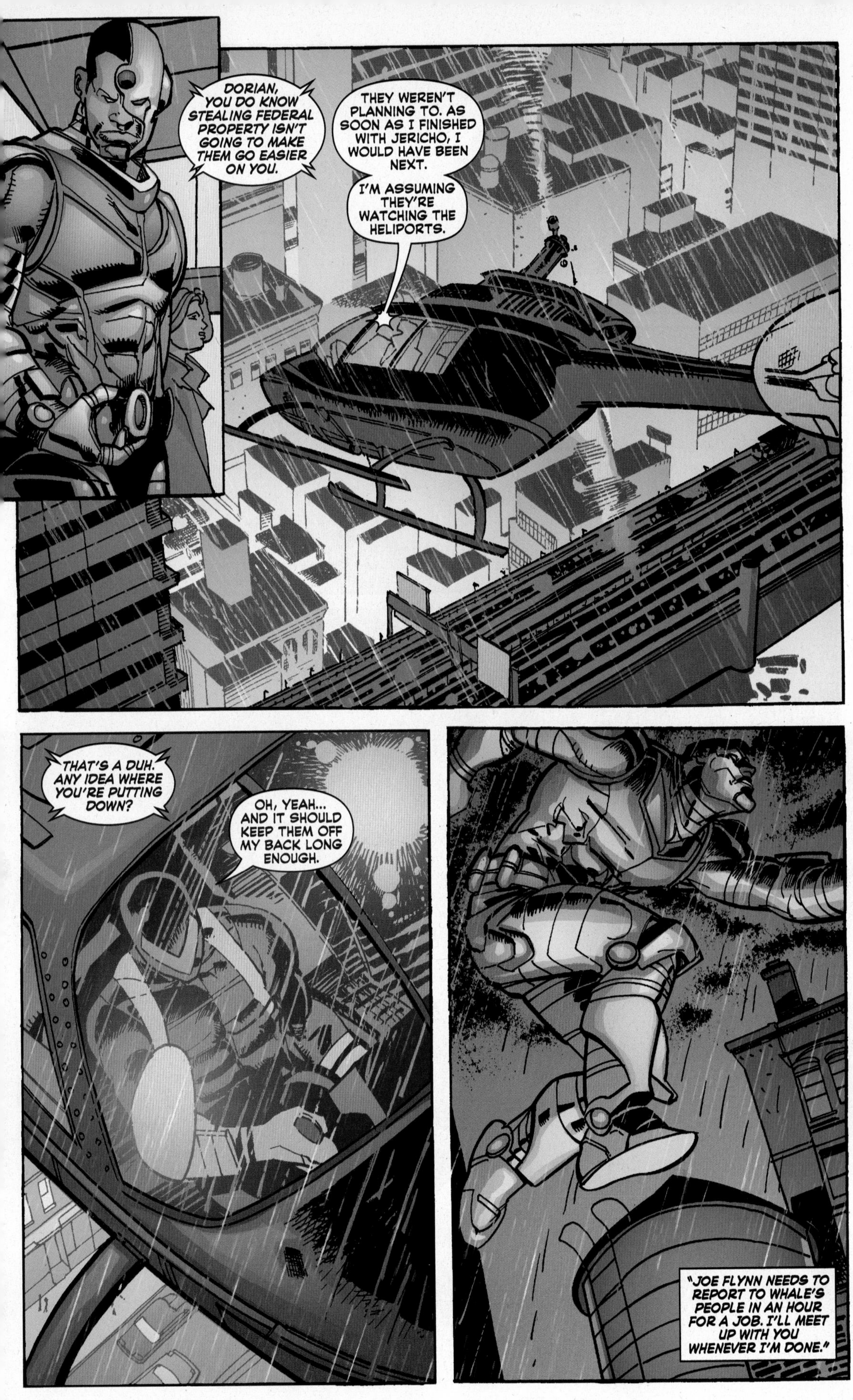
DORIAN, YOU DO KNOW STEALING FEDERAL PROPERTY ISN'T GOING TO MAKE THEM GO EASIER ON YOU.
THEY WEREN'T PLANNING TO. AS SOON AS I FINISHED WITH JERICHO, I WOULD HAVE BEEN NEXT.
I'M ASSUMING THEY'RE WATCHING THE HELIPORTS.
THAT'S A DUH. ANY IDEA WHERE YOU'RE PUTTING DOWN?
OH, YEAH... AND IT SHOULD KEEP THEM OFF MY BACK LONG ENOUGH.
"JOE FLYNN NEEDS TO REPORT TO WHALE'S PEOPLE IN AN HOUR FOR A JOB. I'LL MEET UP WITH YOU WHENEVER I'M DONE."

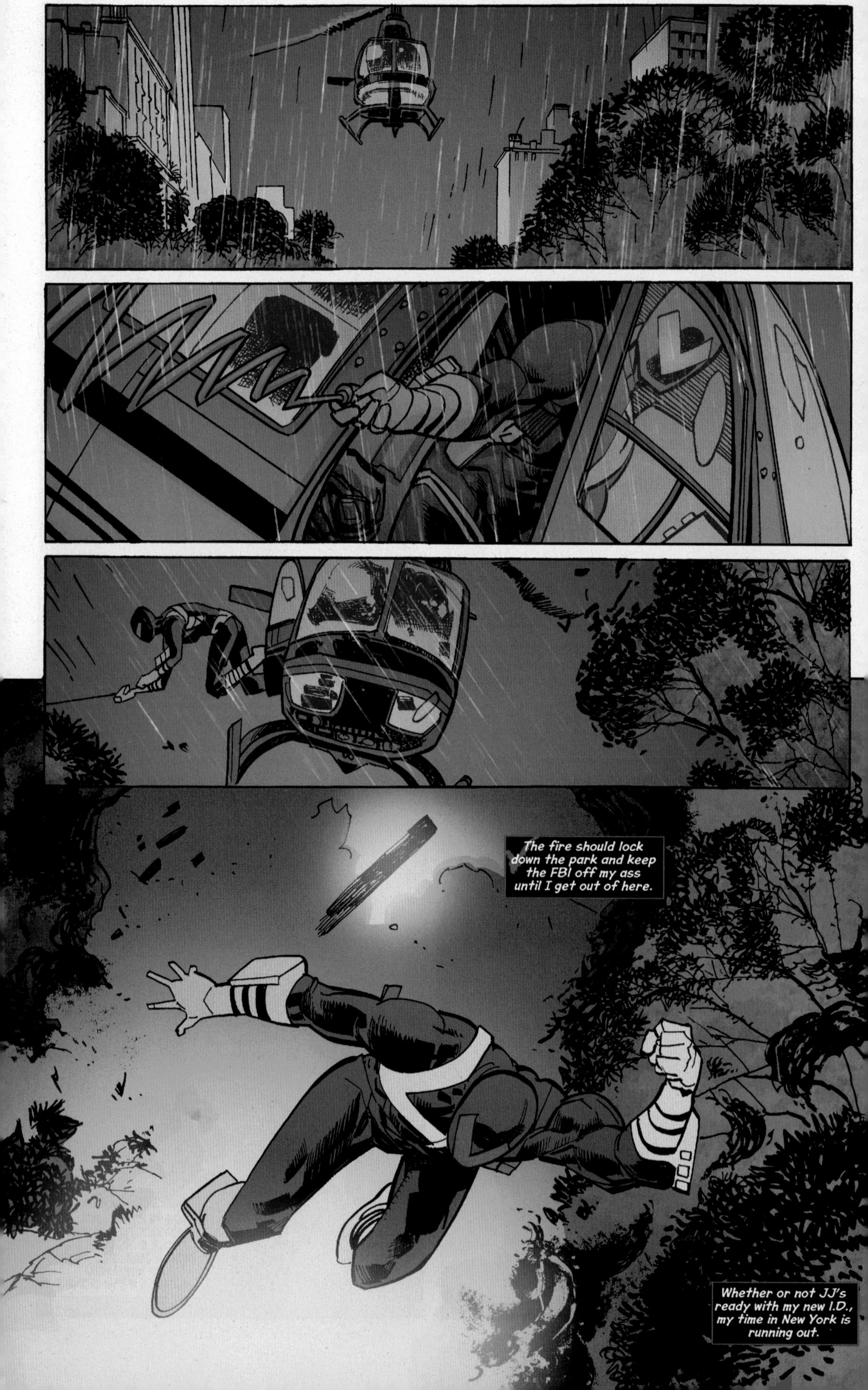
The fire should lock down the park and keep the FBI off my ass until I get out of here.
Whether or not JJ's ready with my new I.D., my time in New York is running out.

I land, safe. But then my mask mic picks up footsteps. Not cops. Something... heavier.

I don't want another fight this soon but I'm ready for whatever.

I COULD'VE KILLED YOU.

NOT LIKELY.

WE GOT WORD ON JOEY.

YOU KNOW WHERE HE IS?

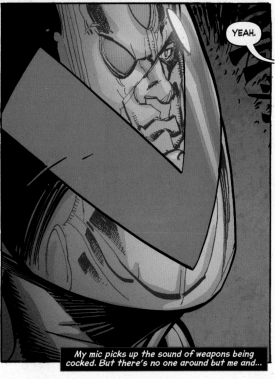

YEAH.

My mic picks up the sound of weapons being cocked. But there's no one around but me and...

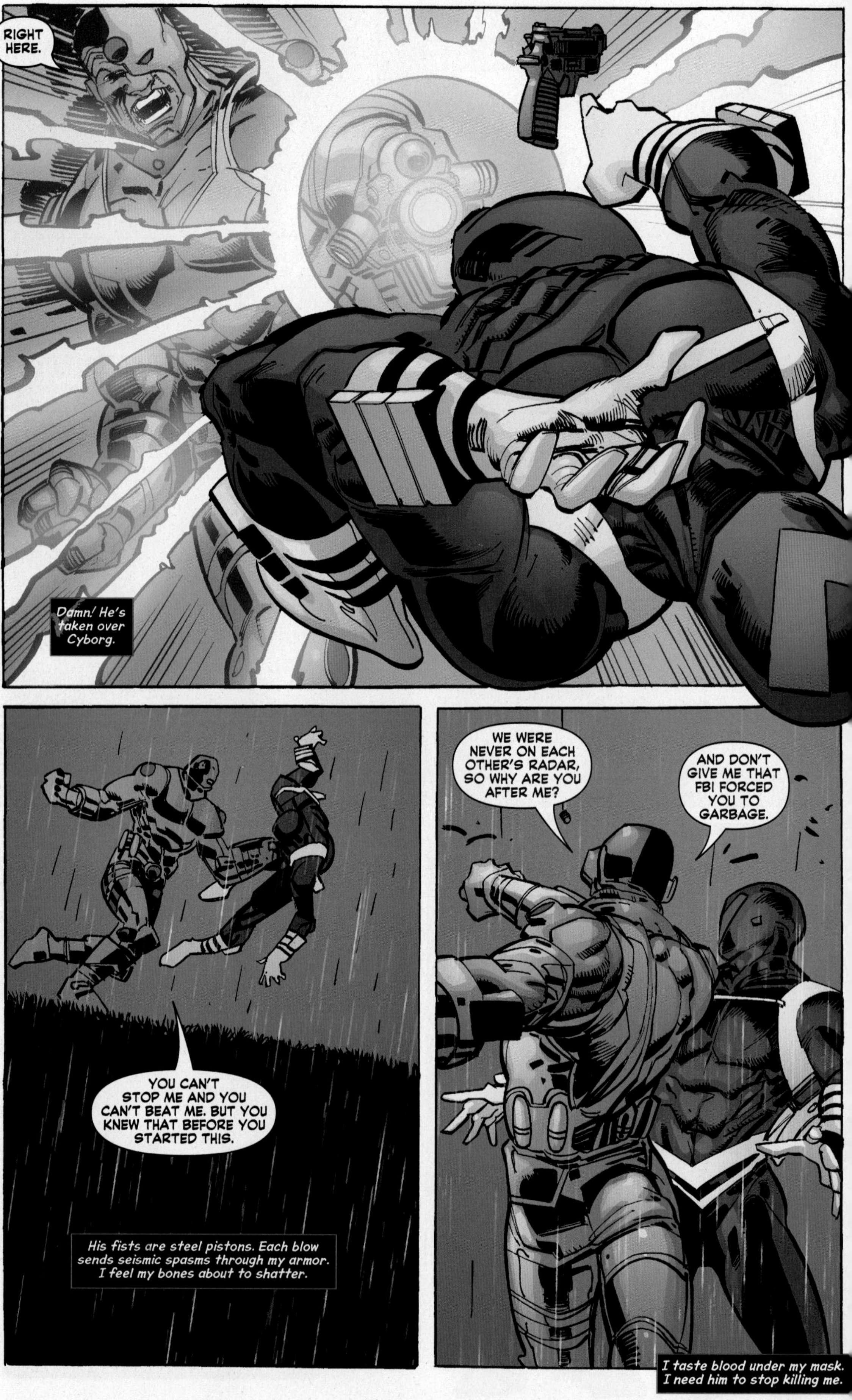
RIGHT HERE.
Damn! He's taken over Cyborg.
YOU CAN'T STOP ME AND YOU CAN'T BEAT ME. BUT YOU KNEW THAT BEFORE YOU STARTED THIS.
His fists are steel pistons. Each blow sends seismic spasms through my armor. I feel my bones about to shatter.
WE WERE NEVER ON EACH OTHER'S RADAR, SO WHY ARE YOU AFTER ME?
AND DON'T GIVE ME THAT FBI FORCED YOU TO GARBAGE.
I taste blood under my mask. I need him to stop killing me.

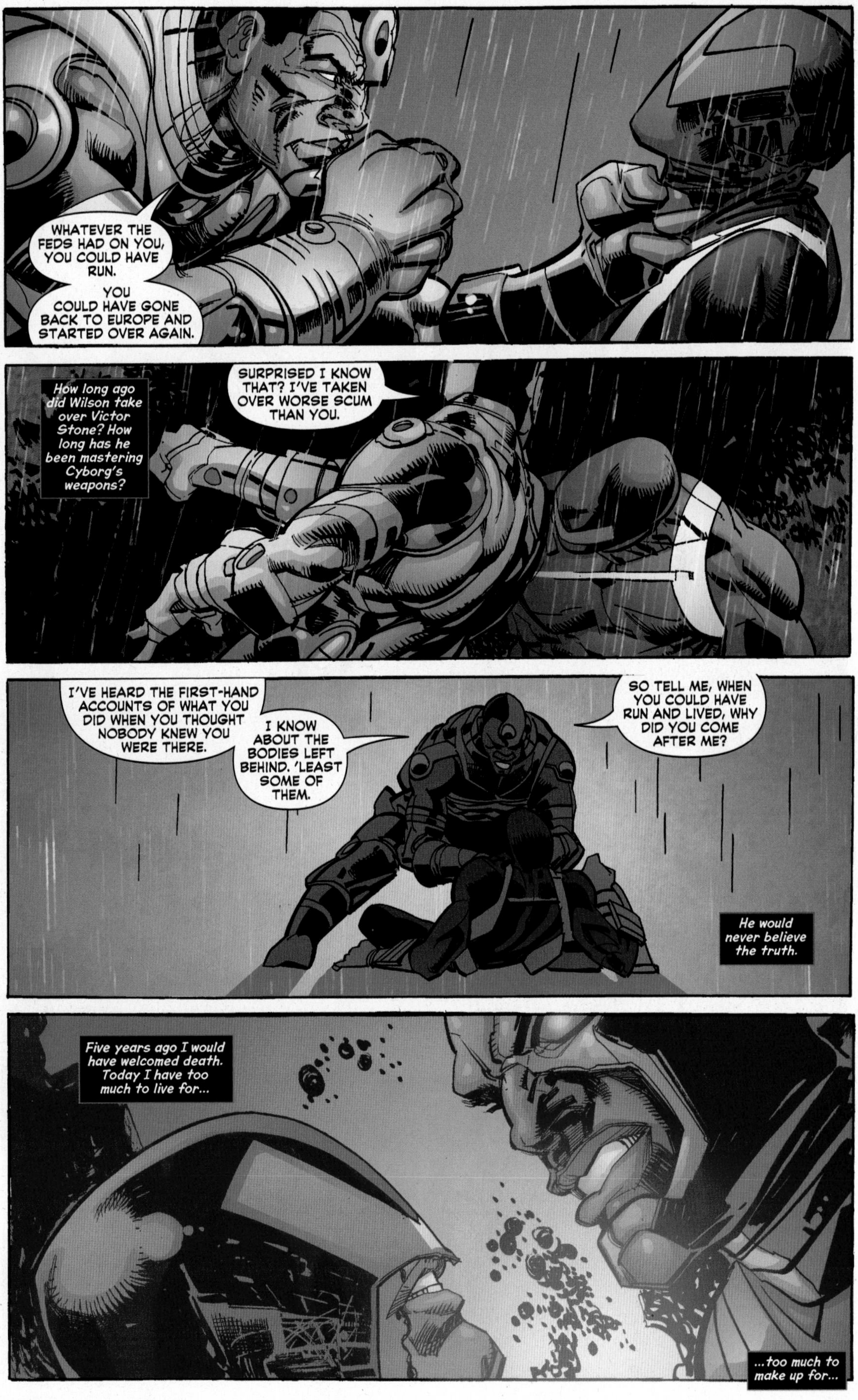
WHATEVER THE FEDS HAD ON YOU, YOU COULD HAVE RUN.
YOU COULD HAVE GONE BACK TO EUROPE AND STARTED OVER AGAIN.
How long ago did Wilson take over Victor Stone? How long has he been mastering Cyborg's weapons?
SURPRISED I KNOW THAT? I'VE TAKEN OVER WORSE SCUM THAN YOU.
I'VE HEARD THE FIRST-HAND ACCOUNTS OF WHAT YOU DID WHEN YOU THOUGHT NOBODY KNEW YOU WERE THERE.
I KNOW ABOUT THE BODIES LEFT BEHIND. 'LEAST SOME OF THEM.
SO TELL ME, WHEN YOU COULD HAVE RUN AND LIVED, WHY DID YOU COME AFTER ME?
He would never believe the truth.
Five years ago I would have welcomed death. Today I have too much to live for...
...too much to make up for...

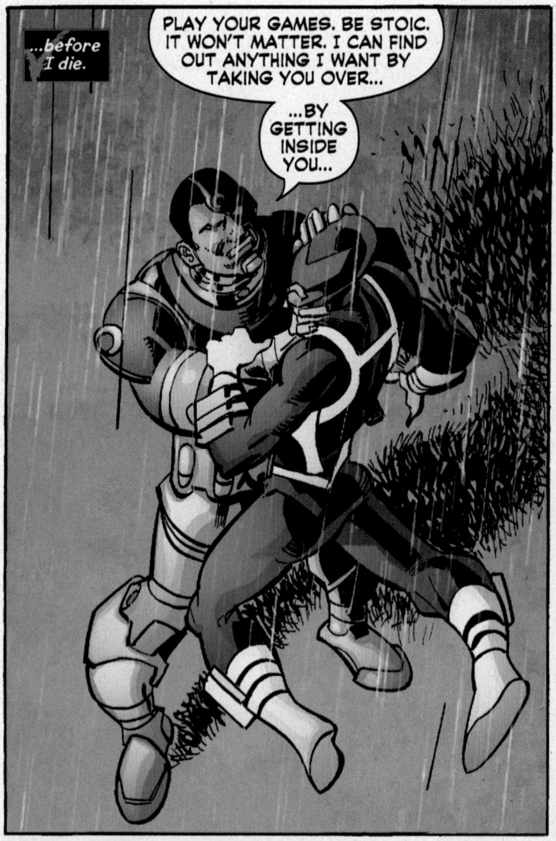
...before I die.
PLAY YOUR GAMES. BE STOIC. IT WON'T MATTER. I CAN FIND OUT ANYTHING I WANT BY TAKING YOU OVER...
...BY GETTING INSIDE YOU...

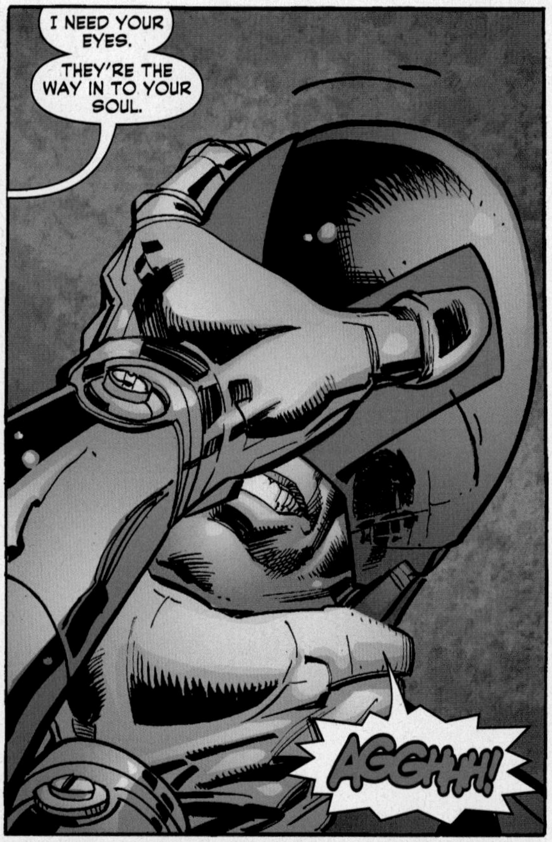
I NEED YOUR EYES.
THEY'RE THE WAY IN TO YOUR SOUL.
AGGHH!

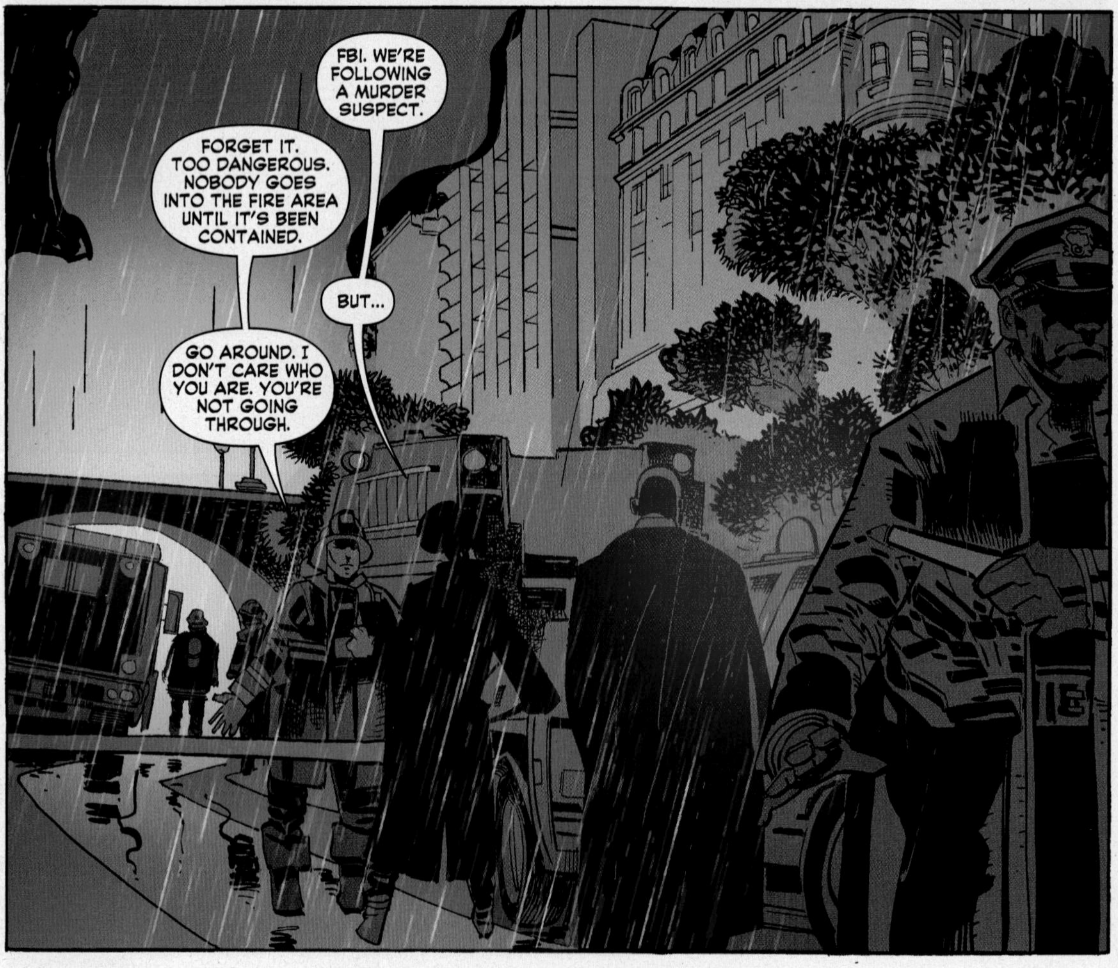
FBI. WE'RE FOLLOWING A MURDER SUSPECT.
FORGET IT. TOO DANGEROUS. NOBODY GOES INTO THE FIRE AREA UNTIL IT'S BEEN CONTAINED.
BUT...
GO AROUND. I DON'T CARE WHO YOU ARE. YOU'RE NOT GOING THROUGH.

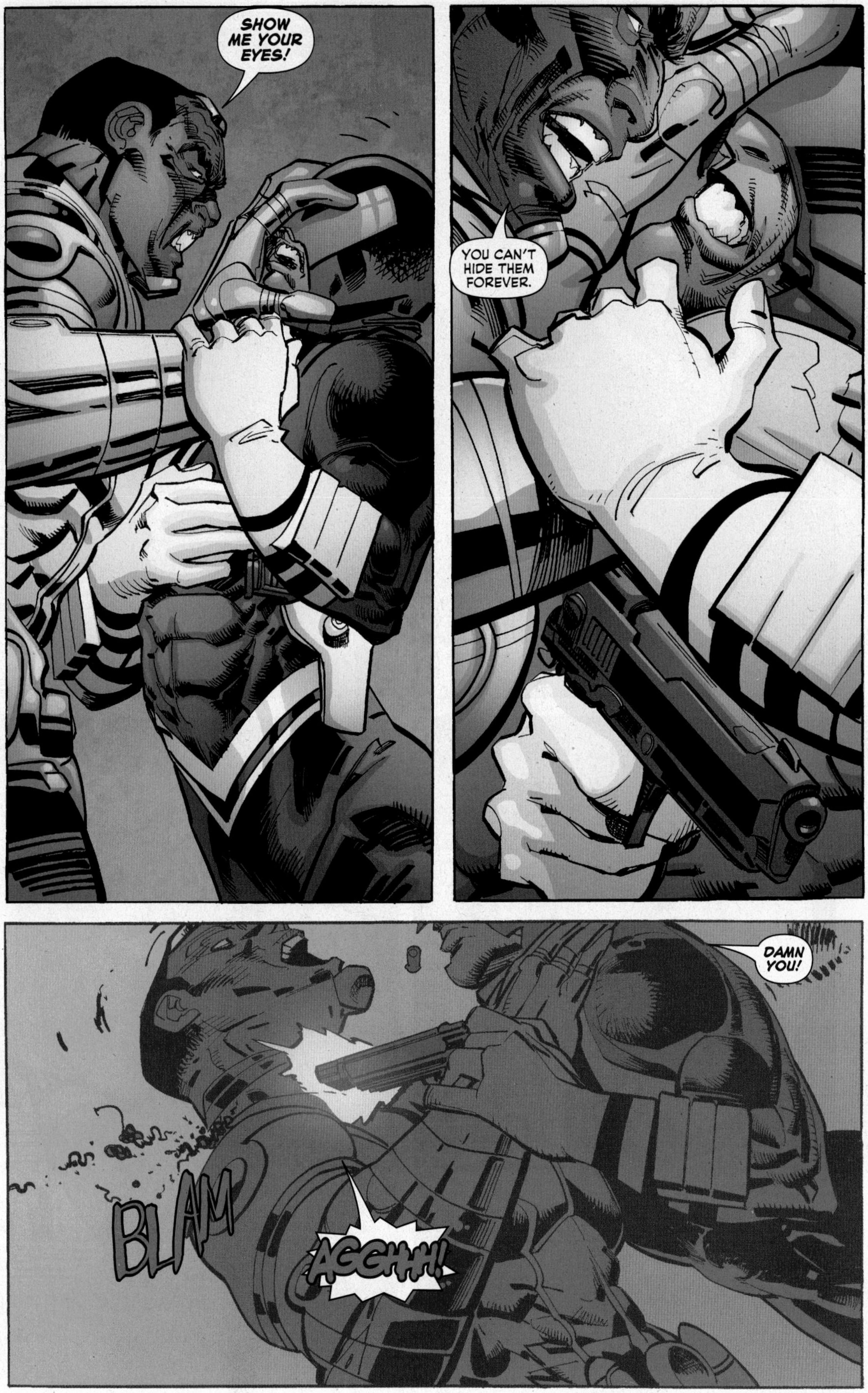
SHOW ME YOUR EYES!
YOU CAN'T HIDE THEM FOREVER.
DAMN YOU!
BLAM
AGGHHH!

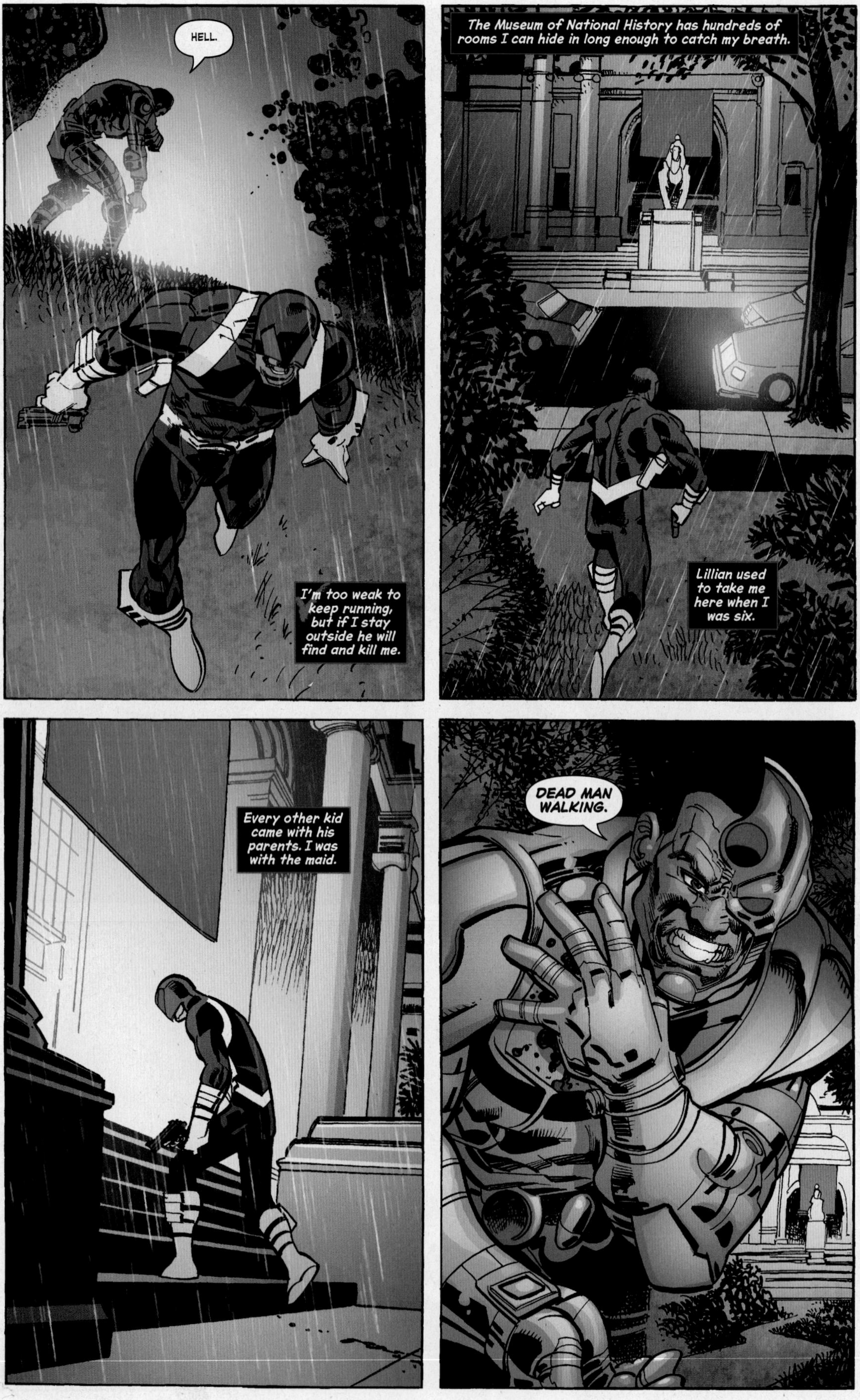
HELL.
I'm too weak to keep running, but if I stay outside he will find and kill me.
The Museum of National History has hundreds of rooms I can hide in long enough to catch my breath.
Lillian used to take me here when I was six.
Every other kid came with his parents. I was with the maid.
DEAD MAN WALKING.

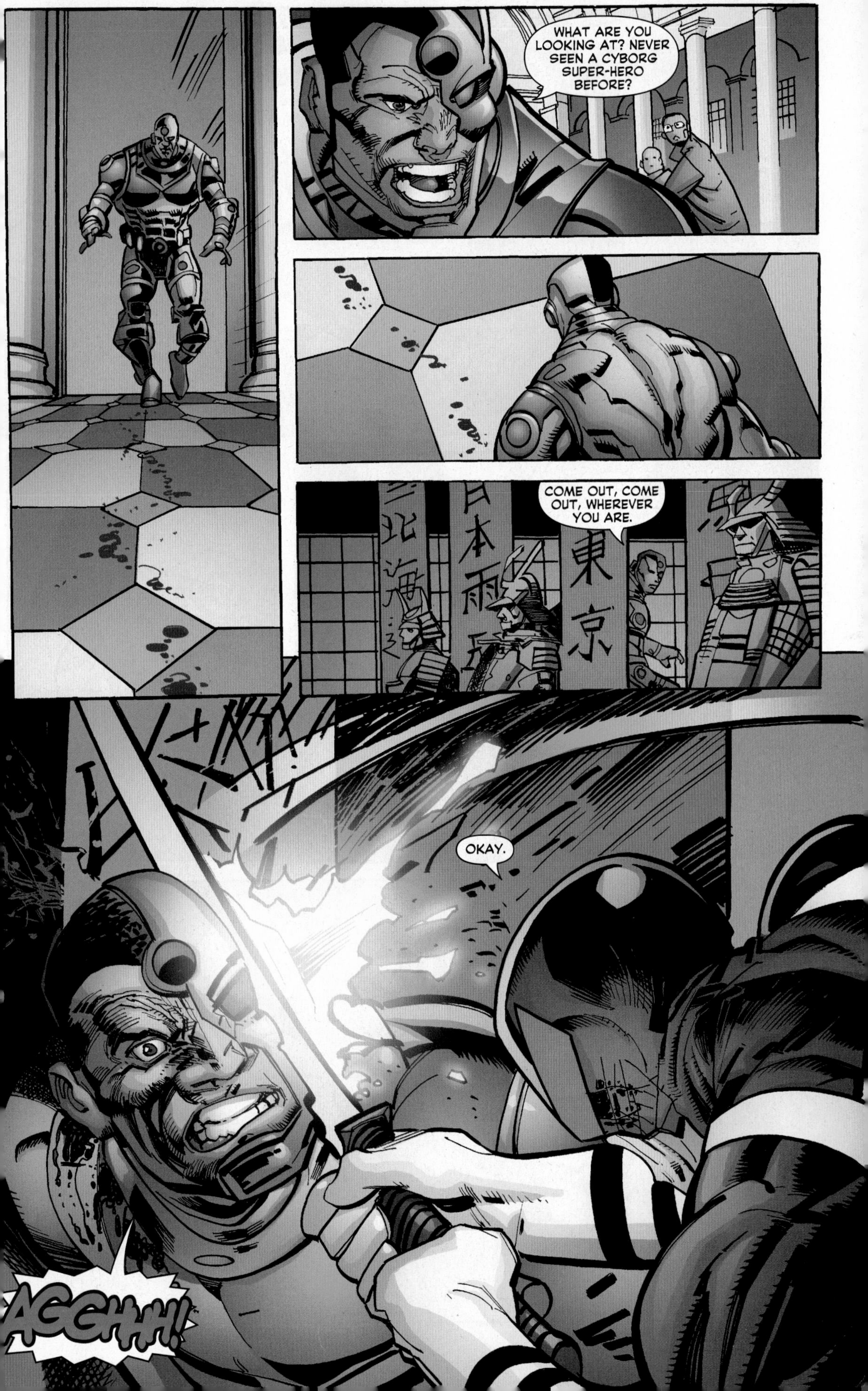
WHAT ARE YOU LOOKING AT? NEVER SEEN A CYBORG SUPER-HERO BEFORE?
COME OUT, COME OUT, WHEREVER YOU ARE.
日本
東京
OKAY.
AGGHHH!

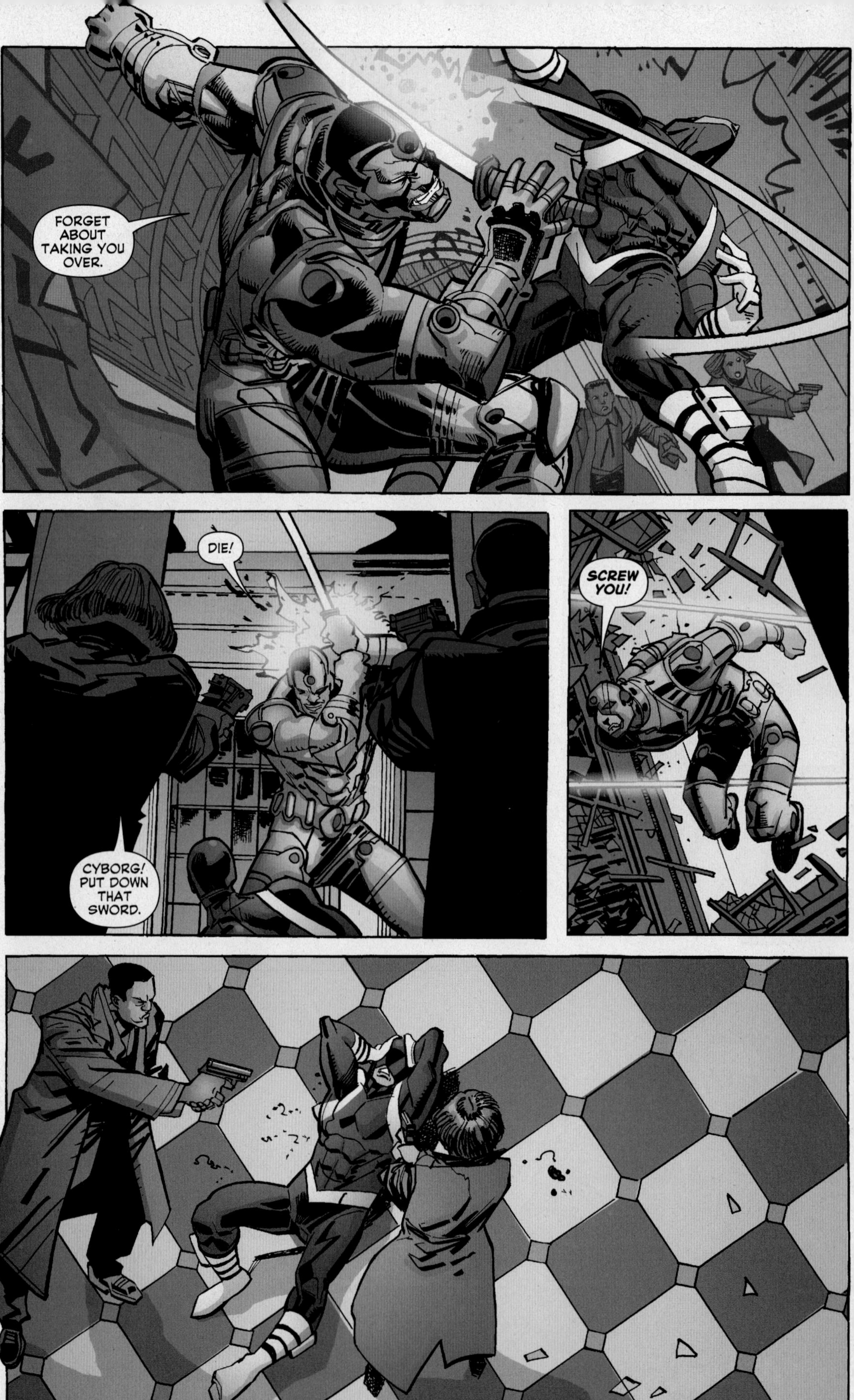
FORGET ABOUT TAKING YOU OVER.
DIE!
CYBORG! PUT DOWN THAT SWORD.
SCREW YOU!

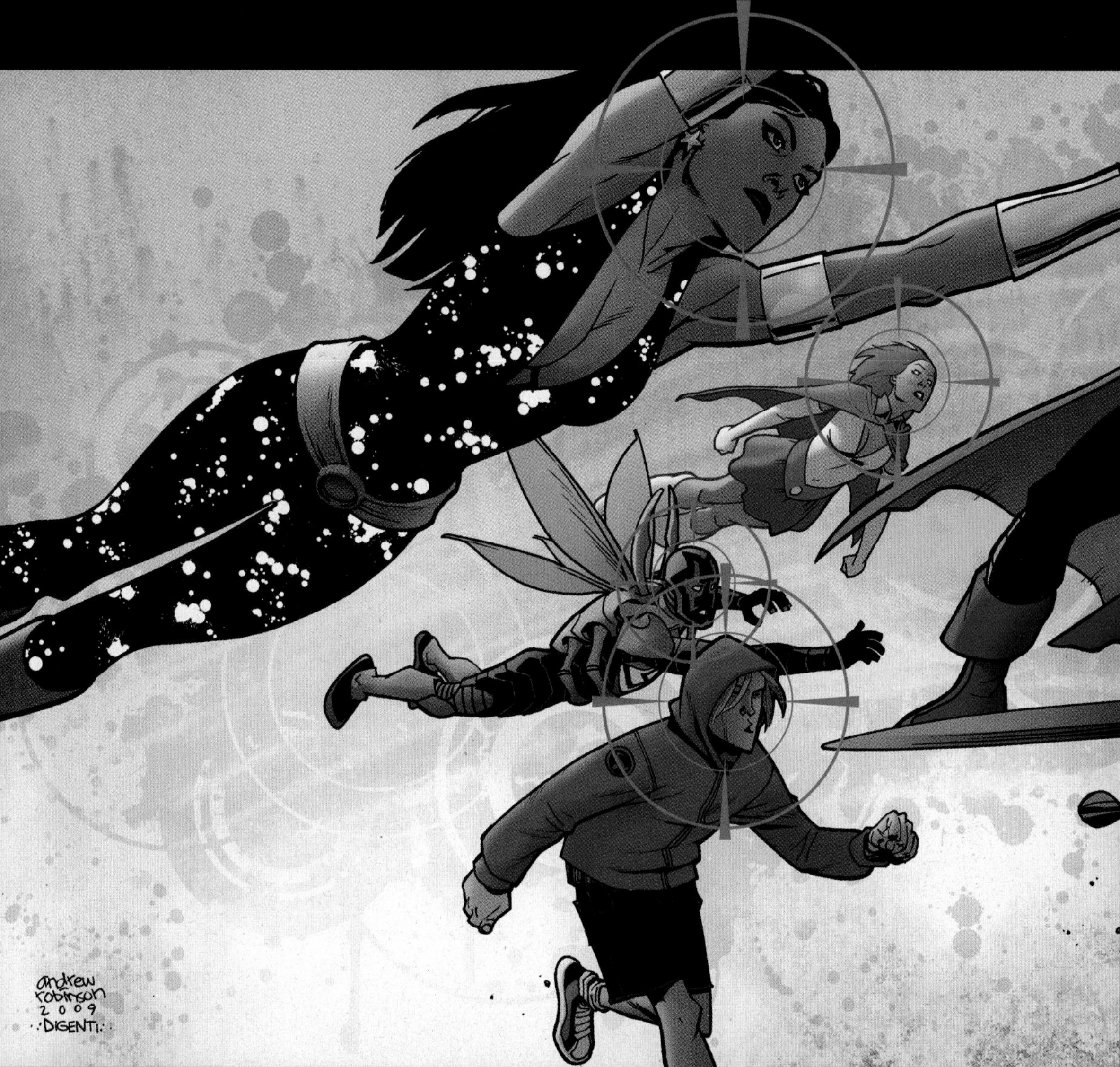
andrew robinson 2009
·DIGENTI·

Deathtrap Part 1

Sean McKeever
Writer

Angel Unzueta
Pencils

Wayne Faucher
Inks

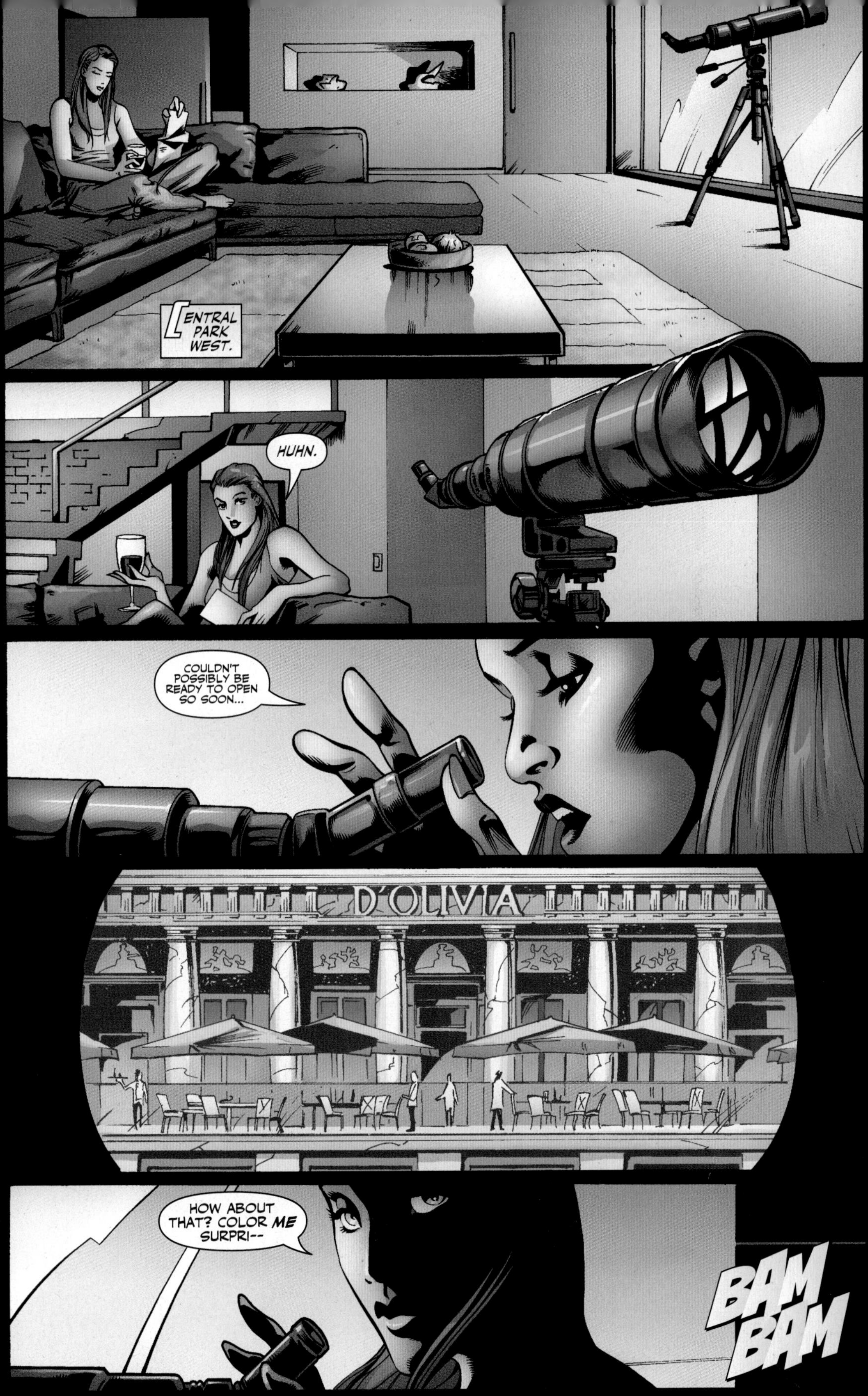

CENTRAL PARK WEST.
HUHN.
COULDN'T POSSIBLY BE READY TO OPEN SO SOON...
D'OLIVIA
HOW ABOUT THAT? COLOR *ME* SURPRI--
BAM BAM

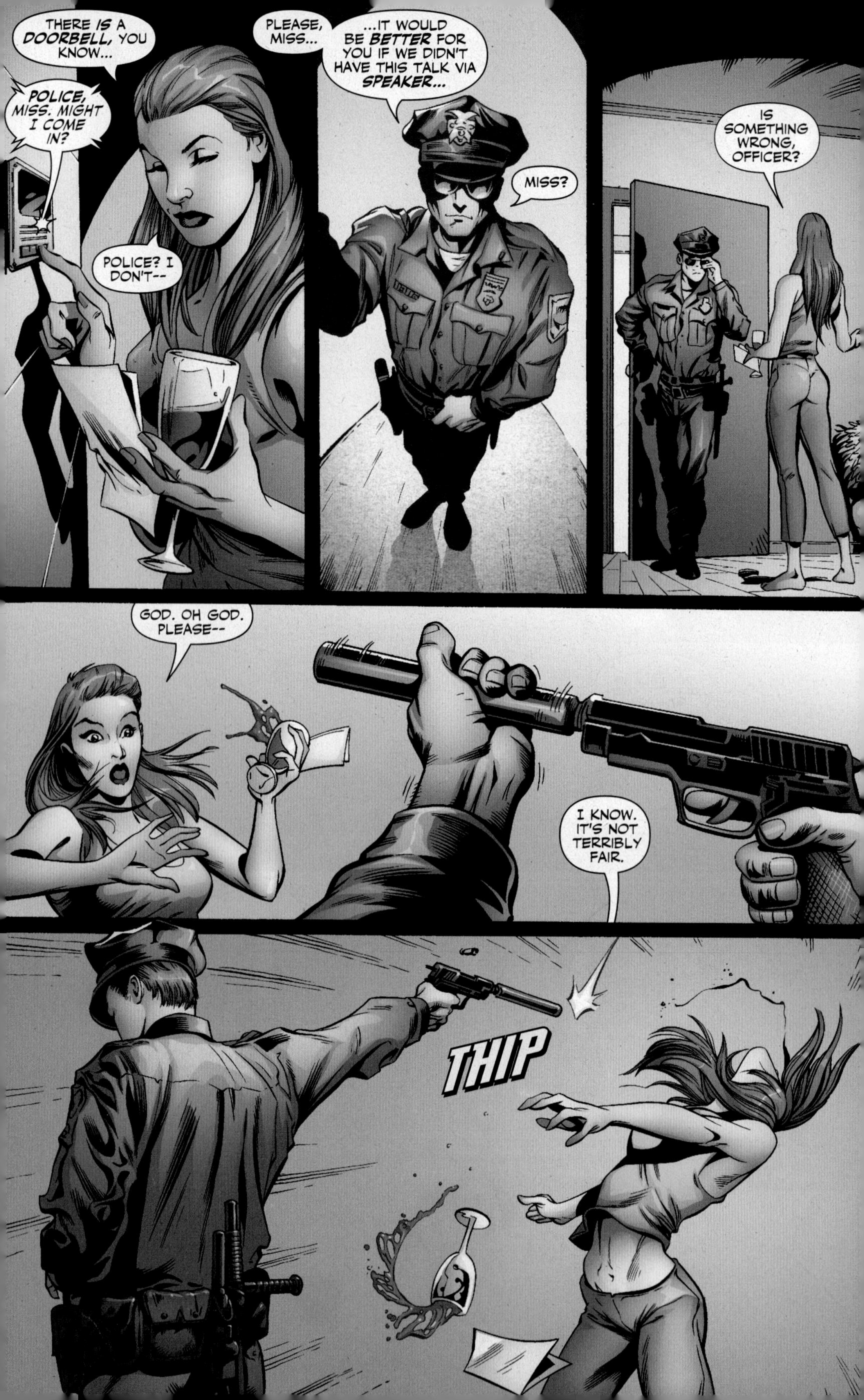
THERE IS A DOORBELL, YOU KNOW...
POLICE, MISS. MIGHT I COME IN?
POLICE? I DON'T--
PLEASE, MISS...
...IT WOULD BE BETTER FOR YOU IF WE DIDN'T HAVE THIS TALK VIA SPEAKER...
MISS?
IS SOMETHING WRONG, OFFICER?
GOD. OH GOD. PLEASE--
I KNOW. IT'S NOT TERRIBLY FAIR.
THIP

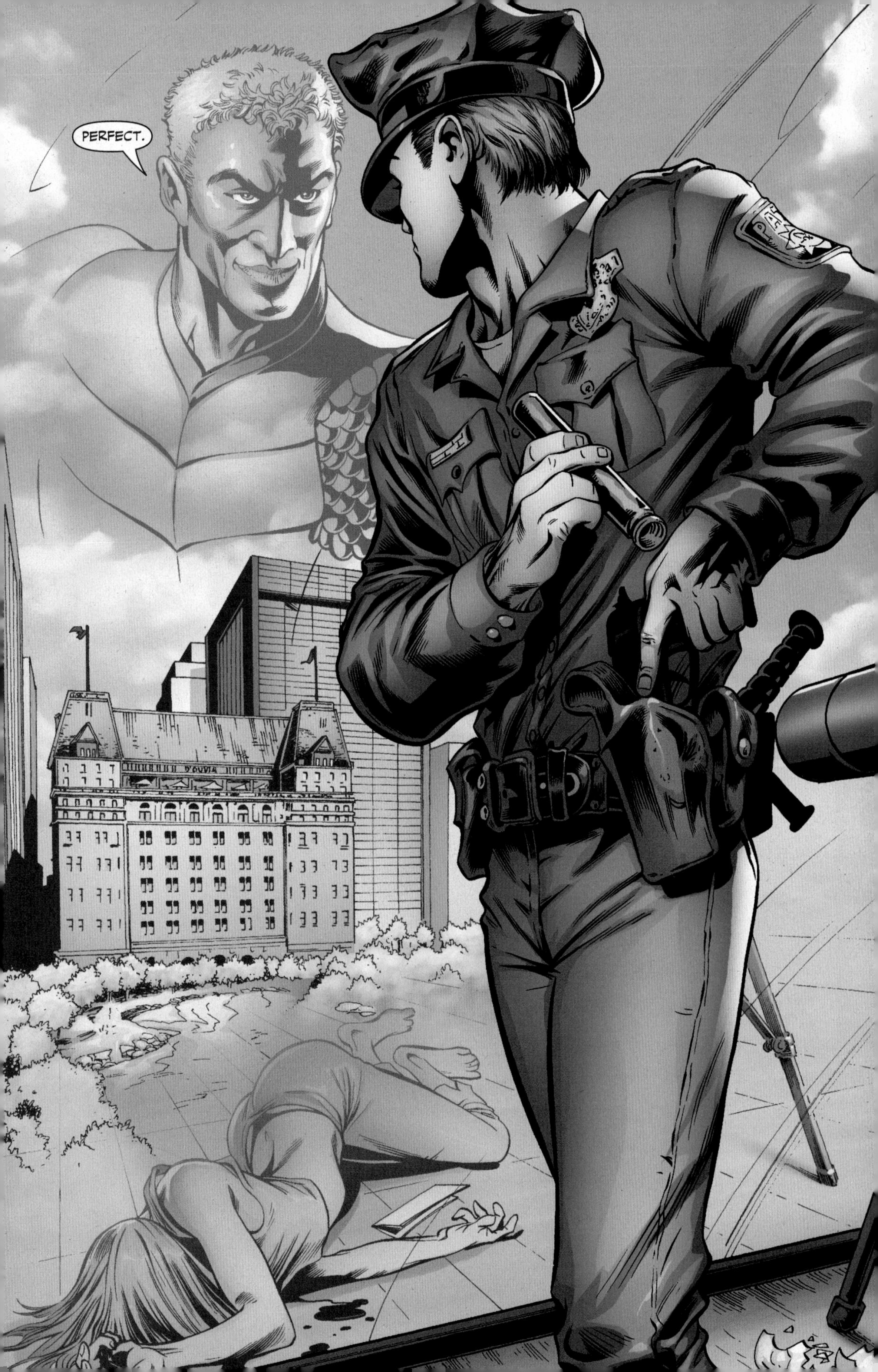
PERFECT.

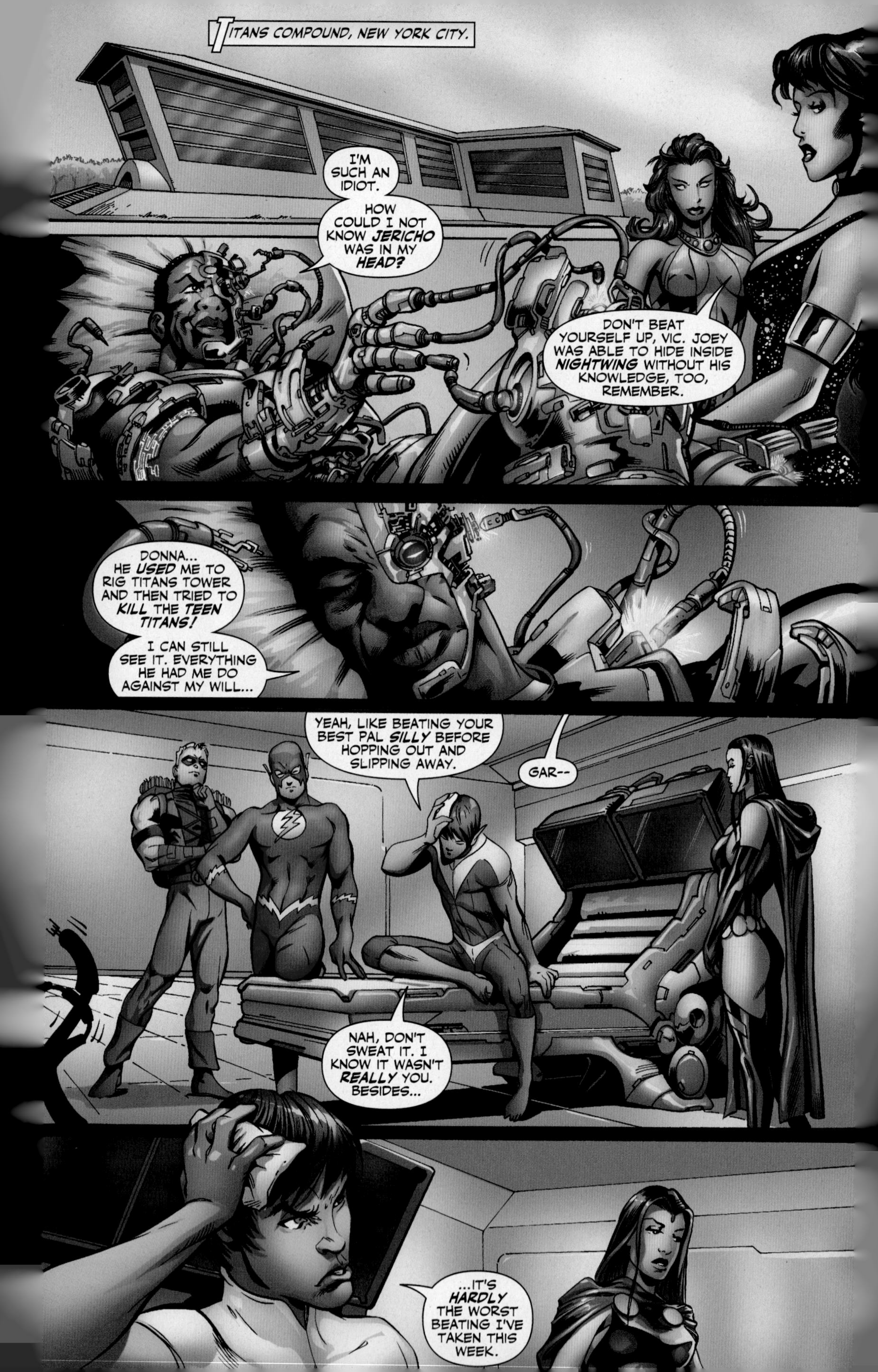
TITANS COMPOUND, NEW YORK CITY.
I'M SUCH AN IDIOT.
HOW COULD I NOT KNOW JERICHO WAS IN MY HEAD?
DON'T BEAT YOURSELF UP, VIC. JOEY WAS ABLE TO HIDE INSIDE NIGHTWING WITHOUT HIS KNOWLEDGE, TOO, REMEMBER.
DONNA... HE USED ME TO RIG TITANS TOWER AND THEN TRIED TO KILL THE TEEN TITANS!
I CAN STILL SEE IT. EVERYTHING HE HAD ME DO AGAINST MY WILL...
YEAH, LIKE BEATING YOUR BEST PAL SILLY BEFORE HOPPING OUT AND SLIPPING AWAY.
GAR--
NAH, DON'T SWEAT IT. I KNOW IT WASN'T REALLY YOU. BESIDES...
...IT'S HARDLY THE WORST BEATING I'VE TAKEN THIS WEEK.

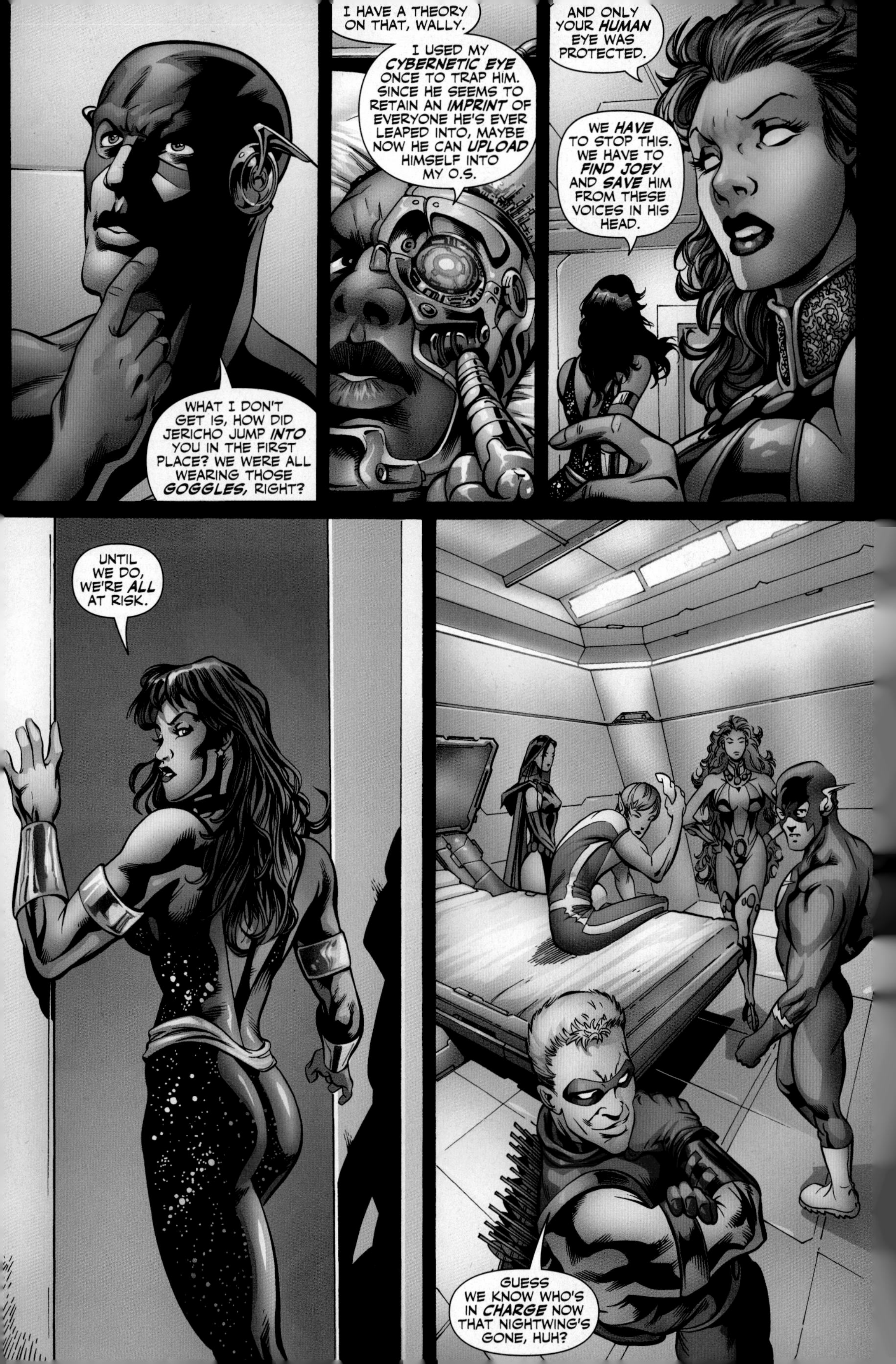

WHAT I DON'T GET IS, HOW DID JERICHO JUMP *INTO* YOU IN THE FIRST PLACE? WE WERE ALL WEARING THOSE *GOGGLES*, RIGHT?
I HAVE A THEORY ON THAT, WALLY.
I USED MY *CYBERNETIC EYE* ONCE TO TRAP HIM. SINCE HE SEEMS TO RETAIN AN *IMPRINT* OF EVERYONE HE'S EVER LEAPED INTO, MAYBE NOW HE CAN *UPLOAD* HIMSELF INTO MY O.S.
AND ONLY YOUR *HUMAN* EYE WAS PROTECTED.
WE *HAVE* TO STOP THIS. WE HAVE TO *FIND JOEY* AND *SAVE* HIM FROM THESE VOICES IN HIS HEAD.
UNTIL WE DO, WE'RE *ALL* AT RISK.
GUESS WE KNOW WHO'S IN *CHARGE* NOW THAT NIGHTWING'S GONE, HUH?

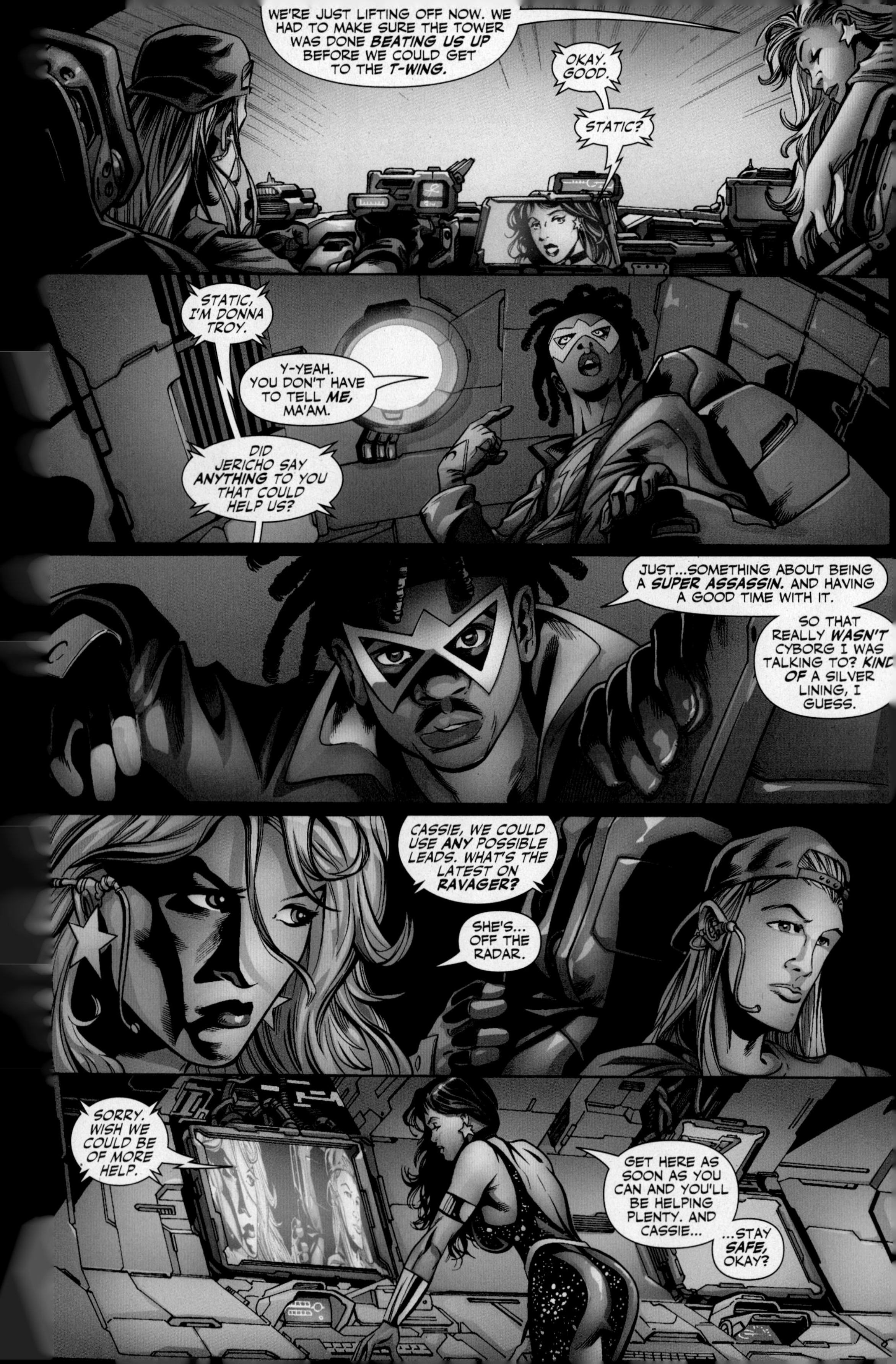

WE'RE JUST LIFTING OFF NOW. WE HAD TO MAKE SURE THE TOWER WAS DONE BEATING US UP BEFORE WE COULD GET TO THE T-WING.
OKAY. GOOD.
STATIC?
STATIC, I'M DONNA TROY.
Y-YEAH. YOU DON'T HAVE TO TELL ME, MA'AM.
DID JERICHO SAY ANYTHING TO YOU THAT COULD HELP US?
JUST...SOMETHING ABOUT BEING A SUPER ASSASSIN. AND HAVING A GOOD TIME WITH IT.
SO THAT REALLY WASN'T CYBORG I WAS TALKING TO? KIND OF A SILVER LINING, I GUESS.
CASSIE, WE COULD USE ANY POSSIBLE LEADS. WHAT'S THE LATEST ON RAVAGER?
SHE'S... OFF THE RADAR.
SORRY. WISH WE COULD BE OF MORE HELP.
GET HERE AS SOON AS YOU CAN AND YOU'LL BE HELPING PLENTY. AND CASSIE...
...STAY SAFE, OKAY?

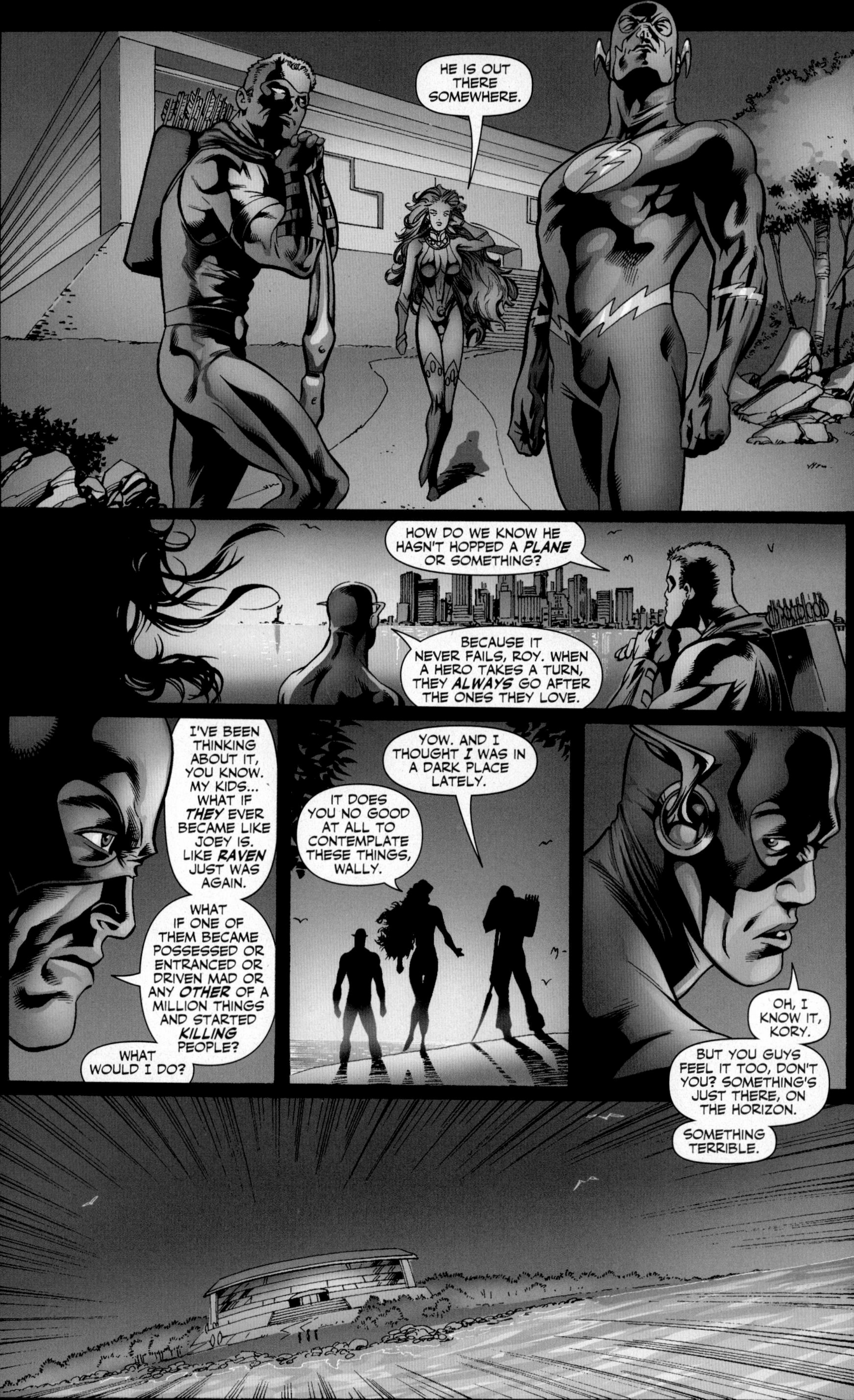
HE IS OUT THERE SOMEWHERE.
HOW DO WE KNOW HE HASN'T HOPPED A PLANE OR SOMETHING?
BECAUSE IT NEVER FAILS, ROY. WHEN A HERO TAKES A TURN, THEY ALWAYS GO AFTER THE ONES THEY LOVE.
I'VE BEEN THINKING ABOUT IT, YOU KNOW. MY KIDS... WHAT IF THEY EVER BECAME LIKE JOEY IS. LIKE RAVEN JUST WAS AGAIN.
WHAT IF ONE OF THEM BECAME POSSESSED OR ENTRANCED OR DRIVEN MAD OR ANY OTHER OF A MILLION THINGS AND STARTED KILLING PEOPLE?
WHAT WOULD I DO?
YOW. AND I THOUGHT I WAS IN A DARK PLACE LATELY.
IT DOES YOU NO GOOD AT ALL TO CONTEMPLATE THESE THINGS, WALLY.
OH, I KNOW IT, KORY.
BUT YOU GUYS FEEL IT TOO, DON'T YOU? SOMETHING'S JUST THERE, ON THE HORIZON.
SOMETHING TERRIBLE.

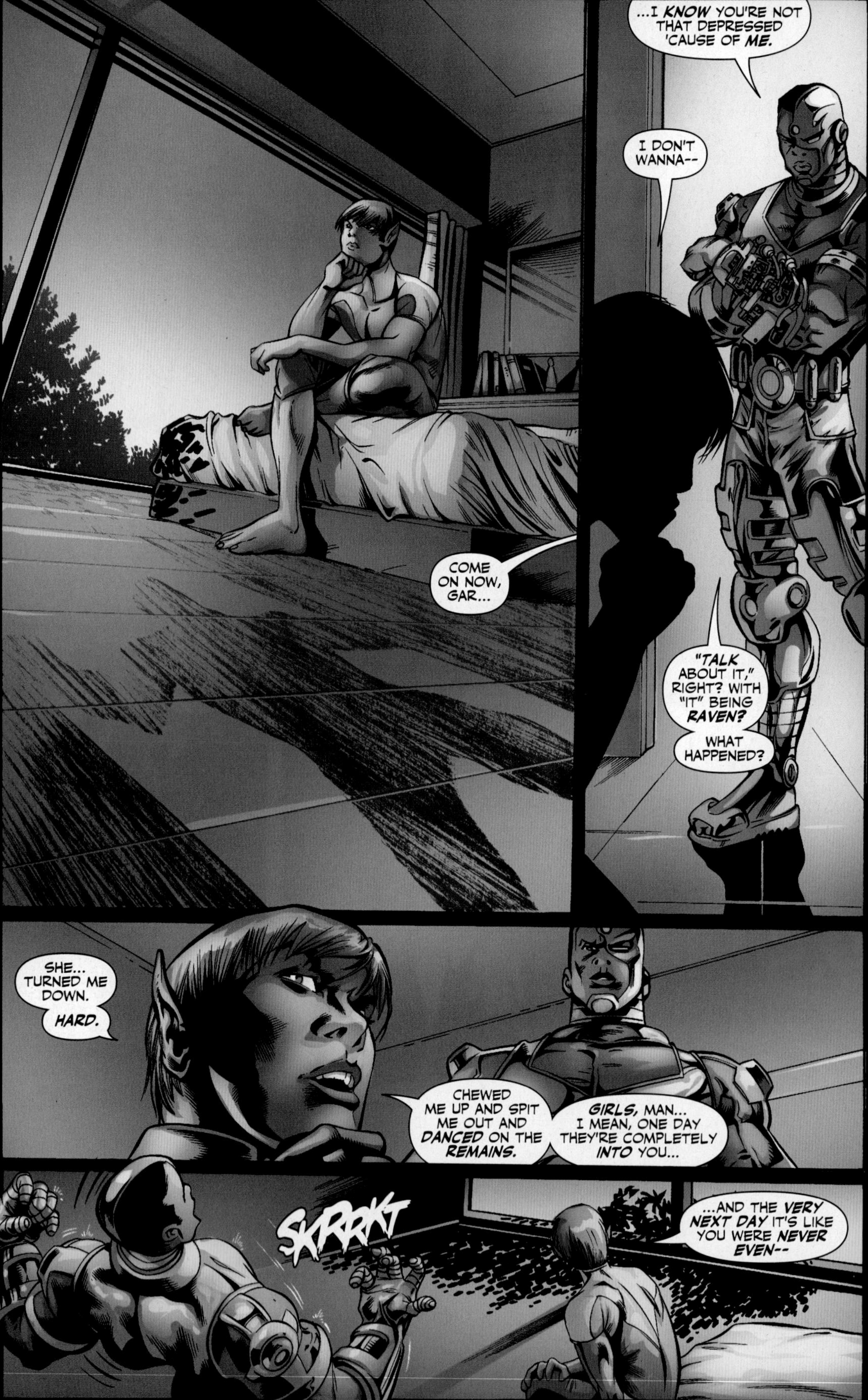
...I **KNOW** YOU'RE NOT THAT DEPRESSED 'CAUSE OF **ME.**
I DON'T WANNA--
COME ON NOW, GAR...
"TALK ABOUT IT," RIGHT? WITH "IT" BEING **RAVEN?**
WHAT HAPPENED?
SHE... TURNED ME DOWN. **HARD.**
CHEWED ME UP AND SPIT ME OUT AND **DANCED** ON THE **REMAINS.**
GIRLS, MAN... I MEAN, ONE DAY THEY'RE COMPLETELY **INTO** YOU...
SKRRKT
...AND THE **VERY NEXT DAY** IT'S LIKE YOU WERE **NEVER EVEN--**

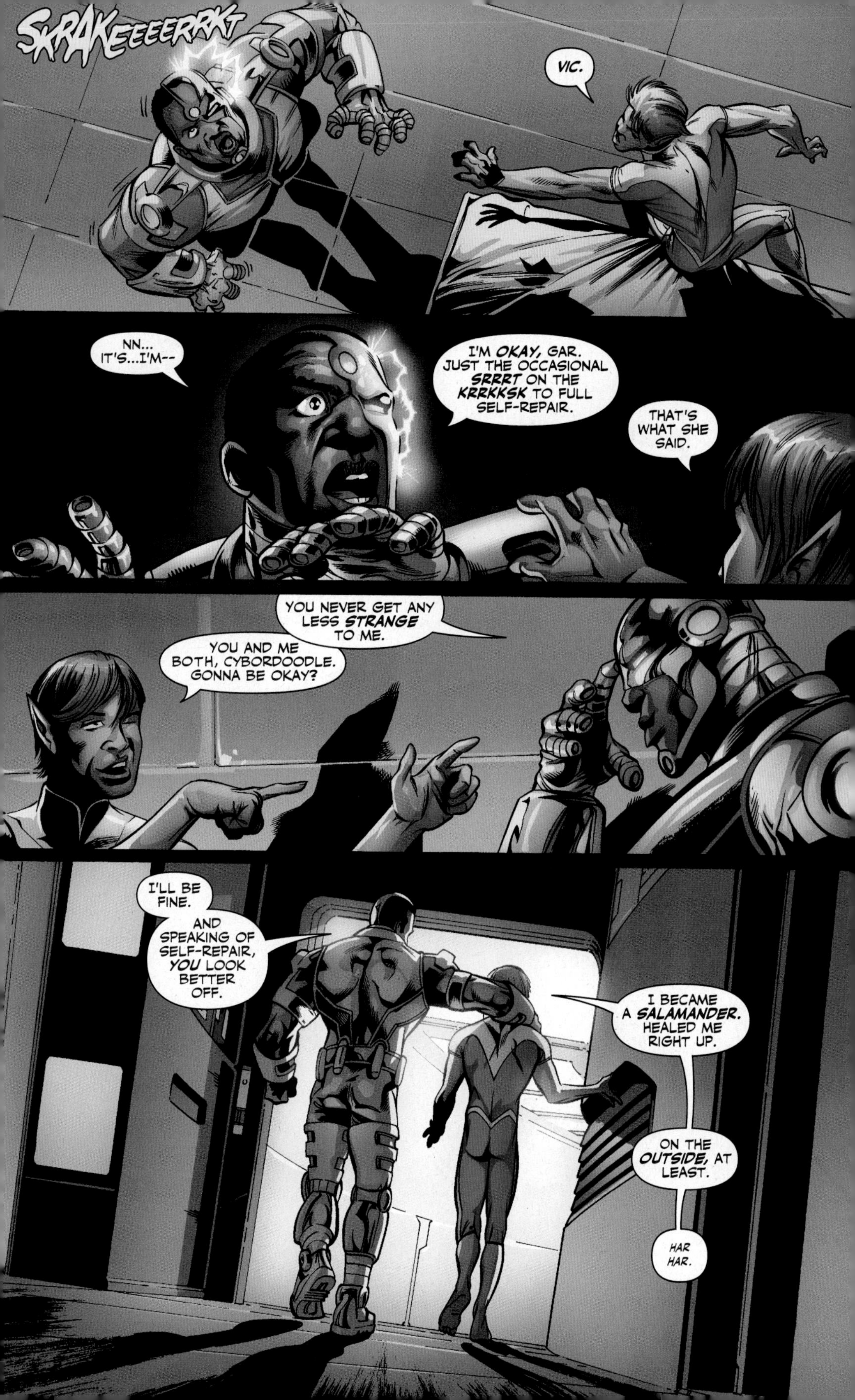
SKRAKEEEEERRKT
VIC.
NN... IT'S...I'M--
I'M OKAY, GAR. JUST THE OCCASIONAL SRRRT ON THE KRRKKSK TO FULL SELF-REPAIR.
THAT'S WHAT SHE SAID.
YOU NEVER GET ANY LESS STRANGE TO ME.
YOU AND ME BOTH, CYBORDOODLE. GONNA BE OKAY?
I'LL BE FINE.
AND SPEAKING OF SELF-REPAIR, YOU LOOK BETTER OFF.
I BECAME A SALAMANDER. HEALED ME RIGHT UP.
ON THE OUTSIDE, AT LEAST.
HAR HAR.

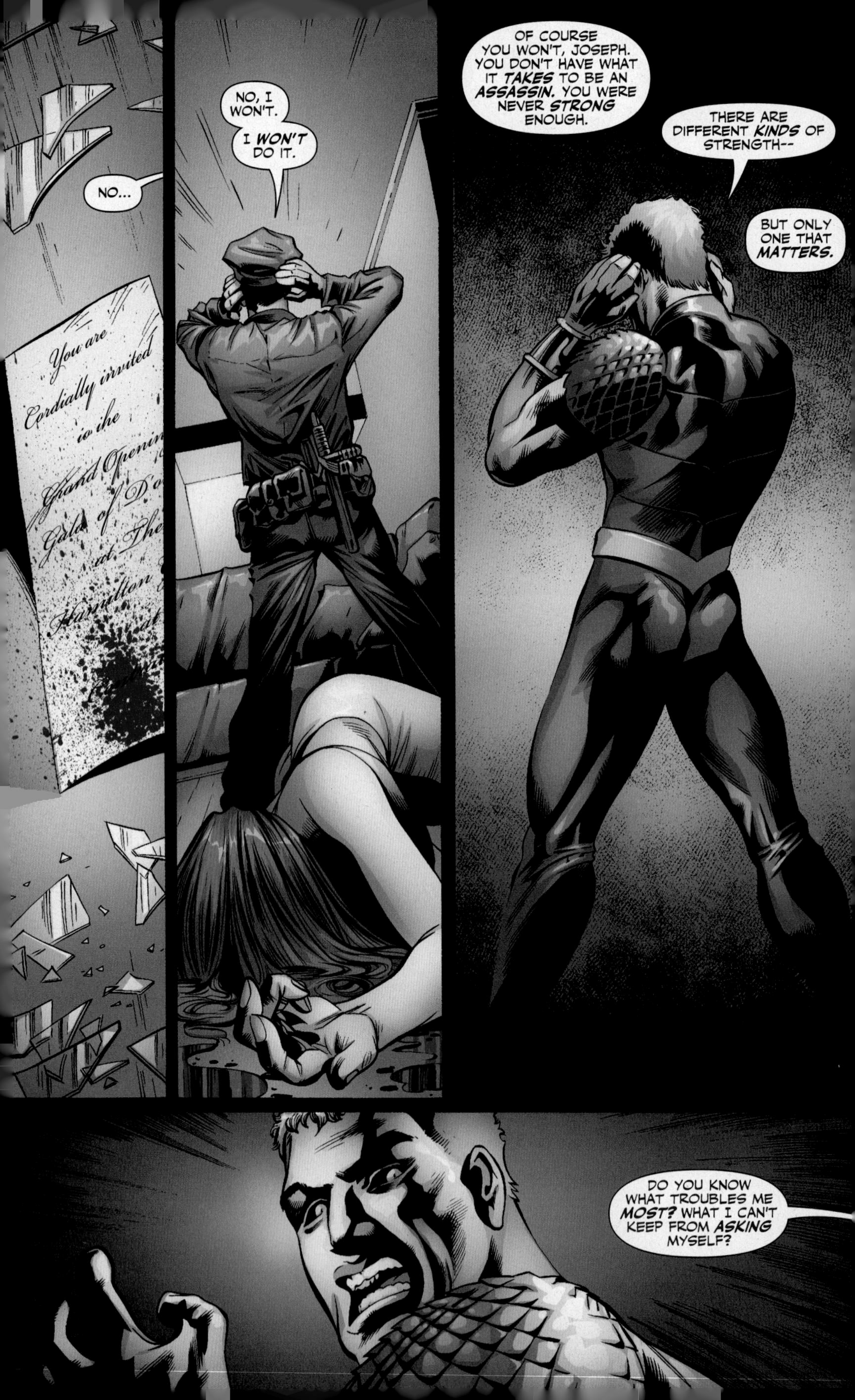
NO...
You are Cordially invited to the Grand Openin Gala of D'o at The Hamilton
NO, I WON'T.
I WON'T DO IT.
OF COURSE YOU WON'T, JOSEPH. YOU DON'T HAVE WHAT IT TAKES TO BE AN ASSASSIN. YOU WERE NEVER STRONG ENOUGH.
THERE ARE DIFFERENT KINDS OF STRENGTH--
BUT ONLY ONE THAT MATTERS.
DO YOU KNOW WHAT TROUBLES ME MOST? WHAT I CAN'T KEEP FROM ASKING MYSELF?

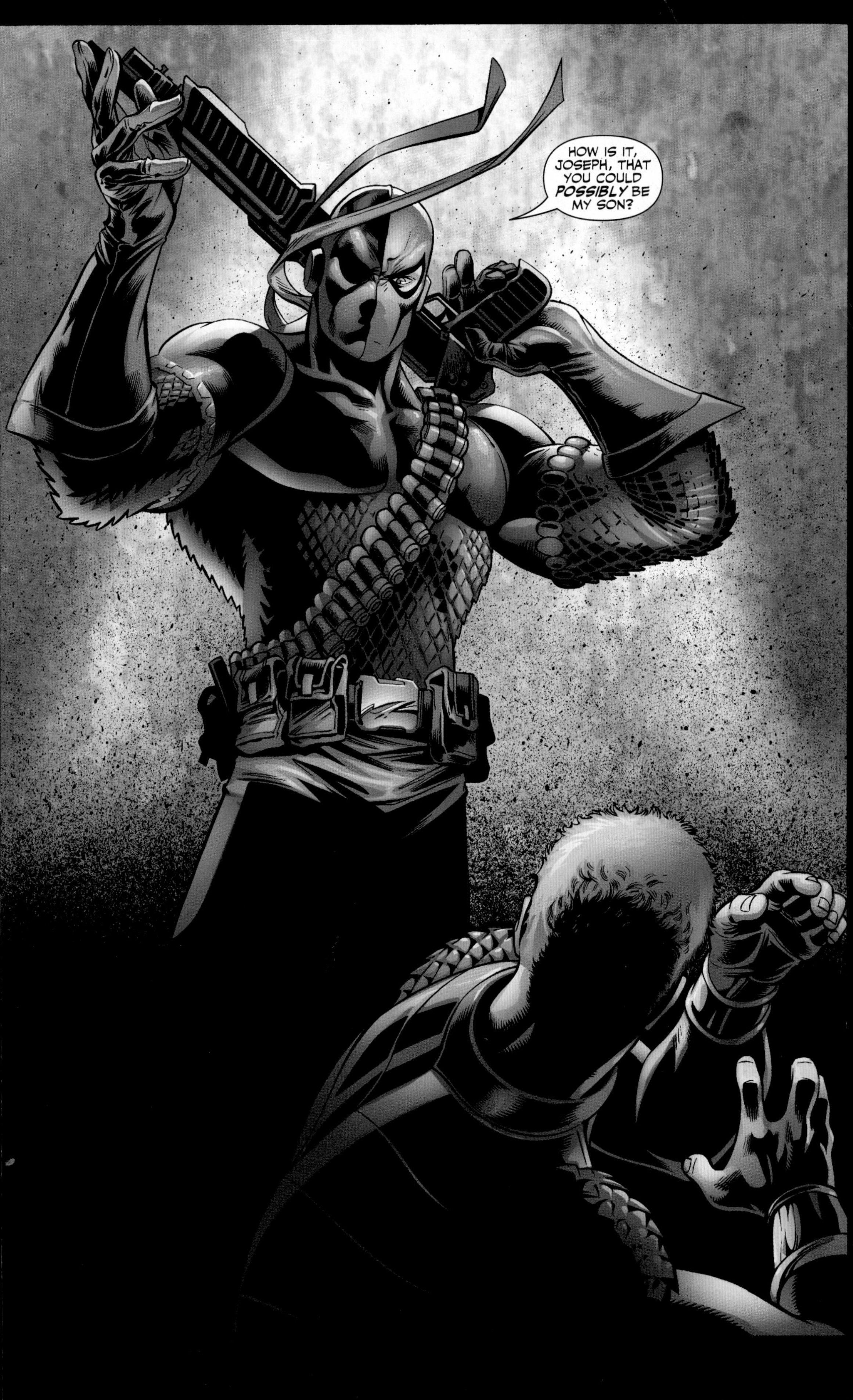
HOW IS IT, JOSEPH, THAT YOU COULD *POSSIBLY* BE MY SON?

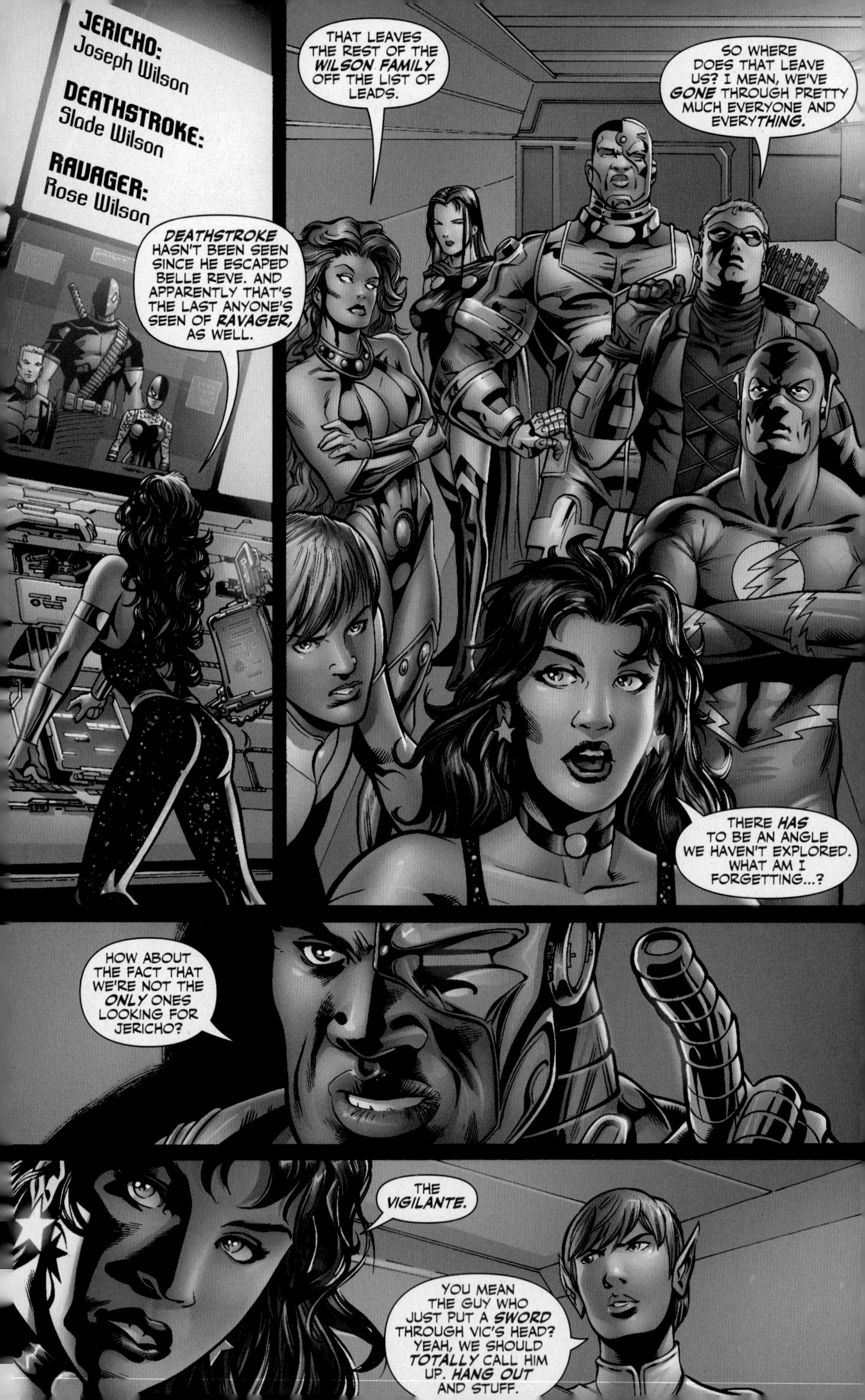
JERICHO: Joseph Wilson
DEATHSTROKE: Slade Wilson
RAVAGER: Rose Wilson
DEATHSTROKE HASN'T BEEN SEEN SINCE HE ESCAPED BELLE REVE. AND APPARENTLY THAT'S THE LAST ANYONE'S SEEN OF RAVAGER, AS WELL.
THAT LEAVES THE REST OF THE WILSON FAMILY OFF THE LIST OF LEADS.
SO WHERE DOES THAT LEAVE US? I MEAN, WE'VE GONE THROUGH PRETTY MUCH EVERYONE AND EVERYTHING.
THERE HAS TO BE AN ANGLE WE HAVEN'T EXPLORED. WHAT AM I FORGETTING...?
HOW ABOUT THE FACT THAT WE'RE NOT THE ONLY ONES LOOKING FOR JERICHO?
THE VIGILANTE.
YOU MEAN THE GUY WHO JUST PUT A SWORD THROUGH VIC'S HEAD? YEAH, WE SHOULD TOTALLY CALL HIM UP. HANG OUT AND STUFF.

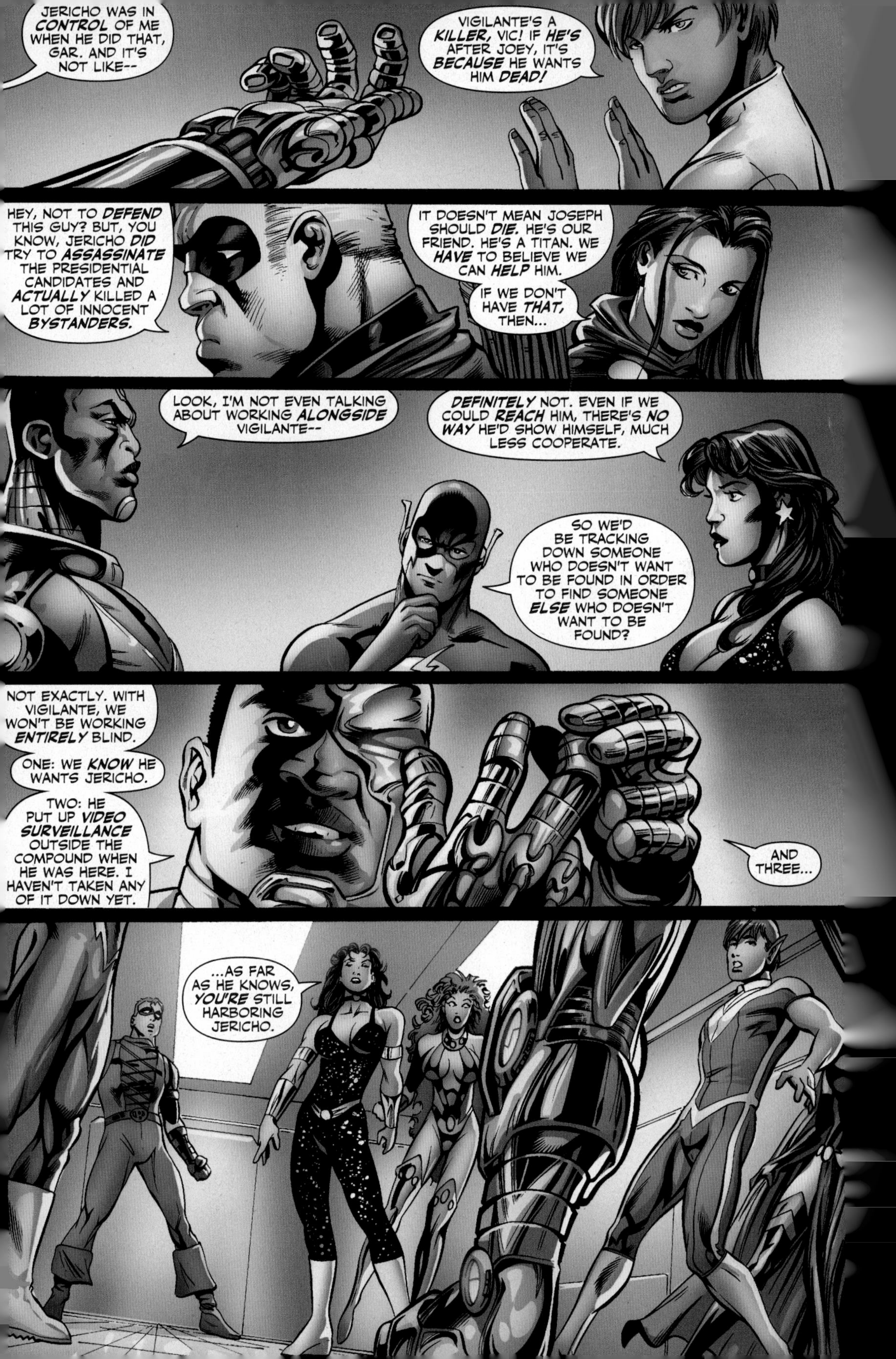
JERICHO WAS IN CONTROL OF ME WHEN HE DID THAT, GAR. AND IT'S NOT LIKE--
VIGILANTE'S A KILLER, VIC! IF HE'S AFTER JOEY, IT'S BECAUSE HE WANTS HIM DEAD!
HEY, NOT TO DEFEND THIS GUY? BUT, YOU KNOW, JERICHO DID TRY TO ASSASSINATE THE PRESIDENTIAL CANDIDATES AND ACTUALLY KILLED A LOT OF INNOCENT BYSTANDERS.
IT DOESN'T MEAN JOSEPH SHOULD DIE. HE'S OUR FRIEND. HE'S A TITAN. WE HAVE TO BELIEVE WE CAN HELP HIM.
IF WE DON'T HAVE THAT, THEN...
LOOK, I'M NOT EVEN TALKING ABOUT WORKING ALONGSIDE VIGILANTE--
DEFINITELY NOT. EVEN IF WE COULD REACH HIM, THERE'S NO WAY HE'D SHOW HIMSELF, MUCH LESS COOPERATE.
SO WE'D BE TRACKING DOWN SOMEONE WHO DOESN'T WANT TO BE FOUND IN ORDER TO FIND SOMEONE ELSE WHO DOESN'T WANT TO BE FOUND?
NOT EXACTLY. WITH VIGILANTE, WE WON'T BE WORKING ENTIRELY BLIND.
ONE: WE KNOW HE WANTS JERICHO.
TWO: HE PUT UP VIDEO SURVEILLANCE OUTSIDE THE COMPOUND WHEN HE WAS HERE. I HAVEN'T TAKEN ANY OF IT DOWN YET.
AND THREE...
...AS FAR AS HE KNOWS, YOU'RE STILL HARBORING JERICHO.

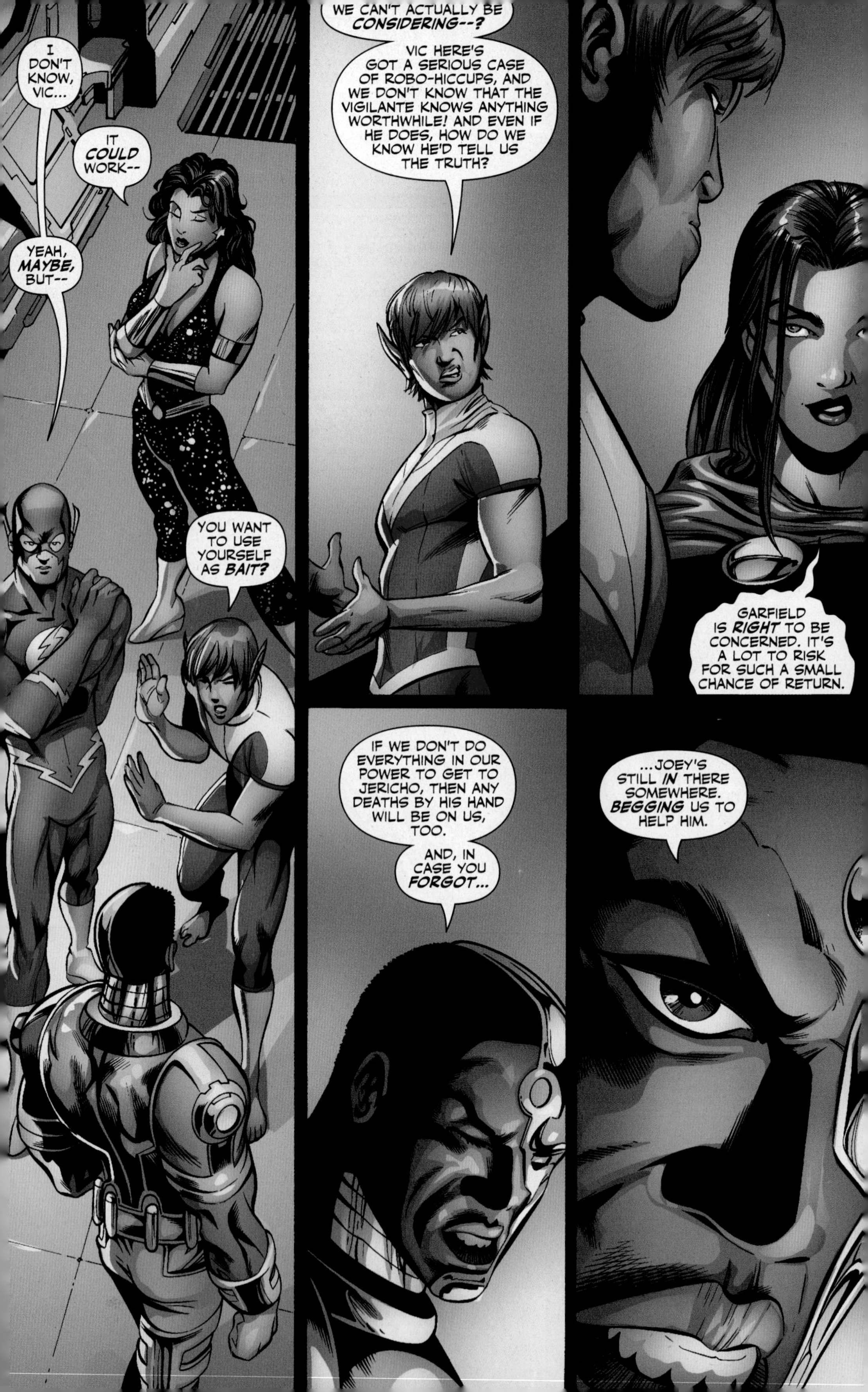
I DON'T KNOW, VIC...
IT COULD WORK--
YEAH, MAYBE, BUT--
YOU WANT TO USE YOURSELF AS BAIT?
WE CAN'T ACTUALLY BE CONSIDERING--?
VIC HERE'S GOT A SERIOUS CASE OF ROBO-HICCUPS, AND WE DON'T KNOW THAT THE VIGILANTE KNOWS ANYTHING WORTHWHILE! AND EVEN IF HE DOES, HOW DO WE KNOW HE'D TELL US THE TRUTH?
GARFIELD IS RIGHT TO BE CONCERNED. IT'S A LOT TO RISK FOR SUCH A SMALL CHANCE OF RETURN.
IF WE DON'T DO EVERYTHING IN OUR POWER TO GET TO JERICHO, THEN ANY DEATHS BY HIS HAND WILL BE ON US, TOO.
AND, IN CASE YOU FORGOT...
...JOEY'S STILL IN THERE SOMEWHERE. BEGGING US TO HELP HIM.

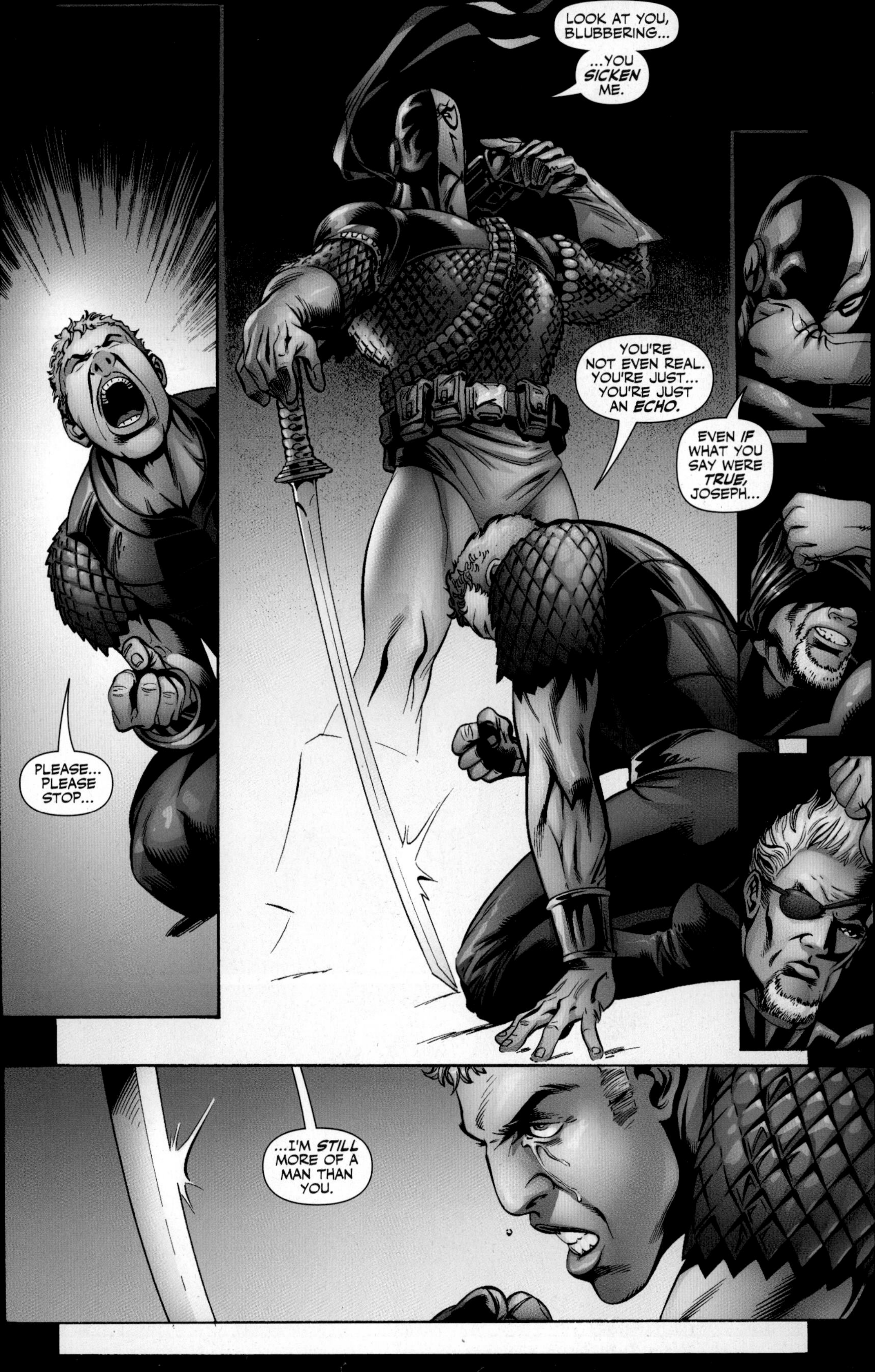

LOOK AT YOU, BLUBBERING...
...YOU *SICKEN* ME.
PLEASE... PLEASE STOP...
YOU'RE NOT EVEN REAL. YOU'RE JUST... YOU'RE JUST AN *ECHO.*
EVEN *IF* WHAT YOU SAY WERE *TRUE,* JOSEPH...
...I'M *STILL* MORE OF A MAN THAN YOU.

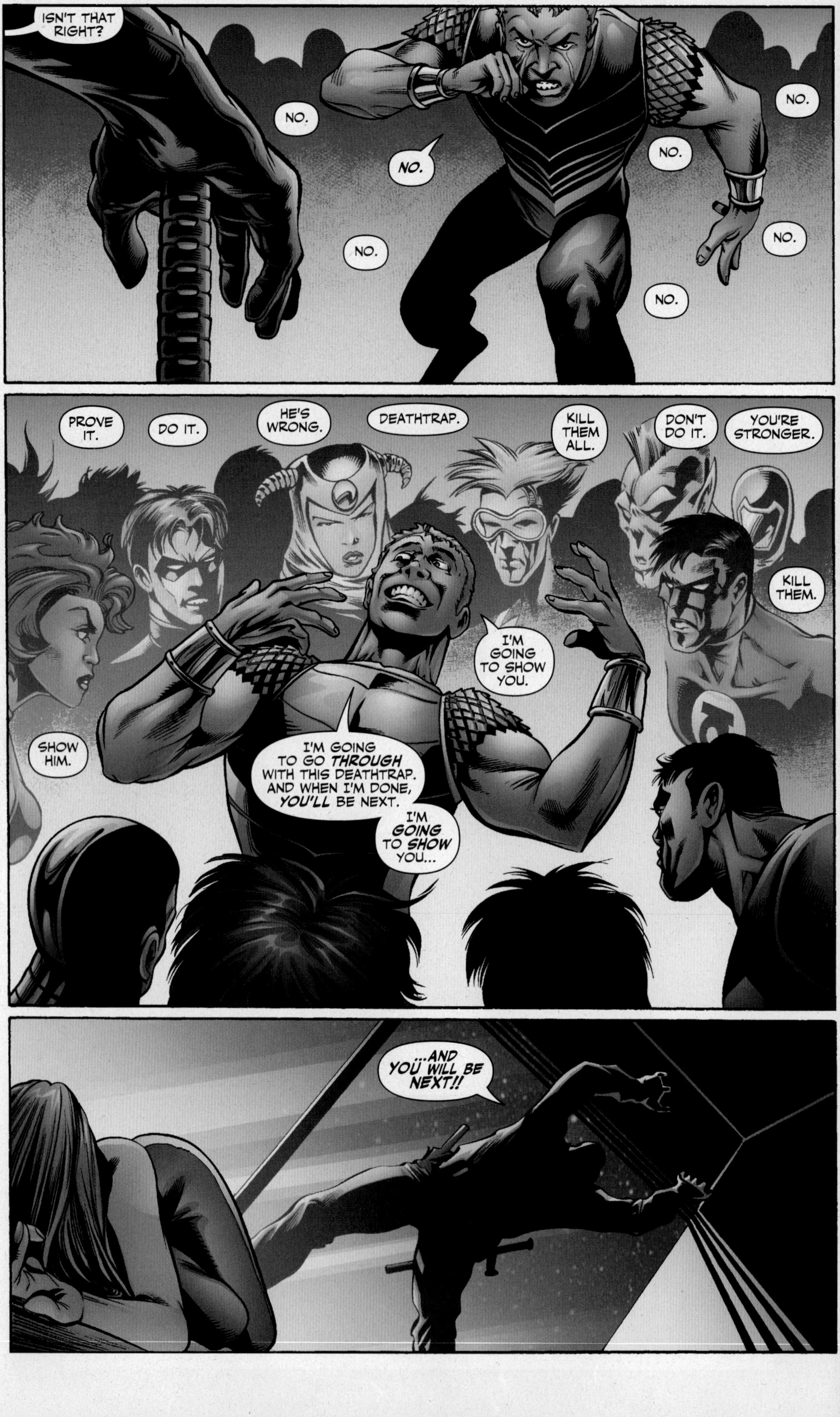
ISN'T THAT RIGHT?
NO.
NO.
NO.
NO.
NO.
NO.
NO.
PROVE IT.
DO IT.
HE'S WRONG.
DEATHTRAP.
KILL THEM ALL.
DON'T DO IT.
YOU'RE STRONGER.
KILL THEM.
I'M GOING TO SHOW YOU.
SHOW HIM.
I'M GOING TO GO THROUGH WITH THIS DEATHTRAP. AND WHEN I'M DONE, YOU'LL BE NEXT.
I'M GOING TO SHOW YOU...
...AND YOU WILL BE NEXT!!

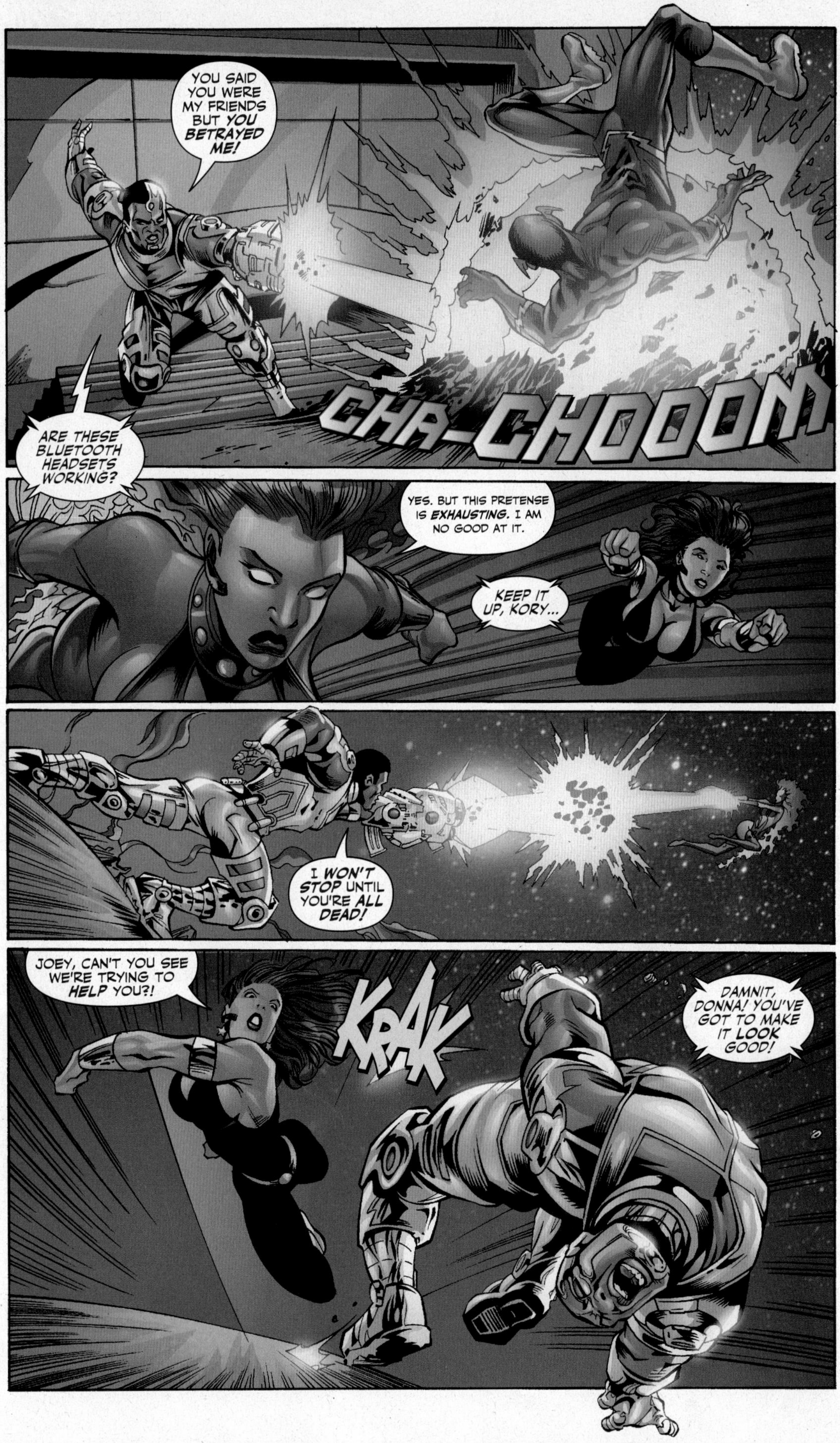
YOU SAID YOU WERE MY FRIENDS BUT YOU BETRAYED ME!
CHA-CHOOOM
ARE THESE BLUETOOTH HEADSETS WORKING?
YES. BUT THIS PRETENSE IS EXHAUSTING. I AM NO GOOD AT IT.
KEEP IT UP, KORY...
I WON'T STOP UNTIL YOU'RE ALL DEAD!
JOEY, CAN'T YOU SEE WE'RE TRYING TO HELP YOU?!
KRAK
DAMNIT, DONNA! YOU'VE GOT TO MAKE IT LOOK GOOD!

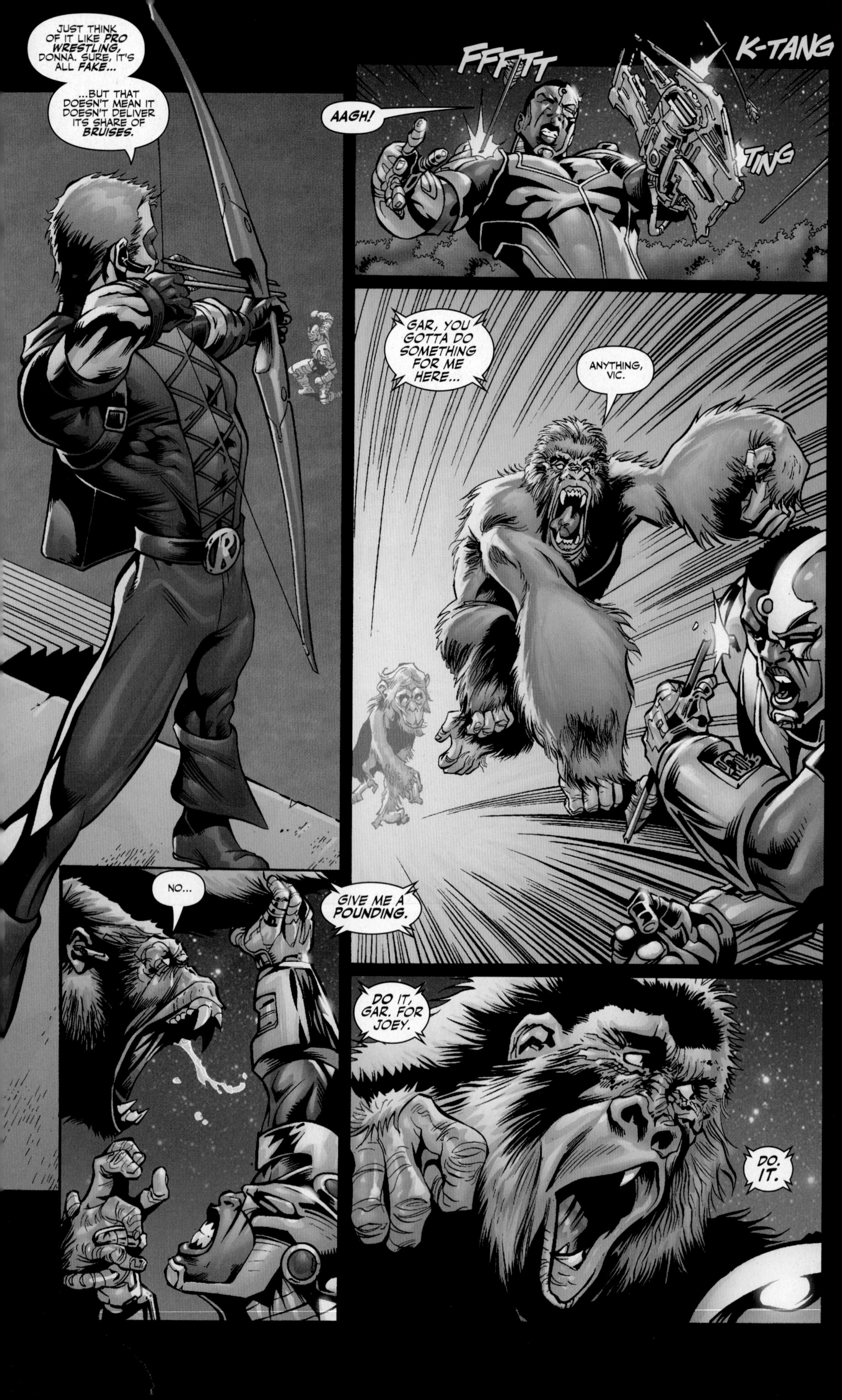
JUST THINK OF IT LIKE PRO WRESTLING, DONNA. SURE, IT'S ALL FAKE...
...BUT THAT DOESN'T MEAN IT DOESN'T DELIVER ITS SHARE OF BRUISES.
FFFTTT
K-TANG
AAGH!
TING
GAR, YOU GOTTA DO SOMETHING FOR ME HERE...
ANYTHING, VIC.
NO...
GIVE ME A POUNDING.
DO IT, GAR. FOR JOEY.
DO. IT.

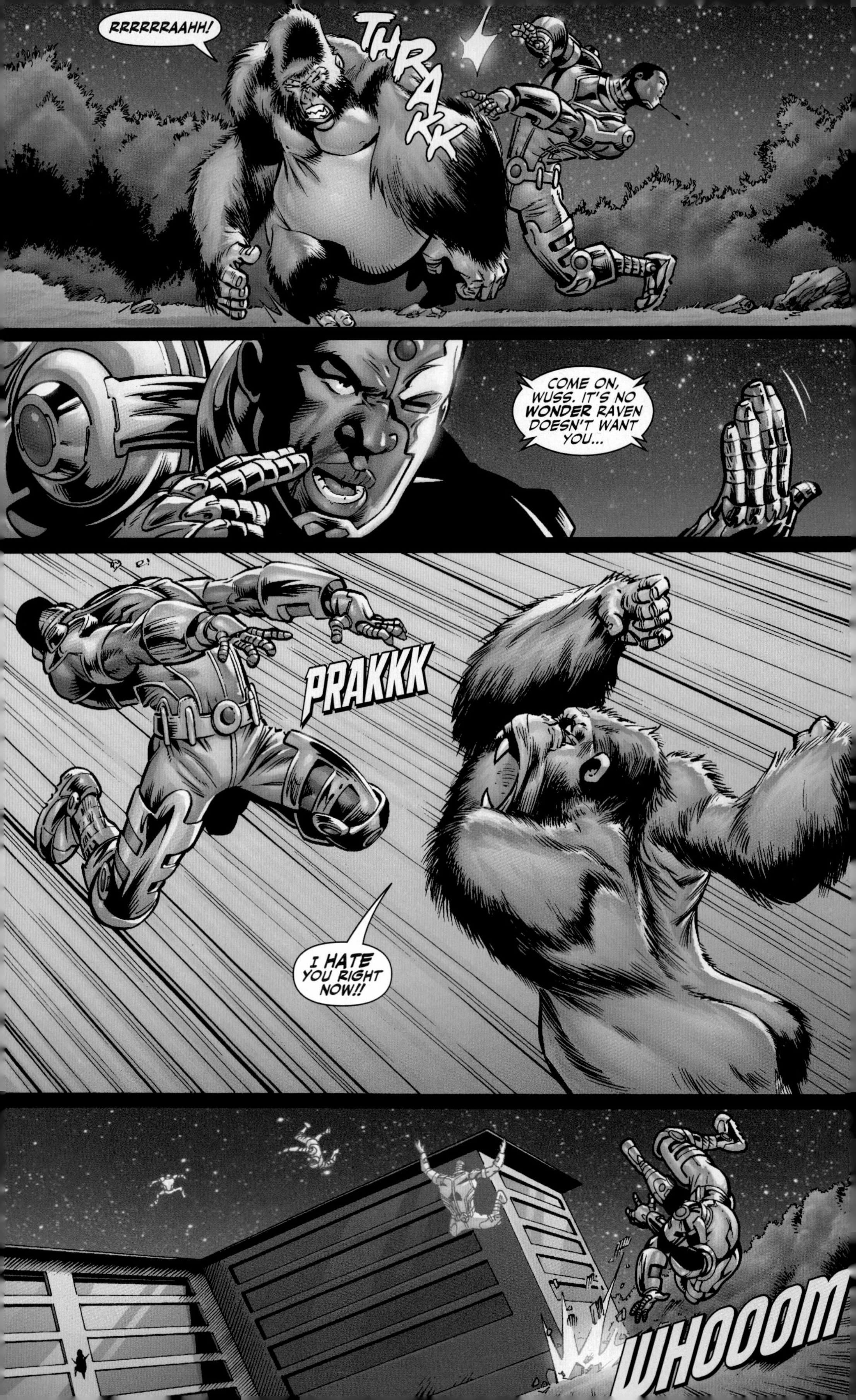
RRRRRRAAHH!
THRAKK
COME ON, WUSS. IT'S NO WONDER RAVEN DOESN'T WANT YOU...
PRAKKK
I HATE YOU RIGHT NOW!!
WHOOOM

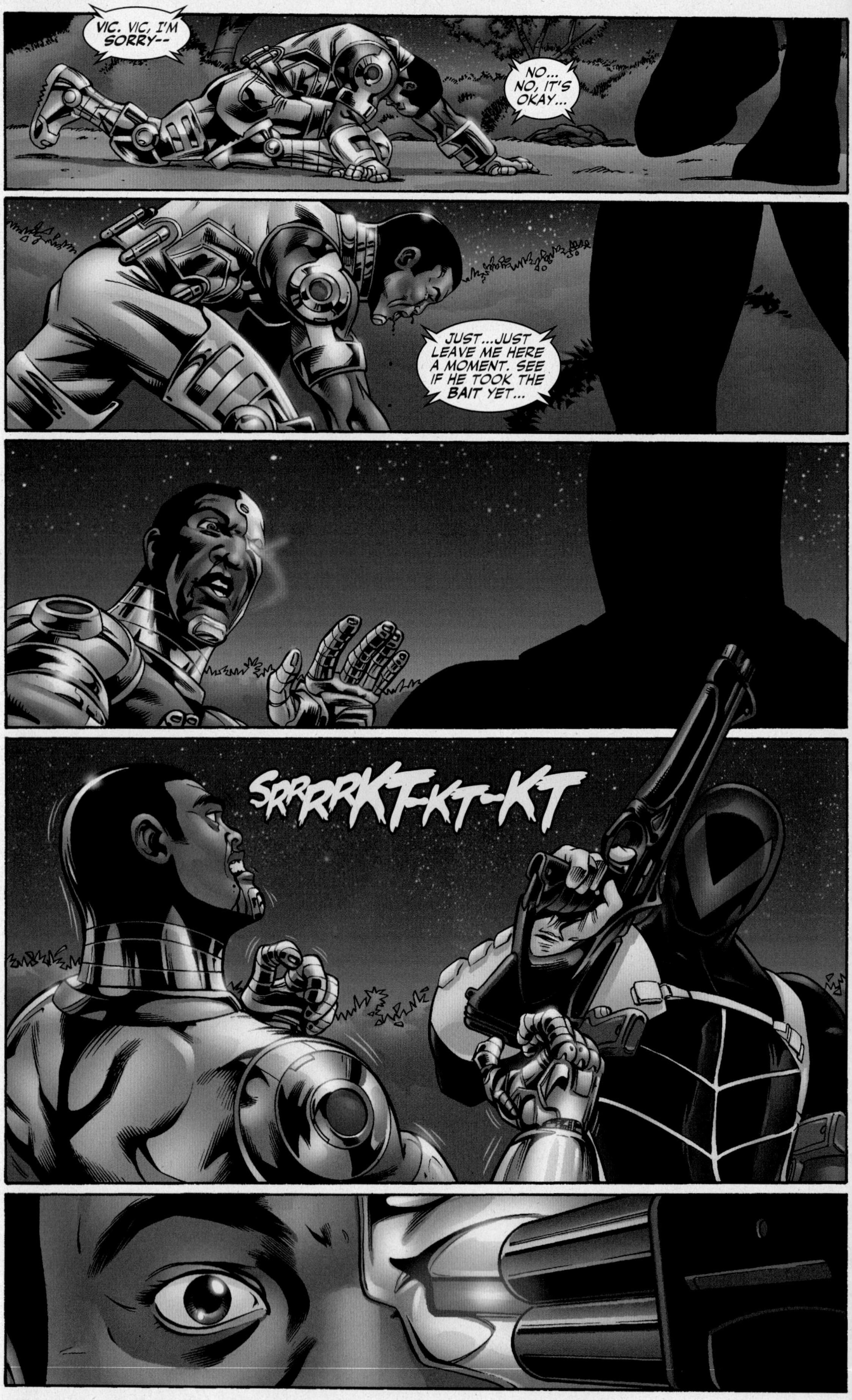
VIC. VIC, I'M SORRY--
NO... NO, IT'S OKAY...
JUST...JUST LEAVE ME HERE A MOMENT. SEE IF HE TOOK THE BAIT YET...
SRRRRKT-KT-KT

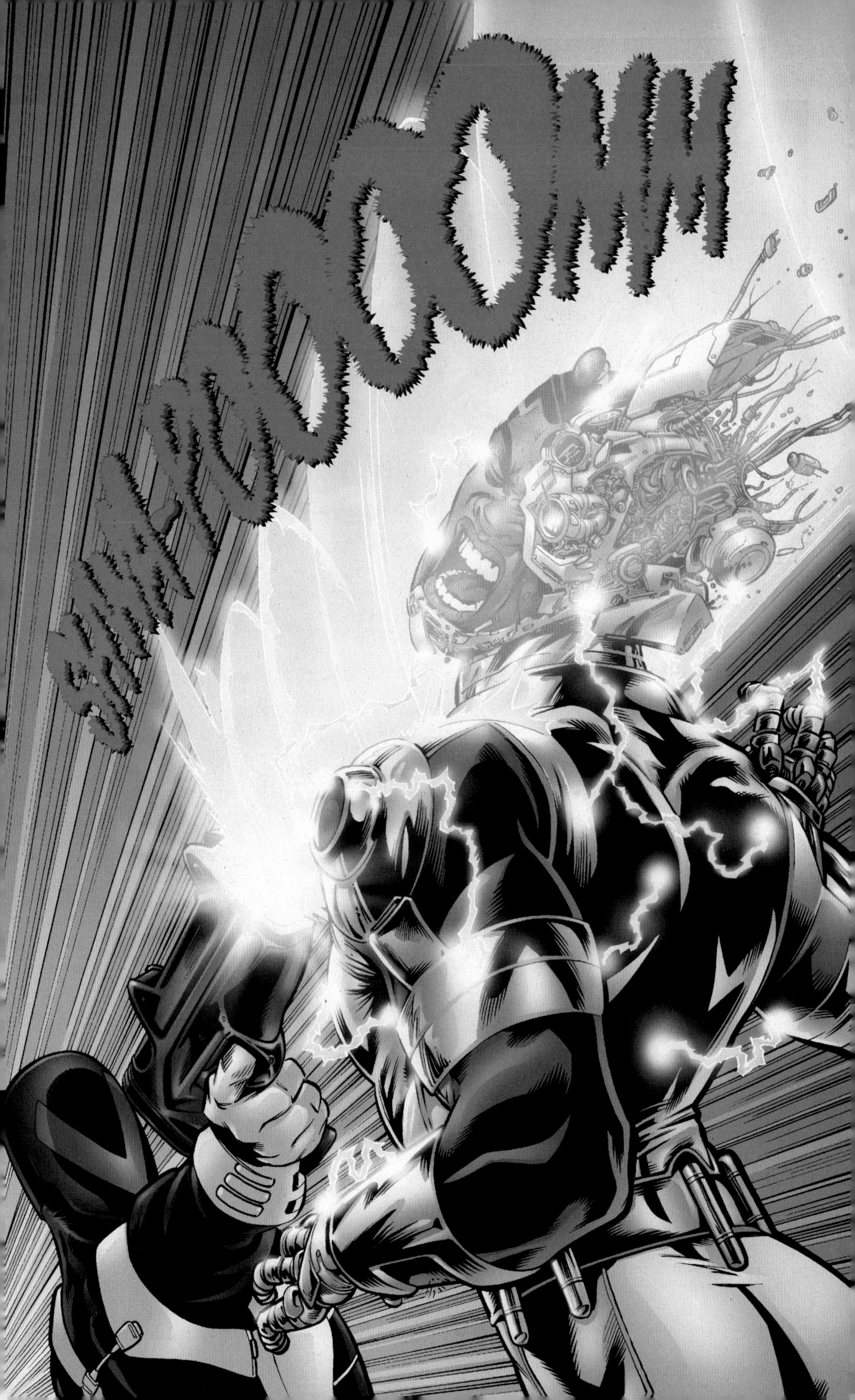
SHKROOOOMM

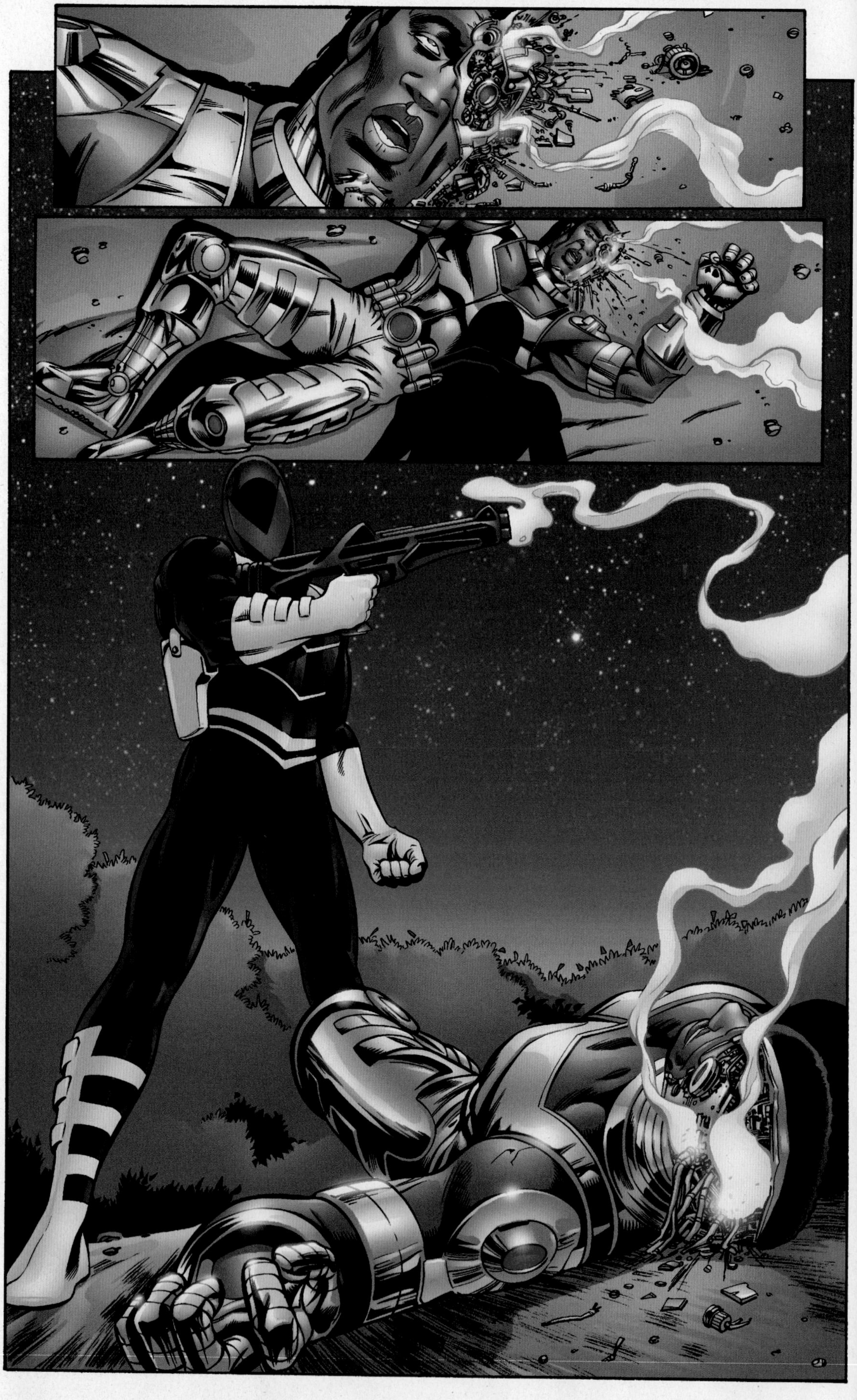

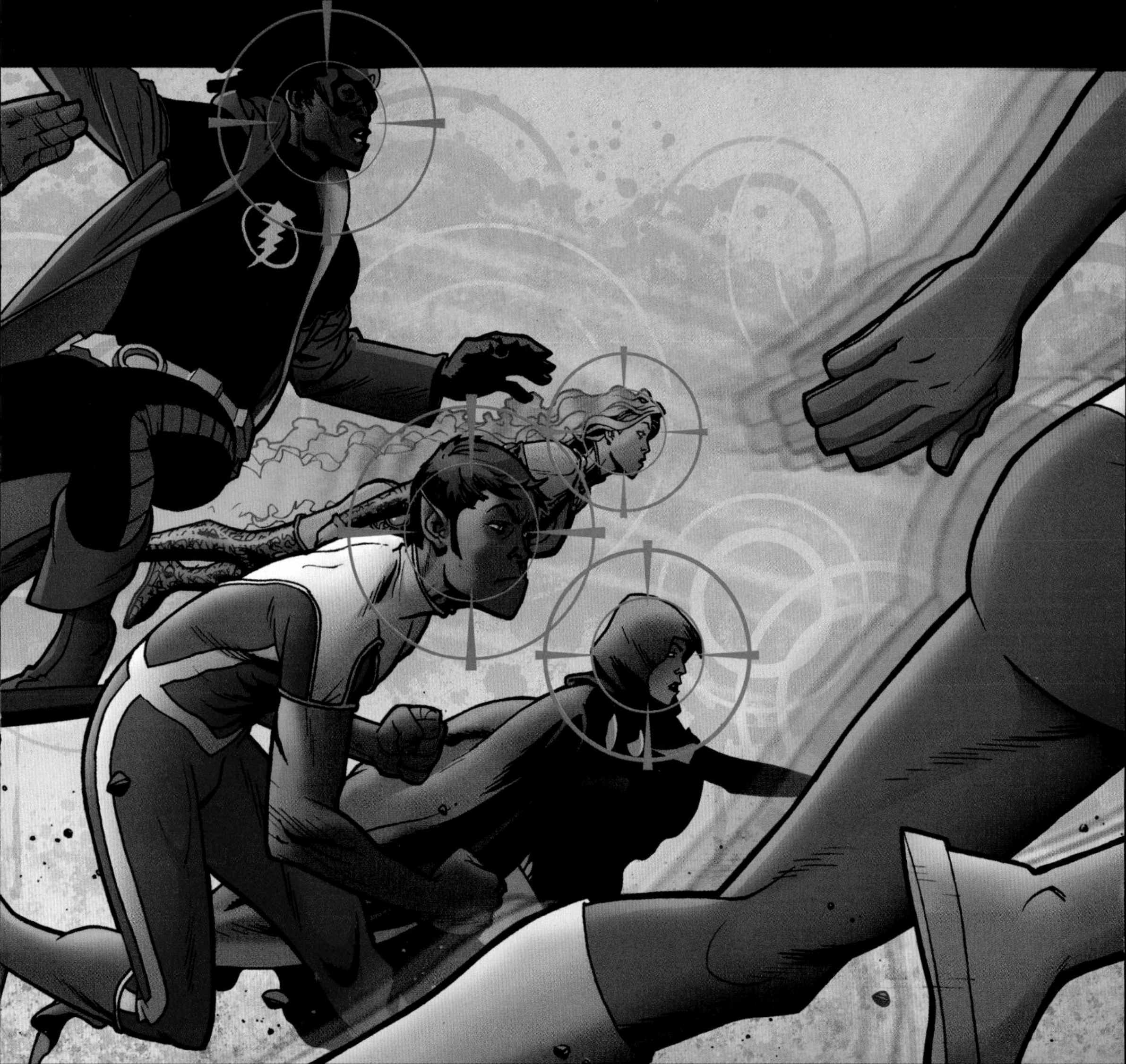

Deathtrap Part 2

Marv Wolfman
Writer

Tom Lyle
Layouts

Scott Hanna

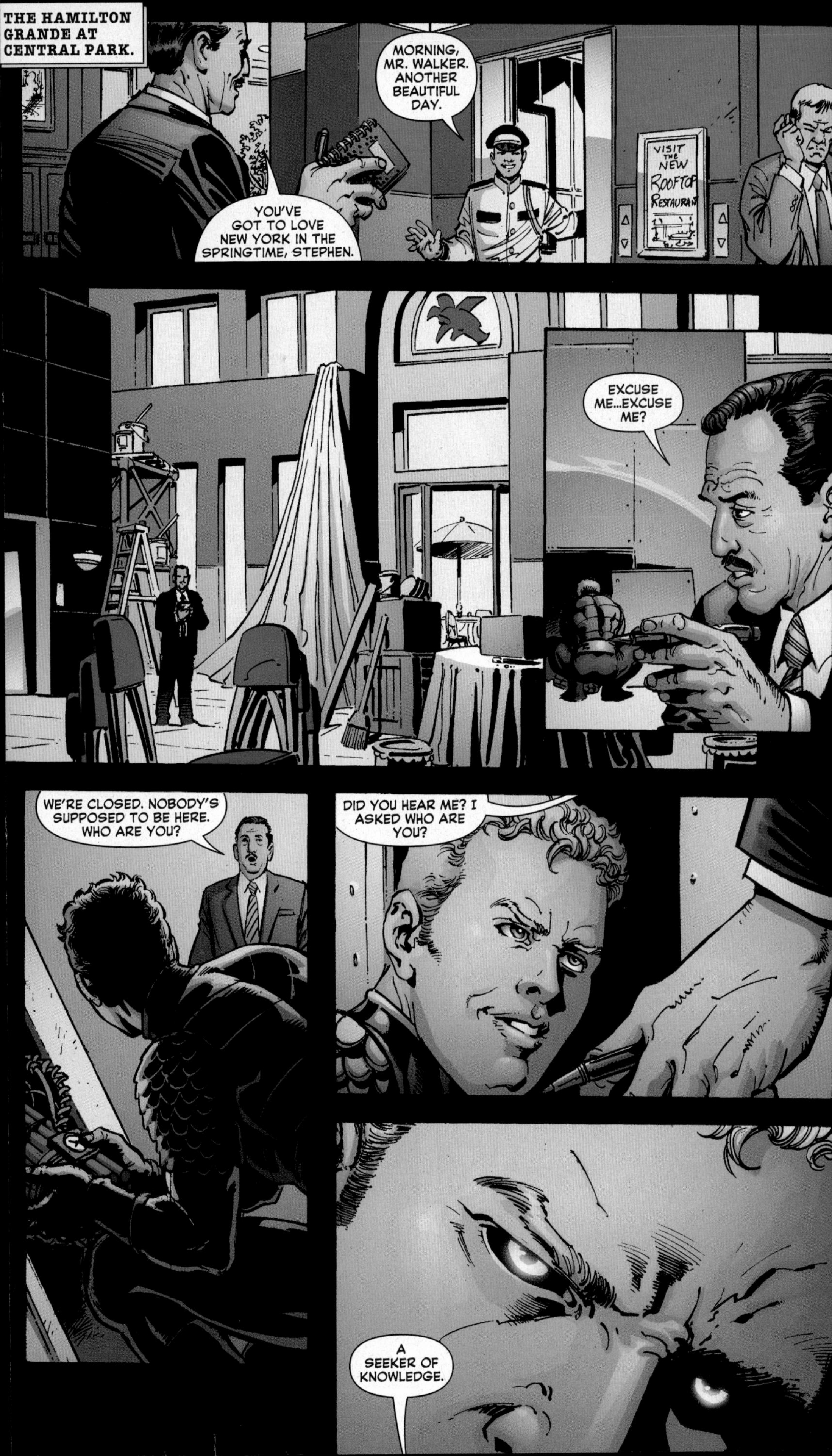
THE HAMILTON GRANDE AT CENTRAL PARK.
MORNING, MR. WALKER. ANOTHER BEAUTIFUL DAY.
YOU'VE GOT TO LOVE NEW YORK IN THE SPRINGTIME, STEPHEN.
VISIT THE NEW ROOFTOP RESTAURANT
EXCUSE ME...EXCUSE ME?
WE'RE CLOSED. NOBODY'S SUPPOSED TO BE HERE. WHO ARE YOU?
DID YOU HEAR ME? I ASKED WHO ARE YOU?
A SEEKER OF KNOWLEDGE.

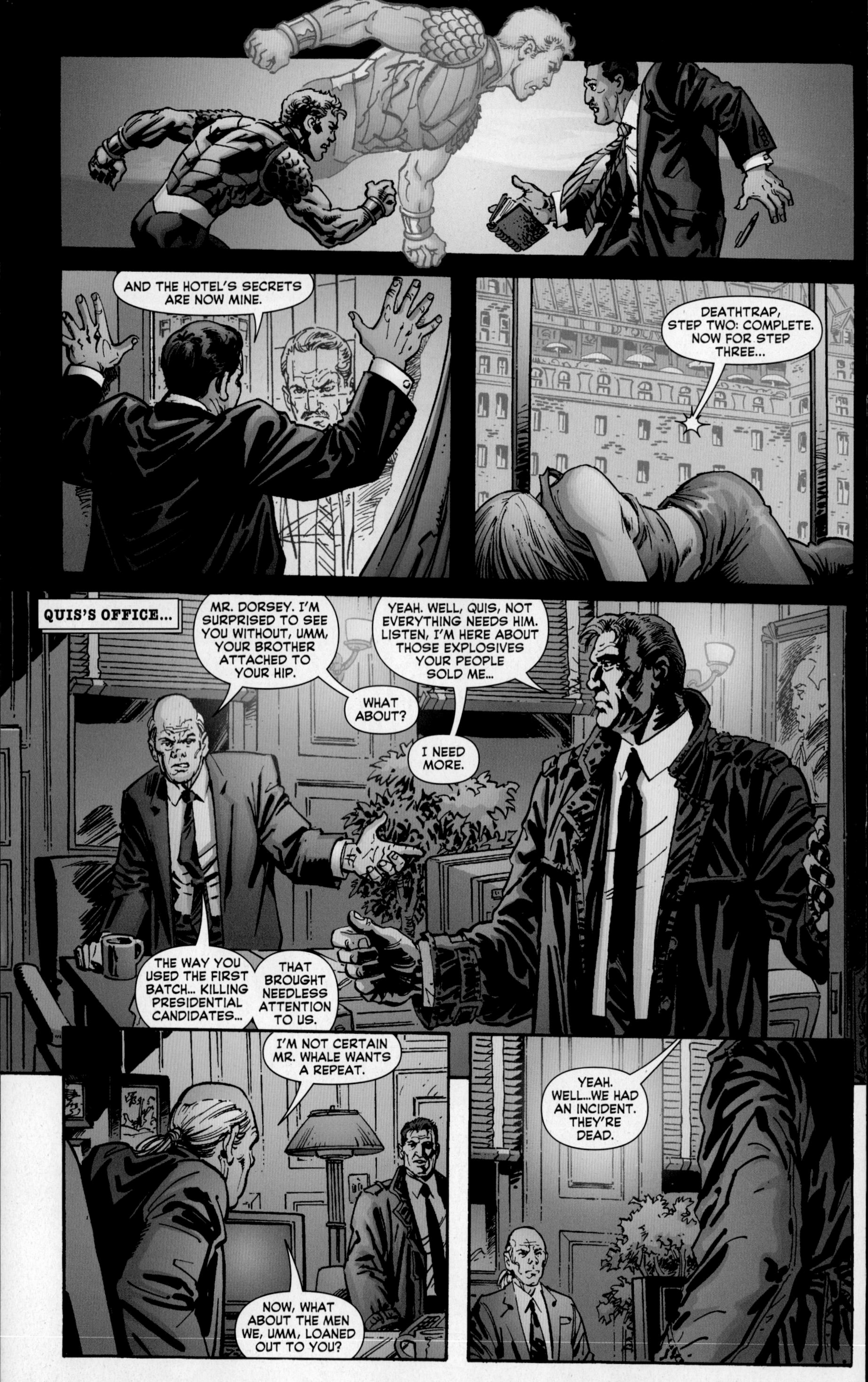
AND THE HOTEL'S SECRETS ARE NOW MINE.
DEATHTRAP, STEP TWO: COMPLETE. NOW FOR STEP THREE...
QUIS'S OFFICE...
MR. DORSEY. I'M SURPRISED TO SEE YOU WITHOUT, UMM, YOUR BROTHER ATTACHED TO YOUR HIP.
YEAH. WELL, QUIS, NOT EVERYTHING NEEDS HIM. LISTEN, I'M HERE ABOUT THOSE EXPLOSIVES YOUR PEOPLE SOLD ME...
WHAT ABOUT?
I NEED MORE.
THE WAY YOU USED THE FIRST BATCH... KILLING PRESIDENTIAL CANDIDATES...
THAT BROUGHT NEEDLESS ATTENTION TO US.
I'M NOT CERTAIN MR. WHALE WANTS A REPEAT.
NOW, WHAT ABOUT THE MEN WE, UMM, LOANED OUT TO YOU?
YEAH. WELL...WE HAD AN INCIDENT. THEY'RE DEAD.

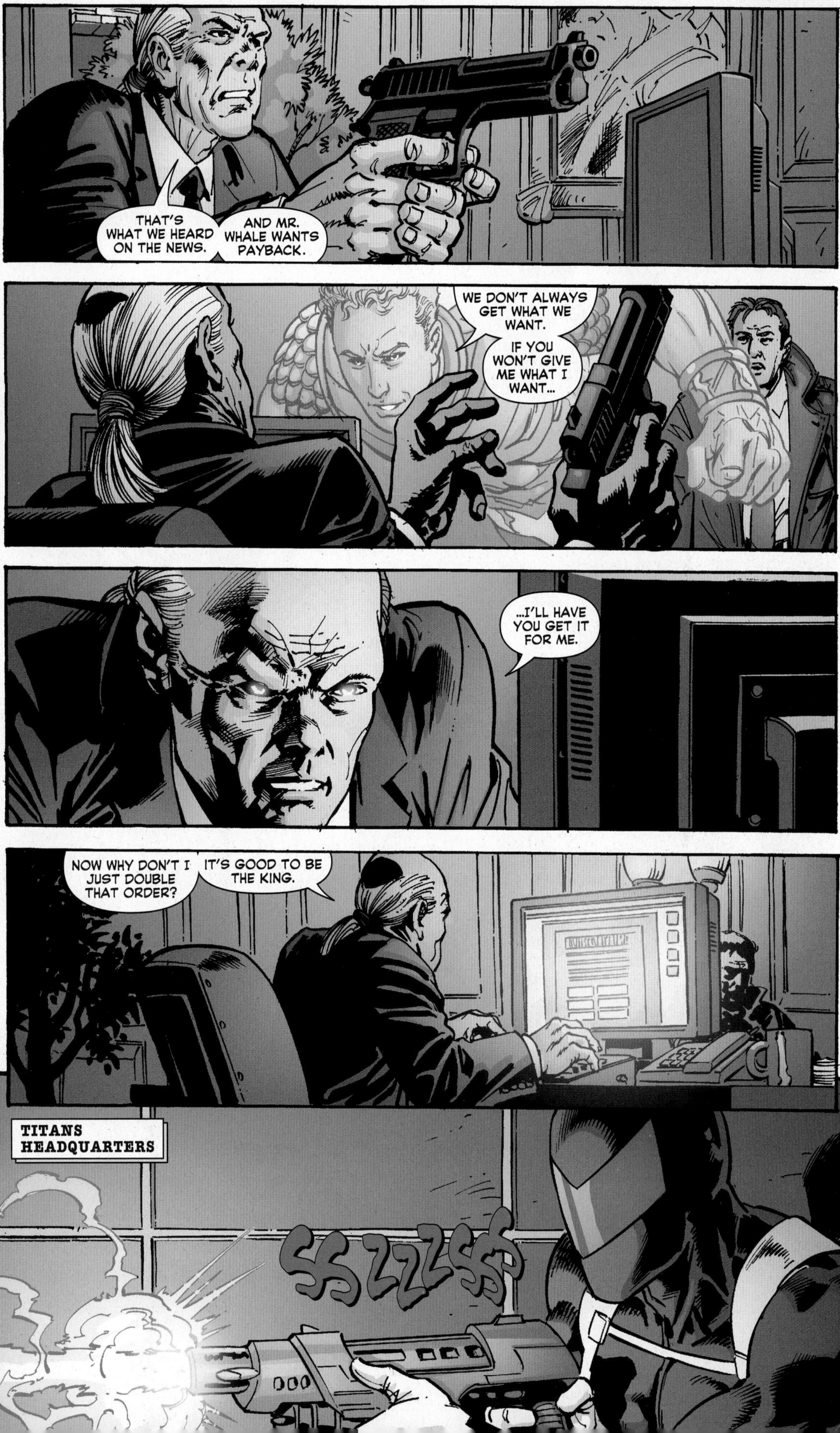
THAT'S WHAT WE HEARD ON THE NEWS.
AND MR. WHALE WANTS PAYBACK.
WE DON'T ALWAYS GET WHAT WE WANT.
IF YOU WON'T GIVE ME WHAT I WANT...
...I'LL HAVE YOU GET IT FOR ME.
NOW WHY DON'T I JUST DOUBLE THAT ORDER?
IT'S GOOD TO BE THE KING.
TITANS HEADQUARTERS
SSZZZSS

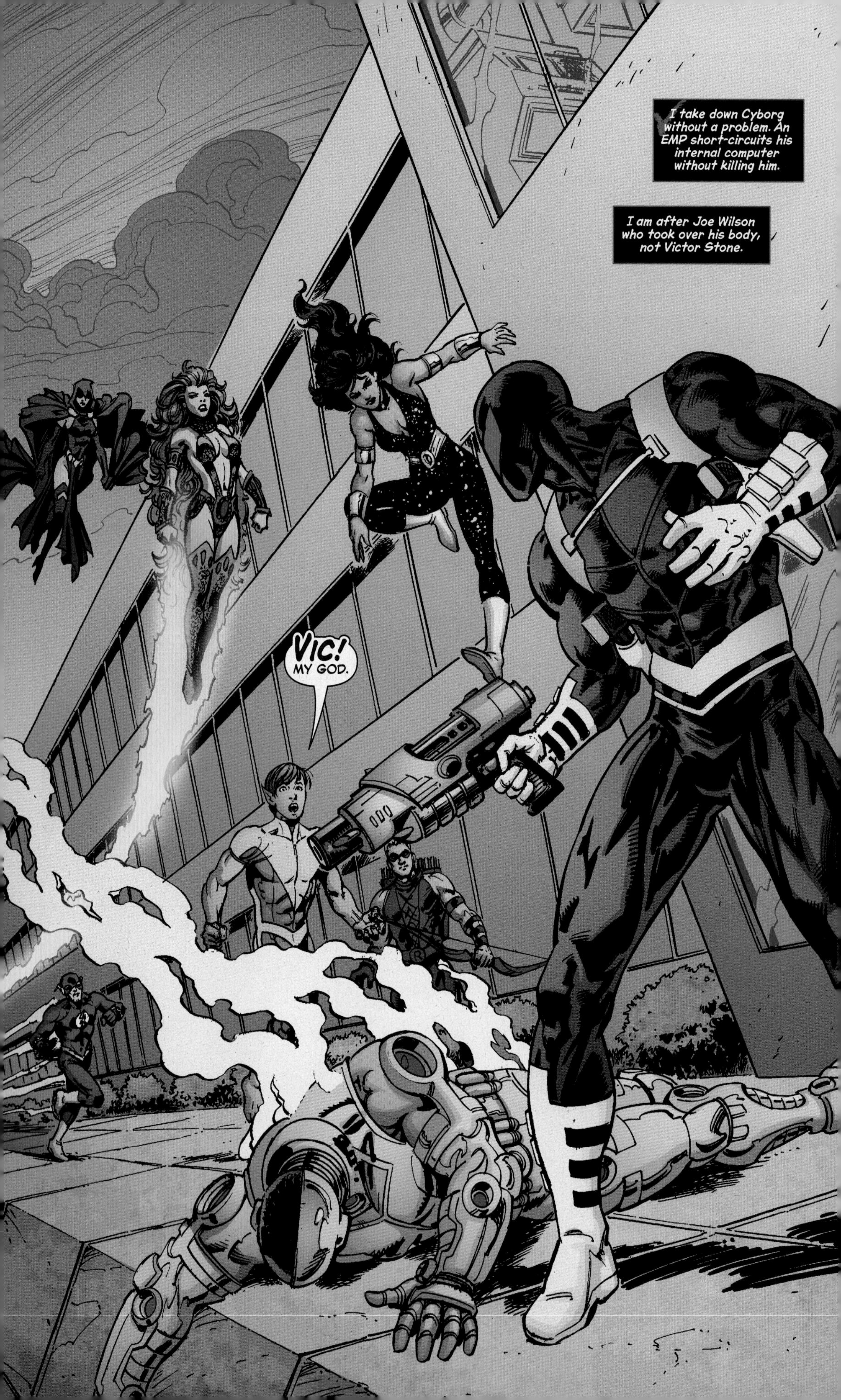

I take down Cyborg without a problem. An EMP short-circuits his internal computer without killing him.
I am after Joe Wilson who took over his body, not Victor Stone.
VIC! MY GOD.

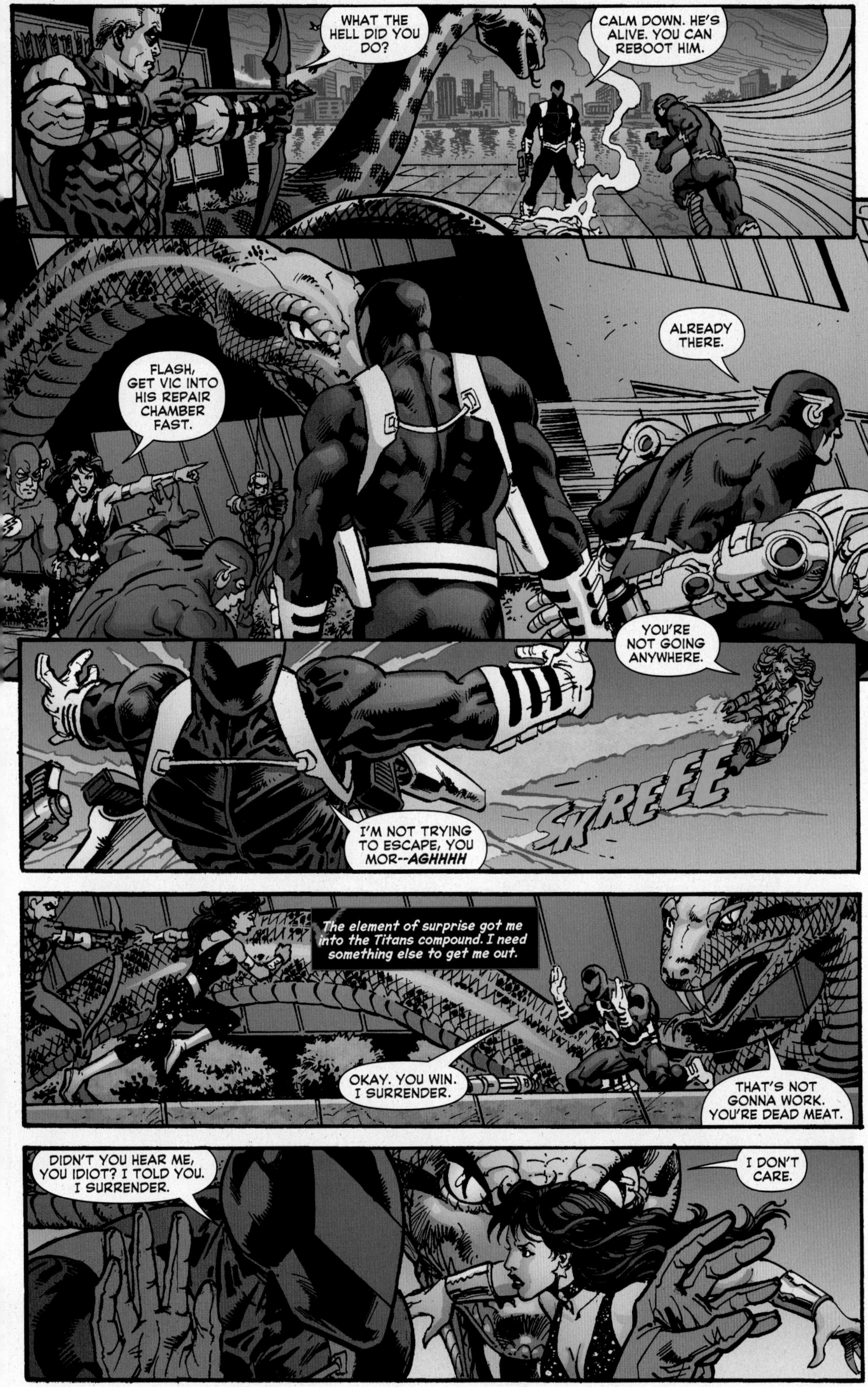
WHAT THE HELL DID YOU DO?
CALM DOWN. HE'S ALIVE. YOU CAN REBOOT HIM.
FLASH, GET VIC INTO HIS REPAIR CHAMBER FAST.
ALREADY THERE.
YOU'RE NOT GOING ANYWHERE.
I'M NOT TRYING TO ESCAPE, YOU MOR--*AGHHHH*
SKREEE
The element of surprise got me into the Titans compound. I need something else to get me out.
OKAY. YOU WIN. I SURRENDER.
THAT'S NOT GONNA WORK. YOU'RE DEAD MEAT.
DIDN'T YOU HEAR ME, YOU IDIOT? I TOLD YOU. I SURRENDER.
I DON'T CARE.

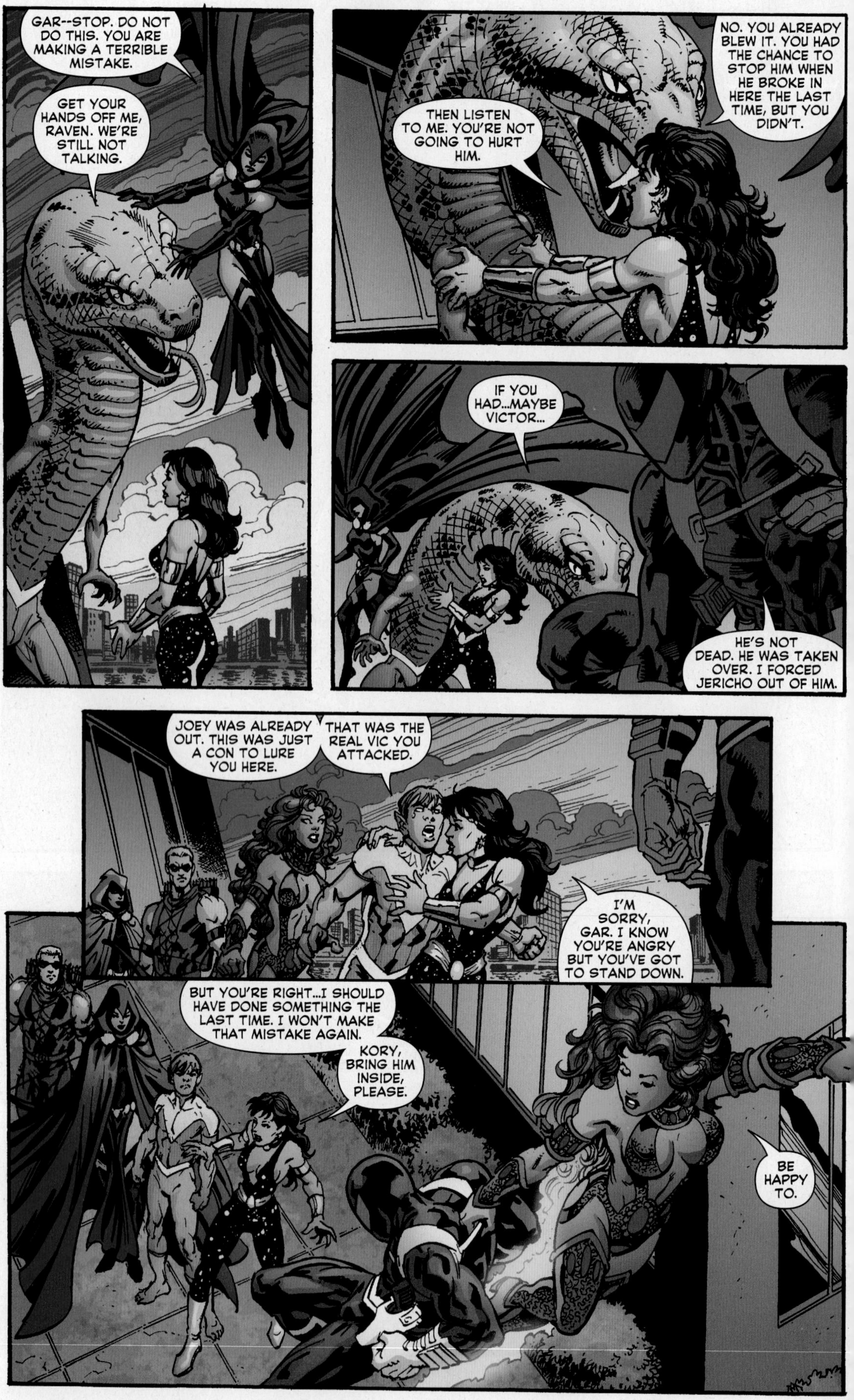
GAR--STOP. DO NOT DO THIS. YOU ARE MAKING A TERRIBLE MISTAKE.
GET YOUR HANDS OFF ME, RAVEN. WE'RE STILL NOT TALKING.
THEN LISTEN TO ME. YOU'RE NOT GOING TO HURT HIM.
NO. YOU ALREADY BLEW IT. YOU HAD THE CHANCE TO STOP HIM WHEN HE BROKE IN HERE THE LAST TIME, BUT YOU DIDN'T.
IF YOU HAD...MAYBE VICTOR...
HE'S NOT DEAD. HE WAS TAKEN OVER. I FORCED JERICHO OUT OF HIM.
JOEY WAS ALREADY OUT. THIS WAS JUST A CON TO LURE YOU HERE.
THAT WAS THE REAL VIC YOU ATTACKED.
I'M SORRY, GAR. I KNOW YOU'RE ANGRY BUT YOU'VE GOT TO STAND DOWN.
BUT YOU'RE RIGHT...I SHOULD HAVE DONE SOMETHING THE LAST TIME. I WON'T MAKE THAT MISTAKE AGAIN.
KORY, BRING HIM INSIDE, PLEASE.
BE HAPPY TO.

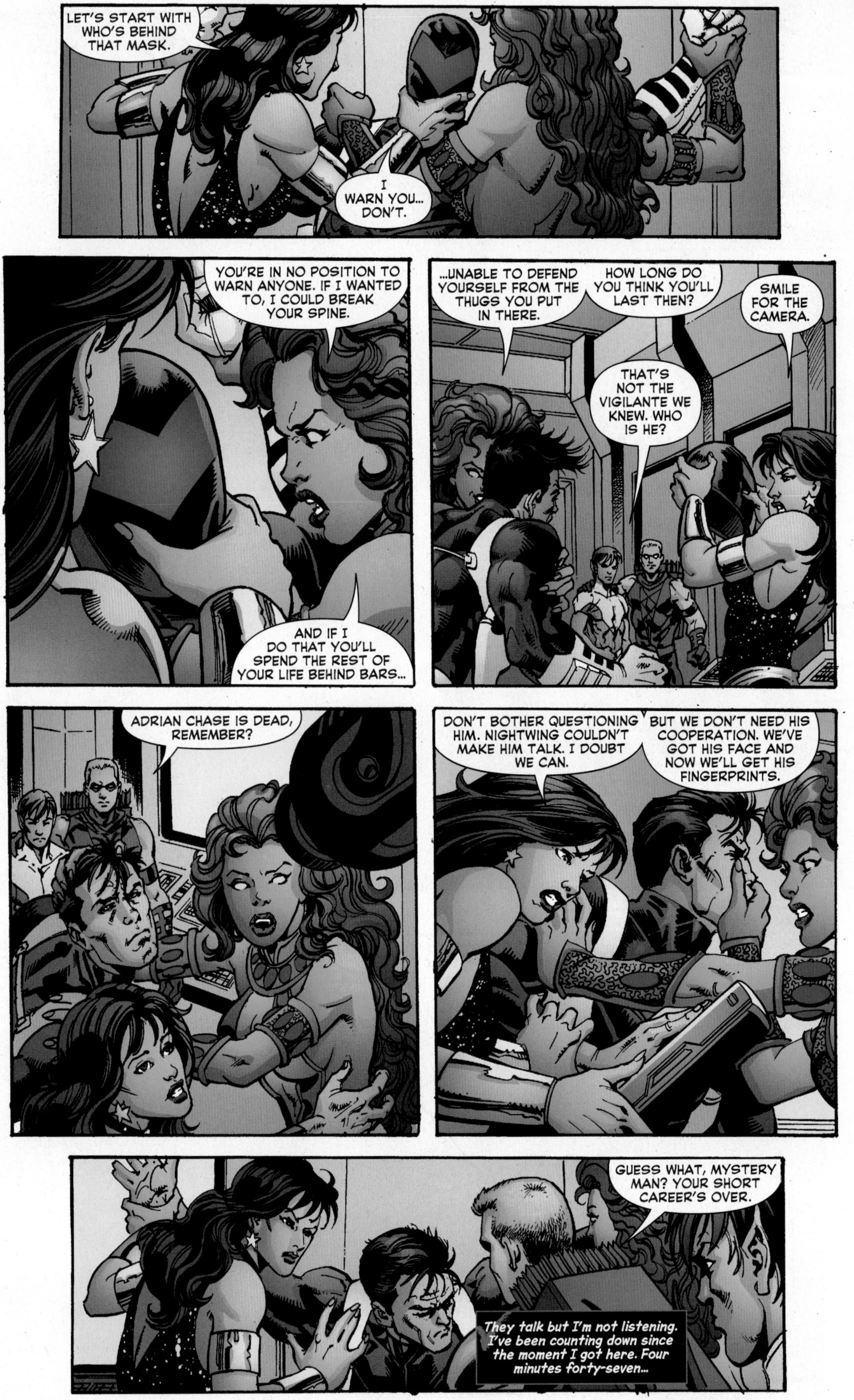
LET'S START WITH WHO'S BEHIND THAT MASK.
I WARN YOU... DON'T.
YOU'RE IN NO POSITION TO WARN ANYONE. IF I WANTED TO, I COULD BREAK YOUR SPINE.
AND IF I DO THAT YOU'LL SPEND THE REST OF YOUR LIFE BEHIND BARS...
...UNABLE TO DEFEND YOURSELF FROM THE THUGS YOU PUT IN THERE.
HOW LONG DO YOU THINK YOU'LL LAST THEN?
SMILE FOR THE CAMERA.
THAT'S NOT THE VIGILANTE WE KNEW. WHO IS HE?
ADRIAN CHASE IS DEAD, REMEMBER?
DON'T BOTHER QUESTIONING HIM. NIGHTWING COULDN'T MAKE HIM TALK. I DOUBT WE CAN.
BUT WE DON'T NEED HIS COOPERATION. WE'VE GOT HIS FACE AND NOW WE'LL GET HIS FINGERPRINTS.
GUESS WHAT, MYSTERY MAN? YOUR SHORT CAREER'S OVER.
They talk but I'm not listening. I've been counting down since the moment I got here. Four minutes forty-seven...

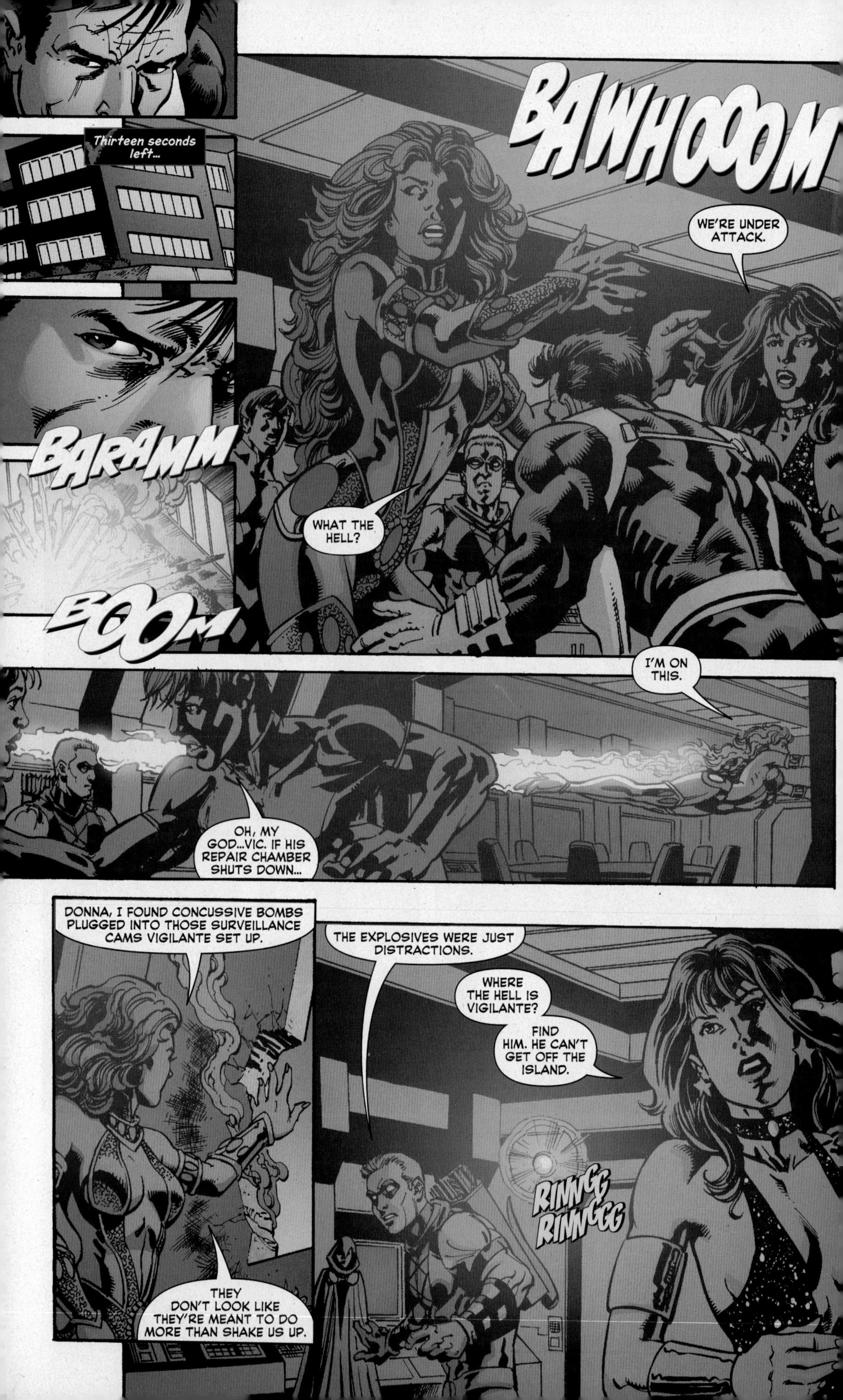
Thirteen seconds left...
BARAMM
BOOM
BAWHOOOM
WE'RE UNDER ATTACK.
WHAT THE HELL?
I'M ON THIS.
OH, MY GOD...VIC. IF HIS REPAIR CHAMBER SHUTS DOWN...
DONNA, I FOUND CONCUSSIVE BOMBS PLUGGED INTO THOSE SURVEILLANCE CAMS VIGILANTE SET UP.
THEY DON'T LOOK LIKE THEY'RE MEANT TO DO MORE THAN SHAKE US UP.
THE EXPLOSIVES WERE JUST DISTRACTIONS.
WHERE THE HELL IS VIGILANTE?
FIND HIM. HE CAN'T GET OFF THE ISLAND.
RINNGG RINNGGG

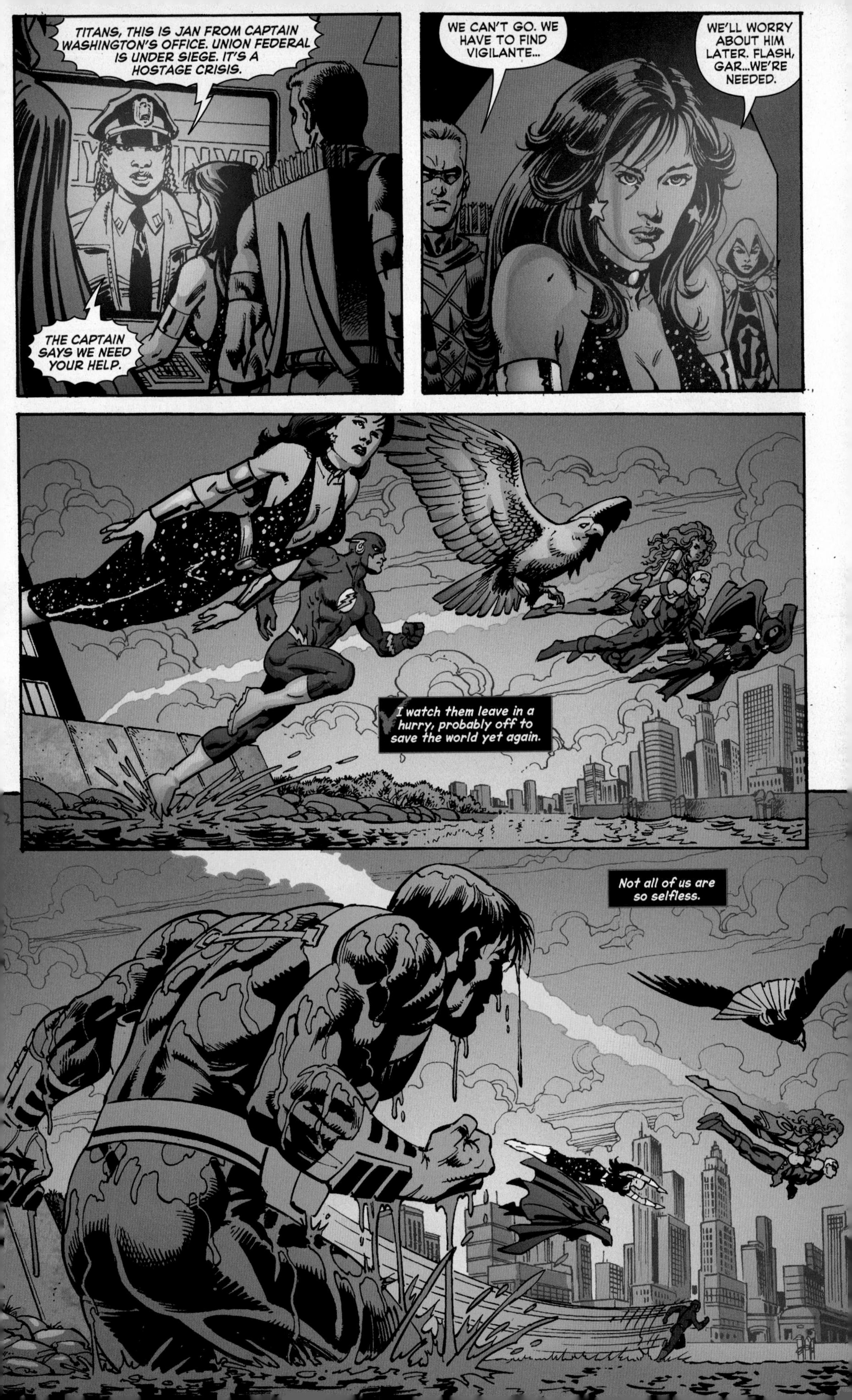
TITANS, THIS IS JAN FROM CAPTAIN WASHINGTON'S OFFICE. UNION FEDERAL IS UNDER SIEGE. IT'S A HOSTAGE CRISIS.
THE CAPTAIN SAYS WE NEED YOUR HELP.
WE CAN'T GO. WE HAVE TO FIND VIGILANTE...
WE'LL WORRY ABOUT HIM LATER. FLASH, GAR...WE'RE NEEDED.
I watch them leave in a hurry, probably off to save the world yet again.
Not all of us are so selfless.

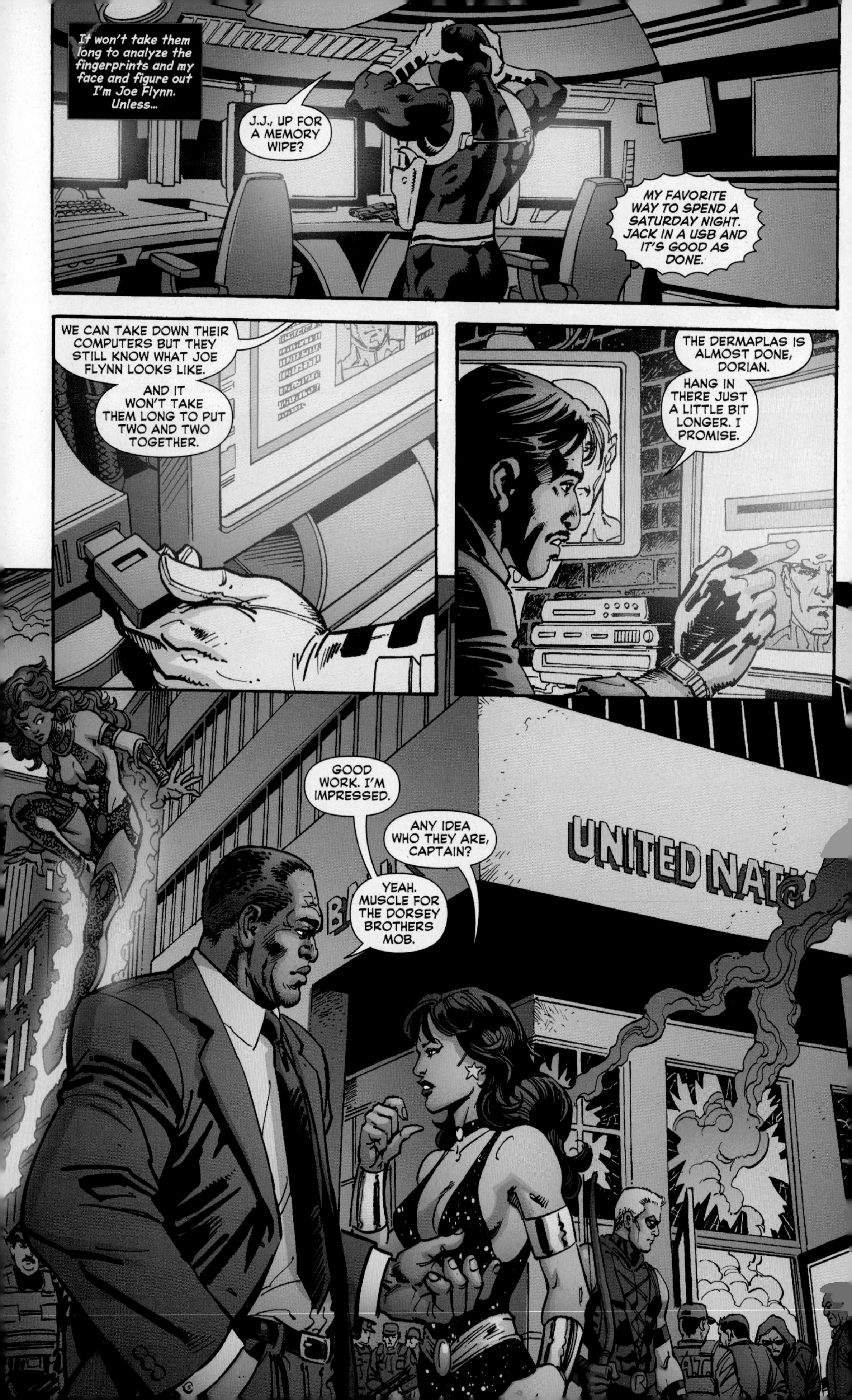
It won't take them long to analyze the fingerprints and my face and figure out I'm Joe Flynn. Unless...
J.J., UP FOR A MEMORY WIPE?
MY FAVORITE WAY TO SPEND A SATURDAY NIGHT. JACK IN A USB AND IT'S GOOD AS DONE.
WE CAN TAKE DOWN THEIR COMPUTERS BUT THEY STILL KNOW WHAT JOE FLYNN LOOKS LIKE.
AND IT WON'T TAKE THEM LONG TO PUT TWO AND TWO TOGETHER.
THE DERMAPLAS IS ALMOST DONE, DORIAN.
HANG IN THERE JUST A LITTLE BIT LONGER. I PROMISE.
GOOD WORK. I'M IMPRESSED.
ANY IDEA WHO THEY ARE, CAPTAIN?
YEAH. MUSCLE FOR THE DORSEY BROTHERS MOB.
UNITED NATI

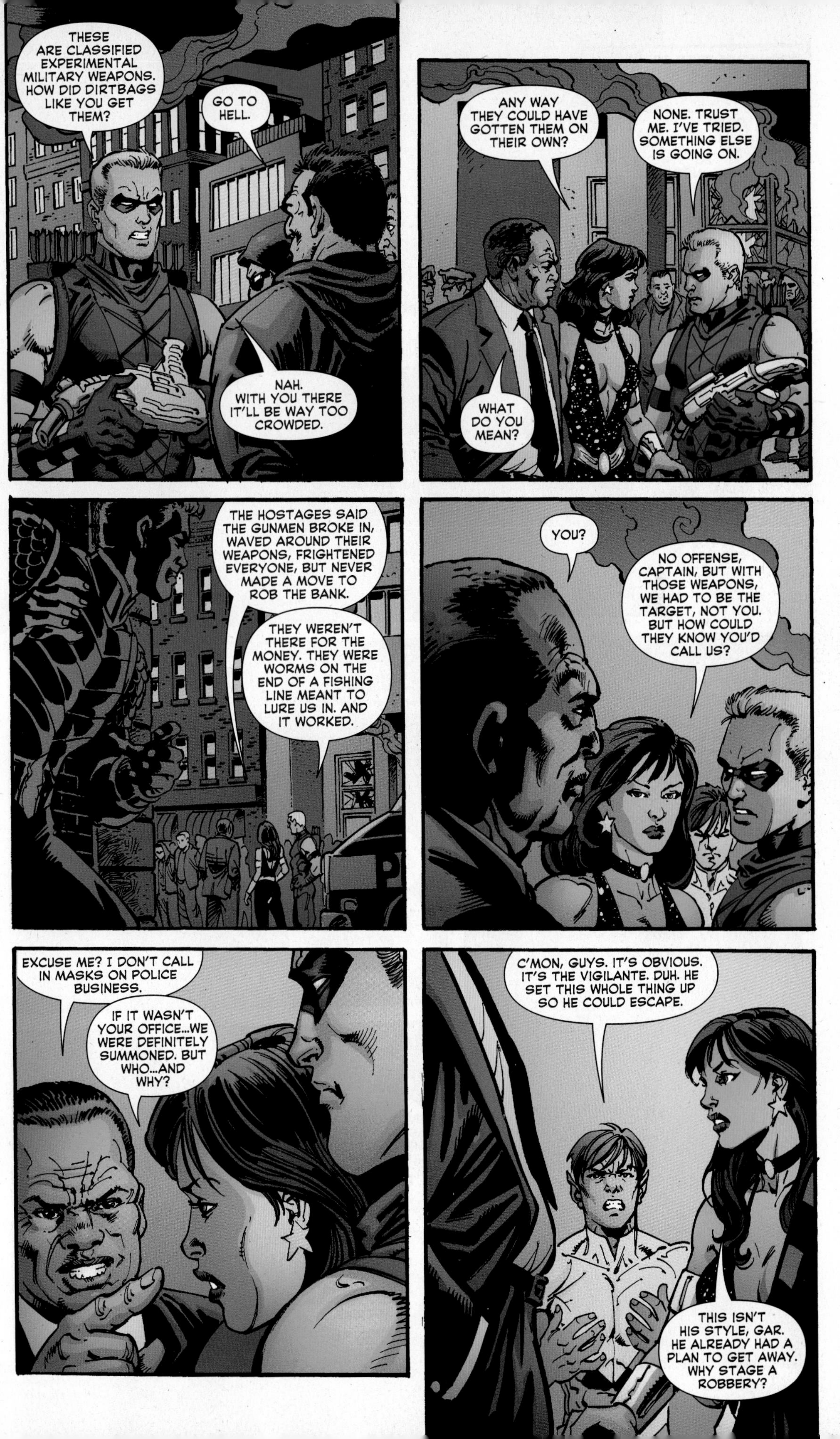
THESE ARE CLASSIFIED EXPERIMENTAL MILITARY WEAPONS. HOW DID DIRTBAGS LIKE YOU GET THEM?
GO TO HELL.
NAH. WITH YOU THERE IT'LL BE WAY TOO CROWDED.
ANY WAY THEY COULD HAVE GOTTEN THEM ON THEIR OWN?
NONE. TRUST ME. I'VE TRIED. SOMETHING ELSE IS GOING ON.
WHAT DO YOU MEAN?
THE HOSTAGES SAID THE GUNMEN BROKE IN, WAVED AROUND THEIR WEAPONS, FRIGHTENED EVERYONE, BUT NEVER MADE A MOVE TO ROB THE BANK.
THEY WEREN'T THERE FOR THE MONEY. THEY WERE WORMS ON THE END OF A FISHING LINE MEANT TO LURE US IN. AND IT WORKED.
YOU?
NO OFFENSE, CAPTAIN, BUT WITH THOSE WEAPONS, WE HAD TO BE THE TARGET, NOT YOU. BUT HOW COULD THEY KNOW YOU'D CALL US?
EXCUSE ME? I DON'T CALL IN MASKS ON POLICE BUSINESS.
IF IT WASN'T YOUR OFFICE...WE WERE DEFINITELY SUMMONED. BUT WHO...AND WHY?
C'MON, GUYS. IT'S OBVIOUS. IT'S THE VIGILANTE. DUH. HE SET THIS WHOLE THING UP SO HE COULD ESCAPE.
THIS ISN'T HIS STYLE, GAR. HE ALREADY HAD A PLAN TO GET AWAY. WHY STAGE A ROBBERY?

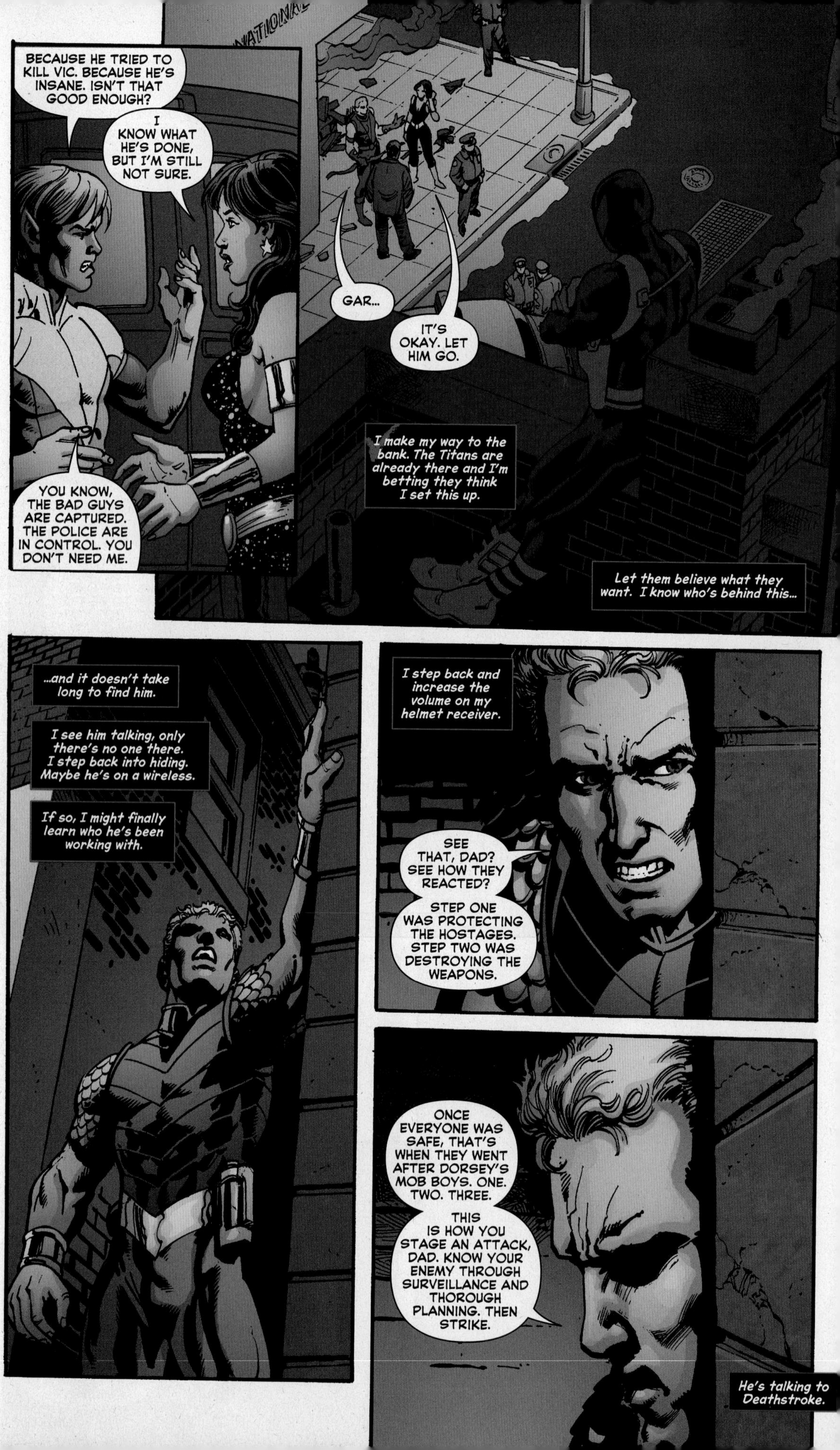
BECAUSE HE TRIED TO KILL VIC. BECAUSE HE'S INSANE. ISN'T THAT GOOD ENOUGH?
I KNOW WHAT HE'S DONE, BUT I'M STILL NOT SURE.
YOU KNOW, THE BAD GUYS ARE CAPTURED. THE POLICE ARE IN CONTROL. YOU DON'T NEED ME.
NATIONAL
GAR...
IT'S OKAY. LET HIM GO.
I make my way to the bank. The Titans are already there and I'm betting they think I set this up.
Let them believe what they want. I know who's behind this...
...and it doesn't take long to find him.
I see him talking, only there's no one there. I step back into hiding. Maybe he's on a wireless.
If so, I might finally learn who he's been working with.
I step back and increase the volume on my helmet receiver.
SEE THAT, DAD? SEE HOW THEY REACTED?
STEP ONE WAS PROTECTING THE HOSTAGES. STEP TWO WAS DESTROYING THE WEAPONS.
ONCE EVERYONE WAS SAFE, THAT'S WHEN THEY WENT AFTER DORSEY'S MOB BOYS. ONE. TWO. THREE.
THIS IS HOW YOU STAGE AN ATTACK, DAD. KNOW YOUR ENEMY THROUGH SURVEILLANCE AND THOROUGH PLANNING. THEN STRIKE.
He's talking to Deathstroke.

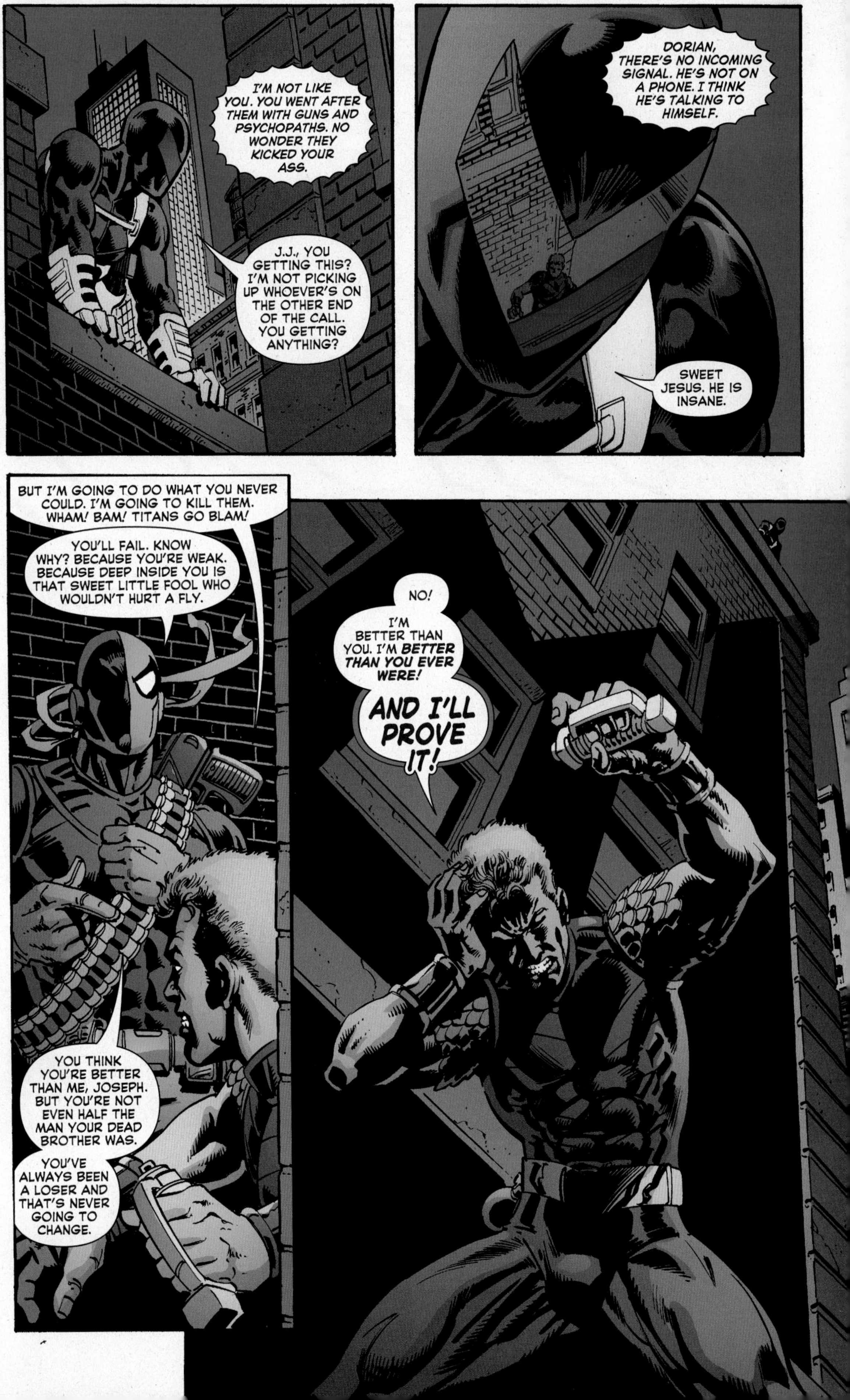

I'M NOT LIKE YOU. YOU WENT AFTER THEM WITH GUNS AND PSYCHOPATHS. NO WONDER THEY KICKED YOUR ASS.
J.J., YOU GETTING THIS? I'M NOT PICKING UP WHOEVER'S ON THE OTHER END OF THE CALL. YOU GETTING ANYTHING?
DORIAN, THERE'S NO INCOMING SIGNAL. HE'S NOT ON A PHONE. I THINK HE'S TALKING TO HIMSELF.
SWEET JESUS. HE IS INSANE.
BUT I'M GOING TO DO WHAT YOU NEVER COULD. I'M GOING TO KILL THEM. WHAM! BAM! TITANS GO BLAM!
YOU'LL FAIL. KNOW WHY? BECAUSE YOU'RE WEAK. BECAUSE DEEP INSIDE YOU IS THAT SWEET LITTLE FOOL WHO WOULDN'T HURT A FLY.
YOU THINK YOU'RE BETTER THAN ME, JOSEPH. BUT YOU'RE NOT EVEN HALF THE MAN YOUR DEAD BROTHER WAS.
YOU'VE ALWAYS BEEN A LOSER AND THAT'S NEVER GOING TO CHANGE.
NO!
I'M BETTER THAN YOU. I'M BETTER THAN YOU EVER WERE!
AND I'LL PROVE IT!

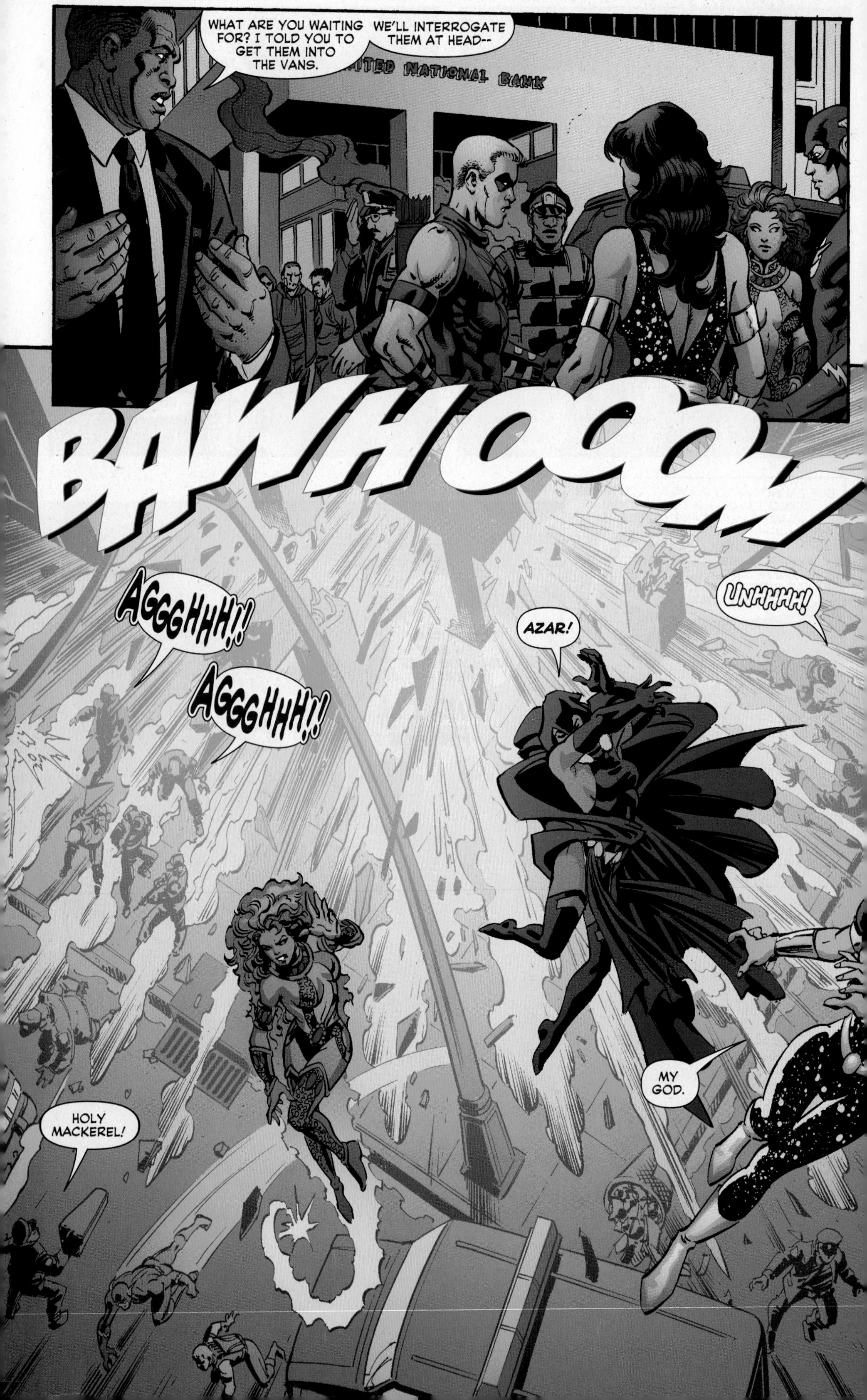
WHAT ARE YOU WAITING FOR? I TOLD YOU TO GET THEM INTO THE VANS.
WE'LL INTERROGATE THEM AT HEAD--
NATIONAL BANK
BAWHOOOM
AGGGHHH!!
AGGGHHH!!
AZAR!
UNHHHH!
HOLY MACKEREL!
MY GOD.

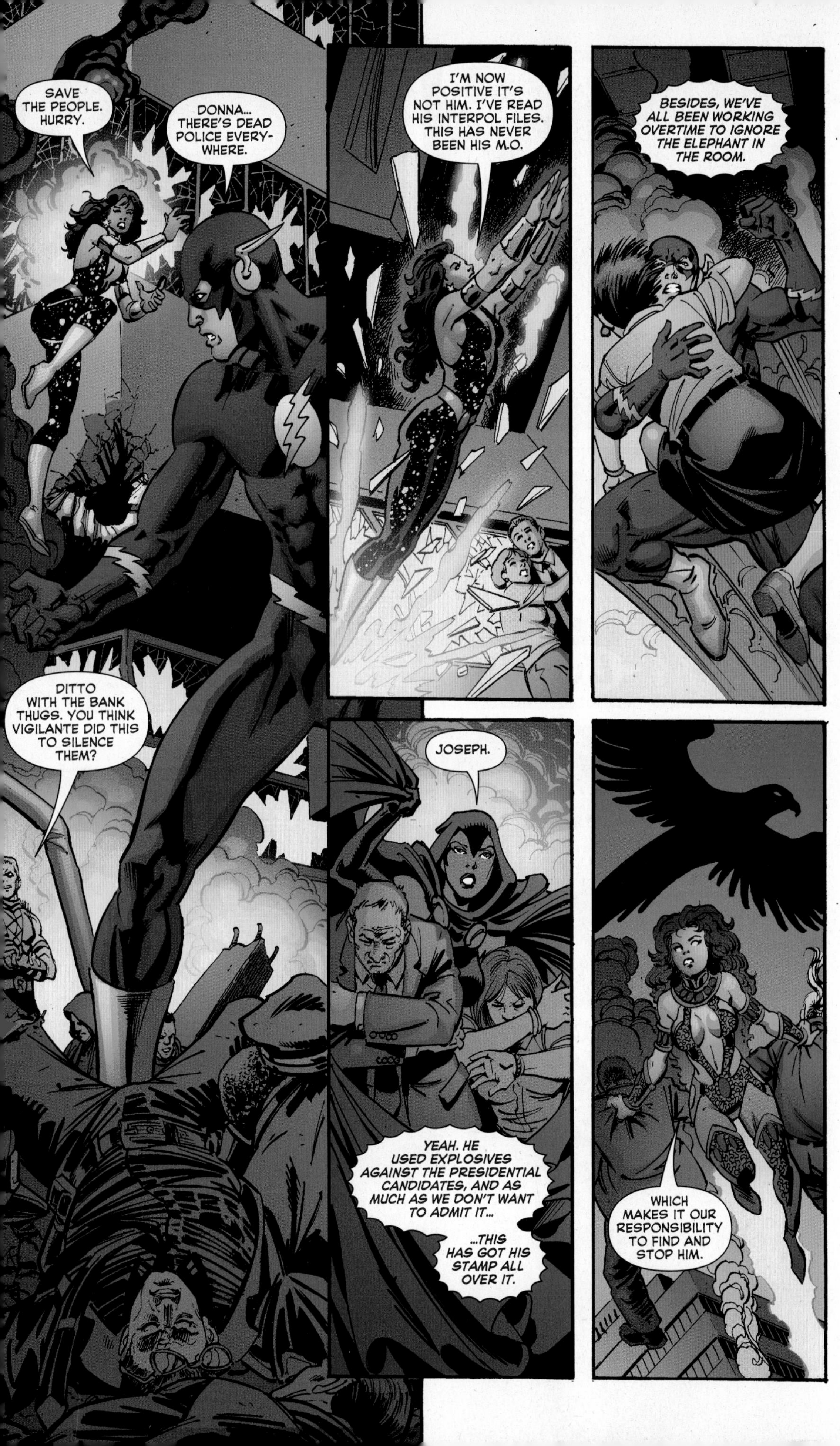
SAVE THE PEOPLE. HURRY.
DONNA... THERE'S DEAD POLICE EVERY-WHERE.
I'M NOW POSITIVE IT'S NOT HIM. I'VE READ HIS INTERPOL FILES. THIS HAS NEVER BEEN HIS M.O.
BESIDES, WE'VE ALL BEEN WORKING OVERTIME TO IGNORE THE ELEPHANT IN THE ROOM.
DITTO WITH THE BANK THUGS. YOU THINK VIGILANTE DID THIS TO SILENCE THEM?
JOSEPH.
YEAH. HE USED EXPLOSIVES AGAINST THE PRESIDENTIAL CANDIDATES, AND AS MUCH AS WE DON'T WANT TO ADMIT IT...
...THIS HAS GOT HIS STAMP ALL OVER IT.
WHICH MAKES IT OUR RESPONSIBILITY TO FIND AND STOP HIM.

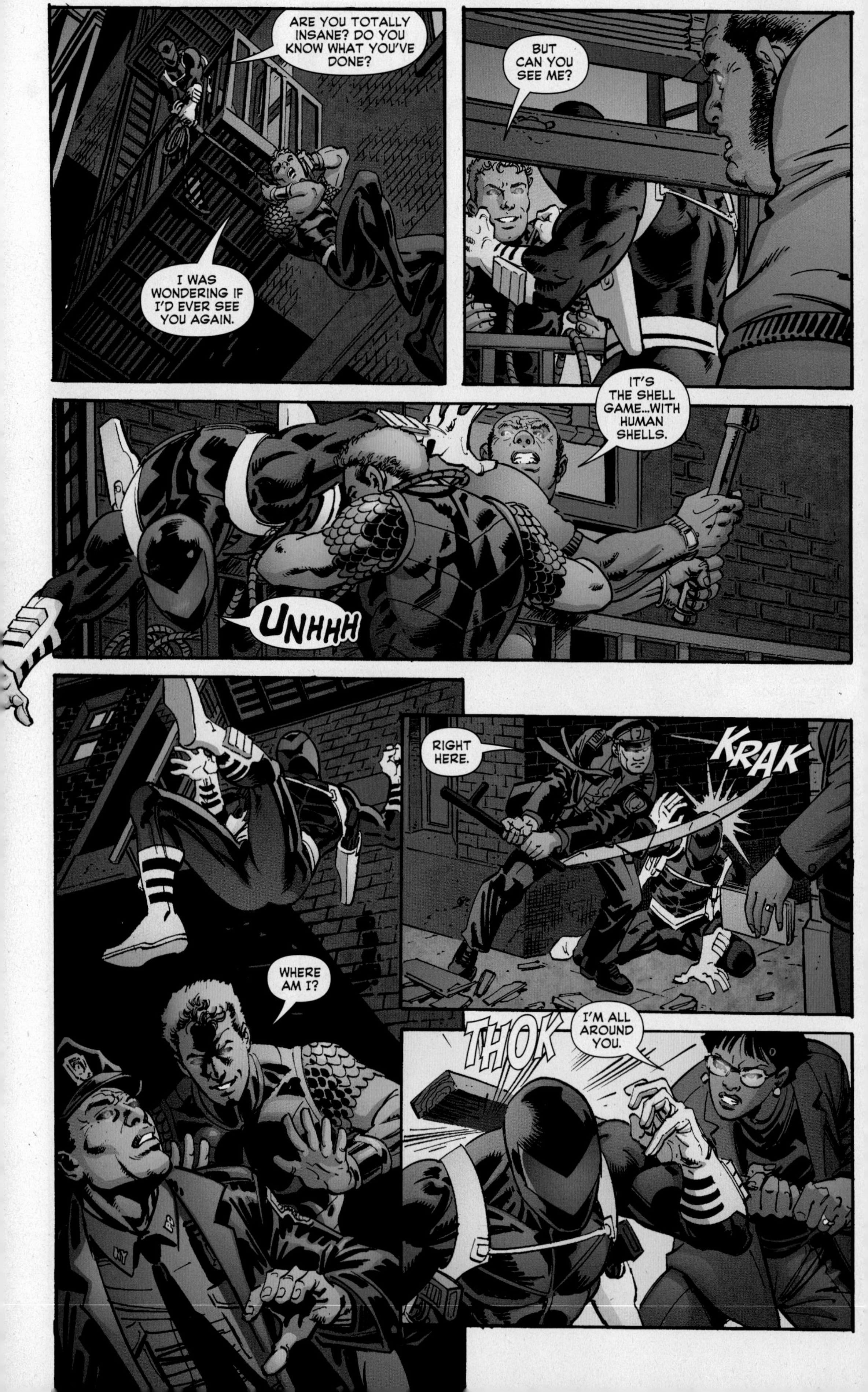
ARE YOU TOTALLY INSANE? DO YOU KNOW WHAT YOU'VE DONE?
I WAS WONDERING IF I'D EVER SEE YOU AGAIN.
BUT CAN YOU SEE ME?
IT'S THE SHELL GAME...WITH HUMAN SHELLS.
UNHHH
RIGHT HERE.
KRAK
WHERE AM I?
THOK
I'M ALL AROUND YOU.

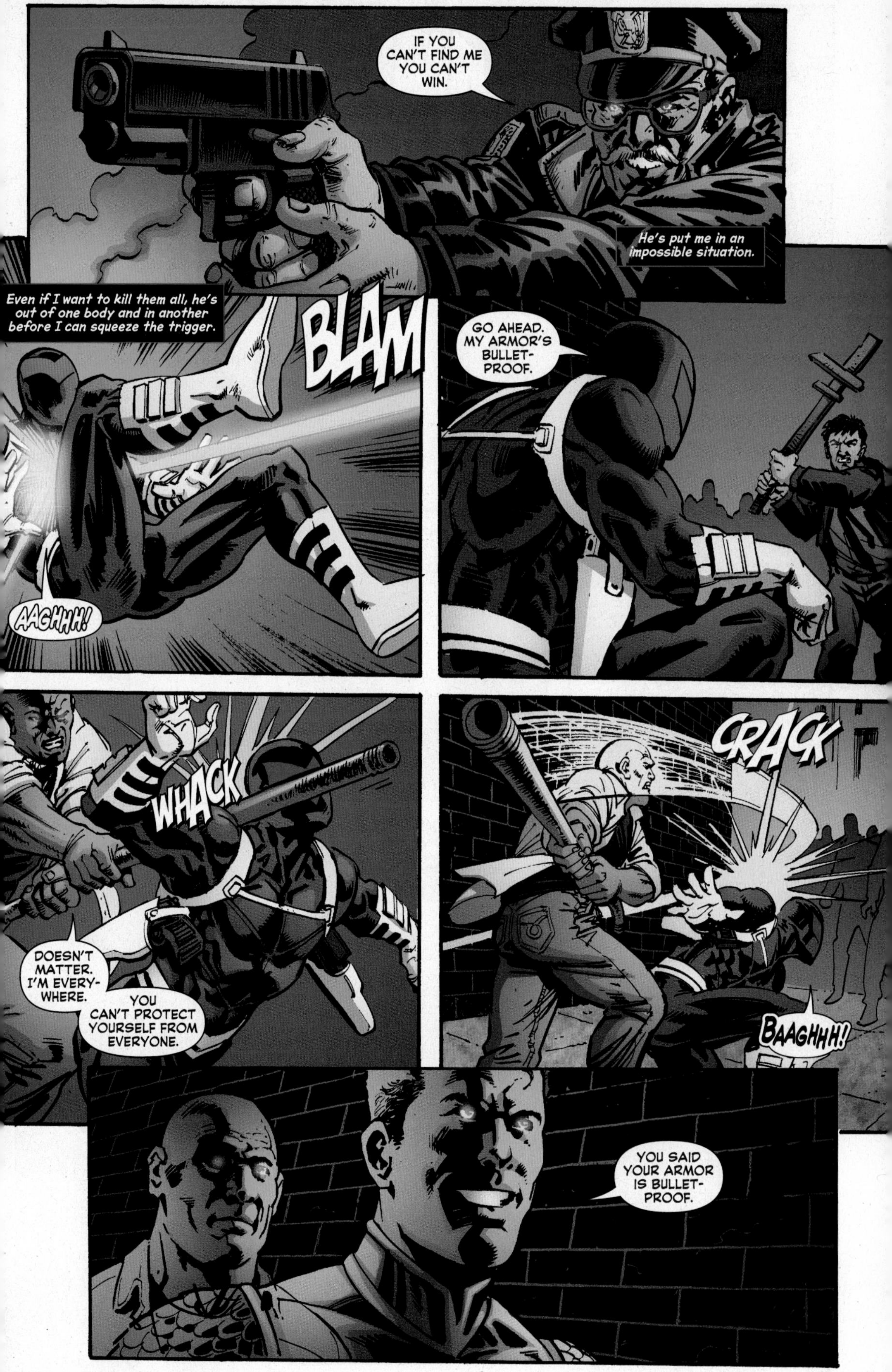
IF YOU CAN'T FIND ME YOU CAN'T WIN.
He's put me in an impossible situation.
Even if I want to kill them all, he's out of one body and in another before I can squeeze the trigger.
BLAM
AAGHHH!
GO AHEAD. MY ARMOR'S BULLET-PROOF.
WHACK
DOESN'T MATTER. I'M EVERY-WHERE.
YOU CAN'T PROTECT YOURSELF FROM EVERYONE.
CRACK
BAAGHHH!
YOU SAID YOUR ARMOR IS BULLET-PROOF.

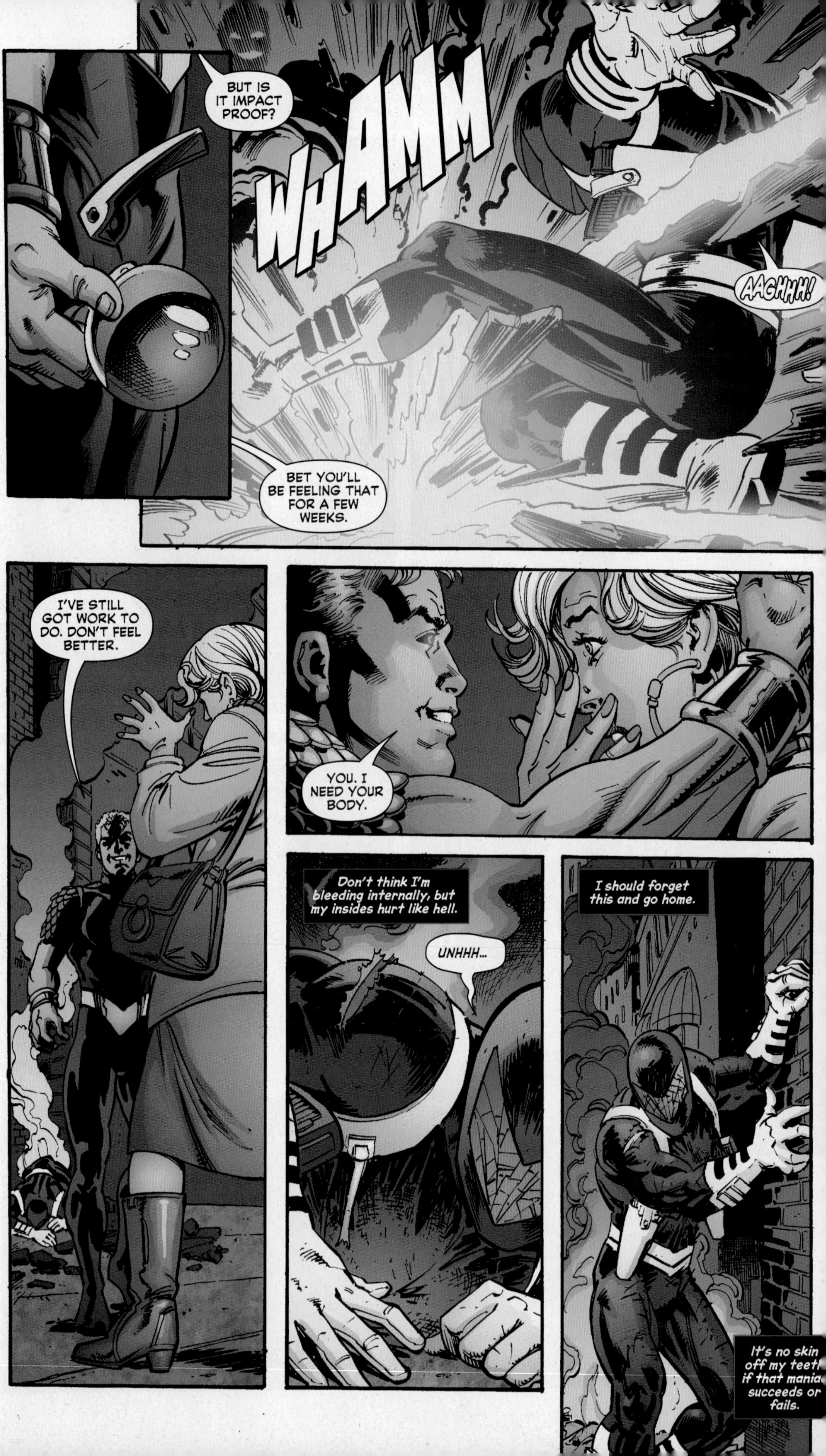
BUT IS IT IMPACT PROOF?
WHAMM
AAGHHH!
BET YOU'LL BE FEELING THAT FOR A FEW WEEKS.
I'VE STILL GOT WORK TO DO. DON'T FEEL BETTER.
YOU. I NEED YOUR BODY.
Don't think I'm bleeding internally, but my insides hurt like hell.
UNHHH...
I should forget this and go home.
It's no skin off my teet if that mania succeeds or fails.

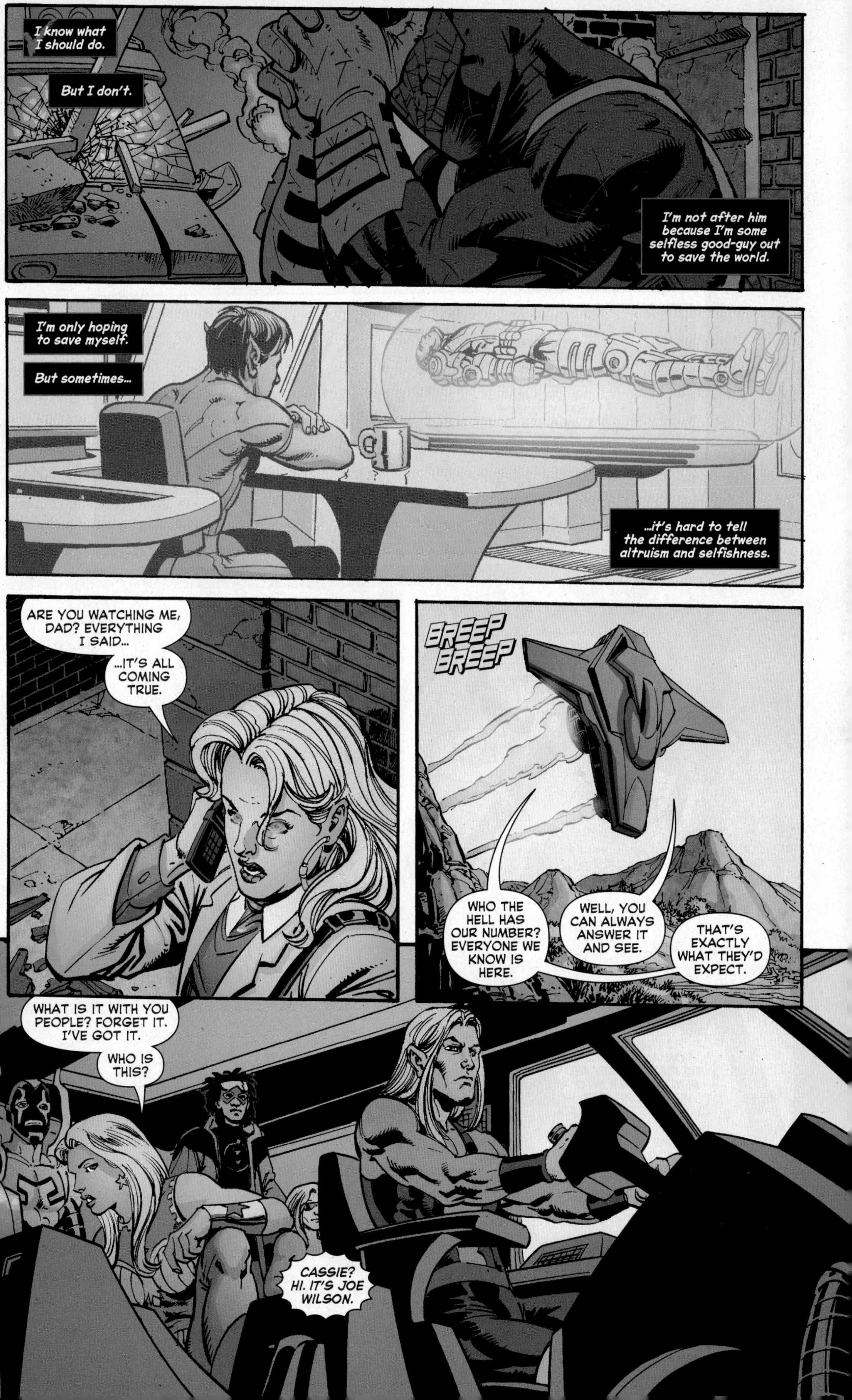
I know what I should do.
But I don't.
I'm not after him because I'm some selfless good-guy out to save the world.
I'm only hoping to save myself.
But sometimes...
...it's hard to tell the difference between altruism and selfishness.
ARE YOU WATCHING ME, DAD? EVERYTHING I SAID...
...IT'S ALL COMING TRUE.
BREEP BREEP
WHO THE HELL HAS OUR NUMBER? EVERYONE WE KNOW IS HERE.
WELL, YOU CAN ALWAYS ANSWER IT AND SEE.
THAT'S EXACTLY WHAT THEY'D EXPECT.
WHAT IS IT WITH YOU PEOPLE? FORGET IT. I'VE GOT IT.
WHO IS THIS?
CASSIE? HI. IT'S JOE WILSON.

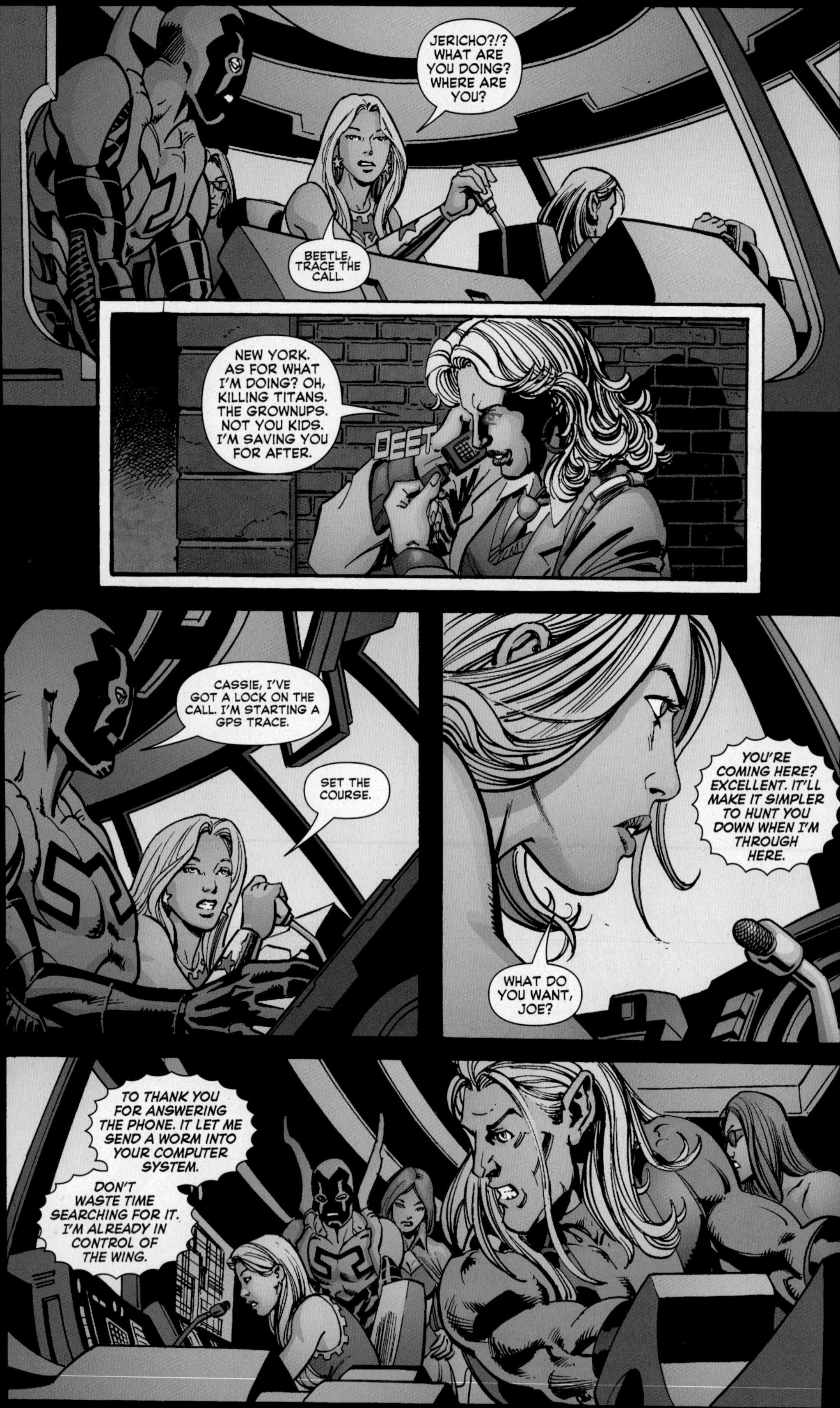
JERICHO?!? WHAT ARE YOU DOING? WHERE ARE YOU?
BEETLE, TRACE THE CALL.
NEW YORK. AS FOR WHAT I'M DOING? OH, KILLING TITANS. THE GROWNUPS. NOT YOU KIDS. I'M SAVING YOU FOR AFTER.
DEET
CASSIE, I'VE GOT A LOCK ON THE CALL. I'M STARTING A GPS TRACE.
SET THE COURSE.
YOU'RE COMING HERE? EXCELLENT. IT'LL MAKE IT SIMPLER TO HUNT YOU DOWN WHEN I'M THROUGH HERE.
WHAT DO YOU WANT, JOE?
TO THANK YOU FOR ANSWERING THE PHONE. IT LET ME SEND A WORM INTO YOUR COMPUTER SYSTEM.
DON'T WASTE TIME SEARCHING FOR IT. I'M ALREADY IN CONTROL OF THE WING.

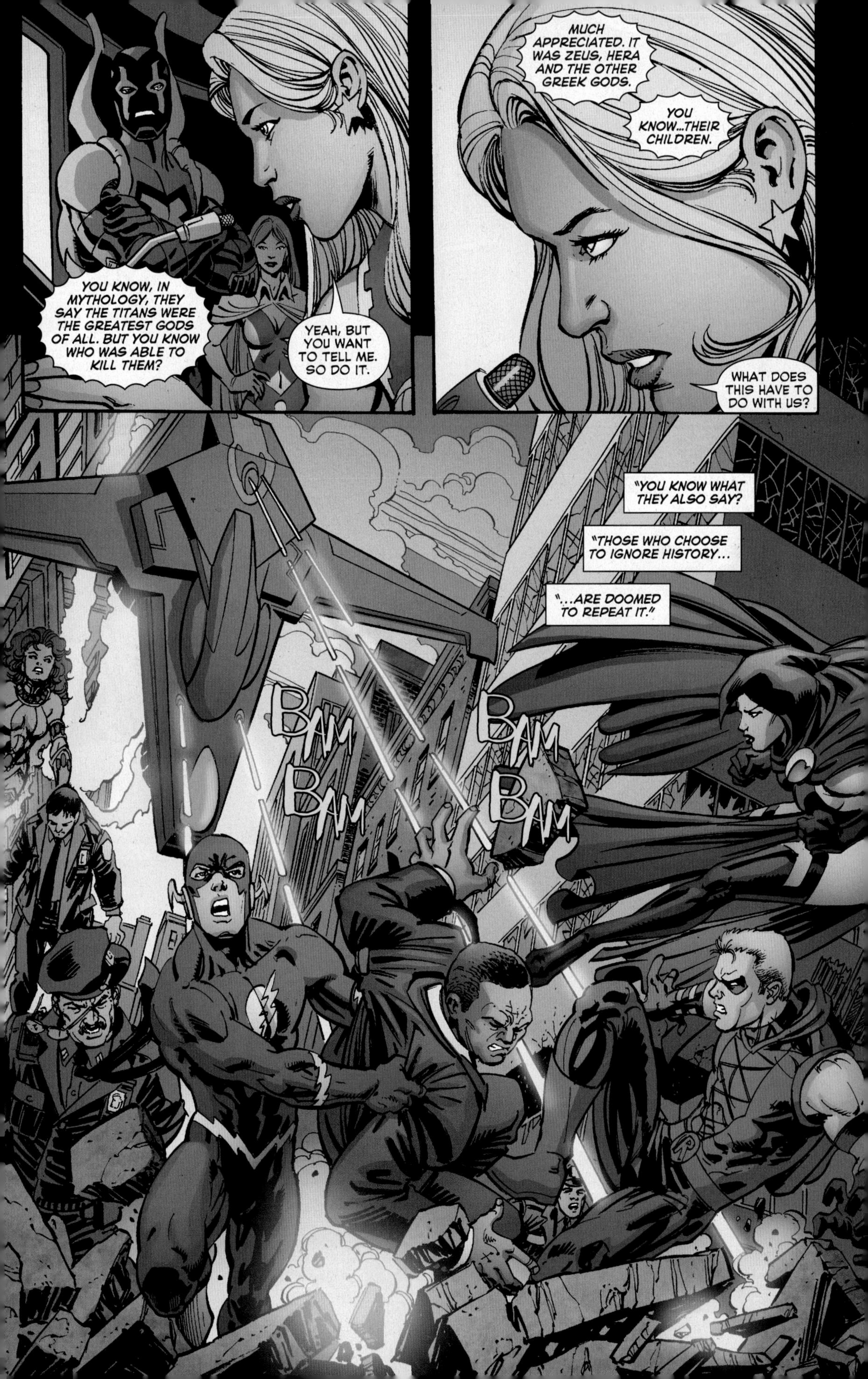
YOU KNOW, IN MYTHOLOGY, THEY SAY THE TITANS WERE THE GREATEST GODS OF ALL. BUT YOU KNOW WHO WAS ABLE TO KILL THEM?
YEAH, BUT YOU WANT TO TELL ME. SO DO IT.
MUCH APPRECIATED. IT WAS ZEUS, HERA AND THE OTHER GREEK GODS.
YOU KNOW...THEIR CHILDREN.
WHAT DOES THIS HAVE TO DO WITH US?
"YOU KNOW WHAT THEY ALSO SAY?
"THOSE WHO CHOOSE TO IGNORE HISTORY...
"...ARE DOOMED TO REPEAT IT."
BAM
BAM
BAM
BAM

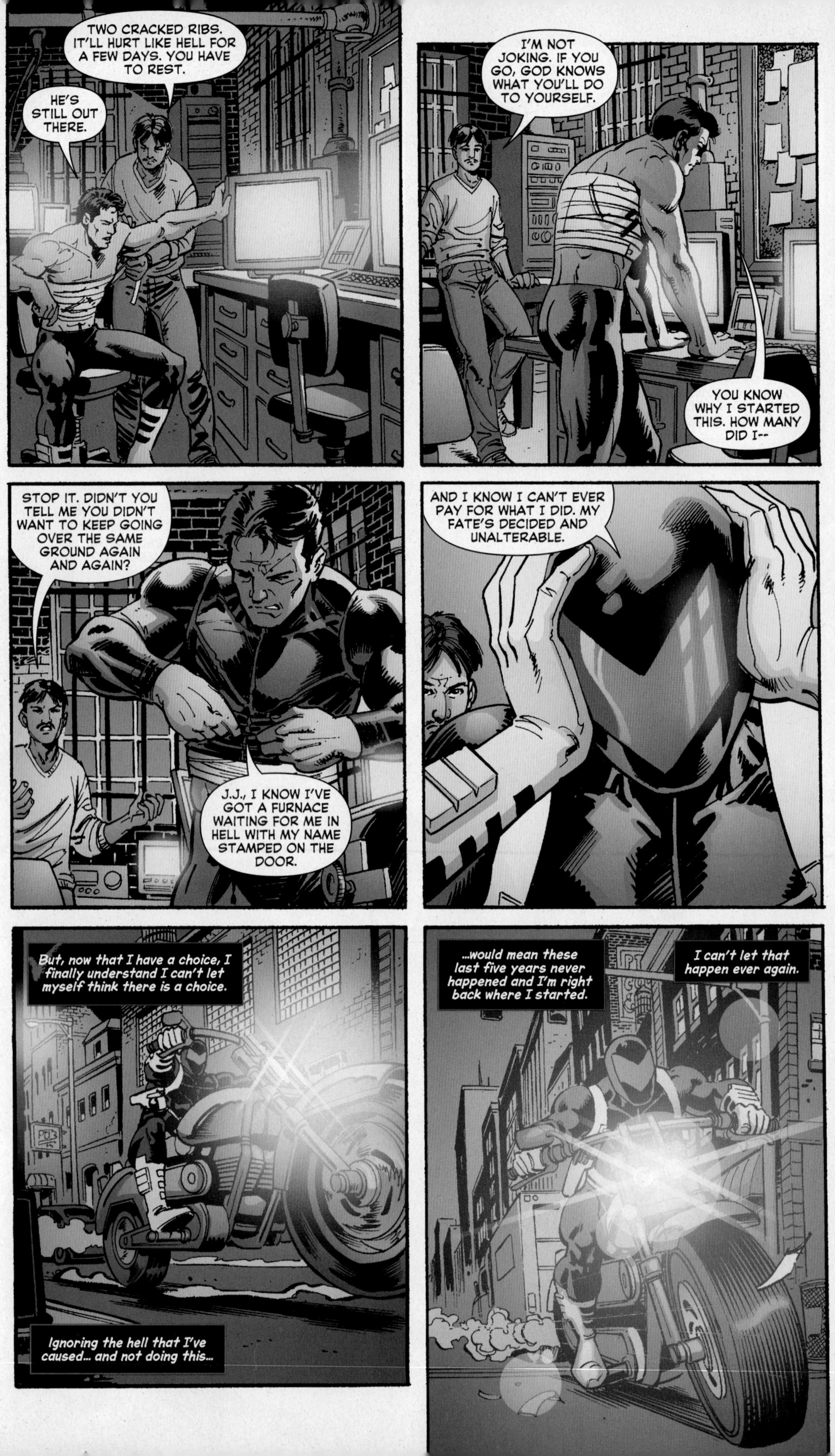
TWO CRACKED RIBS. IT'LL HURT LIKE HELL FOR A FEW DAYS. YOU HAVE TO REST.
HE'S STILL OUT THERE.
I'M NOT JOKING. IF YOU GO, GOD KNOWS WHAT YOU'LL DO TO YOURSELF.
YOU KNOW WHY I STARTED THIS. HOW MANY DID I--
STOP IT. DIDN'T YOU TELL ME YOU DIDN'T WANT TO KEEP GOING OVER THE SAME GROUND AGAIN AND AGAIN?
J.J., I KNOW I'VE GOT A FURNACE WAITING FOR ME IN HELL WITH MY NAME STAMPED ON THE DOOR.
AND I KNOW I CAN'T EVER PAY FOR WHAT I DID. MY FATE'S DECIDED AND UNALTERABLE.
But, now that I have a choice, I finally understand I can't let myself think there is a choice.
Ignoring the hell that I've caused... and not doing this...
...would mean these last five years never happened and I'm right back where I started.
I can't let that happen ever again.

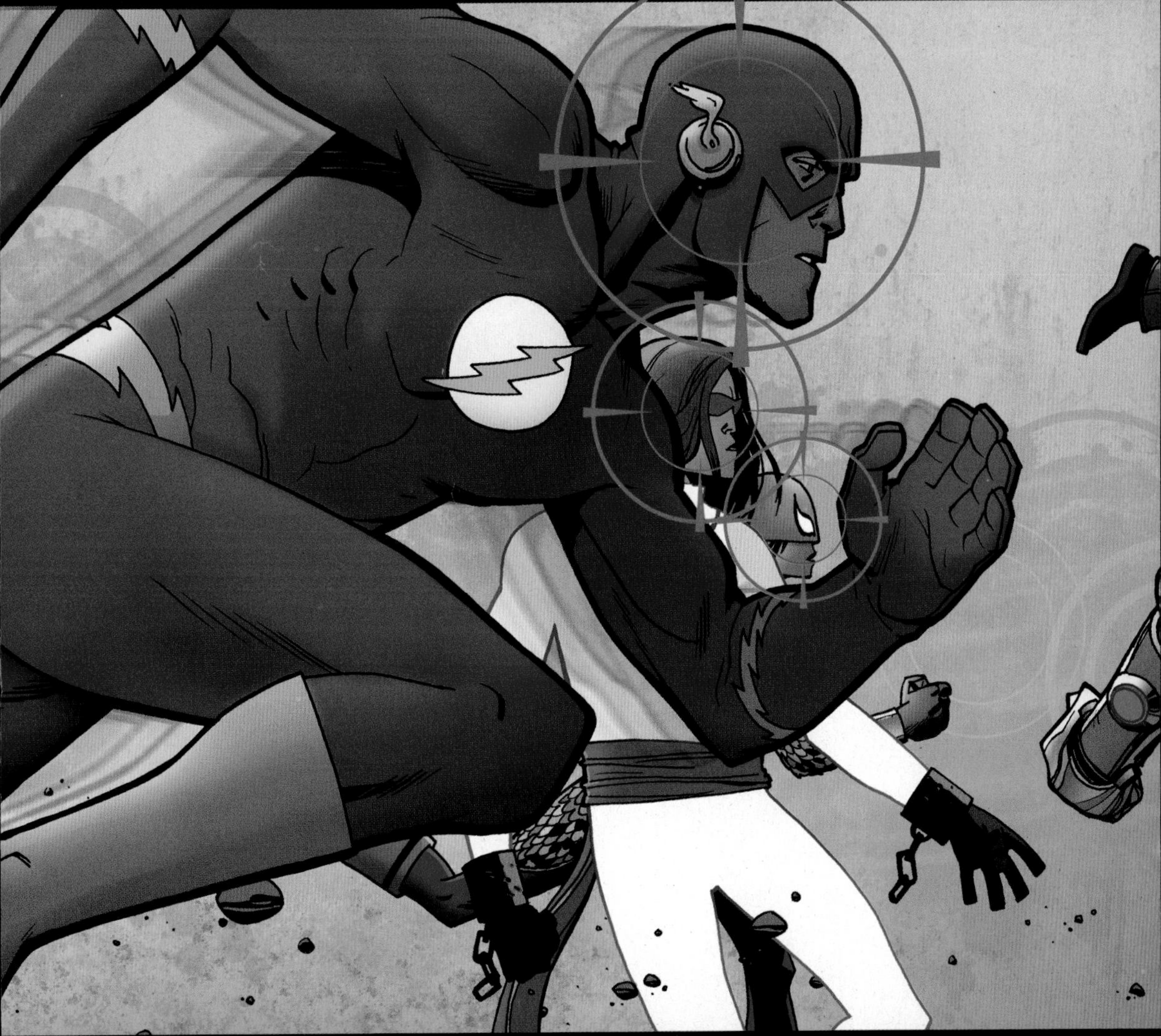

Deathtrap Part 3

Sean McKeever
Writer

Joe Bennett
Pencils

Jack Jadson

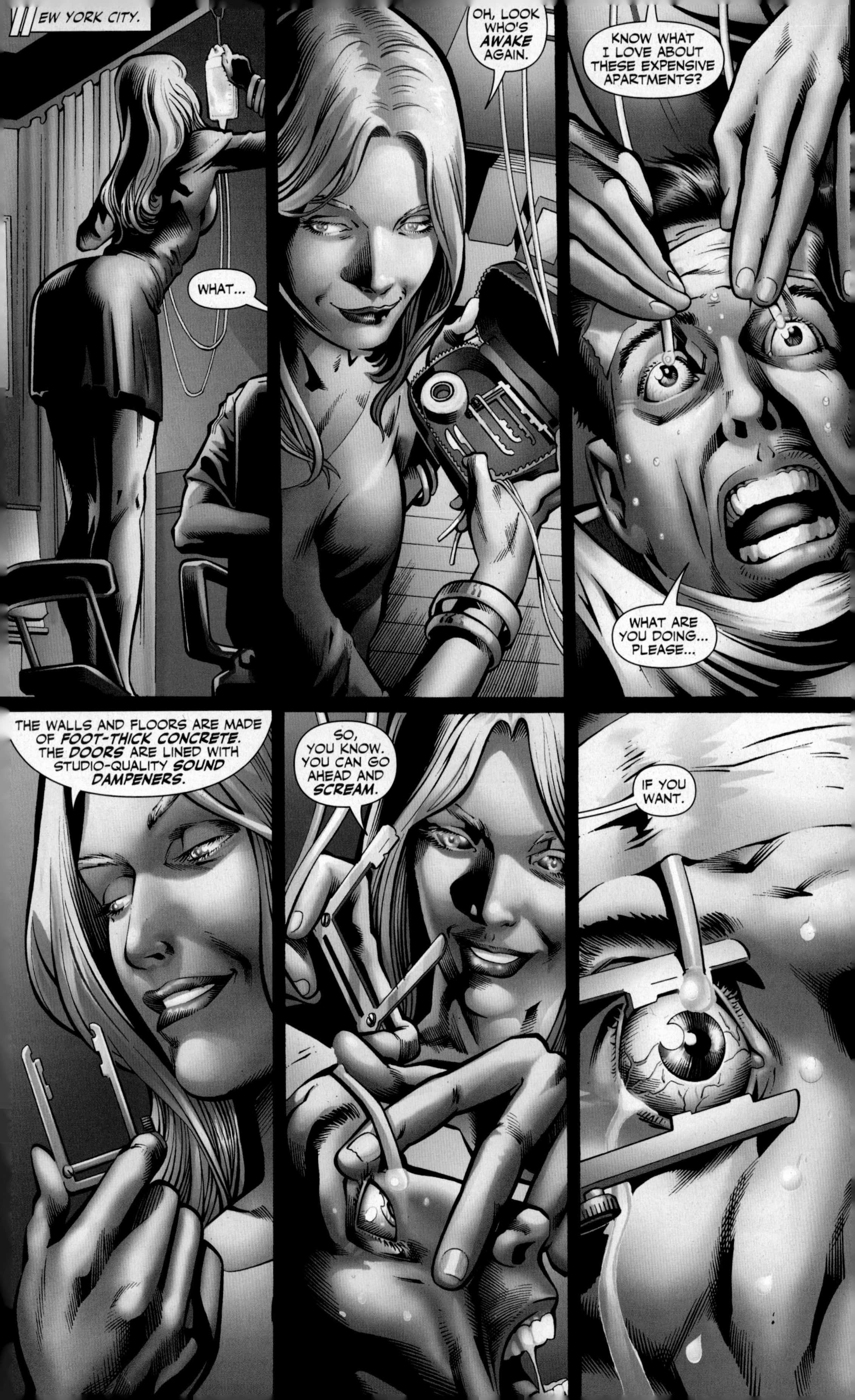
NEW YORK CITY.
WHAT...
OH, LOOK WHO'S AWAKE AGAIN.
KNOW WHAT I LOVE ABOUT THESE EXPENSIVE APARTMENTS?
WHAT ARE YOU DOING... PLEASE...
THE WALLS AND FLOORS ARE MADE OF FOOT-THICK CONCRETE. THE DOORS ARE LINED WITH STUDIO-QUALITY SOUND DAMPENERS.
SO, YOU KNOW. YOU CAN GO AHEAD AND SCREAM.
IF YOU WANT.

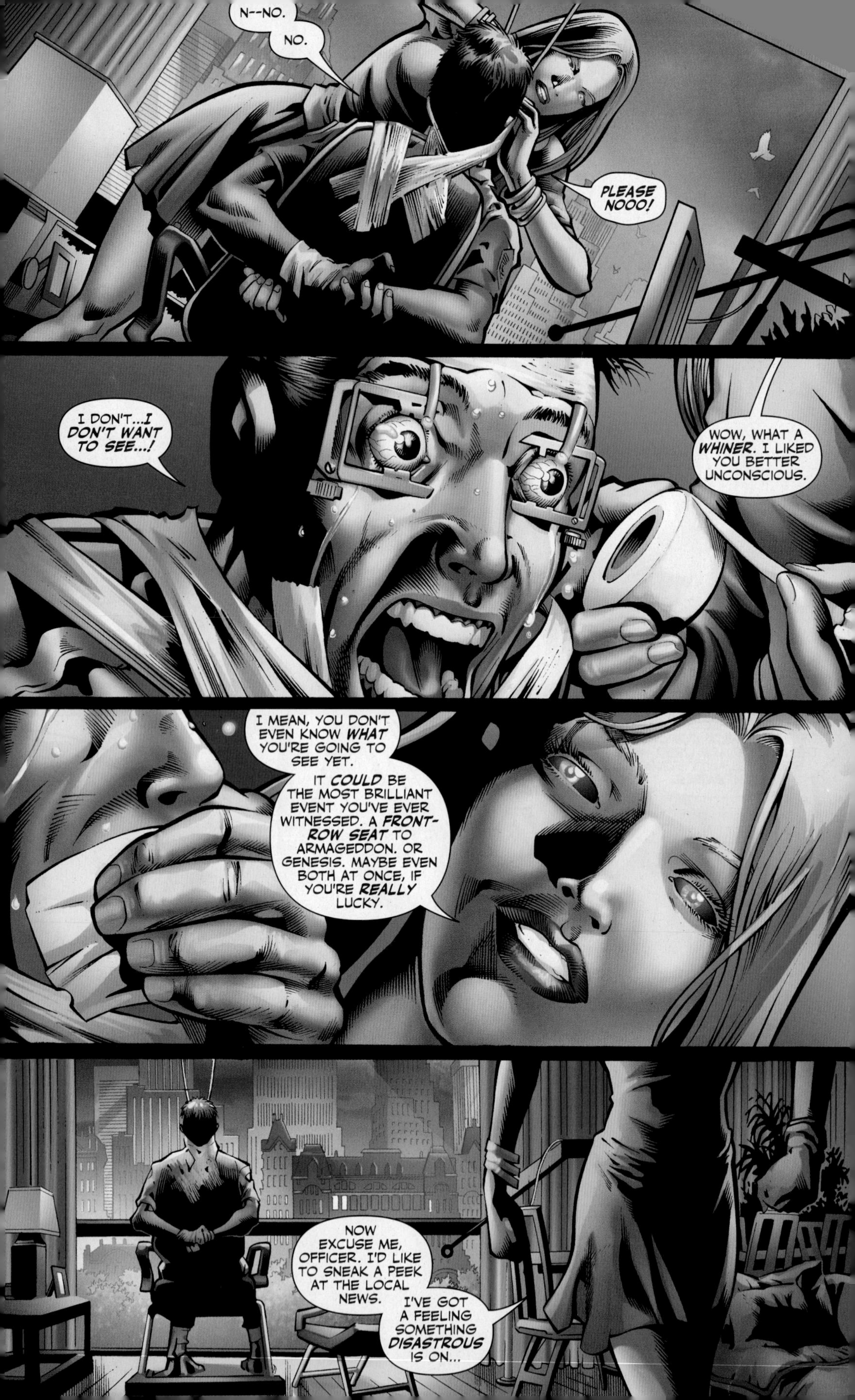
N--NO.
NO.
PLEASE NOOO!
I DON'T...I DON'T WANT TO SEE...!
WOW, WHAT A WHINER. I LIKED YOU BETTER UNCONSCIOUS.
I MEAN, YOU DON'T EVEN KNOW WHAT YOU'RE GOING TO SEE YET.
IT COULD BE THE MOST BRILLIANT EVENT YOU'VE EVER WITNESSED. A FRONT-ROW SEAT TO ARMAGEDDON. OR GENESIS. MAYBE EVEN BOTH AT ONCE, IF YOU'RE REALLY LUCKY.
NOW EXCUSE ME, OFFICER. I'D LIKE TO SNEAK A PEEK AT THE LOCAL NEWS.
I'VE GOT A FEELING SOMETHING DISASTROUS IS ON...

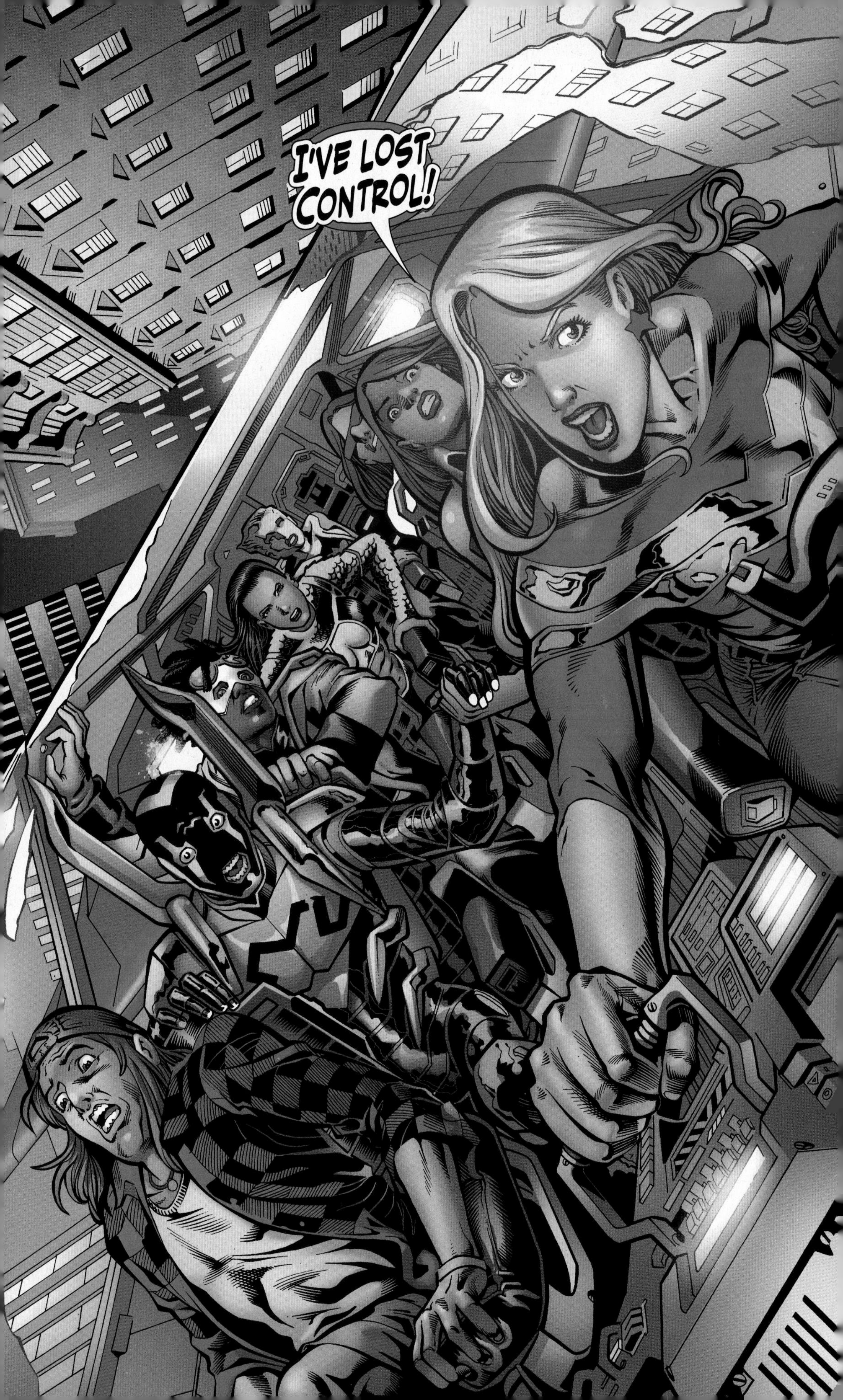
I'VE LOST CONTROL!

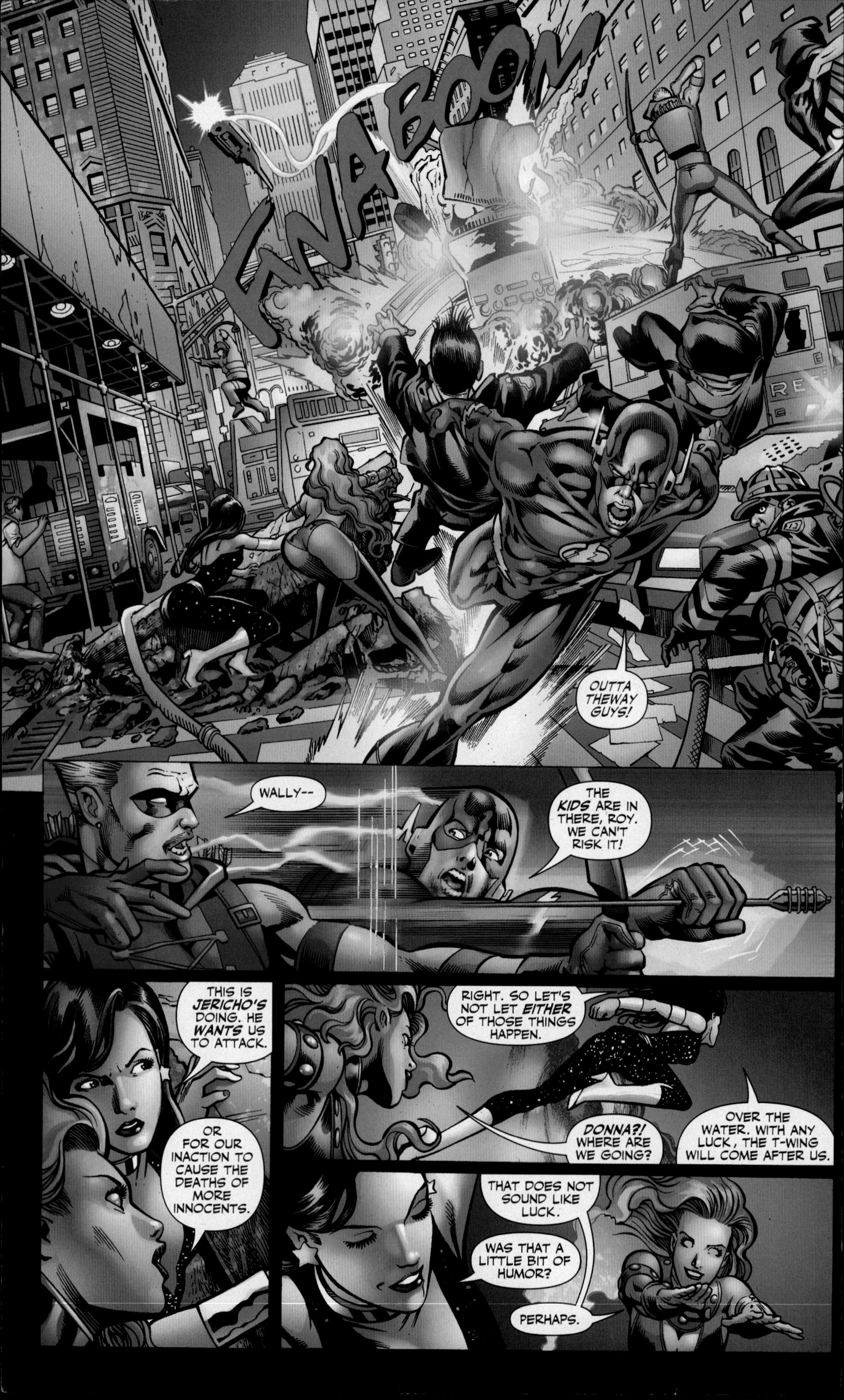
KA-BOOM
OUTTA THEWAY GUYS!
WALLY--
THE KIDS ARE IN THERE, ROY. WE CAN'T RISK IT!
THIS IS JERICHO'S DOING. HE WANTS US TO ATTACK.
OR FOR OUR INACTION TO CAUSE THE DEATHS OF MORE INNOCENTS.
RIGHT. SO LET'S NOT LET EITHER OF THOSE THINGS HAPPEN.
DONNA?! WHERE ARE WE GOING?
OVER THE WATER. WITH ANY LUCK, THE T-WING WILL COME AFTER US.
THAT DOES NOT SOUND LIKE LUCK.
WAS THAT A LITTLE BIT OF HUMOR?
PERHAPS.

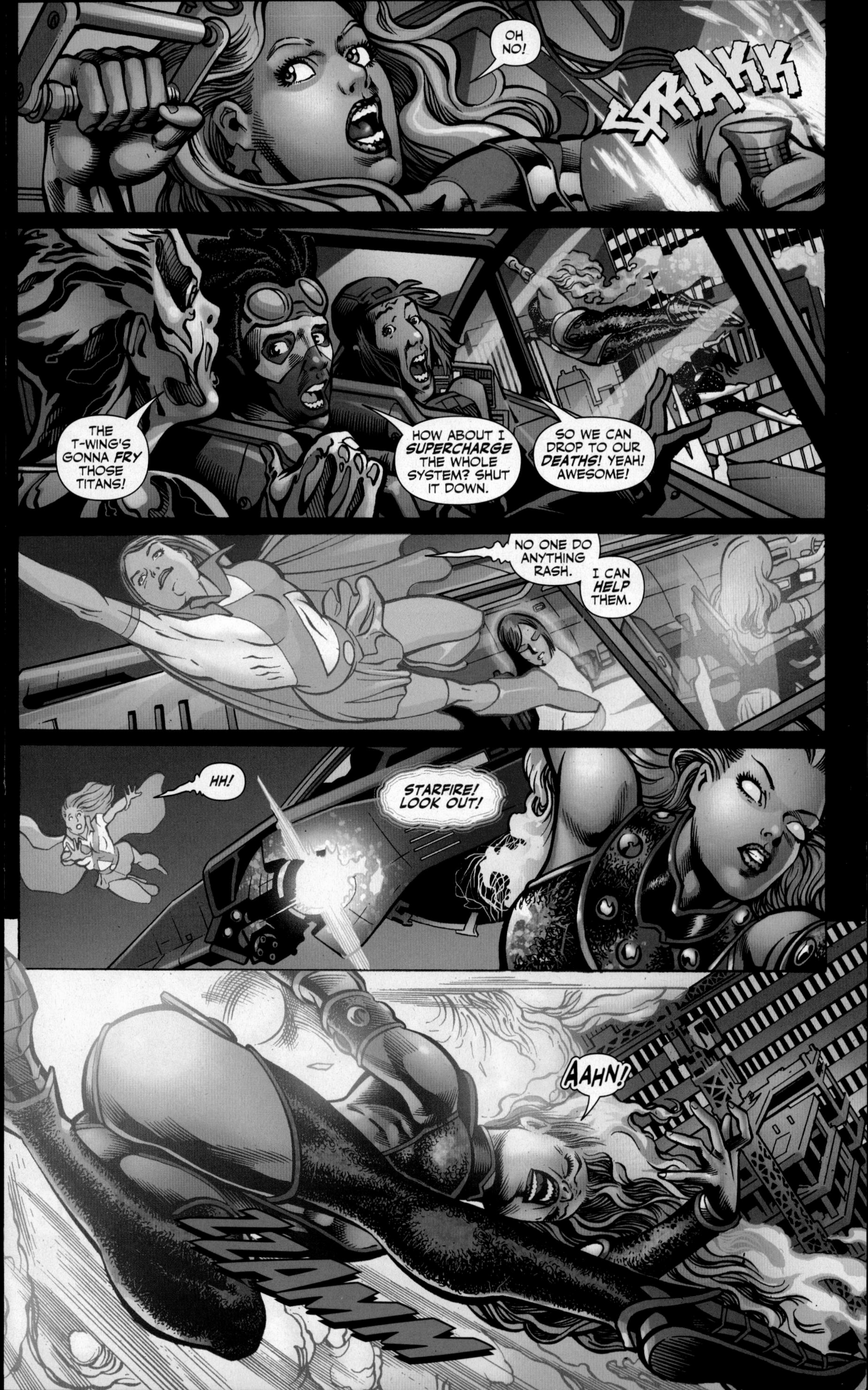
OH NO!
SPRAKK
THE T-WING'S GONNA FRY THOSE TITANS!
HOW ABOUT I SUPERCHARGE THE WHOLE SYSTEM? SHUT IT DOWN.
SO WE CAN DROP TO OUR DEATHS! YEAH! AWESOME!
NO ONE DO ANYTHING RASH.
I CAN HELP THEM.
HH!
STARFIRE! LOOK OUT!
AAHN!
WZAMM

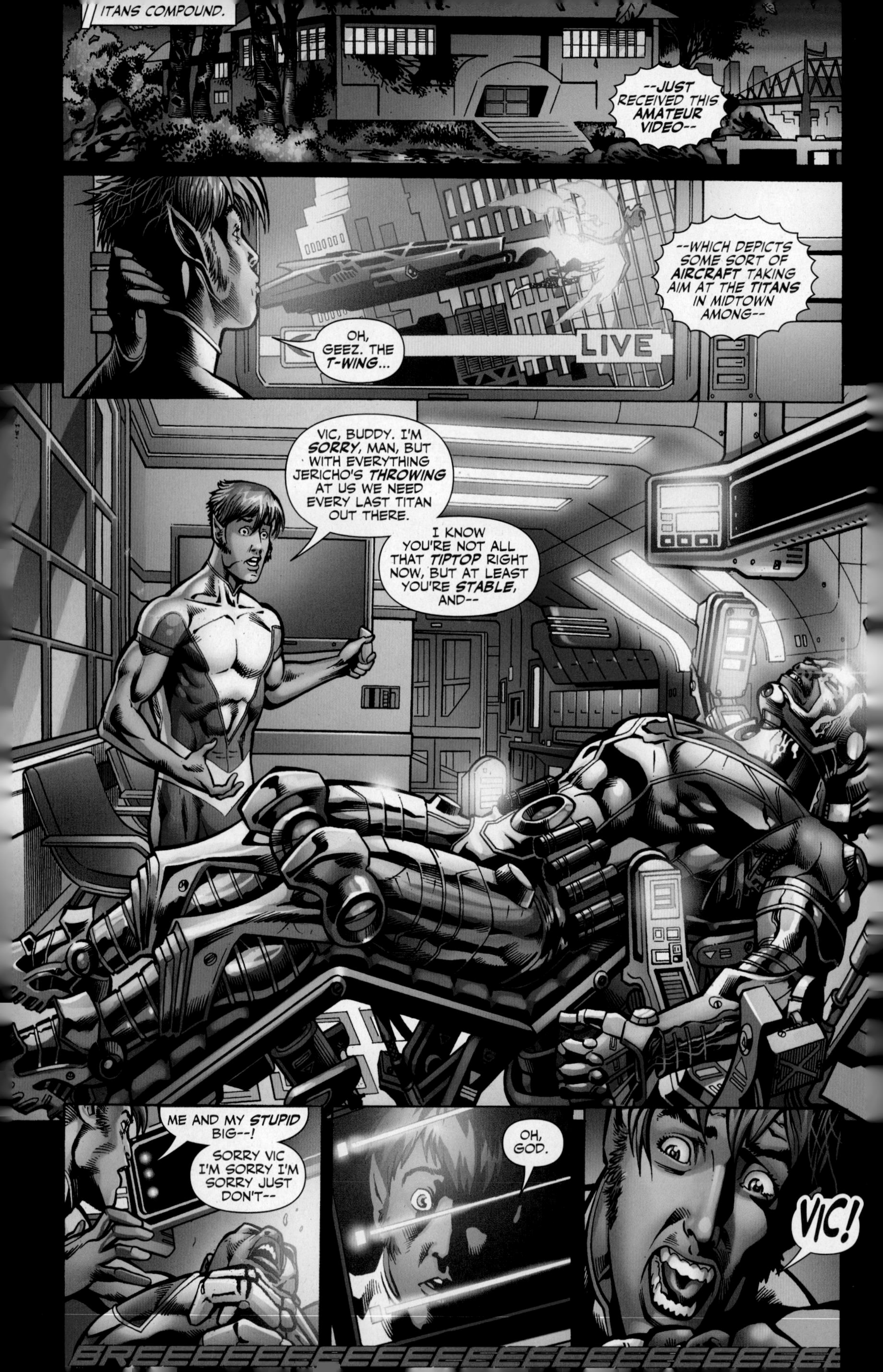
TITANS COMPOUND.
--JUST RECEIVED THIS AMATEUR VIDEO--
--WHICH DEPICTS SOME SORT OF AIRCRAFT TAKING AIM AT THE TITANS IN MIDTOWN AMONG--
LIVE
OH, GEEZ. THE T-WING...
VIC, BUDDY. I'M SORRY, MAN, BUT WITH EVERYTHING JERICHO'S THROWING AT US WE NEED EVERY LAST TITAN OUT THERE.
I KNOW YOU'RE NOT ALL THAT TIPTOP RIGHT NOW, BUT AT LEAST YOU'RE STABLE, AND--
ME AND MY STUPID BIG--!
SORRY VIC I'M SORRY I'M SORRY JUST DON'T--
OH, GOD.
VIC!
BREEEEEEEEEEEEEEEEEEEEEEEEEE

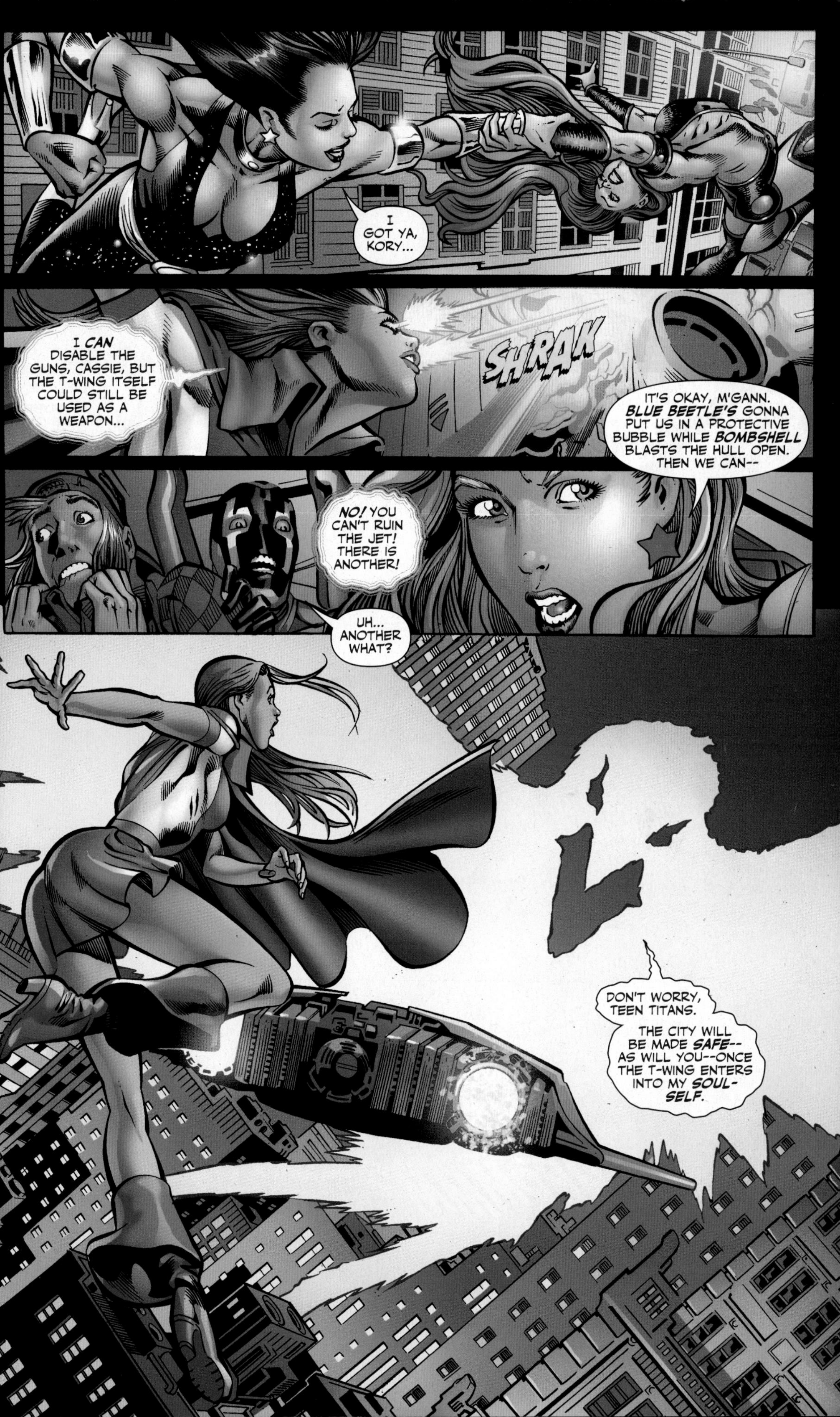

I GOT YA, KORY...
I *CAN* DISABLE THE GUNS, CASSIE, BUT THE T-WING ITSELF COULD STILL BE USED AS A WEAPON...
SHRAK
IT'S OKAY, M'GANN. ***BLUE BEETLE'S*** GONNA PUT US IN A PROTECTIVE BUBBLE WHILE ***BOMBSHELL*** BLASTS THE HULL OPEN. THEN WE CAN--
NO! YOU CAN'T RUIN THE JET! THERE IS ANOTHER!
UH... ANOTHER WHAT?
DON'T WORRY, TEEN TITANS.
THE CITY WILL BE MADE *SAFE*-- AS WILL YOU--ONCE THE T-WING ENTERS INTO MY *SOUL-SELF*.

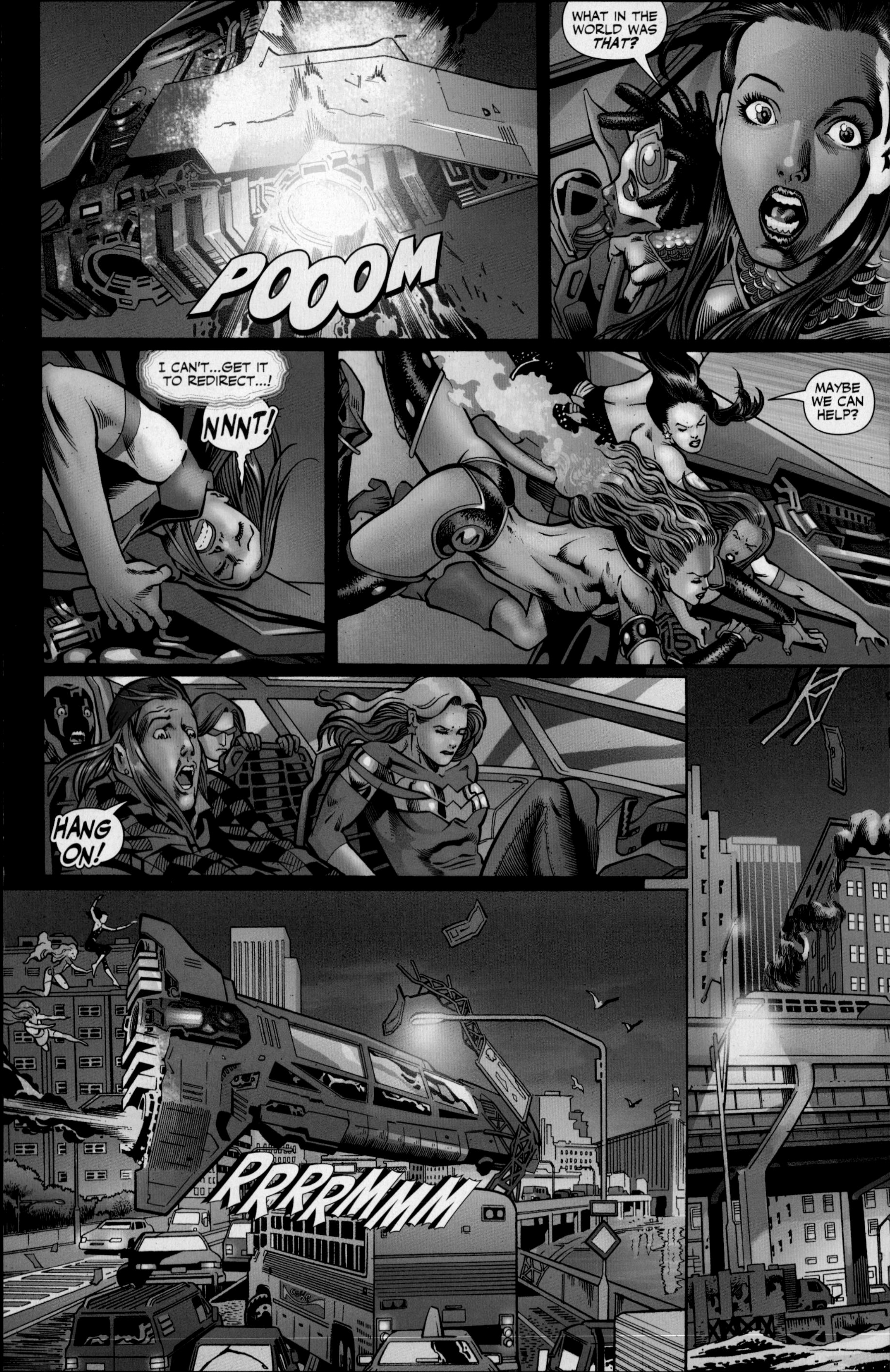
POOOM
WHAT IN THE WORLD WAS THAT?
I CAN'T...GET IT TO REDIRECT...!
NNNT!
MAYBE WE CAN HELP?
HANG ON!
RRRRRMMMM

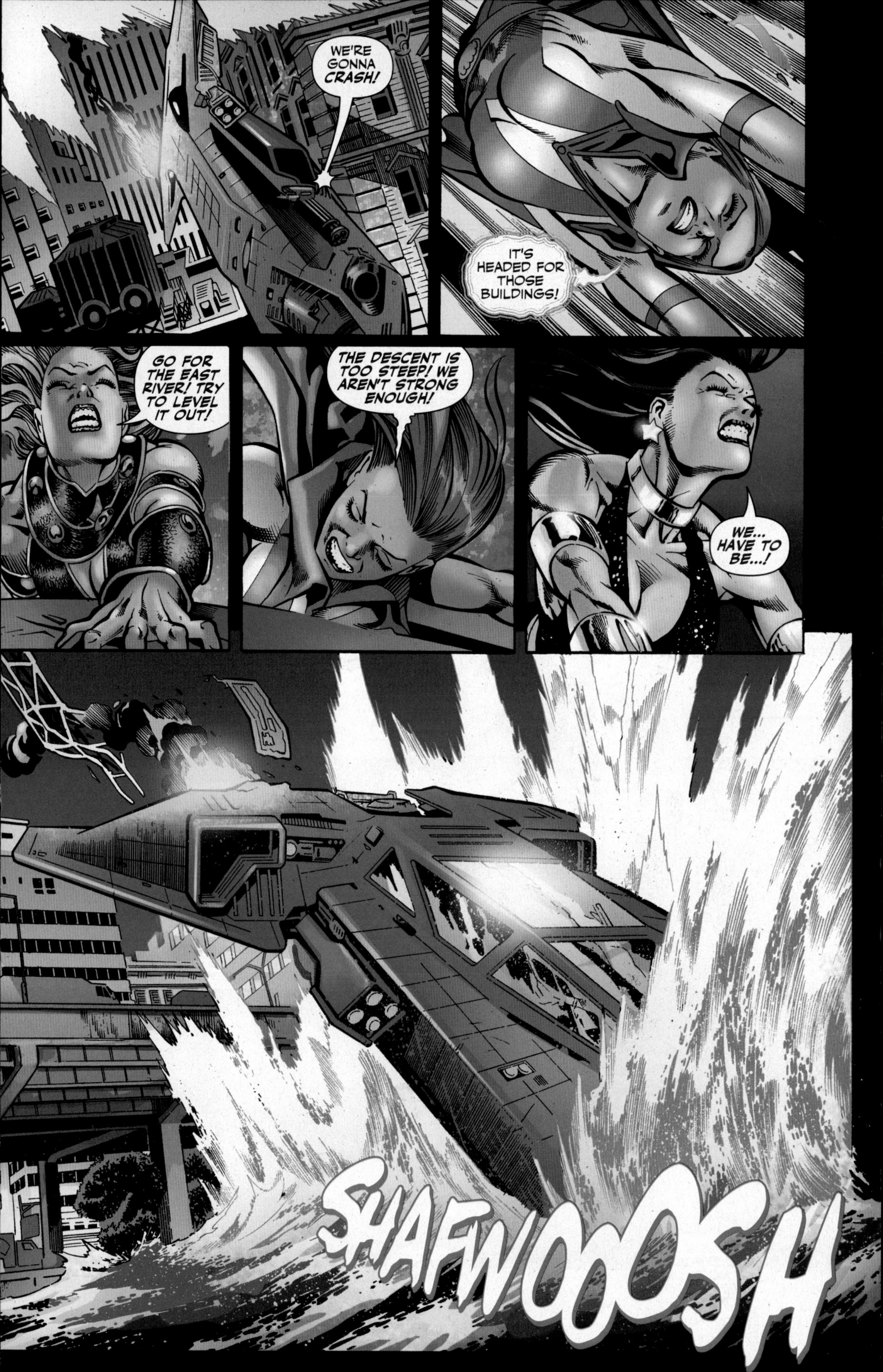
WE'RE GONNA CRASH!
IT'S HEADED FOR THOSE BUILDINGS!
GO FOR THE EAST RIVER! TRY TO LEVEL IT OUT!
THE DESCENT IS TOO STEEP! WE AREN'T STRONG ENOUGH!
WE... HAVE TO BE...!
SHAFWOOOSH

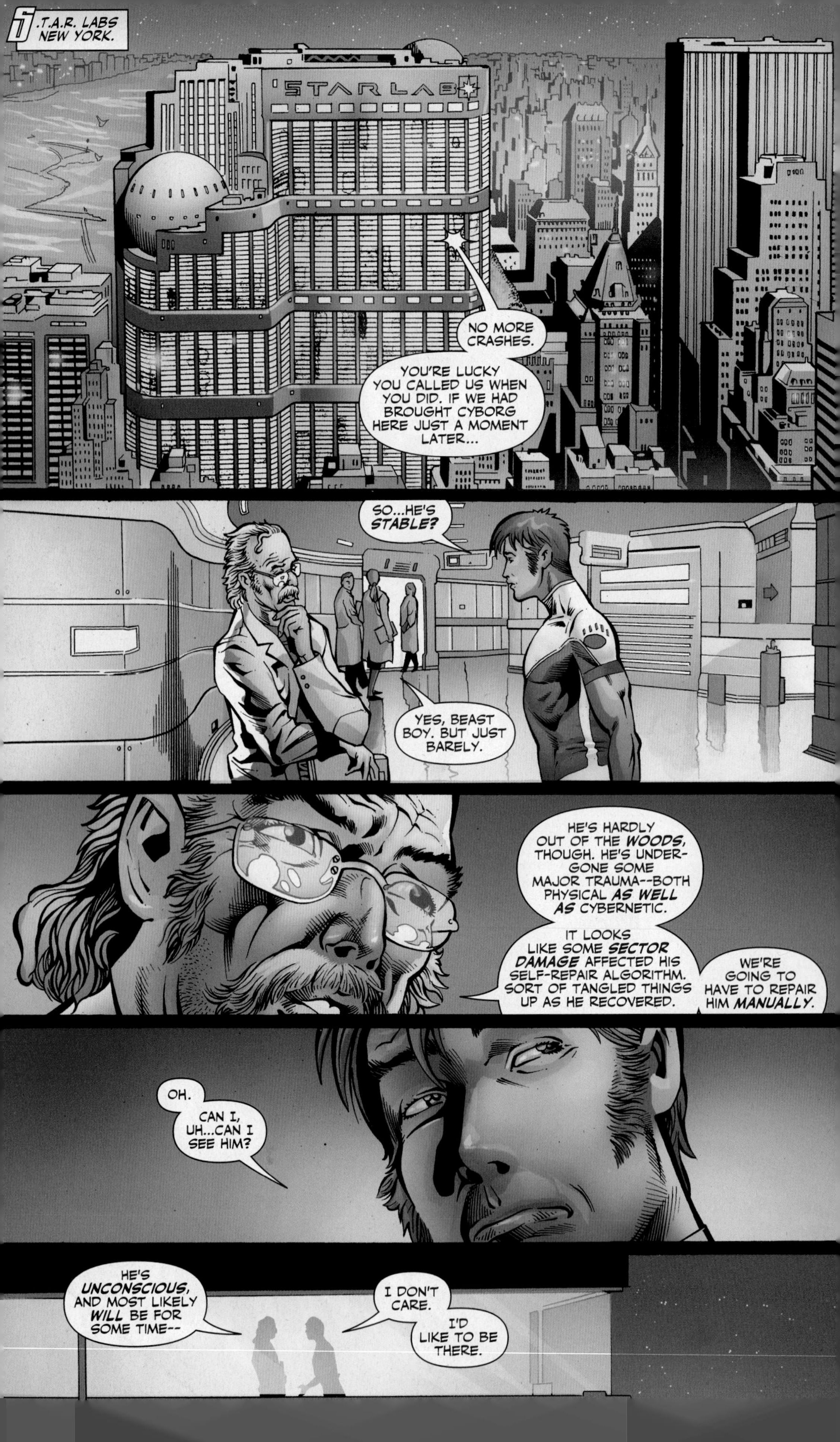
S.T.A.R. LABS NEW YORK.
STAR LABS
NO MORE CRASHES.
YOU'RE LUCKY YOU CALLED US WHEN YOU DID. IF WE HAD BROUGHT CYBORG HERE JUST A MOMENT LATER...
SO...HE'S STABLE?
YES, BEAST BOY. BUT JUST BARELY.
HE'S HARDLY OUT OF THE WOODS, THOUGH. HE'S UNDERGONE SOME MAJOR TRAUMA--BOTH PHYSICAL AS WELL AS CYBERNETIC.
IT LOOKS LIKE SOME SECTOR DAMAGE AFFECTED HIS SELF-REPAIR ALGORITHM. SORT OF TANGLED THINGS UP AS HE RECOVERED.
WE'RE GOING TO HAVE TO REPAIR HIM MANUALLY.
OH.
CAN I, UH...CAN I SEE HIM?
HE'S UNCONSCIOUS, AND MOST LIKELY WILL BE FOR SOME TIME--
I DON'T CARE.
I'D LIKE TO BE THERE.

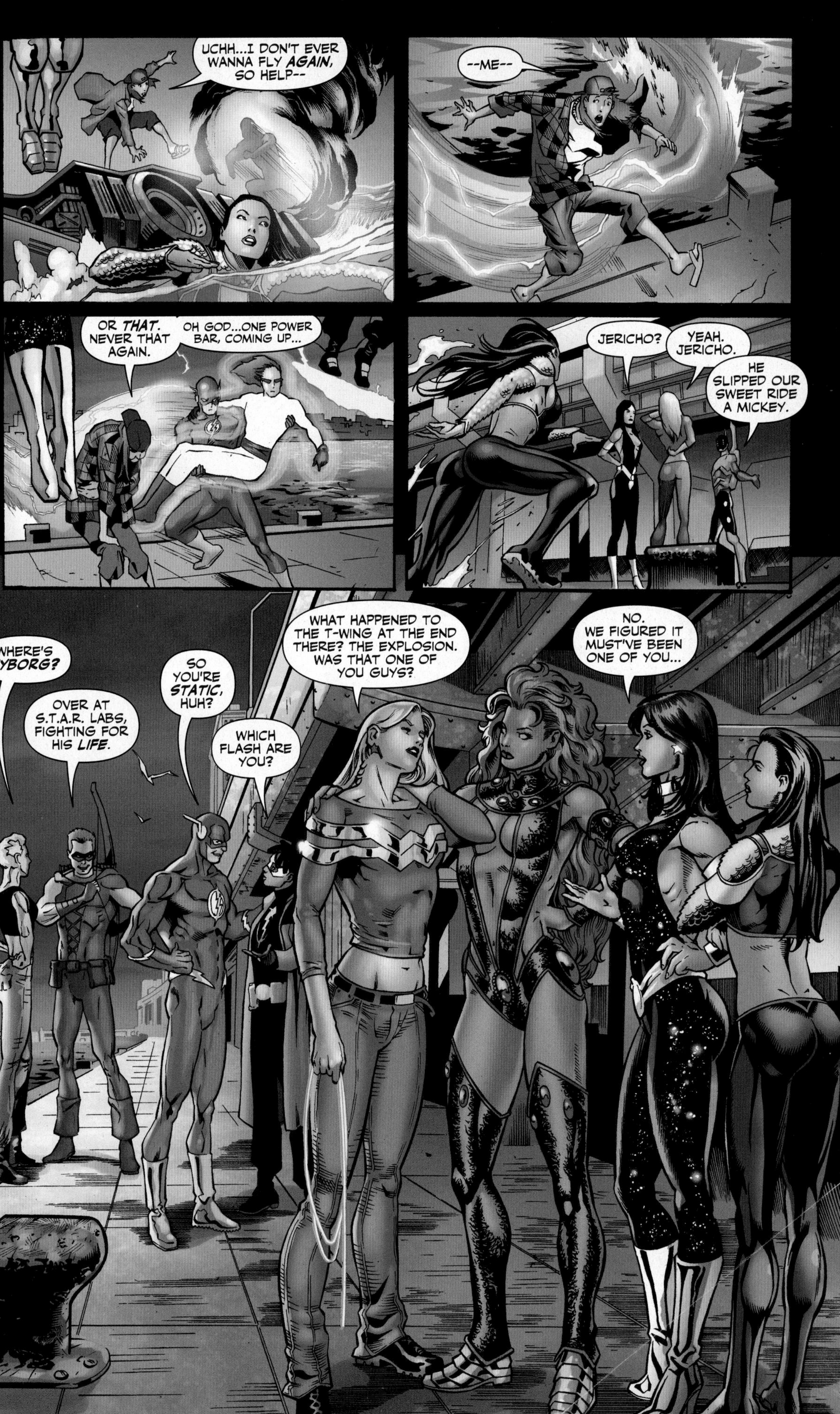
UCHH...I DON'T EVER WANNA FLY AGAIN, SO HELP--
--ME--
OR THAT. NEVER THAT AGAIN.
OH GOD...ONE POWER BAR, COMING UP...
JERICHO?
YEAH. JERICHO.
HE SLIPPED OUR SWEET RIDE A MICKEY.
WHERE'S CYBORG?
OVER AT S.T.A.R. LABS, FIGHTING FOR HIS LIFE.
SO YOU'RE STATIC, HUH?
WHICH FLASH ARE YOU?
WHAT HAPPENED TO THE T-WING AT THE END THERE? THE EXPLOSION. WAS THAT ONE OF YOU GUYS?
NO. WE FIGURED IT MUST'VE BEEN ONE OF YOU...

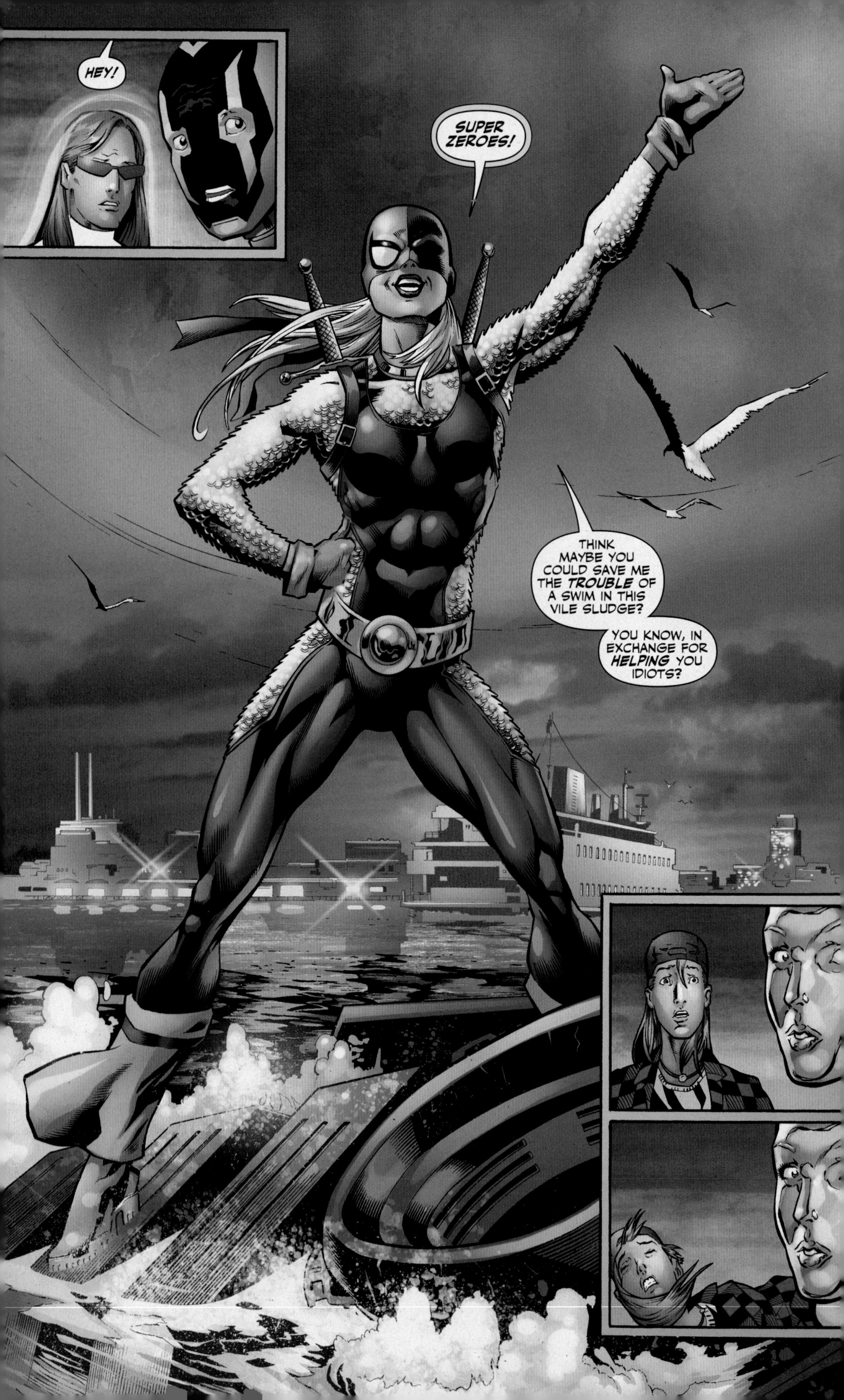
HEY!
SUPER ZEROES!
THINK MAYBE YOU COULD SAVE ME THE TROUBLE OF A SWIM IN THIS VILE SLUDGE?
YOU KNOW, IN EXCHANGE FOR HELPING YOU IDIOTS?

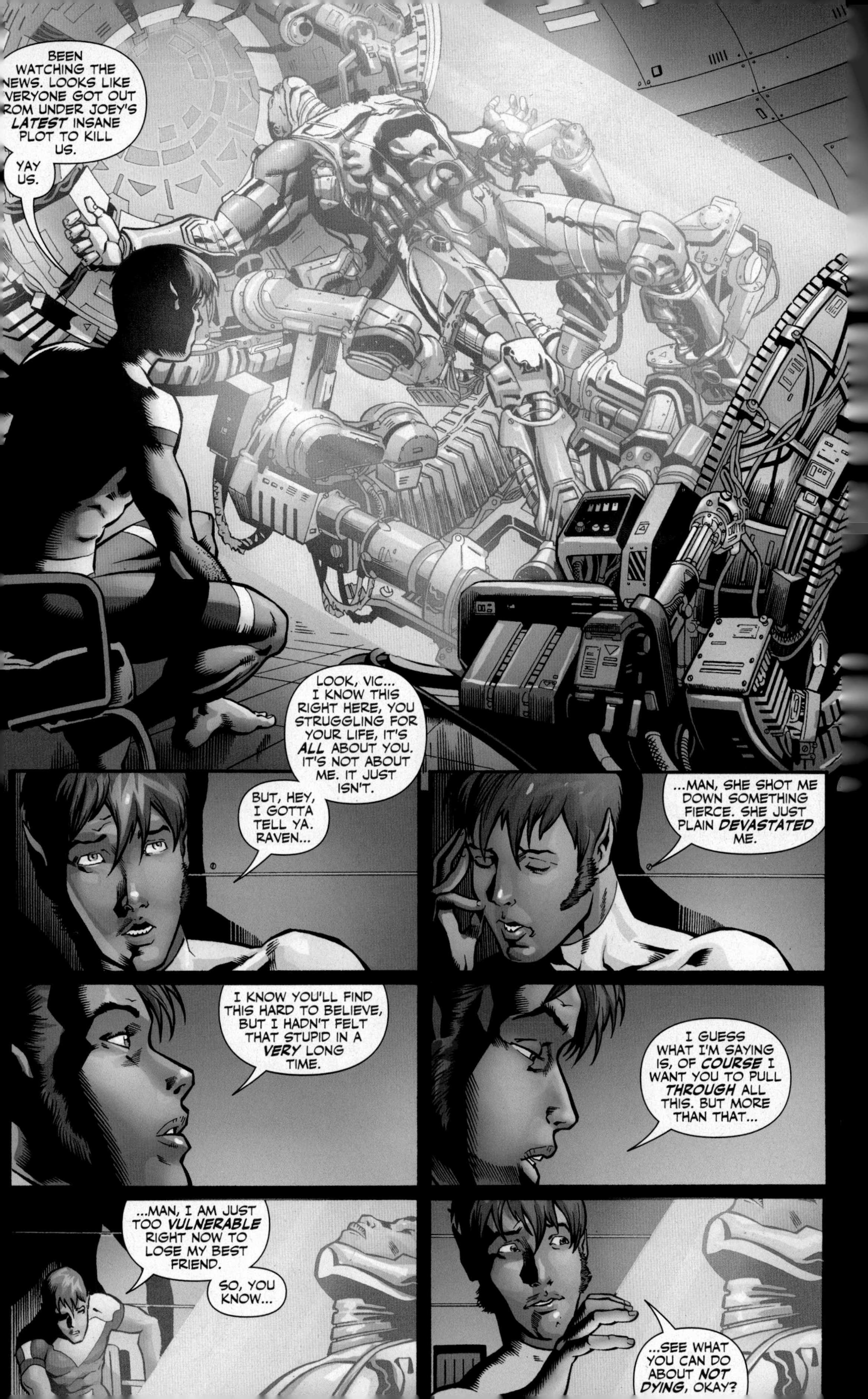
BEEN WATCHING THE NEWS. LOOKS LIKE VERYONE GOT OUT ROM UNDER JOEY'S LATEST INSANE PLOT TO KILL US.
YAY US.
LOOK, VIC... I KNOW THIS RIGHT HERE, YOU STRUGGLING FOR YOUR LIFE, IT'S ALL ABOUT YOU. IT'S NOT ABOUT ME. IT JUST ISN'T.
BUT, HEY, I GOTTA TELL YA. RAVEN...
...MAN, SHE SHOT ME DOWN SOMETHING FIERCE. SHE JUST PLAIN DEVASTATED ME.
I KNOW YOU'LL FIND THIS HARD TO BELIEVE, BUT I HADN'T FELT THAT STUPID IN A VERY LONG TIME.
I GUESS WHAT I'M SAYING IS, OF COURSE I WANT YOU TO PULL THROUGH ALL THIS. BUT MORE THAN THAT...
...MAN, I AM JUST TOO VULNERABLE RIGHT NOW TO LOSE MY BEST FRIEND.
SO, YOU KNOW...
...SEE WHAT YOU CAN DO ABOUT NOT DYING, OKAY?

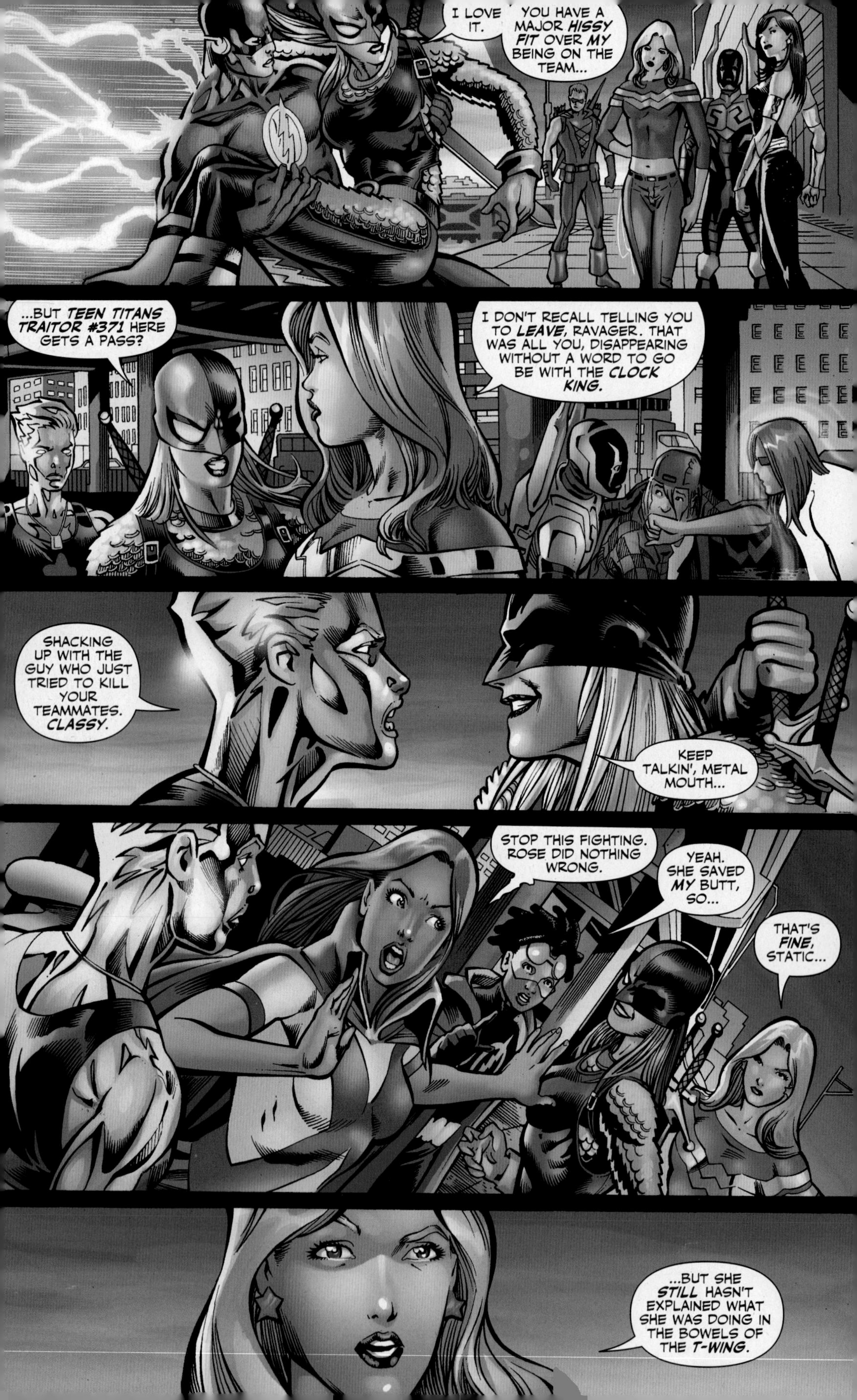

I LOVE IT.
YOU HAVE A MAJOR HISSY FIT OVER MY BEING ON THE TEAM...
...BUT TEEN TITANS TRAITOR #371 HERE GETS A PASS?
I DON'T RECALL TELLING YOU TO LEAVE, RAVAGER. THAT WAS ALL YOU, DISAPPEARING WITHOUT A WORD TO GO BE WITH THE CLOCK KING.
SHACKING UP WITH THE GUY WHO JUST TRIED TO KILL YOUR TEAMMATES. CLASSY.
KEEP TALKIN', METAL MOUTH...
STOP THIS FIGHTING. ROSE DID NOTHING WRONG.
YEAH. SHE SAVED MY BUTT, SO...
THAT'S FINE, STATIC...
...BUT SHE STILL HASN'T EXPLAINED WHAT SHE WAS DOING IN THE BOWELS OF THE T-WING.

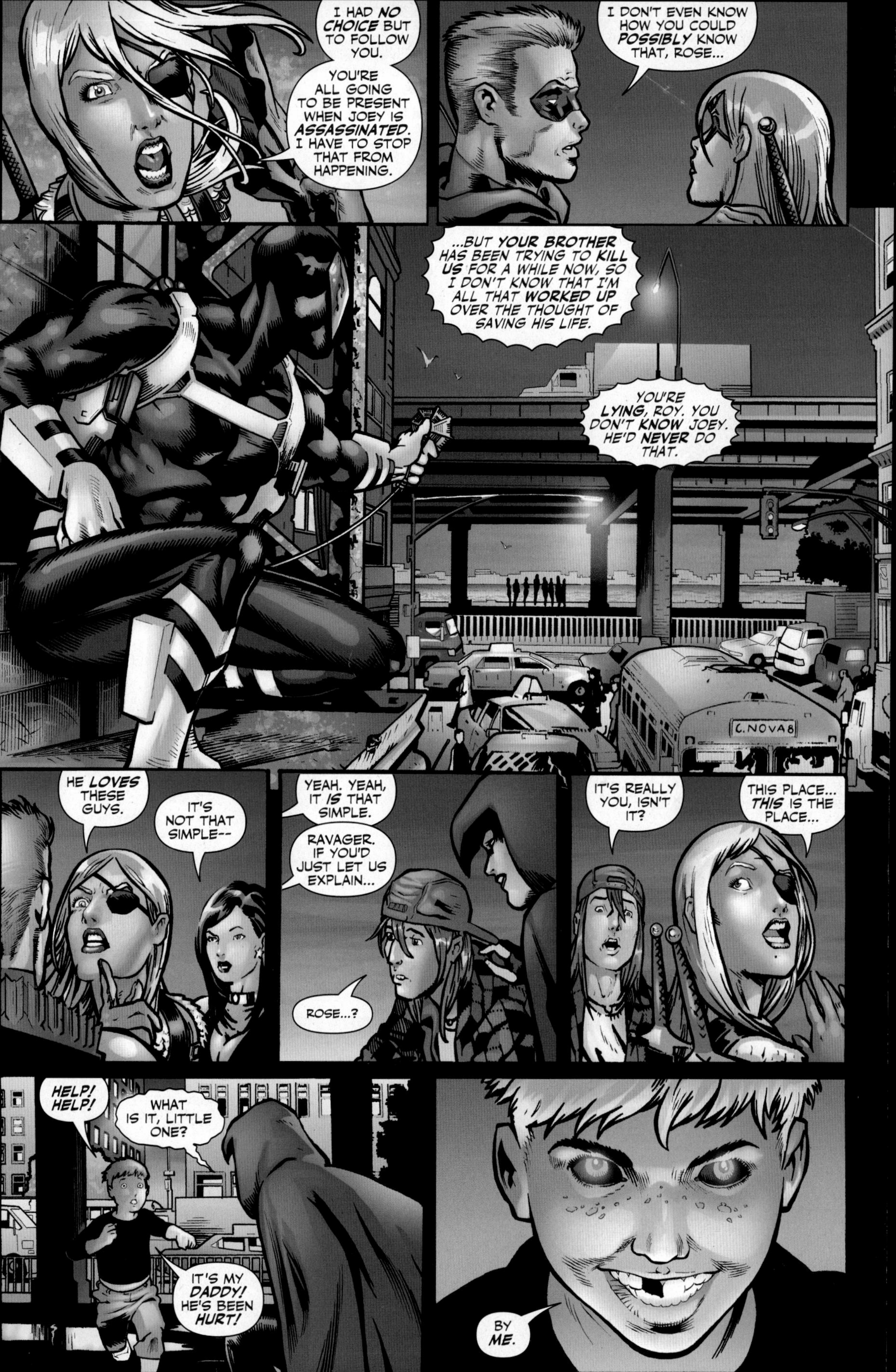
I HAD NO CHOICE BUT TO FOLLOW YOU.
YOU'RE ALL GOING TO BE PRESENT WHEN JOEY IS ASSASSINATED. I HAVE TO STOP THAT FROM HAPPENING.
I DON'T EVEN KNOW HOW YOU COULD POSSIBLY KNOW THAT, ROSE...
...BUT YOUR BROTHER HAS BEEN TRYING TO KILL US FOR A WHILE NOW, SO I DON'T KNOW THAT I'M ALL THAT WORKED UP OVER THE THOUGHT OF SAVING HIS LIFE.
YOU'RE LYING, ROY. YOU DON'T KNOW JOEY. HE'D NEVER DO THAT.
C. NOVA 8
HE LOVES THESE GUYS.
IT'S NOT THAT SIMPLE--
YEAH. YEAH, IT IS THAT SIMPLE.
RAVAGER. IF YOU'D JUST LET US EXPLAIN...
ROSE...?
IT'S REALLY YOU, ISN'T IT?
THIS PLACE... THIS IS THE PLACE...
HELP! HELP!
WHAT IS IT, LITTLE ONE?
IT'S MY DADDY! HE'S BEEN HURT!
BY ME.

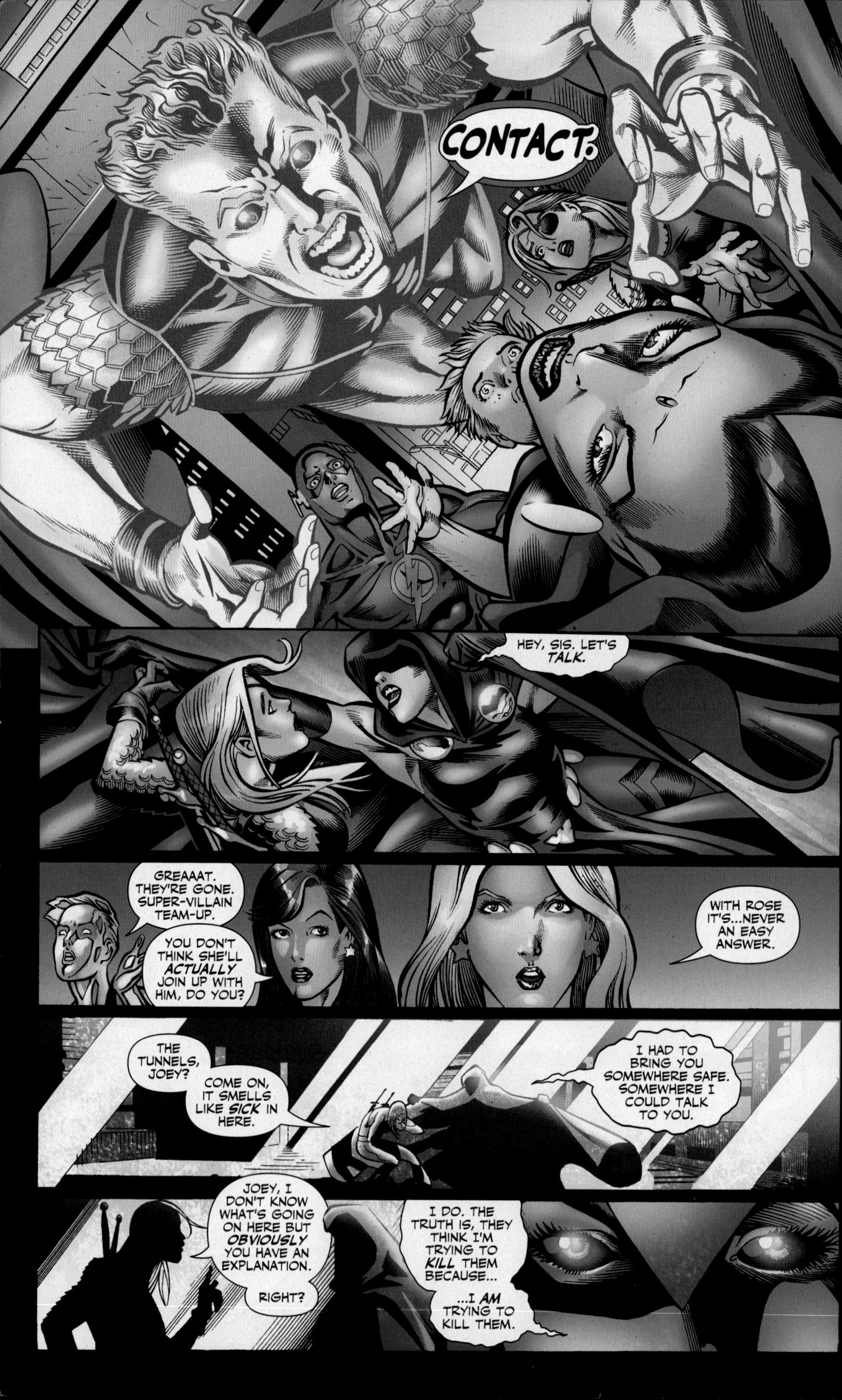
CONTACT.
HEY, SIS. LET'S TALK.
GREAAAT. THEY'RE GONE. SUPER-VILLAIN TEAM-UP.
YOU DON'T THINK SHE'LL ACTUALLY JOIN UP WITH HIM, DO YOU?
WITH ROSE IT'S...NEVER AN EASY ANSWER.
THE TUNNELS, JOEY?
COME ON, IT SMELLS LIKE SICK IN HERE.
I HAD TO BRING YOU SOMEWHERE SAFE. SOMEWHERE I COULD TALK TO YOU.
JOEY, I DON'T KNOW WHAT'S GOING ON HERE BUT OBVIOUSLY YOU HAVE AN EXPLANATION.
RIGHT?
I DO. THE TRUTH IS, THEY THINK I'M TRYING TO KILL THEM BECAUSE...
...I AM TRYING TO KILL THEM.

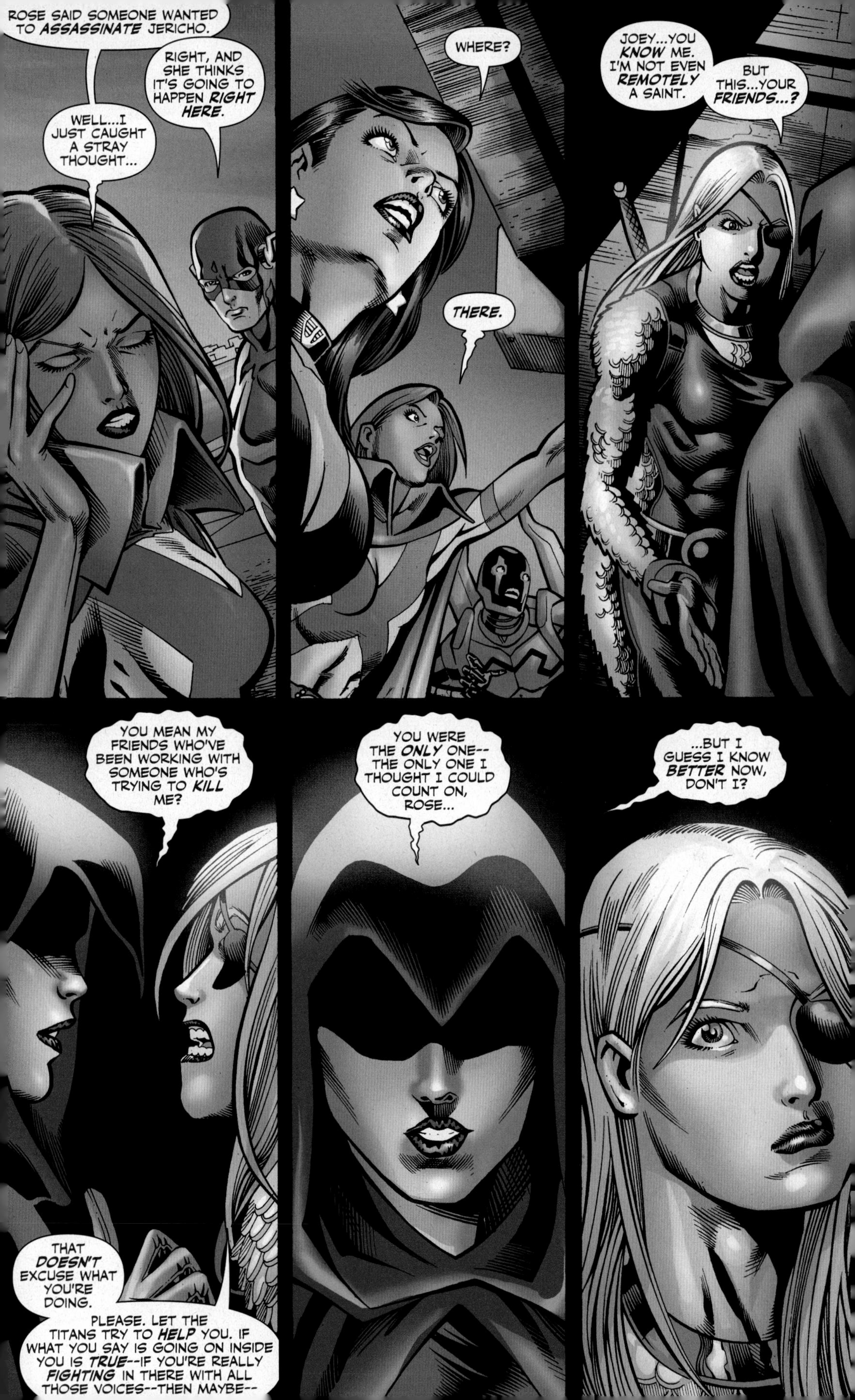
ROSE SAID SOMEONE WANTED TO ASSASSINATE JERICHO.
RIGHT, AND SHE THINKS IT'S GOING TO HAPPEN RIGHT HERE.
WELL...I JUST CAUGHT A STRAY THOUGHT...
WHERE?
THERE.
JOEY...YOU KNOW ME. I'M NOT EVEN REMOTELY A SAINT.
BUT THIS...YOUR FRIENDS...?
YOU MEAN MY FRIENDS WHO'VE BEEN WORKING WITH SOMEONE WHO'S TRYING TO KILL ME?
THAT DOESN'T EXCUSE WHAT YOU'RE DOING.
PLEASE. LET THE TITANS TRY TO HELP YOU. IF WHAT YOU SAY IS GOING ON INSIDE YOU IS TRUE--IF YOU'RE REALLY FIGHTING IN THERE WITH ALL THOSE VOICES--THEN MAYBE--
YOU WERE THE ONLY ONE-- THE ONLY ONE I THOUGHT I COULD COUNT ON, ROSE...
...BUT I GUESS I KNOW BETTER NOW, DON'T I?

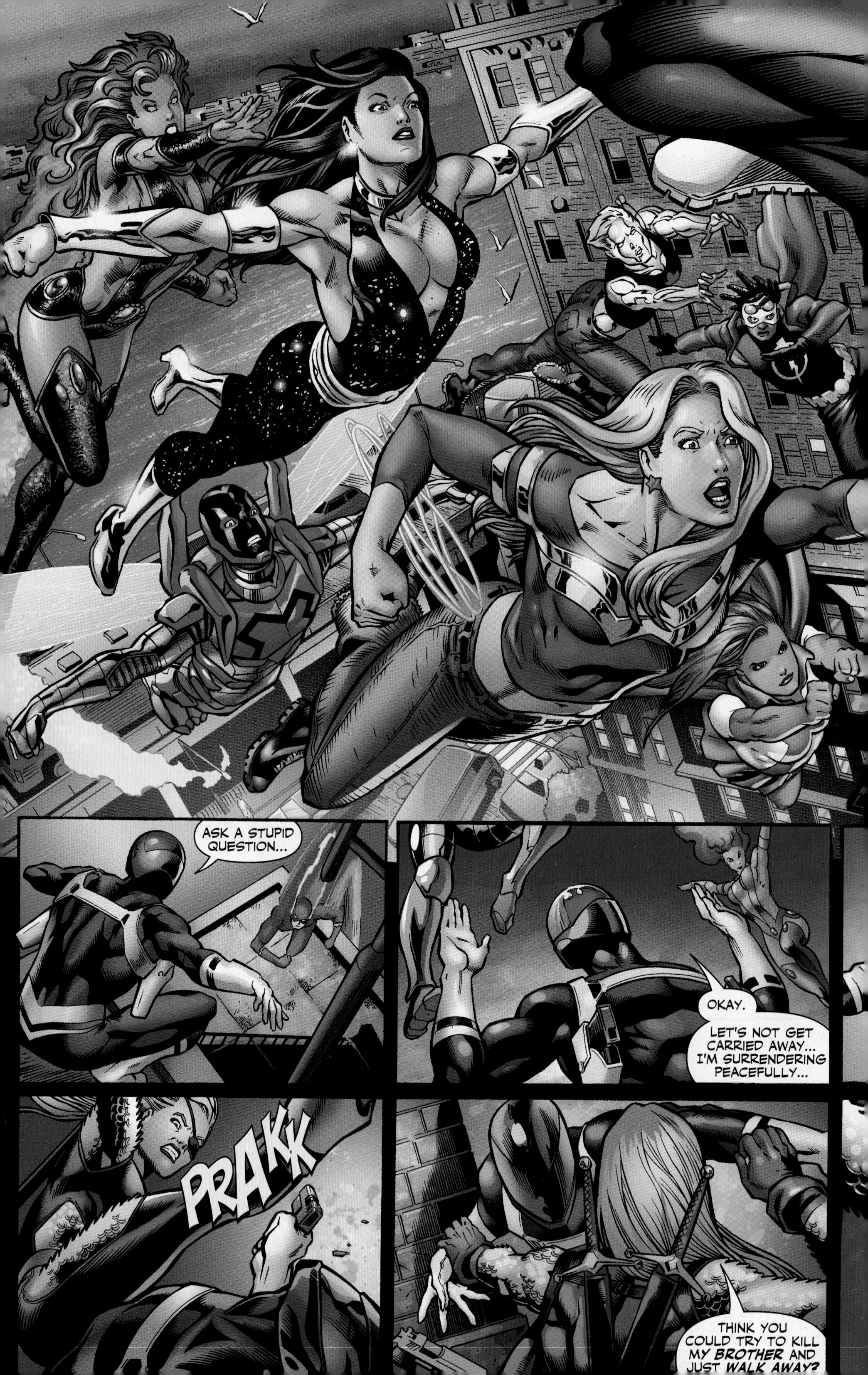
ASK A STUPID QUESTION...
OKAY.
LET'S NOT GET CARRIED AWAY... I'M SURRENDERING PEACEFULLY...
PRAKK
THINK YOU COULD TRY TO KILL MY *BROTHER* AND JUST *WALK AWAY?*

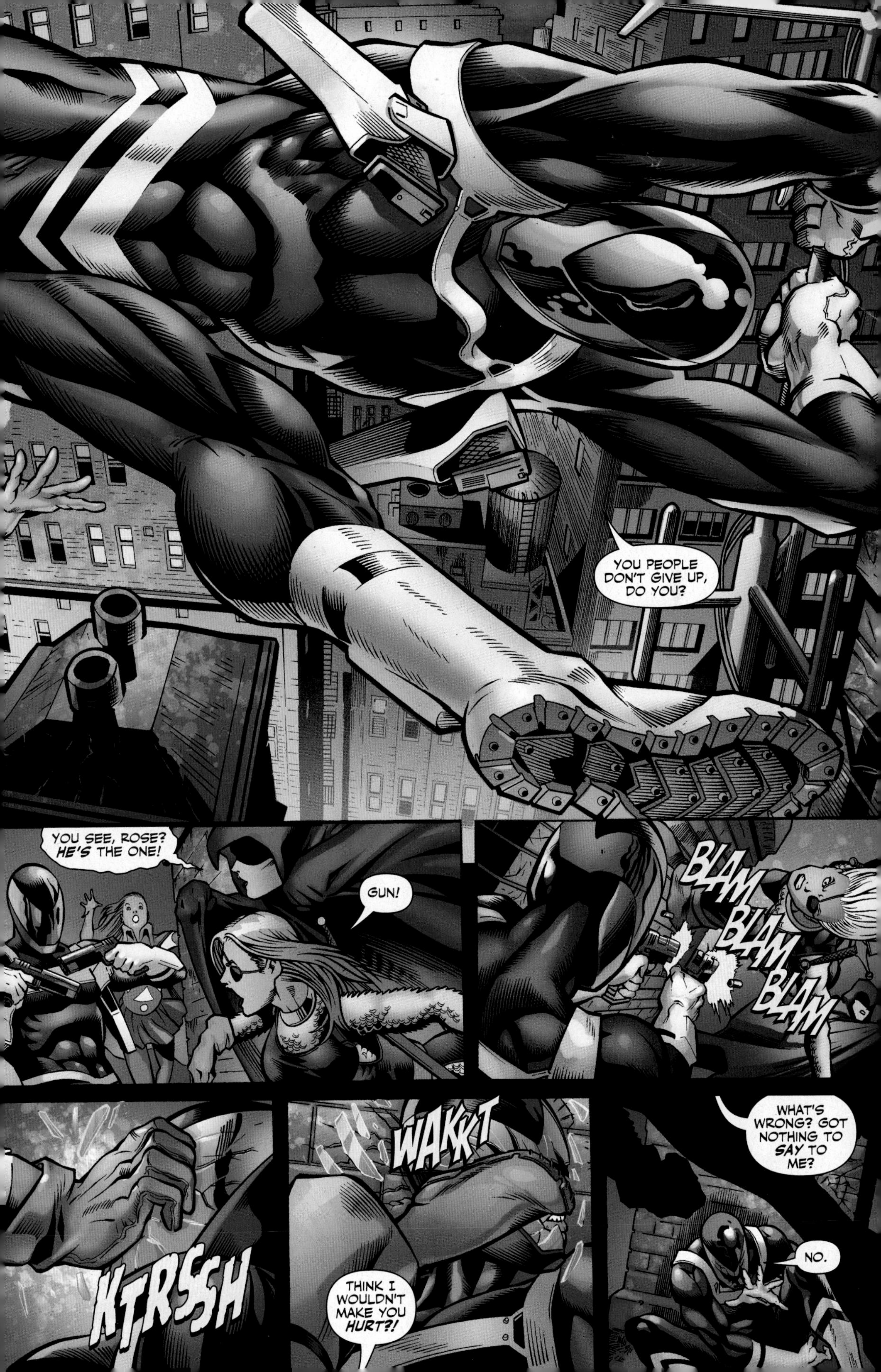

YOU PEOPLE DON'T GIVE UP, DO YOU?
YOU SEE, ROSE? HE'S THE ONE!
GUN!
BLAM BLAM BLAM BLAM
KTRSSH
WAKKT
THINK I WOULDN'T MAKE YOU HURT?!
WHAT'S WRONG? GOT NOTHING TO SAY TO ME?
NO.

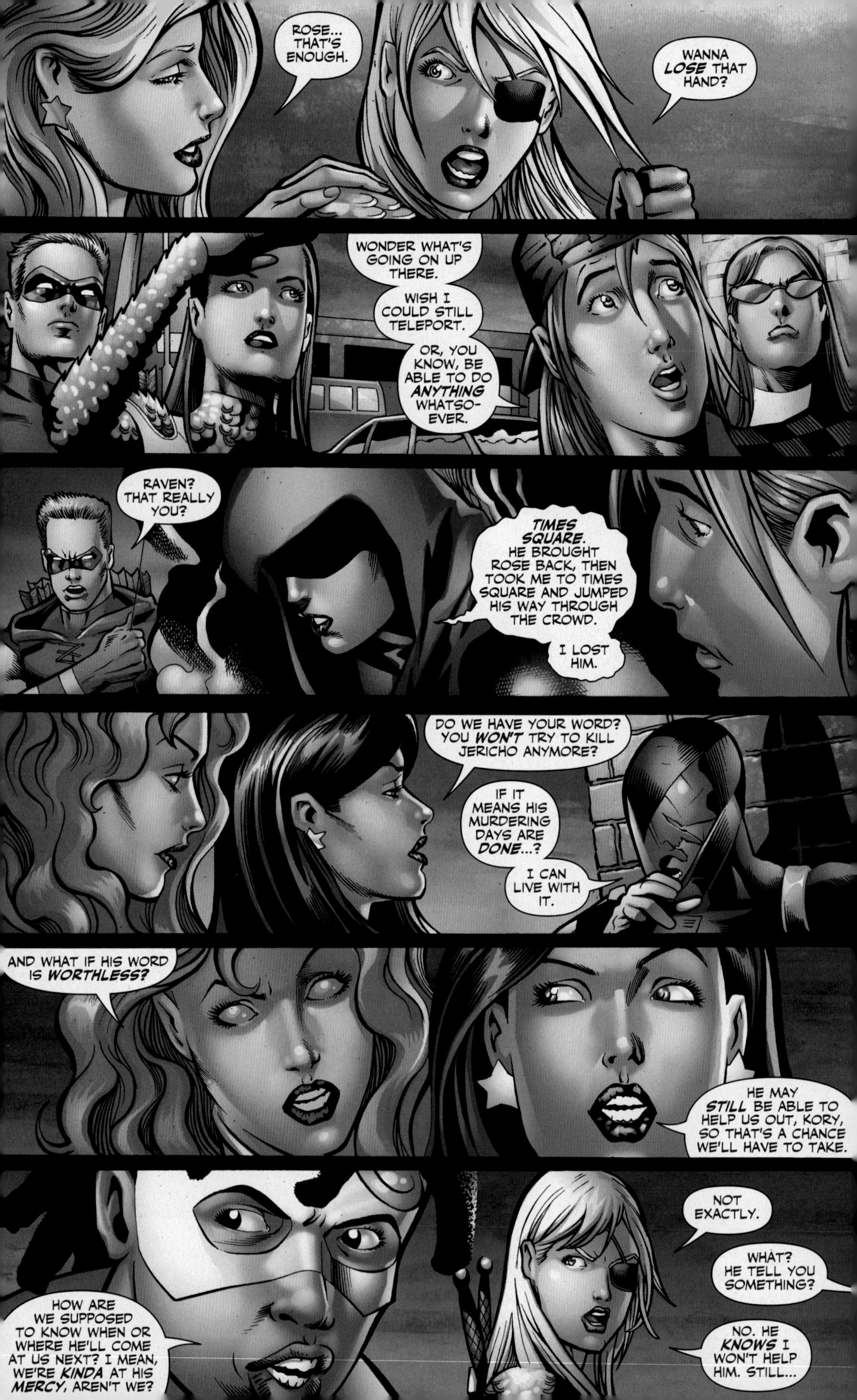
ROSE... THAT'S ENOUGH.
WANNA LOSE THAT HAND?
WONDER WHAT'S GOING ON UP THERE.
WISH I COULD STILL TELEPORT.
OR, YOU KNOW, BE ABLE TO DO ANYTHING WHATSO-EVER.
RAVEN? THAT REALLY YOU?
TIMES SQUARE. HE BROUGHT ROSE BACK, THEN TOOK ME TO TIMES SQUARE AND JUMPED HIS WAY THROUGH THE CROWD.
I LOST HIM.
DO WE HAVE YOUR WORD? YOU WON'T TRY TO KILL JERICHO ANYMORE?
IF IT MEANS HIS MURDERING DAYS ARE DONE...?
I CAN LIVE WITH IT.
AND WHAT IF HIS WORD IS WORTHLESS?
HE MAY STILL BE ABLE TO HELP US OUT, KORY, SO THAT'S A CHANCE WE'LL HAVE TO TAKE.
HOW ARE WE SUPPOSED TO KNOW WHEN OR WHERE HE'LL COME AT US NEXT? I MEAN, WE'RE KINDA AT HIS MERCY, AREN'T WE?
NOT EXACTLY.
WHAT? HE TELL YOU SOMETHING?
NO. HE KNOWS I WON'T HELP HIM. STILL...

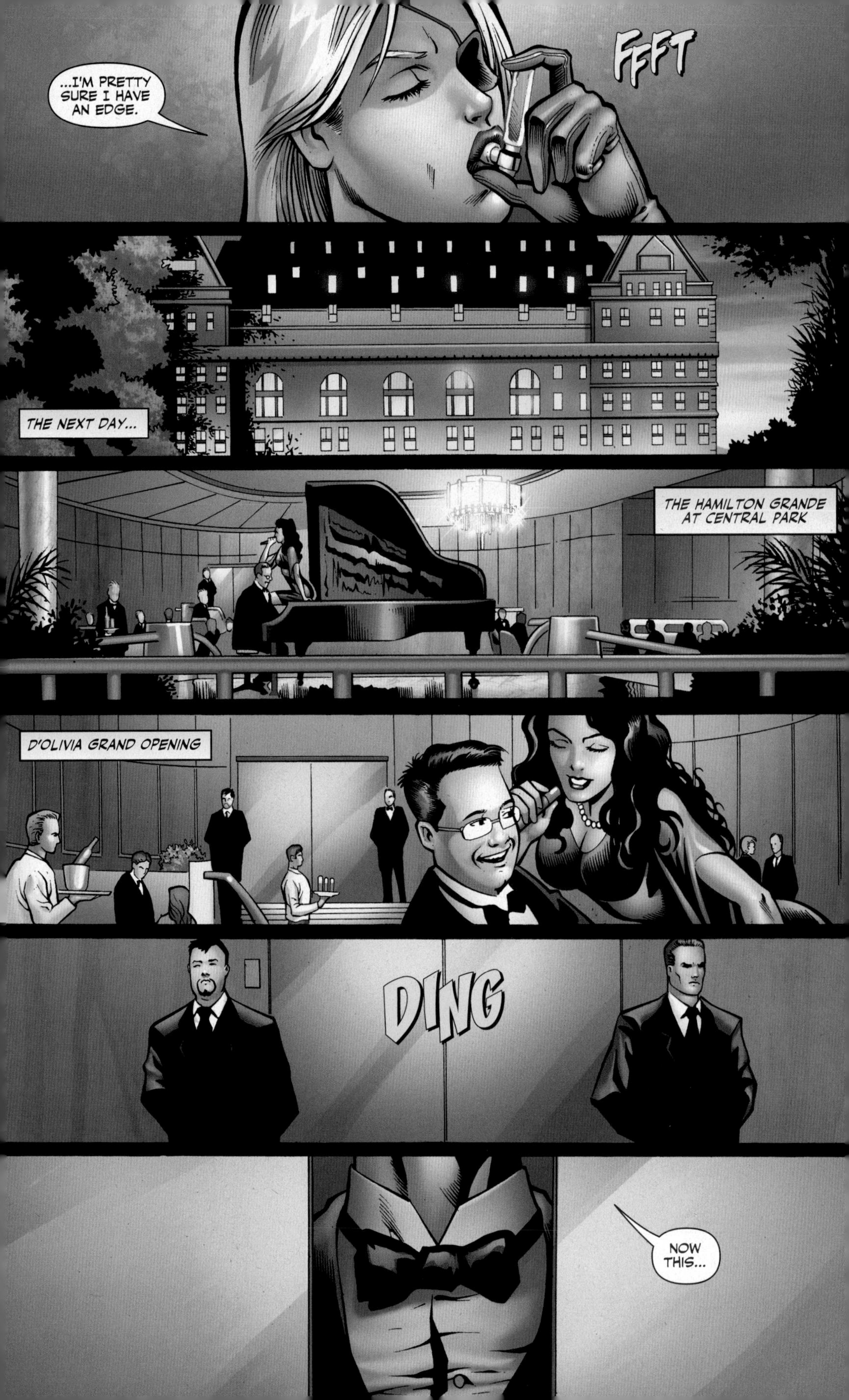
...I'M PRETTY SURE I HAVE AN EDGE.
FFFT
THE NEXT DAY...
THE HAMILTON GRANDE AT CENTRAL PARK
D'OLIVIA GRAND OPENING
DING
NOW THIS...

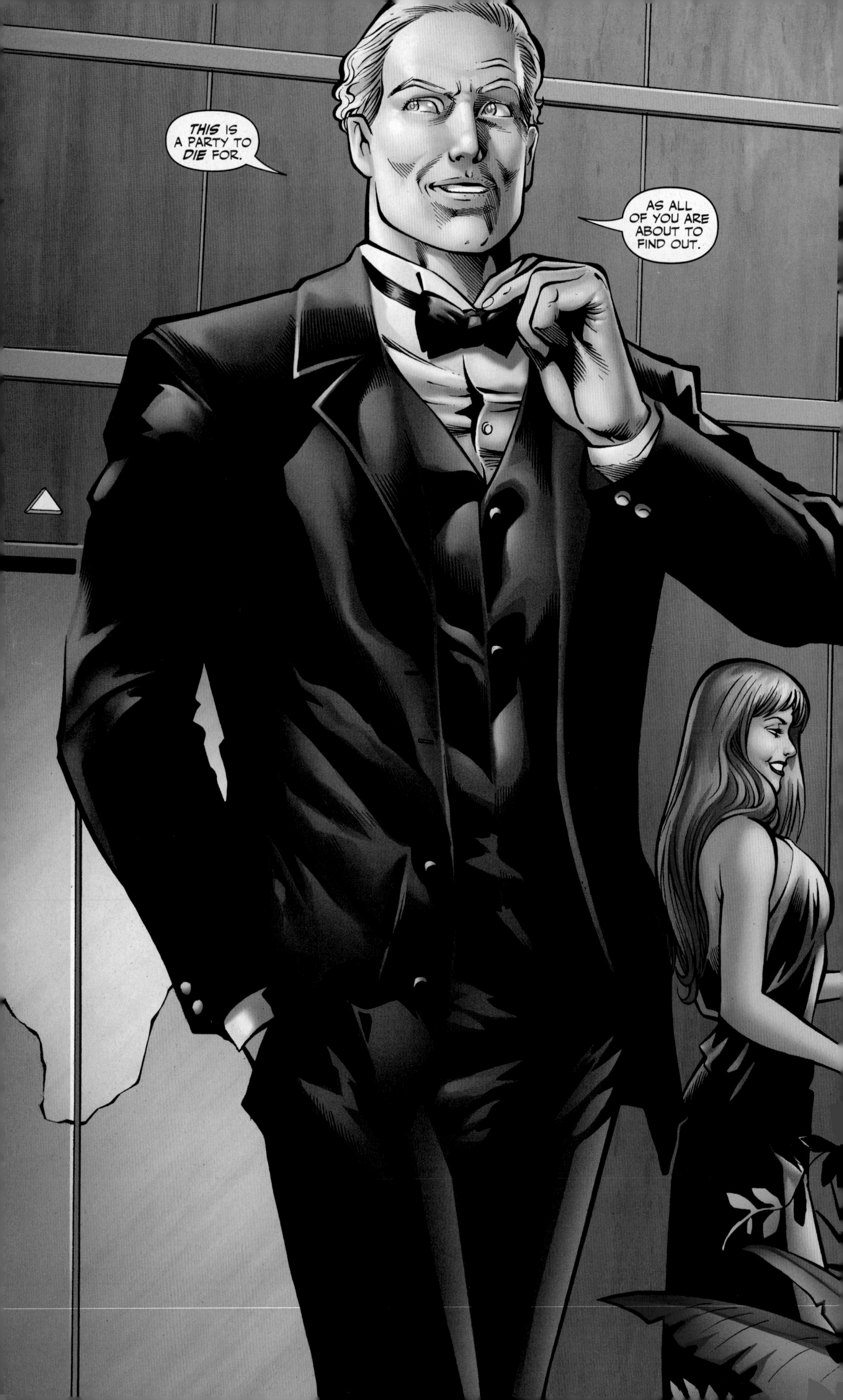
THIS IS A PARTY TO *DIE* FOR.
AS ALL OF YOU ARE ABOUT TO FIND OUT.

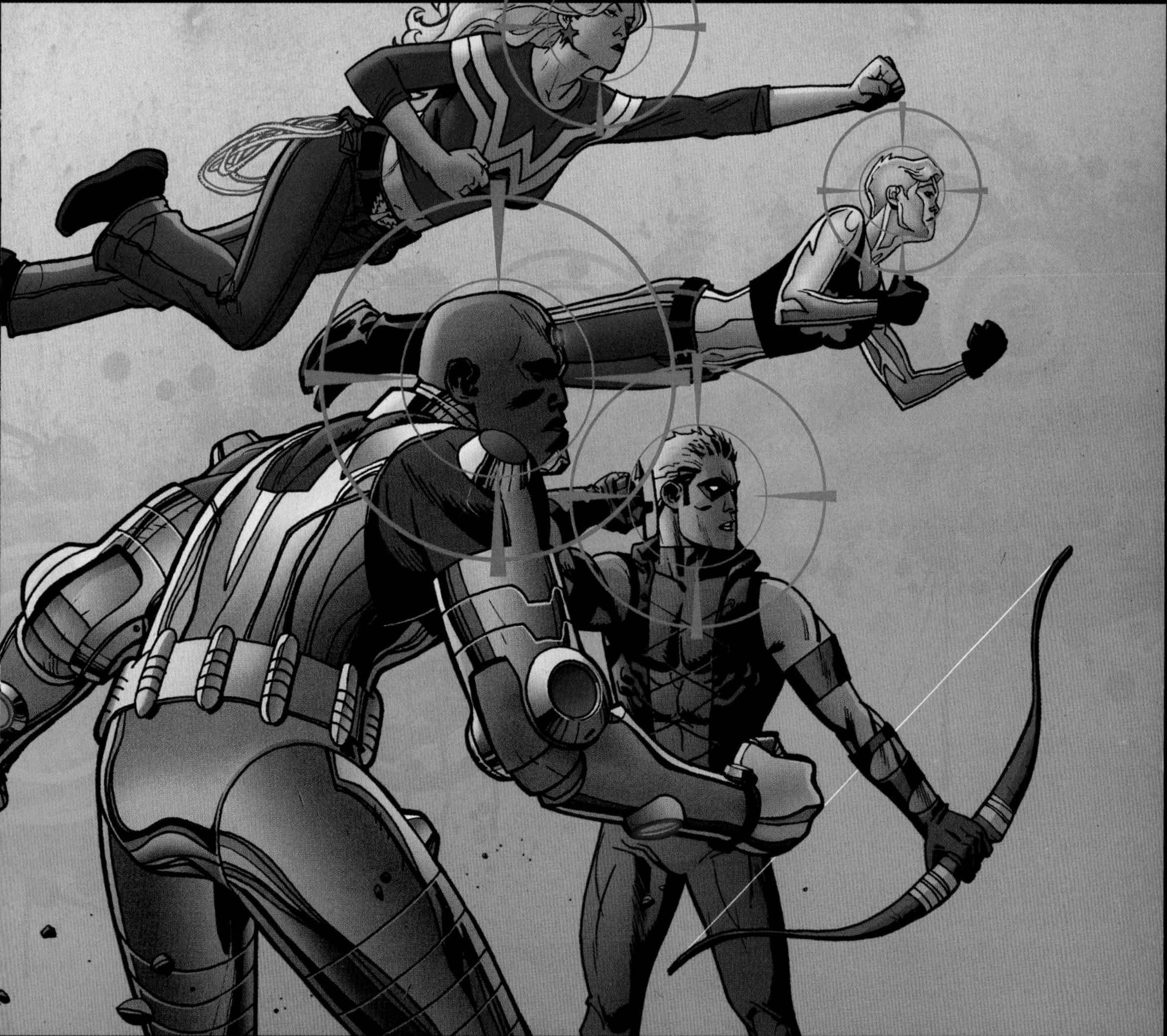

Deathtrap Part 4

Sean McKeever
Writer

Angel Unzueta
Pencils

Wayne Faucher
Inks

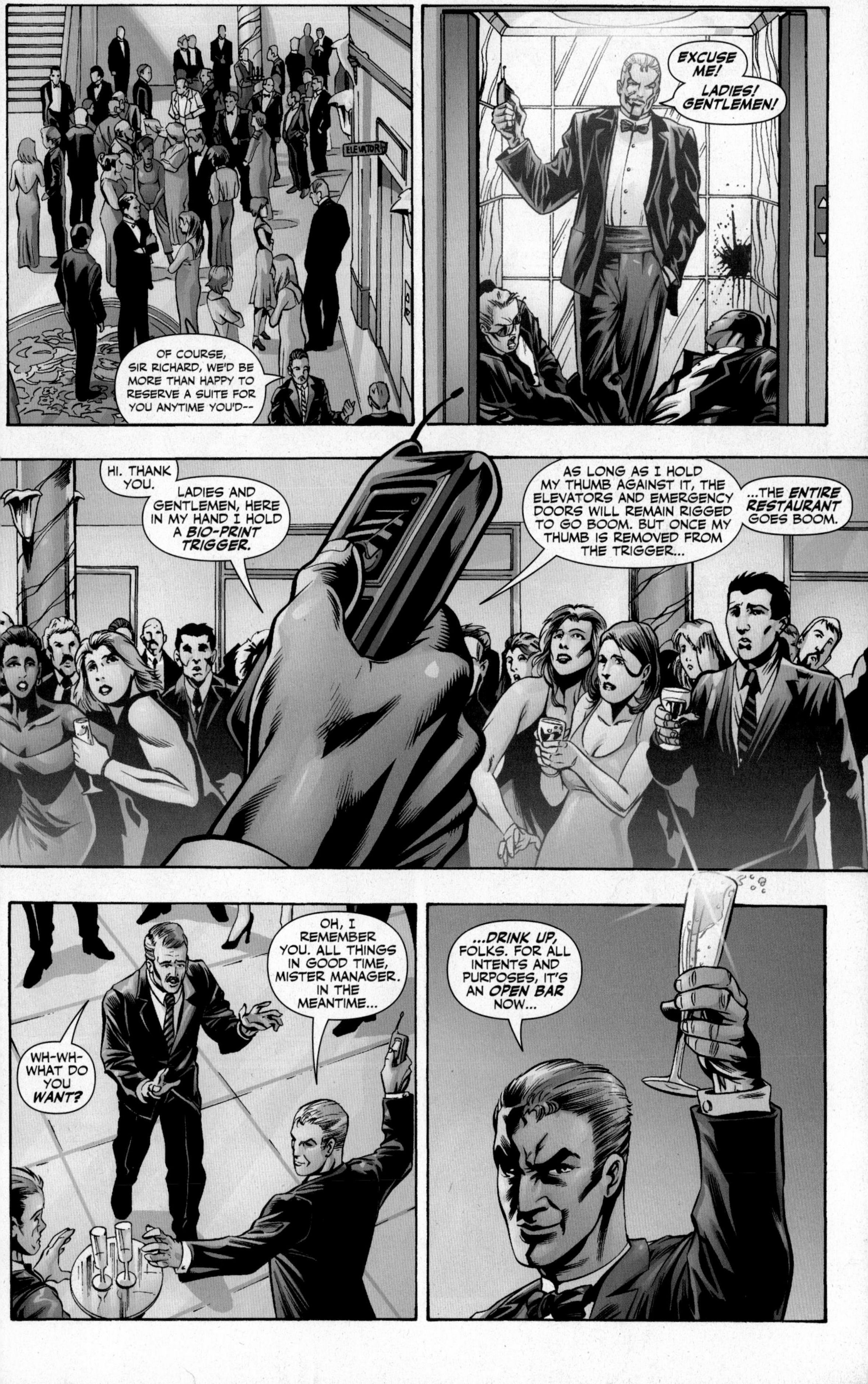
OF COURSE, SIR RICHARD, WE'D BE MORE THAN HAPPY TO RESERVE A SUITE FOR YOU ANYTIME YOU'D--
ELEVATOR
EXCUSE ME!
LADIES! GENTLEMEN!
HI. THANK YOU.
LADIES AND GENTLEMEN, HERE IN MY HAND I HOLD A *BIO-PRINT TRIGGER.*
AS LONG AS I HOLD MY THUMB AGAINST IT, THE ELEVATORS AND EMERGENCY DOORS WILL REMAIN RIGGED TO GO BOOM. BUT ONCE MY THUMB IS REMOVED FROM THE TRIGGER...
...THE *ENTIRE RESTAURANT* GOES BOOM.
WH-WH-WHAT DO YOU *WANT?*
OH, I REMEMBER YOU. ALL THINGS IN GOOD TIME, MISTER MANAGER. IN THE MEANTIME...
...DRINK UP, FOLKS. FOR ALL INTENTS AND PURPOSES, IT'S AN *OPEN BAR* NOW...

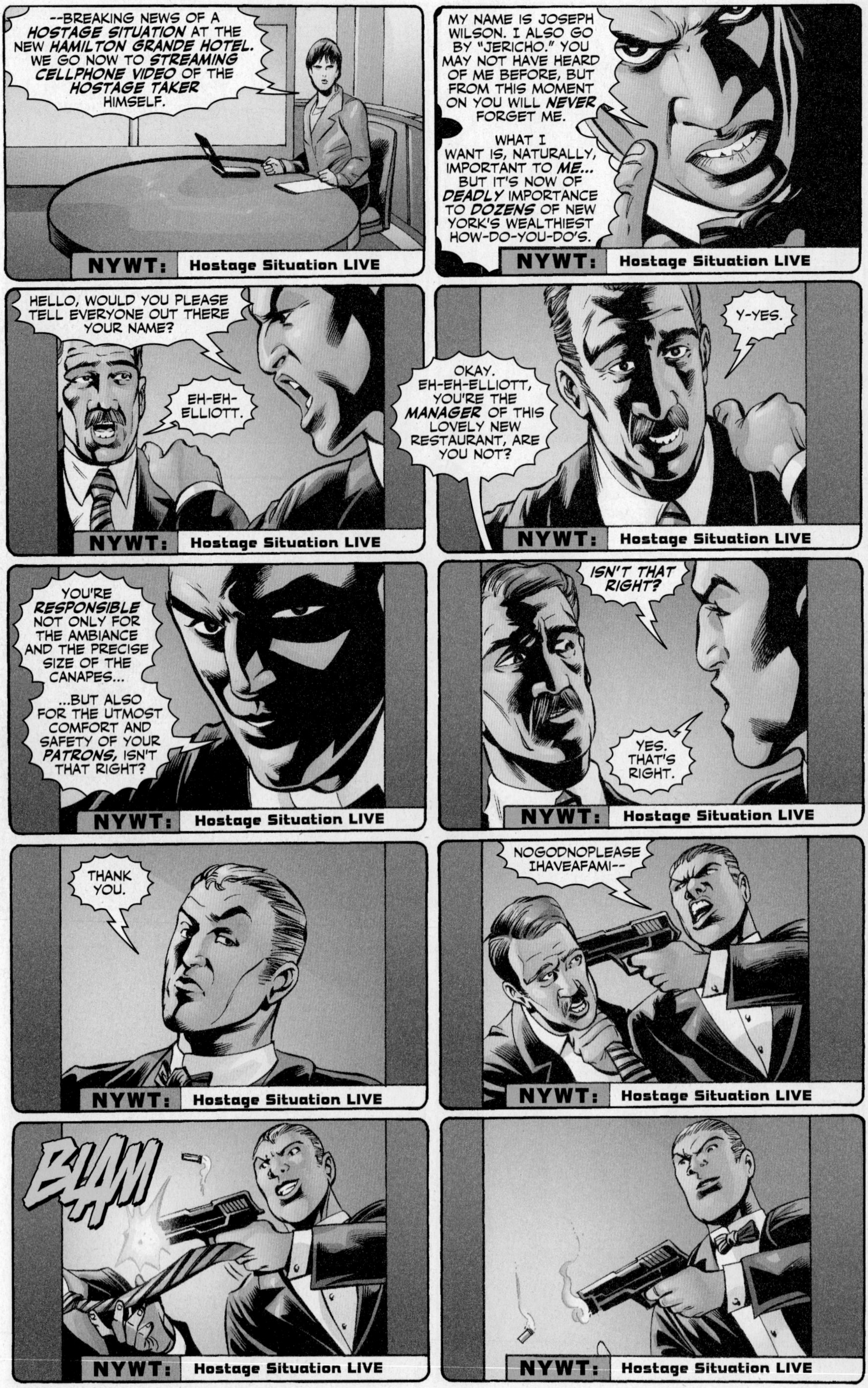
--BREAKING NEWS OF A HOSTAGE SITUATION AT THE NEW HAMILTON GRANDE HOTEL. WE GO NOW TO STREAMING CELLPHONE VIDEO OF THE HOSTAGE TAKER HIMSELF.
NYWT: Hostage Situation LIVE
MY NAME IS JOSEPH WILSON. I ALSO GO BY "JERICHO." YOU MAY NOT HAVE HEARD OF ME BEFORE, BUT FROM THIS MOMENT ON YOU WILL NEVER FORGET ME.
WHAT I WANT IS, NATURALLY, IMPORTANT TO ME... BUT IT'S NOW OF DEADLY IMPORTANCE TO DOZENS OF NEW YORK'S WEALTHIEST HOW-DO-YOU-DO'S.
NYWT: Hostage Situation LIVE
HELLO, WOULD YOU PLEASE TELL EVERYONE OUT THERE YOUR NAME?
EH-EH-ELLIOTT.
NYWT: Hostage Situation LIVE
OKAY. EH-EH-ELLIOTT, YOU'RE THE MANAGER OF THIS LOVELY NEW RESTAURANT, ARE YOU NOT?
Y-YES.
NYWT: Hostage Situation LIVE
YOU'RE RESPONSIBLE NOT ONLY FOR THE AMBIANCE AND THE PRECISE SIZE OF THE CANAPES...
...BUT ALSO FOR THE UTMOST COMFORT AND SAFETY OF YOUR PATRONS, ISN'T THAT RIGHT?
NYWT: Hostage Situation LIVE
ISN'T THAT RIGHT?
YES. THAT'S RIGHT.
NYWT: Hostage Situation LIVE
THANK YOU.
NYWT: Hostage Situation LIVE
NOGODNOPLEASE IHAVEAFAMI--
NYWT: Hostage Situation LIVE
BLAM
NYWT: Hostage Situation LIVE
NYWT: Hostage Situation LIVE

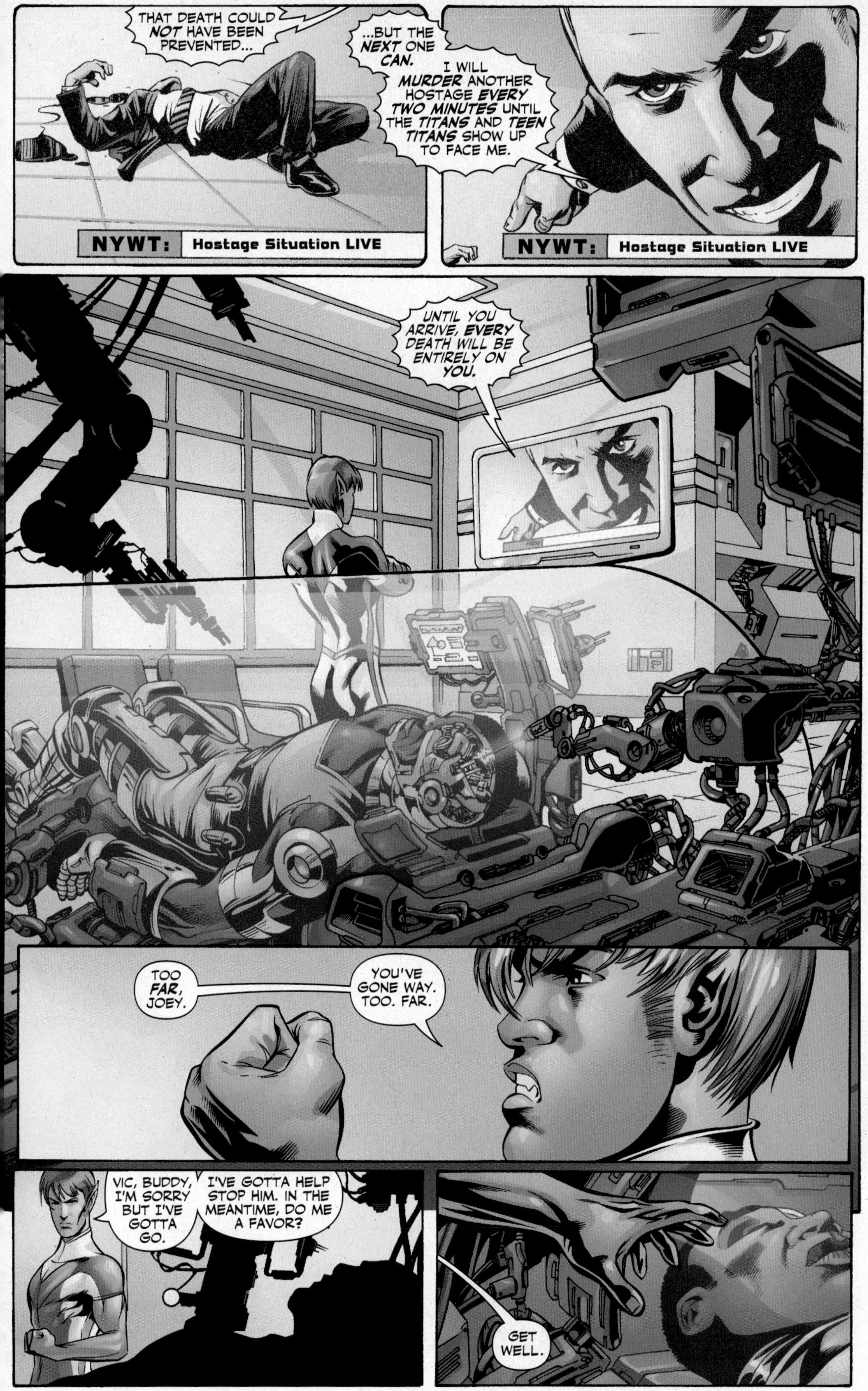
THAT DEATH COULD NOT HAVE BEEN PREVENTED...
NYWT: Hostage Situation LIVE
...BUT THE NEXT ONE CAN.
I WILL MURDER ANOTHER HOSTAGE EVERY TWO MINUTES UNTIL THE TITANS AND TEEN TITANS SHOW UP TO FACE ME.
NYWT: Hostage Situation LIVE
UNTIL YOU ARRIVE, EVERY DEATH WILL BE ENTIRELY ON YOU.
TOO FAR, JOEY.
YOU'VE GONE WAY. TOO. FAR.
VIC, BUDDY, I'M SORRY BUT I'VE GOTTA GO.
I'VE GOTTA HELP STOP HIM. IN THE MEANTIME, DO ME A FAVOR?
GET WELL.

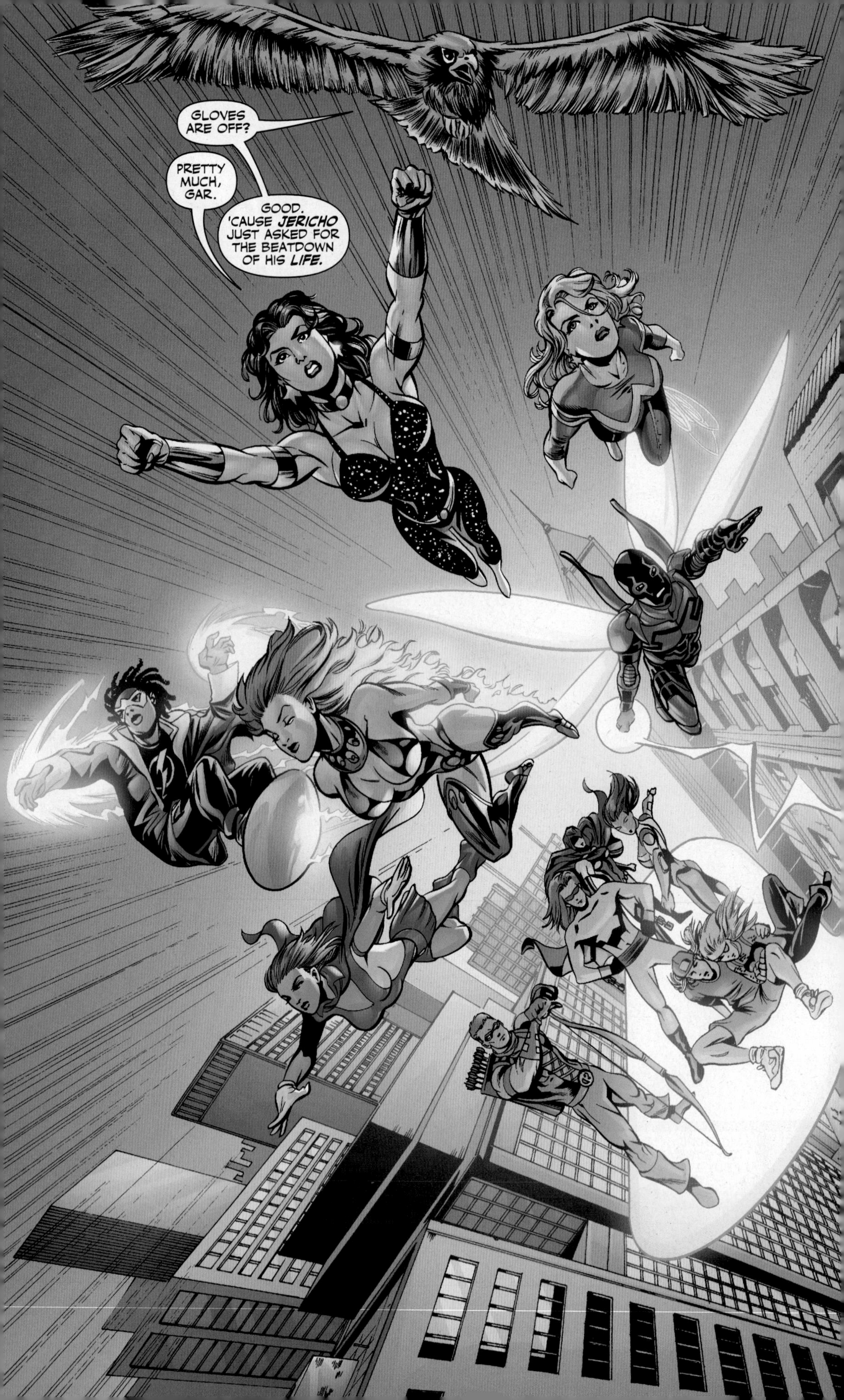
GLOVES ARE OFF?
PRETTY MUCH, GAR.
GOOD. 'CAUSE *JERICHO* JUST ASKED FOR THE BEATDOWN OF HIS *LIFE.*

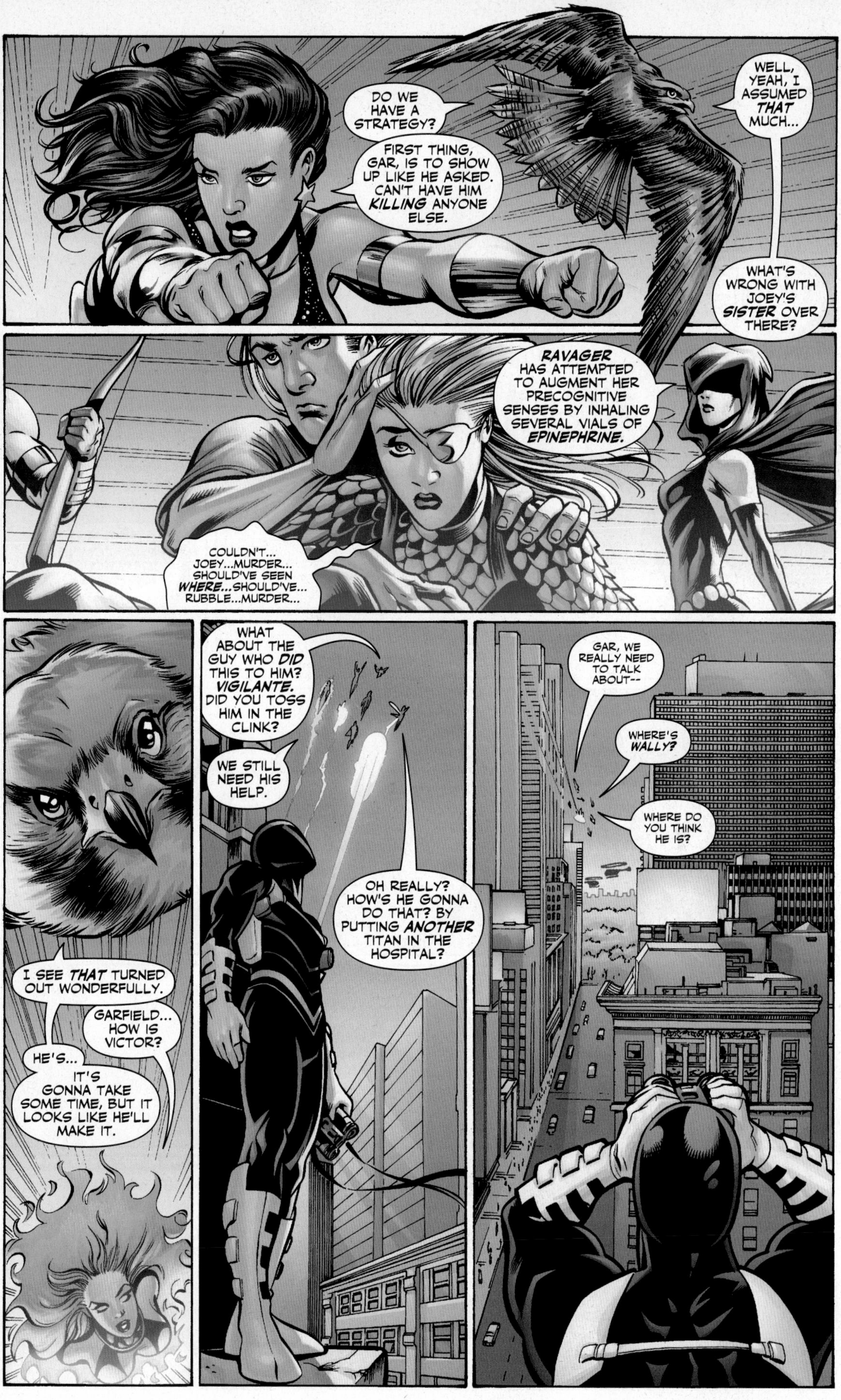
DO WE HAVE A STRATEGY?
FIRST THING, GAR, IS TO SHOW UP LIKE HE ASKED. CAN'T HAVE HIM KILLING ANYONE ELSE.
WELL, YEAH, I ASSUMED THAT MUCH...
WHAT'S WRONG WITH JOEY'S SISTER OVER THERE?
RAVAGER HAS ATTEMPTED TO AUGMENT HER PRECOGNITIVE SENSES BY INHALING SEVERAL VIALS OF EPINEPHRINE.
COULDN'T... JOEY...MURDER... SHOULD'VE SEEN WHERE...SHOULD'VE... RUBBLE...MURDER...
I SEE THAT TURNED OUT WONDERFULLY.
GARFIELD... HOW IS VICTOR?
HE'S...
IT'S GONNA TAKE SOME TIME, BUT IT LOOKS LIKE HE'LL MAKE IT.
WHAT ABOUT THE GUY WHO DID THIS TO HIM? VIGILANTE. DID YOU TOSS HIM IN THE CLINK?
WE STILL NEED HIS HELP.
OH REALLY? HOW'S HE GONNA DO THAT? BY PUTTING ANOTHER TITAN IN THE HOSPITAL?
GAR, WE REALLY NEED TO TALK ABOUT--
WHERE'S WALLY?
WHERE DO YOU THINK HE IS?

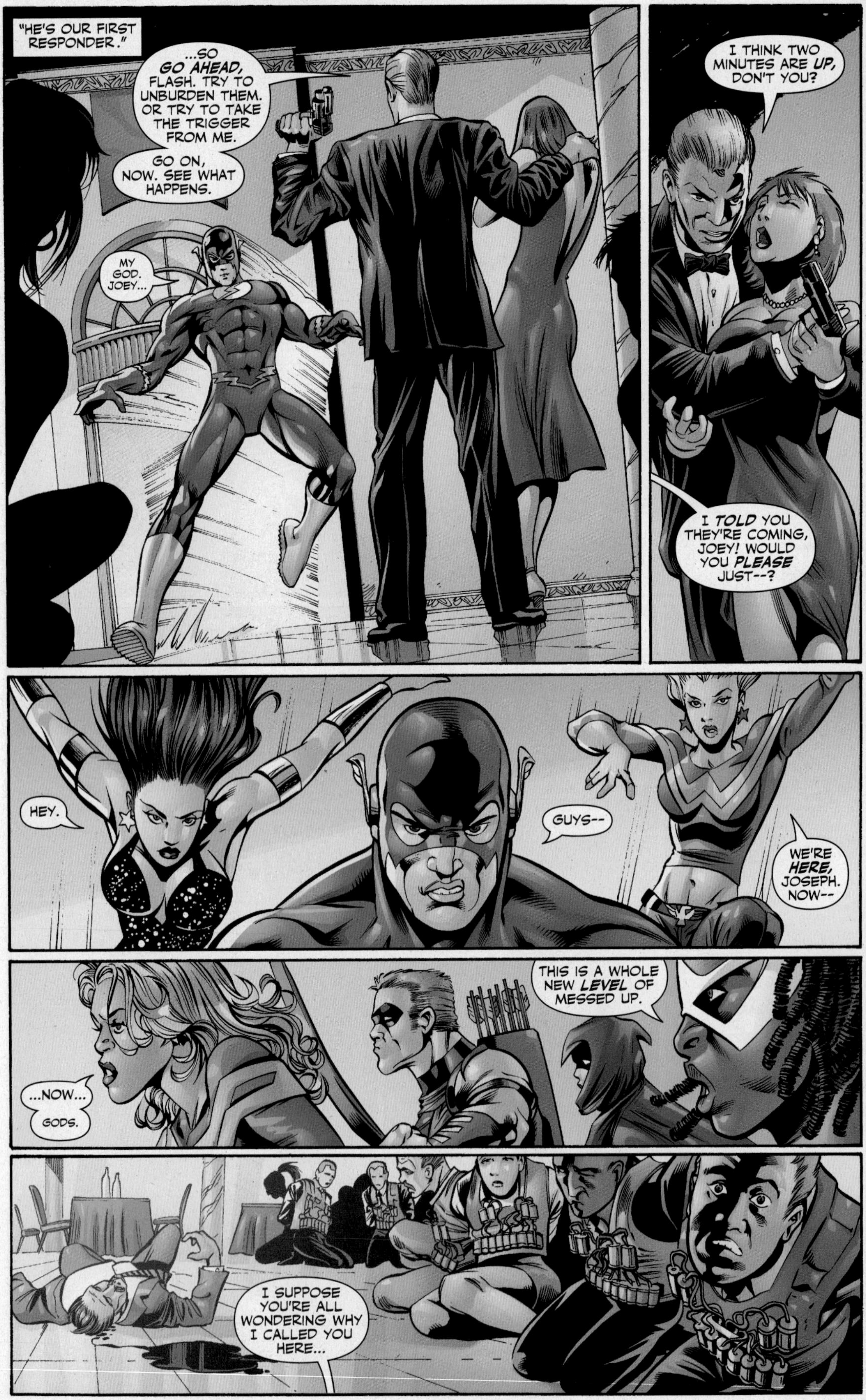
"HE'S OUR FIRST RESPONDER."
...SO GO AHEAD, FLASH. TRY TO UNBURDEN THEM. OR TRY TO TAKE THE TRIGGER FROM ME.
GO ON, NOW. SEE WHAT HAPPENS.
MY GOD. JOEY...
I THINK TWO MINUTES ARE UP, DON'T YOU?
I TOLD YOU THEY'RE COMING, JOEY! WOULD YOU PLEASE JUST--?
HEY.
GUYS--
WE'RE HERE, JOSEPH. NOW--
...NOW...
GODS.
THIS IS A WHOLE NEW LEVEL OF MESSED UP.
I SUPPOSE YOU'RE ALL WONDERING WHY I CALLED YOU HERE...

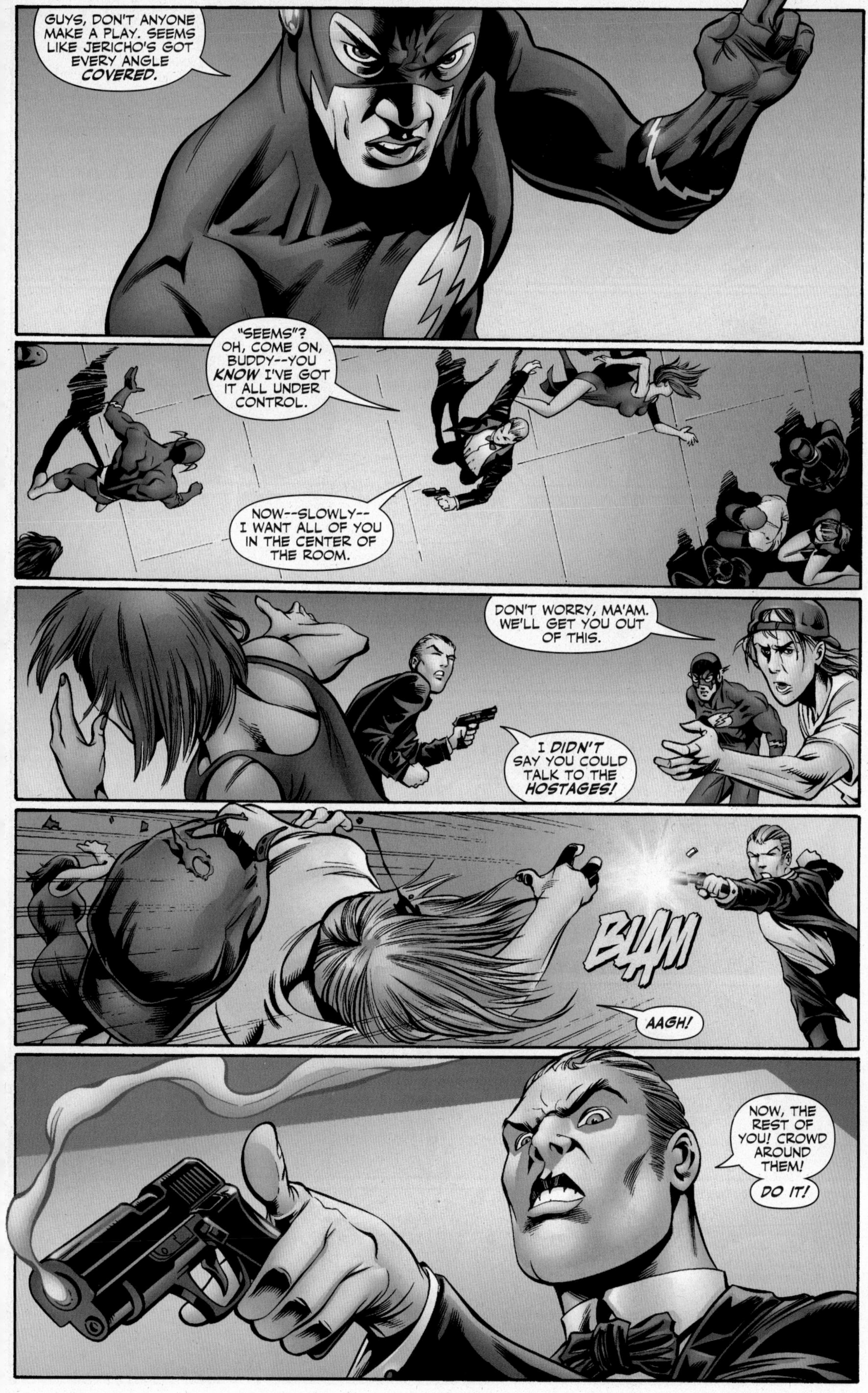
GUYS, DON'T ANYONE MAKE A PLAY. SEEMS LIKE JERICHO'S GOT EVERY ANGLE *COVERED.*
"SEEMS"? OH, COME ON, BUDDY--YOU *KNOW* I'VE GOT IT ALL UNDER CONTROL.
NOW--SLOWLY--I WANT ALL OF YOU IN THE CENTER OF THE ROOM.
DON'T WORRY, MA'AM. WE'LL GET YOU OUT OF THIS.
I *DIDN'T* SAY YOU COULD TALK TO THE *HOSTAGES!*
BLAM
AAGH!
NOW, THE REST OF YOU! CROWD AROUND THEM!
DO IT!

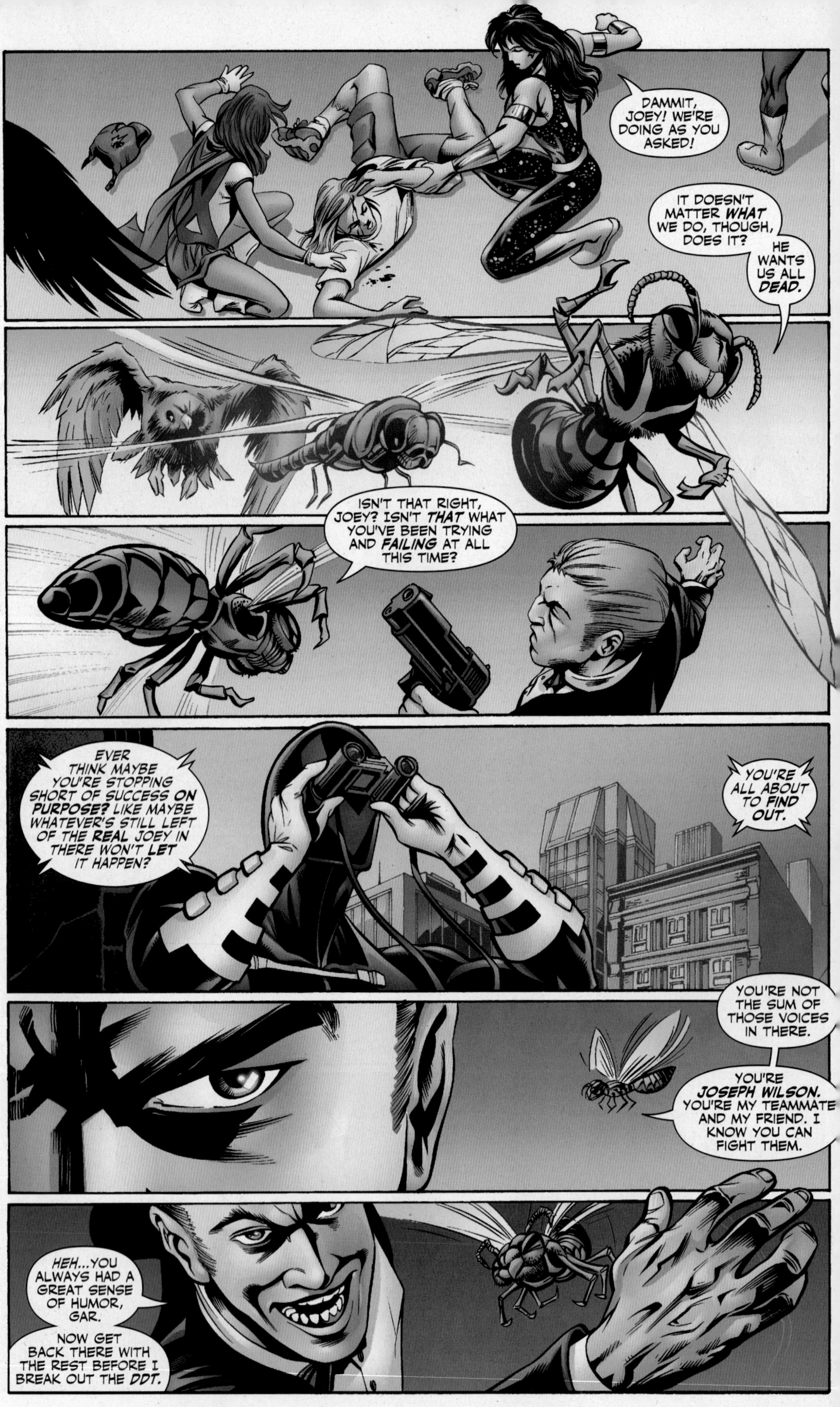
DAMMIT, JOEY! WE'RE DOING AS YOU ASKED!
IT DOESN'T MATTER WHAT WE DO, THOUGH, DOES IT?
HE WANTS US ALL DEAD.
ISN'T THAT RIGHT, JOEY? ISN'T THAT WHAT YOU'VE BEEN TRYING AND FAILING AT ALL THIS TIME?
EVER THINK MAYBE YOU'RE STOPPING SHORT OF SUCCESS ON PURPOSE? LIKE MAYBE WHATEVER'S STILL LEFT OF THE REAL JOEY IN THERE WON'T LET IT HAPPEN?
YOU'RE ALL ABOUT TO FIND OUT.
YOU'RE NOT THE SUM OF THOSE VOICES IN THERE.
YOU'RE JOSEPH WILSON. YOU'RE MY TEAMMATE AND MY FRIEND. I KNOW YOU CAN FIGHT THEM.
HEH...YOU ALWAYS HAD A GREAT SENSE OF HUMOR, GAR.
NOW GET BACK THERE WITH THE REST BEFORE I BREAK OUT THE DDT.

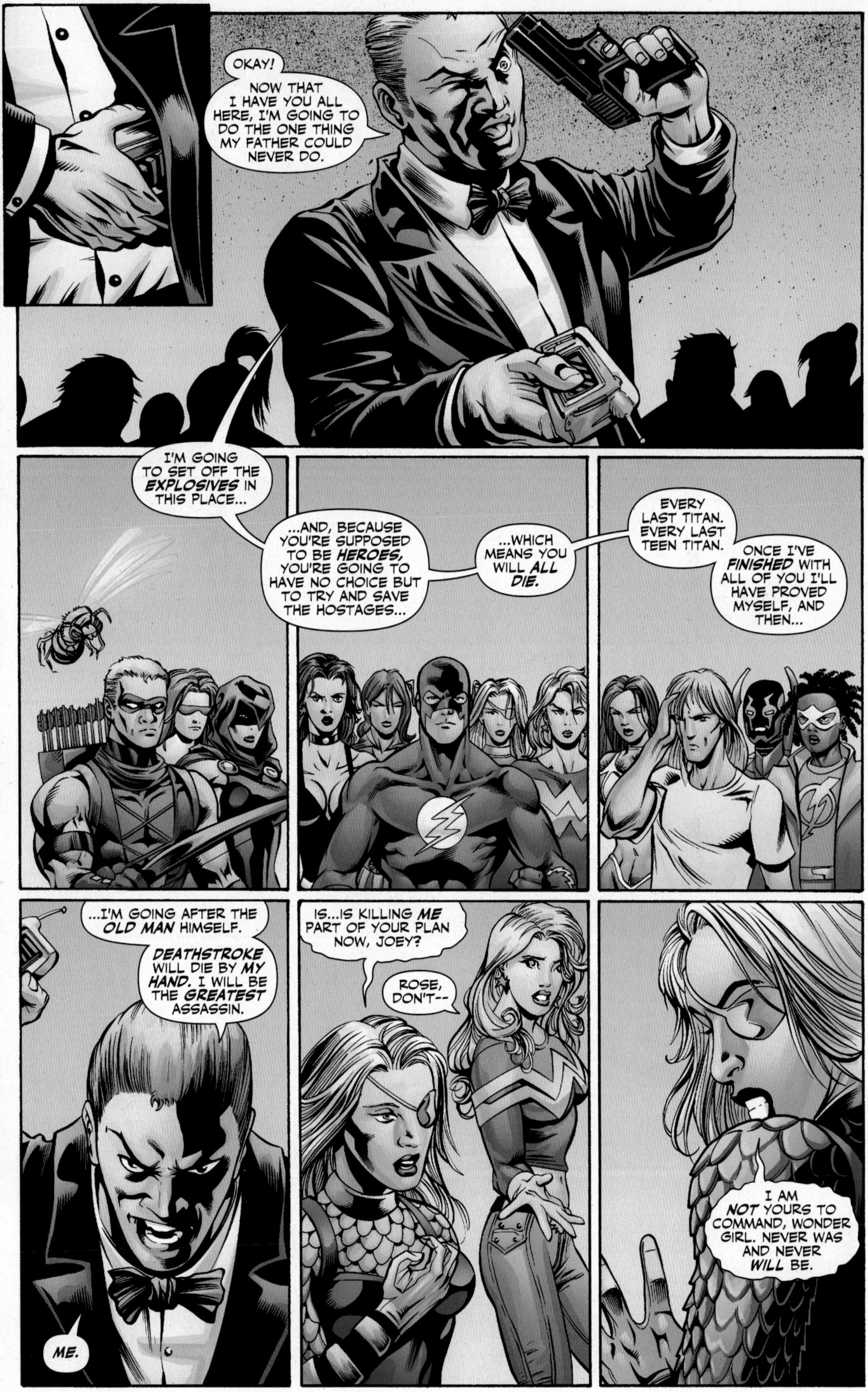
OKAY!
NOW THAT I HAVE YOU ALL HERE, I'M GOING TO DO THE ONE THING MY FATHER COULD NEVER DO.
I'M GOING TO SET OFF THE EXPLOSIVES IN THIS PLACE...
...AND, BECAUSE YOU'RE SUPPOSED TO BE HEROES, YOU'RE GOING TO HAVE NO CHOICE BUT TO TRY AND SAVE THE HOSTAGES...
...WHICH MEANS YOU WILL ALL DIE.
EVERY LAST TITAN. EVERY LAST TEEN TITAN.
ONCE I'VE FINISHED WITH ALL OF YOU I'LL HAVE PROVED MYSELF, AND THEN...
...I'M GOING AFTER THE OLD MAN HIMSELF.
DEATHSTROKE WILL DIE BY MY HAND. I WILL BE THE GREATEST ASSASSIN.
ME.
IS...IS KILLING ME PART OF YOUR PLAN NOW, JOEY?
ROSE, DON'T--
I AM NOT YOURS TO COMMAND, WONDER GIRL. NEVER WAS AND NEVER WILL BE.

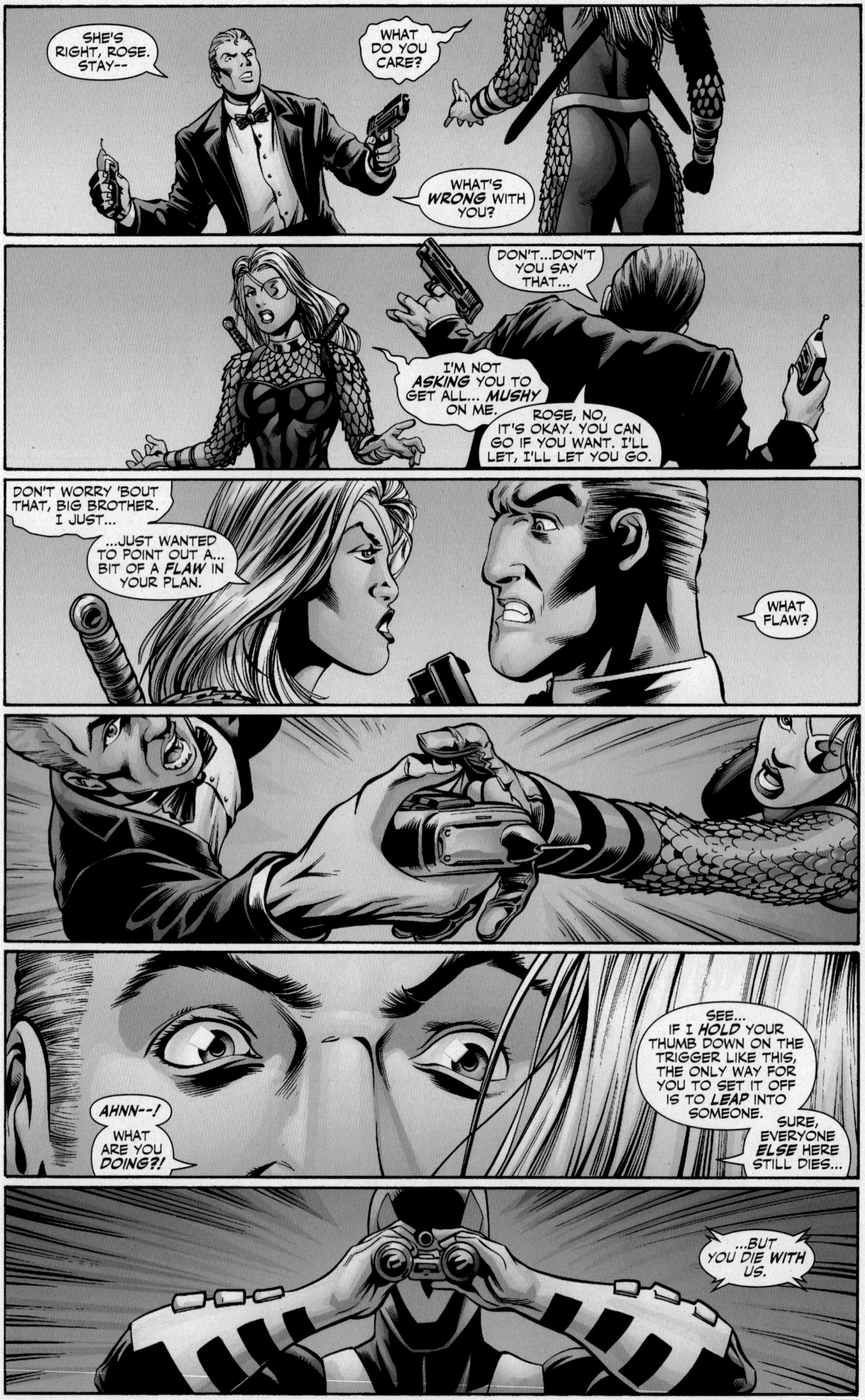
SHE'S RIGHT, ROSE. STAY--
WHAT DO YOU CARE?
WHAT'S WRONG WITH YOU?
DON'T...DON'T YOU SAY THAT...
I'M NOT ASKING YOU TO GET ALL... MUSHY ON ME.
ROSE, NO, IT'S OKAY. YOU CAN GO IF YOU WANT. I'LL LET, I'LL LET YOU GO.
DON'T WORRY 'BOUT THAT, BIG BROTHER. I JUST...
...JUST WANTED TO POINT OUT A... BIT OF A FLAW IN YOUR PLAN.
WHAT FLAW?
AHNN--! WHAT ARE YOU DOING?!
SEE... IF I HOLD YOUR THUMB DOWN ON THE TRIGGER LIKE THIS, THE ONLY WAY FOR YOU TO SET IT OFF IS TO LEAP INTO SOMEONE.
SURE, EVERYONE ELSE HERE STILL DIES...
...BUT YOU DIE WITH US.

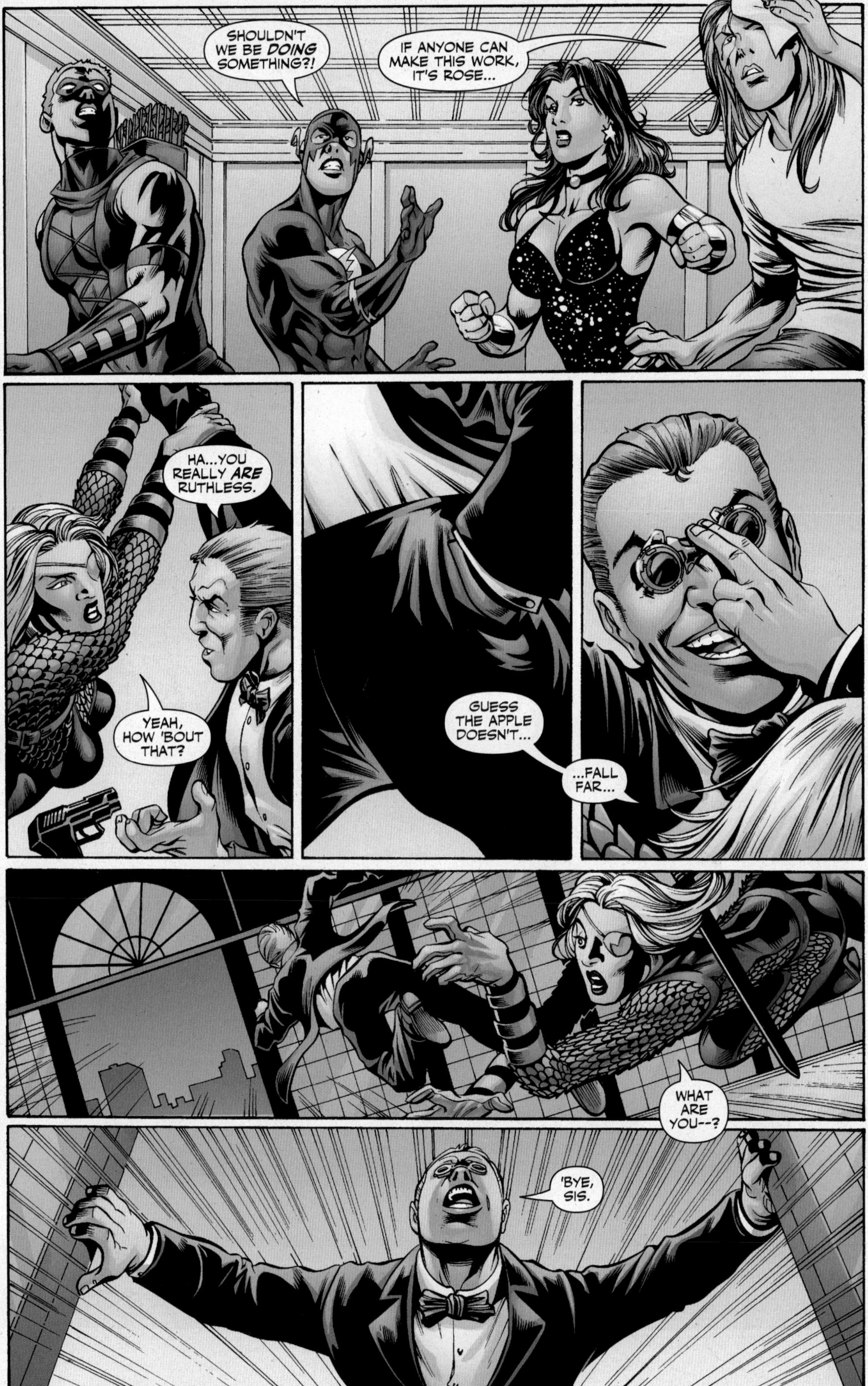
SHOULDN'T WE BE *DOING* SOMETHING?!
IF ANYONE CAN MAKE THIS WORK, IT'S ROSE...
HA...YOU REALLY *ARE* RUTHLESS.
YEAH, HOW 'BOUT THAT?
GUESS THE APPLE DOESN'T...
...FALL FAR...
WHAT ARE YOU--?
'BYE, SIS.

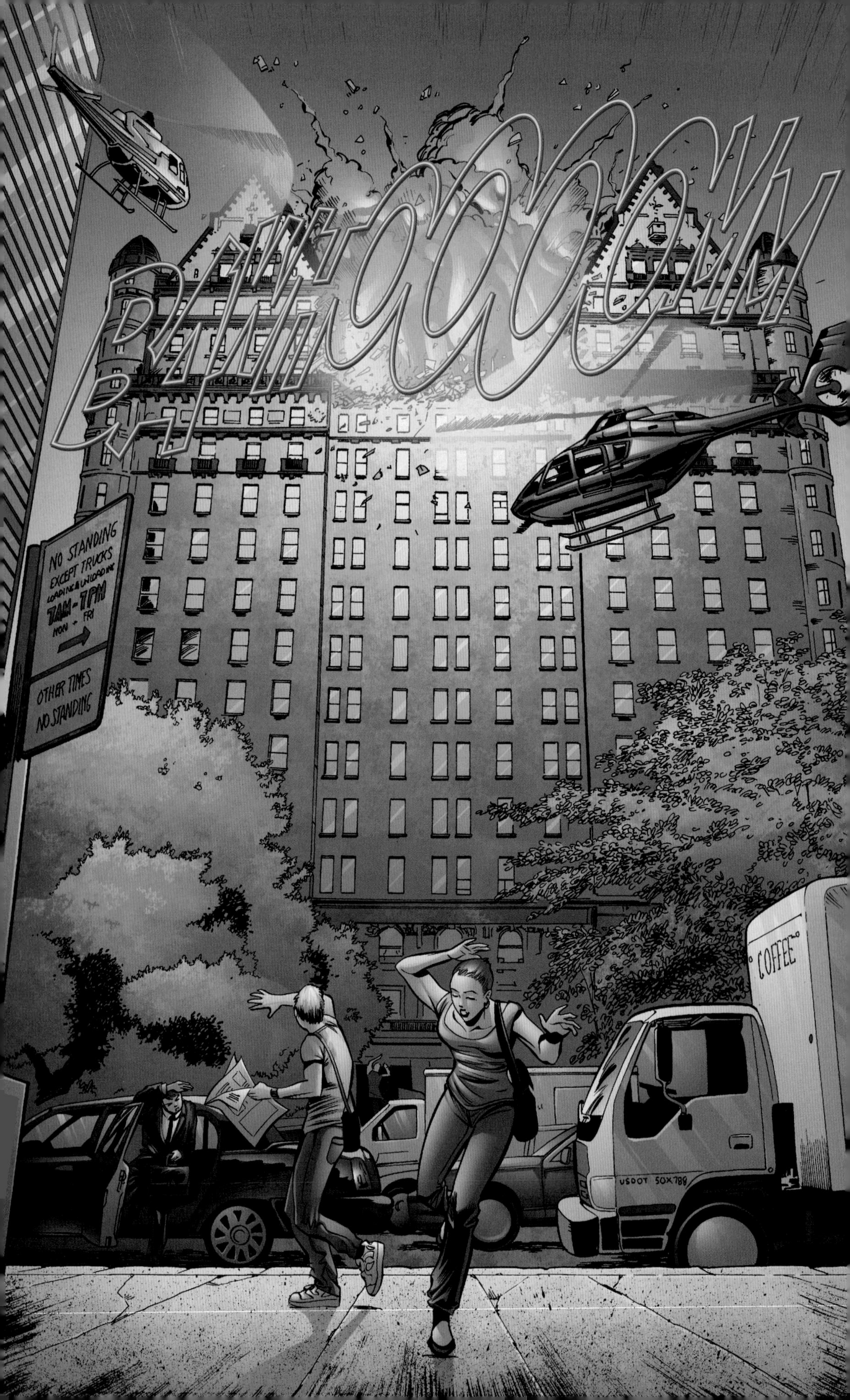
NO STANDING
EXCEPT TRUCKS
LOADING & UNLOADING
7AM - 7PM
MON - FRI
OTHER TIMES
NO STANDING
COFFEE
USDOT 50X788

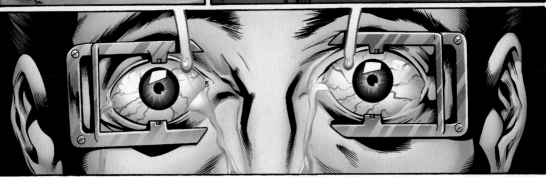

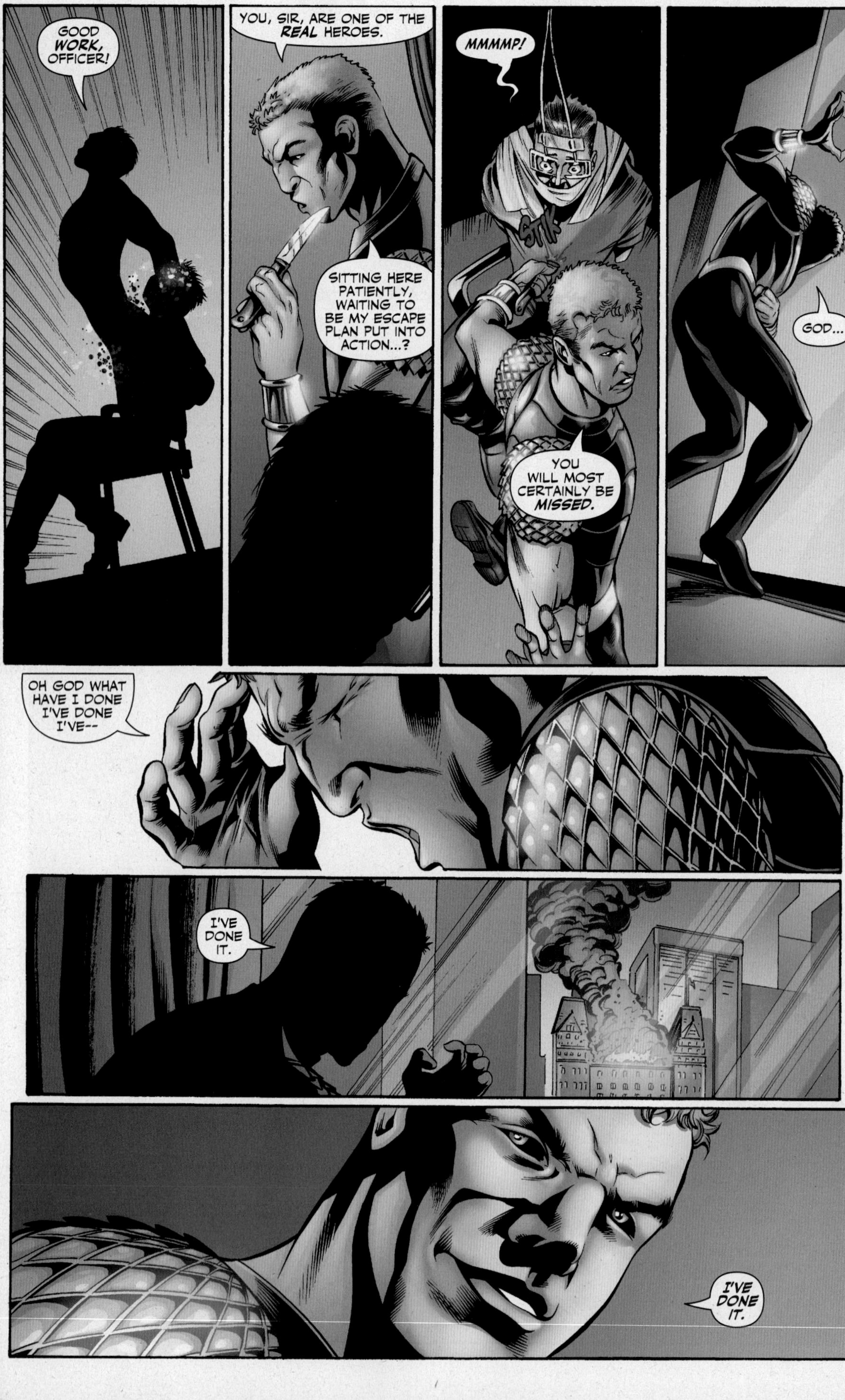
GOOD WORK, OFFICER!
YOU, SIR, ARE ONE OF THE REAL HEROES.
SITTING HERE PATIENTLY, WAITING TO BE MY ESCAPE PLAN PUT INTO ACTION...?
MMMMP!
YOU WILL MOST CERTAINLY BE MISSED.
GOD...
OH GOD WHAT HAVE I DONE I'VE DONE I'VE--
I'VE DONE IT.
I'VE DONE IT.

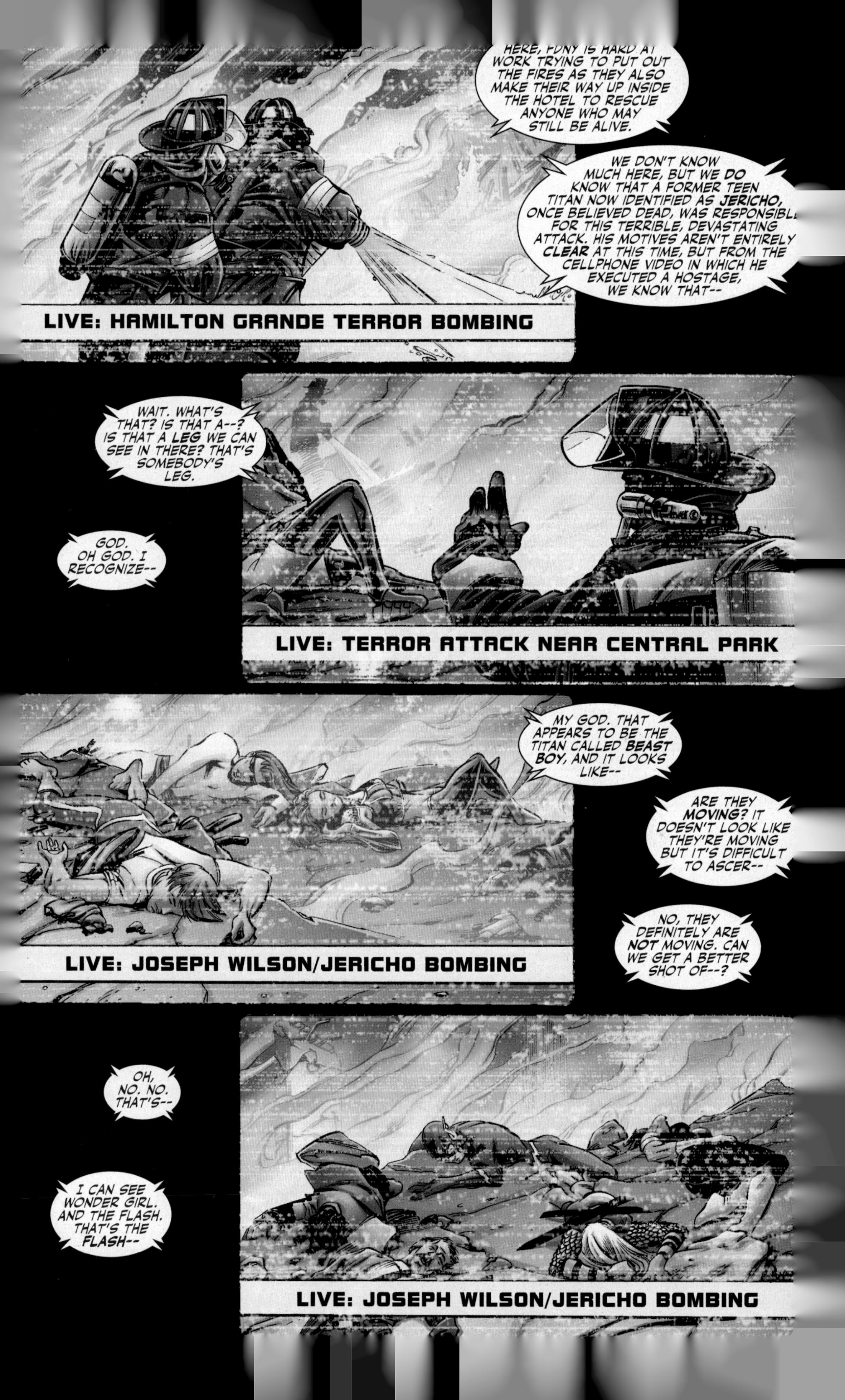
HERE, FDNY IS HARD AT WORK TRYING TO PUT OUT THE FIRES AS THEY ALSO MAKE THEIR WAY UP INSIDE THE HOTEL TO RESCUE ANYONE WHO MAY STILL BE ALIVE.
WE DON'T KNOW MUCH HERE, BUT WE DO KNOW THAT A FORMER TEEN TITAN NOW IDENTIFIED AS JERICHO, ONCE BELIEVED DEAD, WAS RESPONSIBLE FOR THIS TERRIBLE, DEVASTATING ATTACK. HIS MOTIVES AREN'T ENTIRELY CLEAR AT THIS TIME, BUT FROM THE CELLPHONE VIDEO IN WHICH HE EXECUTED A HOSTAGE, WE KNOW THAT--
LIVE: HAMILTON GRANDE TERROR BOMBING
WAIT. WHAT'S THAT? IS THAT A--? IS THAT A LEG WE CAN SEE IN THERE? THAT'S SOMEBODY'S LEG.
GOD. OH GOD. I RECOGNIZE--
LIVE: TERROR ATTACK NEAR CENTRAL PARK
MY GOD. THAT APPEARS TO BE THE TITAN CALLED BEAST BOY, AND IT LOOKS LIKE--
ARE THEY MOVING? IT DOESN'T LOOK LIKE THEY'RE MOVING BUT IT'S DIFFICULT TO ASCER--
NO, THEY DEFINITELY ARE NOT MOVING. CAN WE GET A BETTER SHOT OF--?
LIVE: JOSEPH WILSON/JERICHO BOMBING
OH, NO. NO. THAT'S--
I CAN SEE WONDER GIRL. AND THE FLASH. THAT'S THE FLASH--
LIVE: JOSEPH WILSON/JERICHO BOMBING

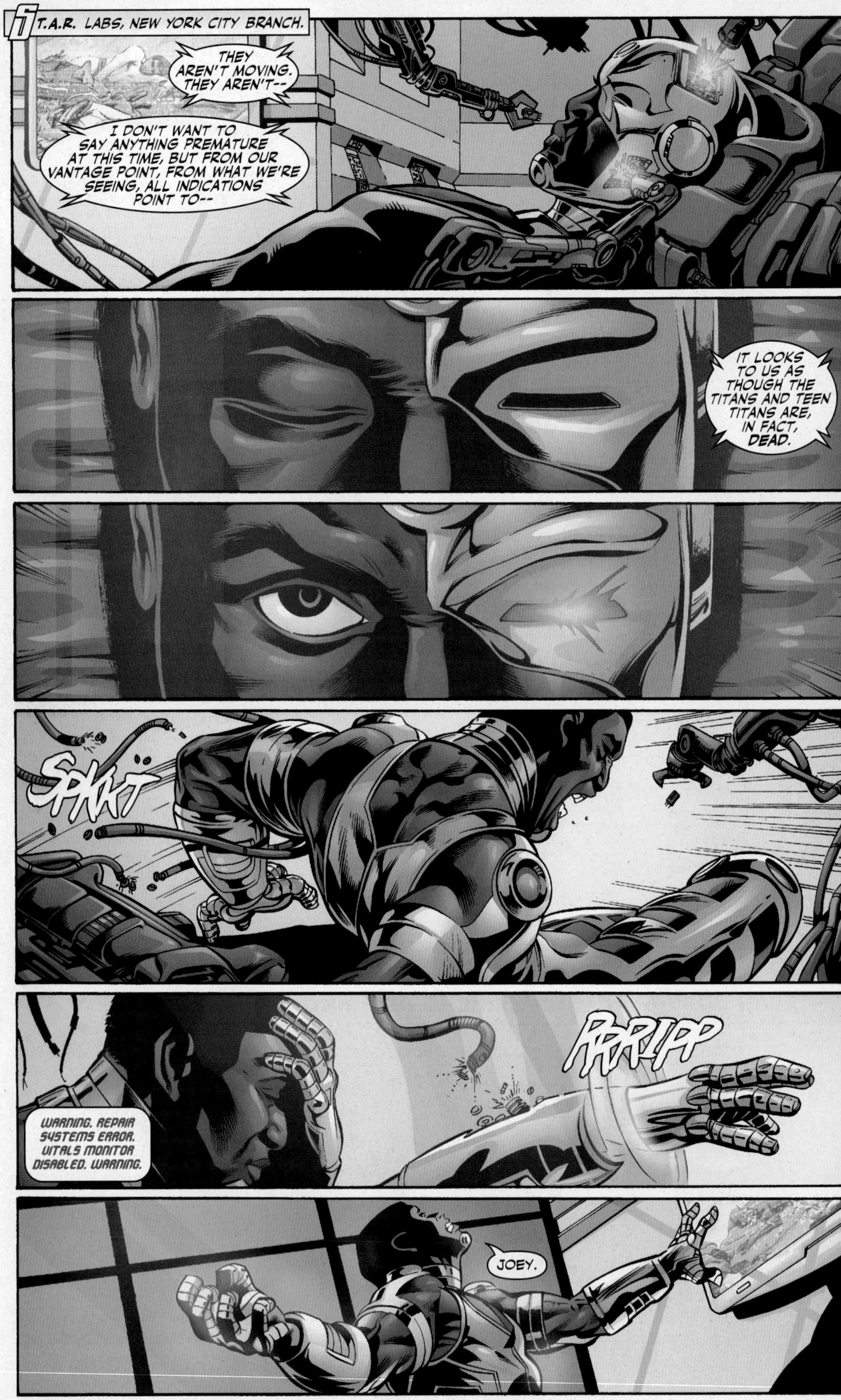
5
T.A.R. LABS, NEW YORK CITY BRANCH.
THEY AREN'T MOVING. THEY AREN'T--
I DON'T WANT TO SAY ANYTHING PREMATURE AT THIS TIME, BUT FROM OUR VANTAGE POINT, FROM WHAT WE'RE SEEING, ALL INDICATIONS POINT TO--
IT LOOKS TO US AS THOUGH THE TITANS AND TEEN TITANS ARE, IN FACT, DEAD.
SPKKT
RRRIPP
WARNING. REPAIR SYSTEMS ERROR. VITALS MONITOR DISABLED. WARNING.
JOEY.

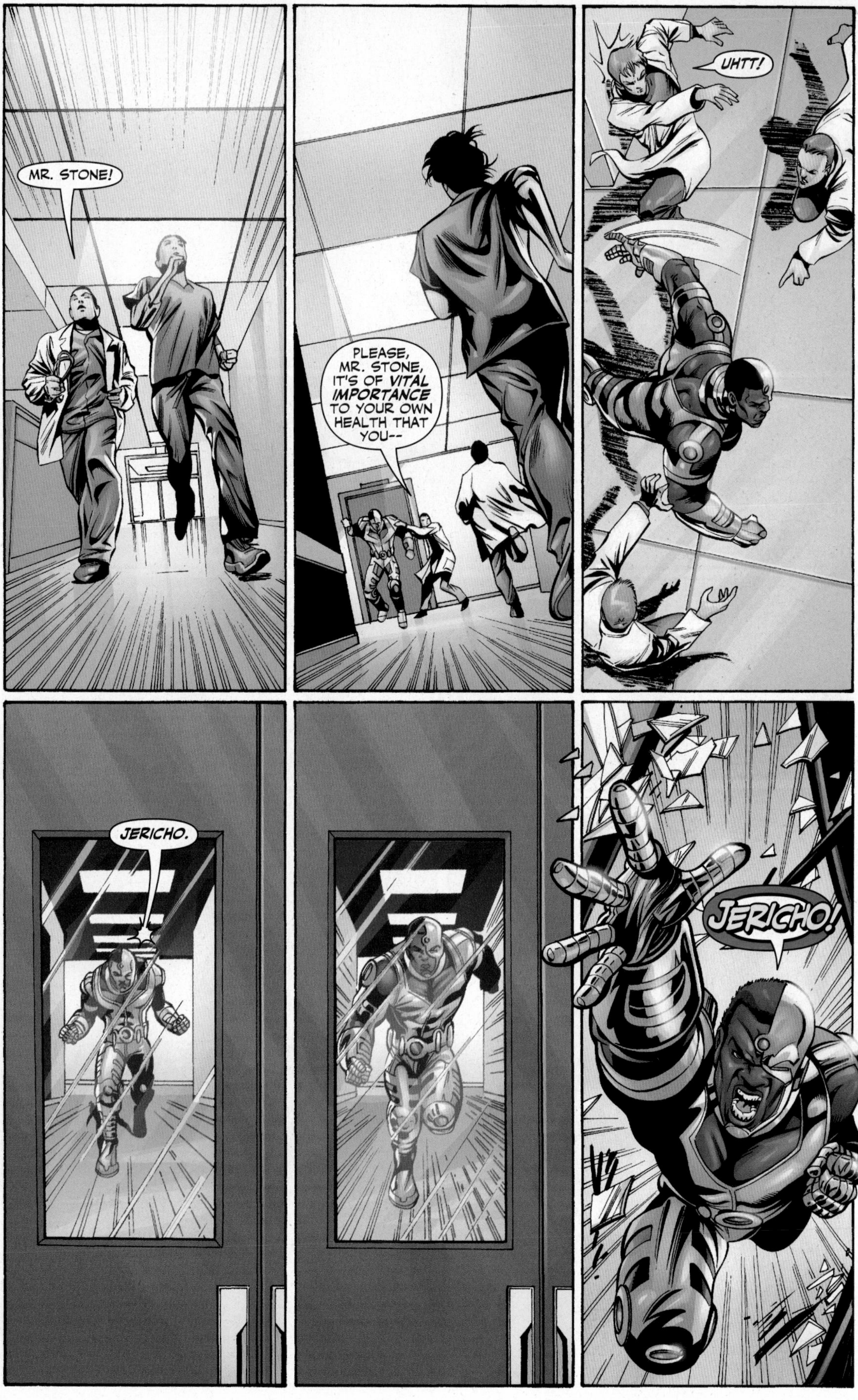
MR. STONE!
PLEASE, MR. STONE, IT'S OF VITAL IMPORTANCE TO YOUR OWN HEALTH THAT YOU--
UHTT!
JERICHO.
JERICHO!

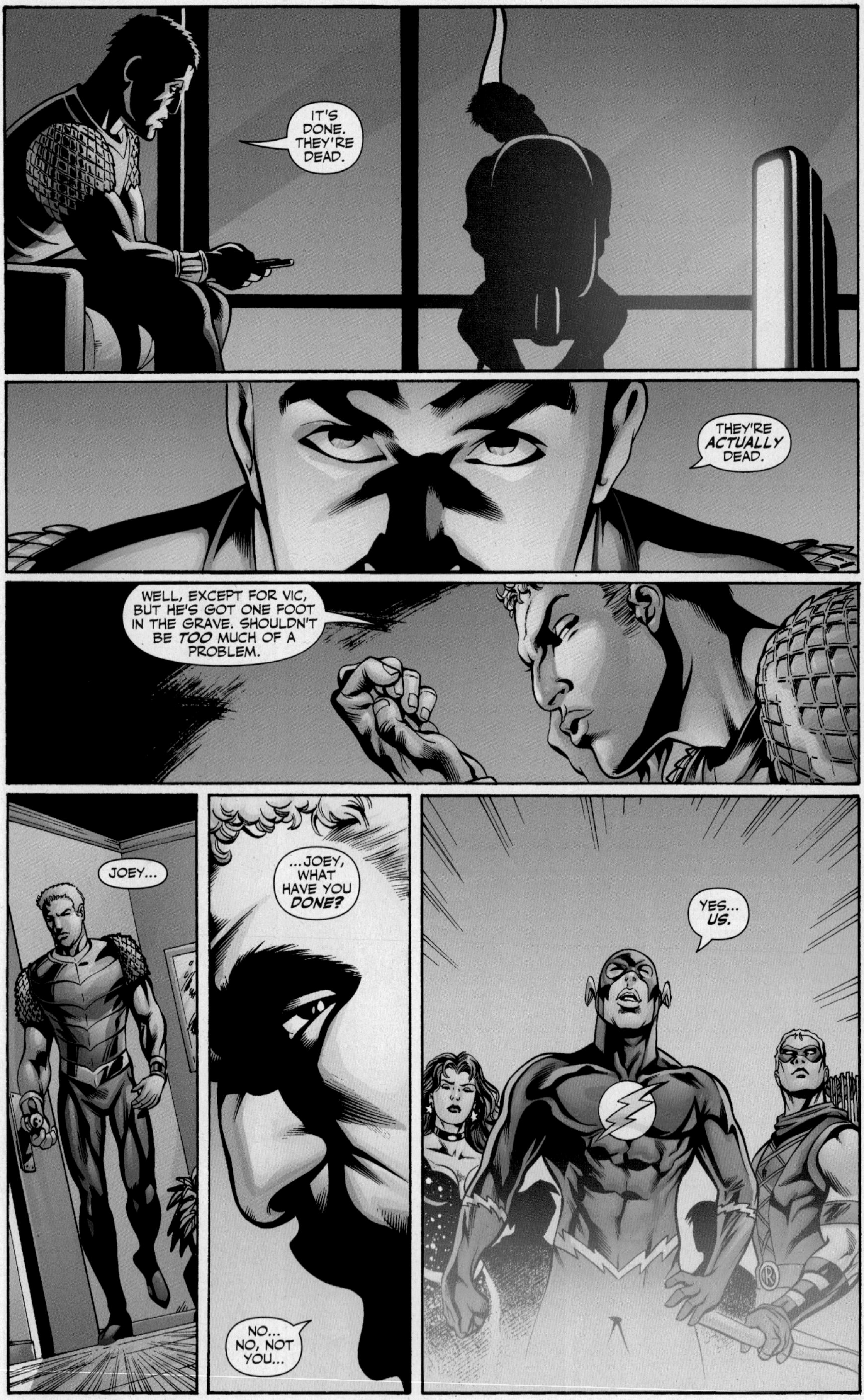
IT'S DONE. THEY'RE DEAD.
THEY'RE *ACTUALLY* DEAD.
WELL, EXCEPT FOR VIC, BUT HE'S GOT ONE FOOT IN THE GRAVE. SHOULDN'T BE *TOO* MUCH OF A PROBLEM.
JOEY...
...JOEY, WHAT HAVE YOU *DONE?*
NO... NO, NOT YOU...
YES... *US.*

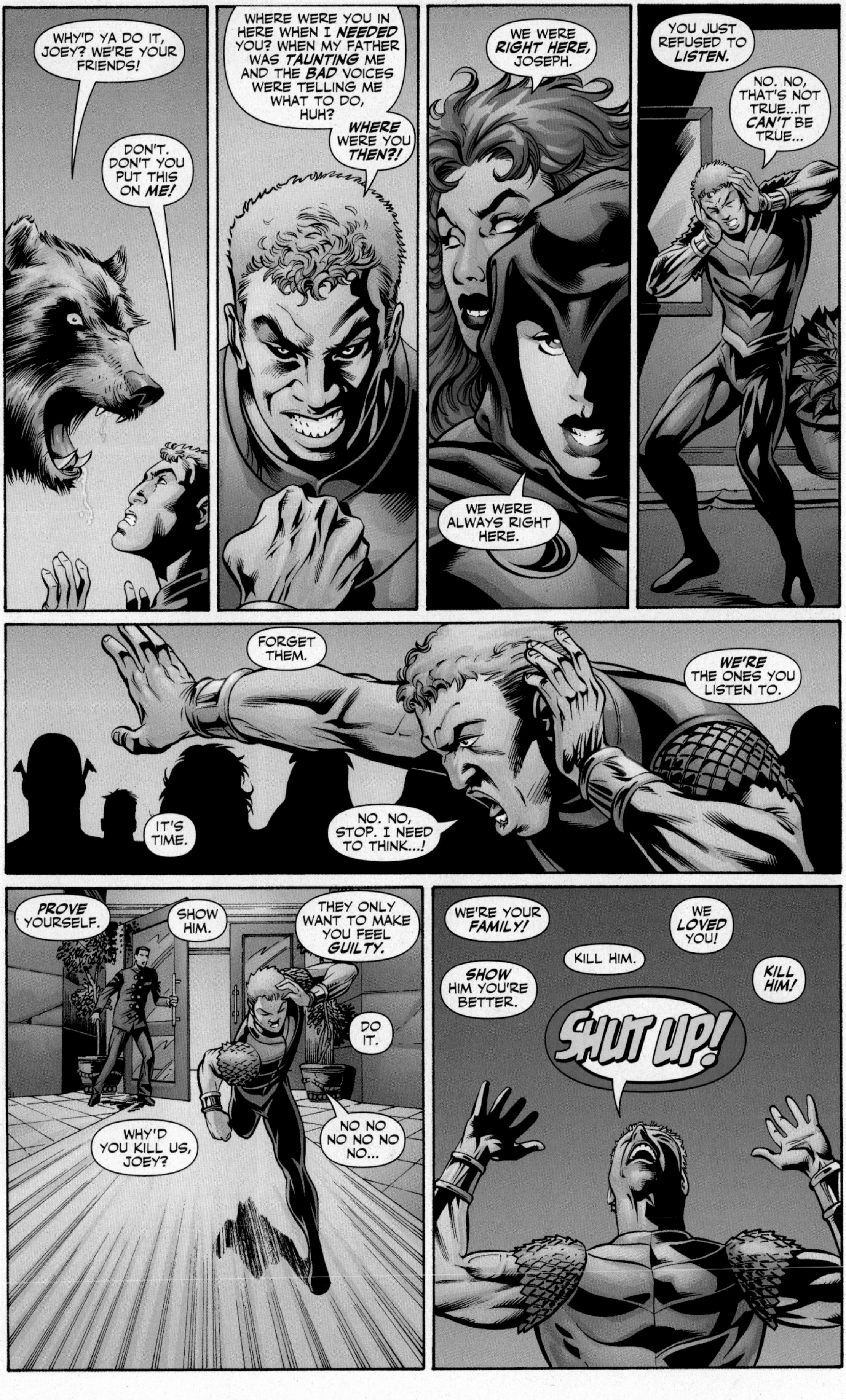
WHY'D YA DO IT, JOEY? WE'RE YOUR FRIENDS!
DON'T. DON'T YOU PUT THIS ON *ME!*
WHERE WERE YOU IN HERE WHEN I *NEEDED* YOU? WHEN MY FATHER WAS *TAUNTING* ME AND THE *BAD* VOICES WERE TELLING ME WHAT TO DO, HUH?
WHERE WERE YOU *THEN?!*
WE WERE *RIGHT HERE,* JOSEPH.
WE WERE ALWAYS RIGHT HERE.
YOU JUST REFUSED TO *LISTEN.*
NO. NO, THAT'S NOT TRUE...IT *CAN'T* BE TRUE...
FORGET THEM.
WE'RE THE ONES YOU LISTEN TO.
IT'S TIME.
NO. NO, STOP. I NEED TO THINK...!
PROVE YOURSELF.
SHOW HIM.
THEY ONLY WANT TO MAKE YOU FEEL *GUILTY.*
DO IT.
WHY'D YOU KILL US, JOEY?
NO NO NO NO NO NO...
WE'RE YOUR *FAMILY!*
WE *LOVED* YOU!
KILL HIM.
SHOW HIM YOU'RE BETTER.
KILL HIM!
SHUT UP!

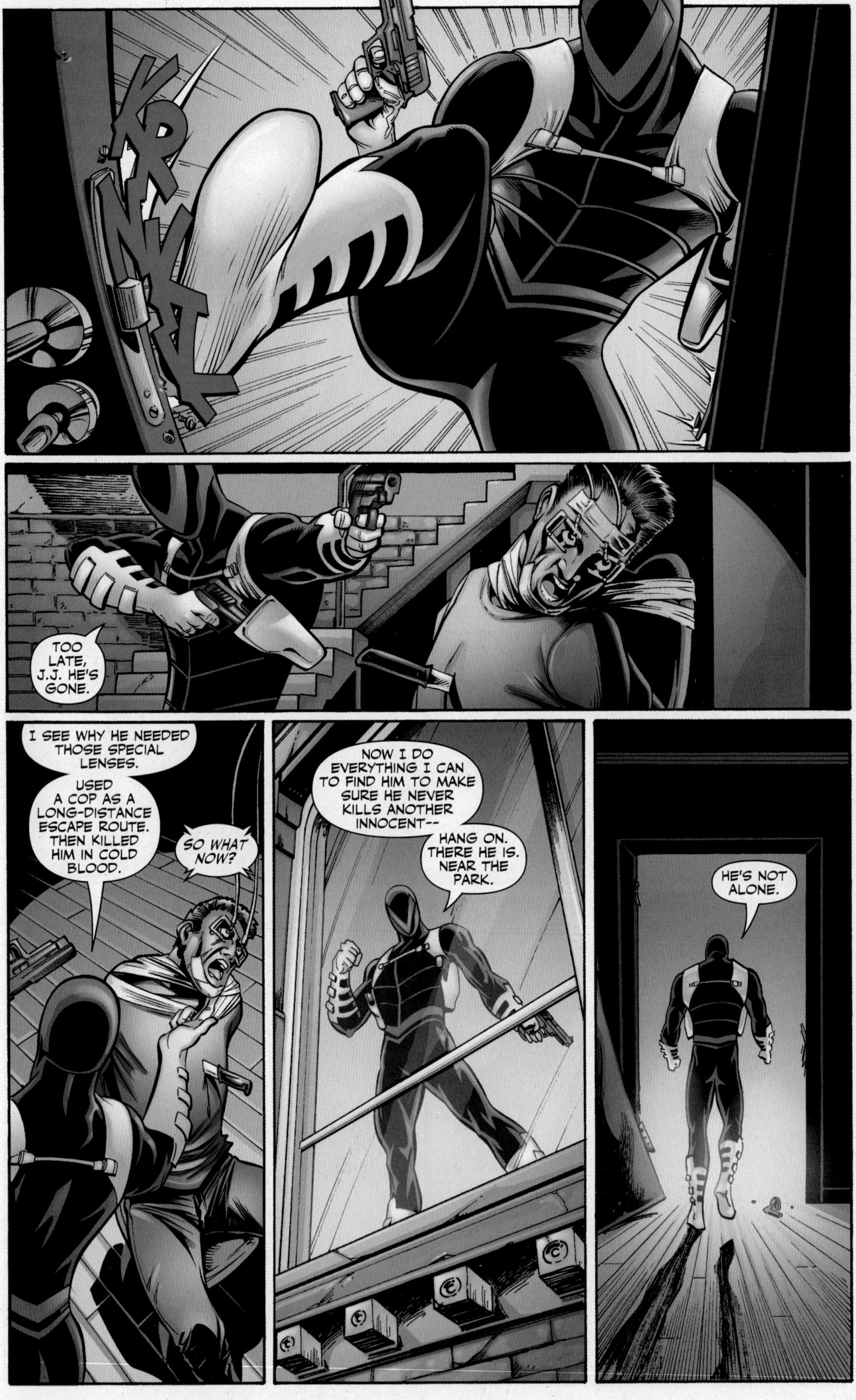
KRNKK
TOO LATE, J.J. HE'S GONE.
I SEE WHY HE NEEDED THOSE SPECIAL LENSES.
USED A COP AS A LONG-DISTANCE ESCAPE ROUTE. THEN KILLED HIM IN COLD BLOOD.
SO WHAT NOW?
NOW I DO EVERYTHING I CAN TO FIND HIM TO MAKE SURE HE NEVER KILLS ANOTHER INNOCENT--
HANG ON. THERE HE IS. NEAR THE PARK.
HE'S NOT ALONE.

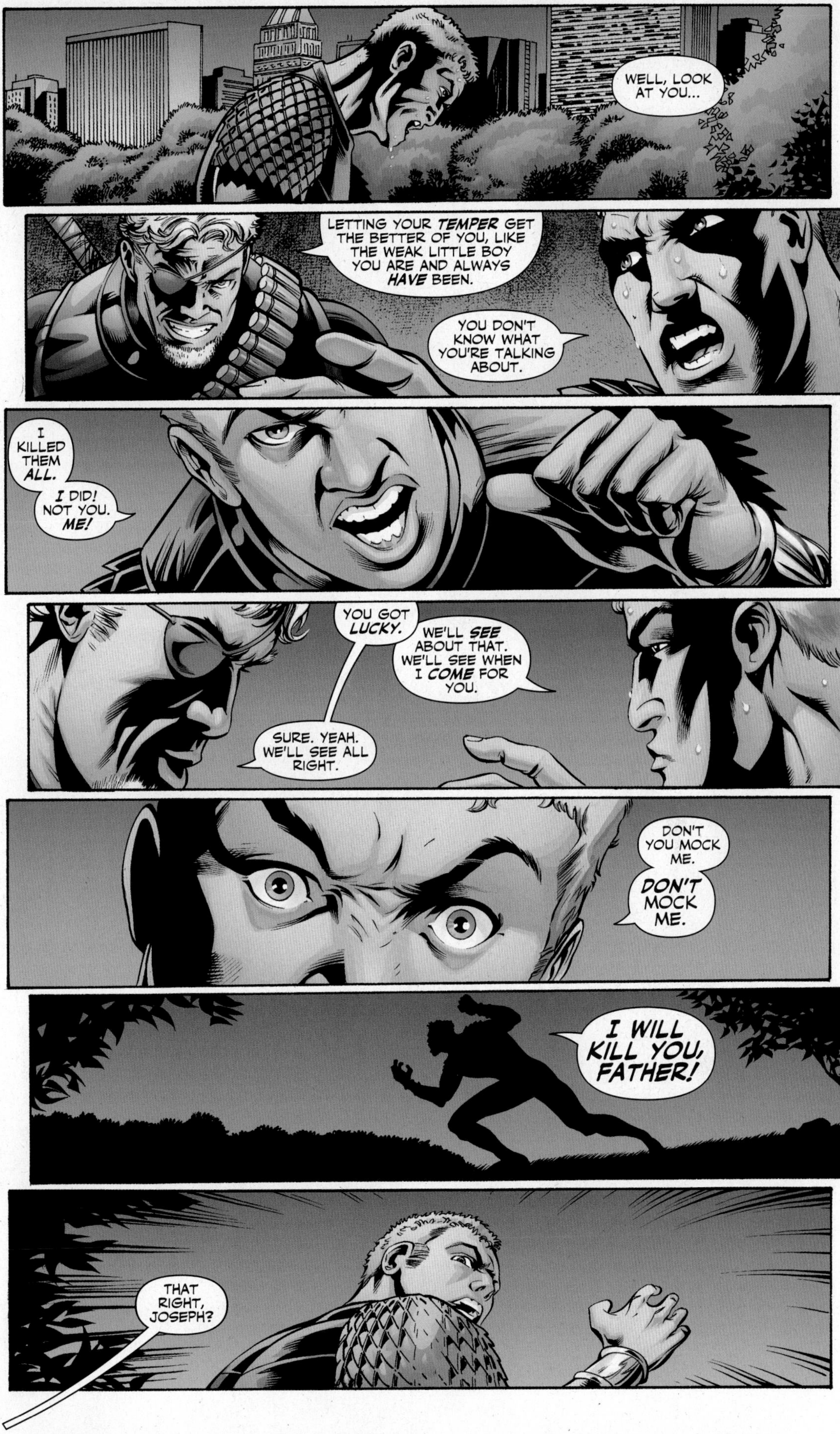
WELL, LOOK AT YOU...
LETTING YOUR TEMPER GET THE BETTER OF YOU, LIKE THE WEAK LITTLE BOY YOU ARE AND ALWAYS HAVE BEEN.
YOU DON'T KNOW WHAT YOU'RE TALKING ABOUT.
I KILLED THEM ALL.
I DID! NOT YOU. ME!
YOU GOT LUCKY.
WE'LL SEE ABOUT THAT. WE'LL SEE WHEN I COME FOR YOU.
SURE. YEAH. WE'LL SEE ALL RIGHT.
DON'T YOU MOCK ME.
DON'T MOCK ME.
I WILL KILL YOU, FATHER!
THAT RIGHT, JOSEPH?

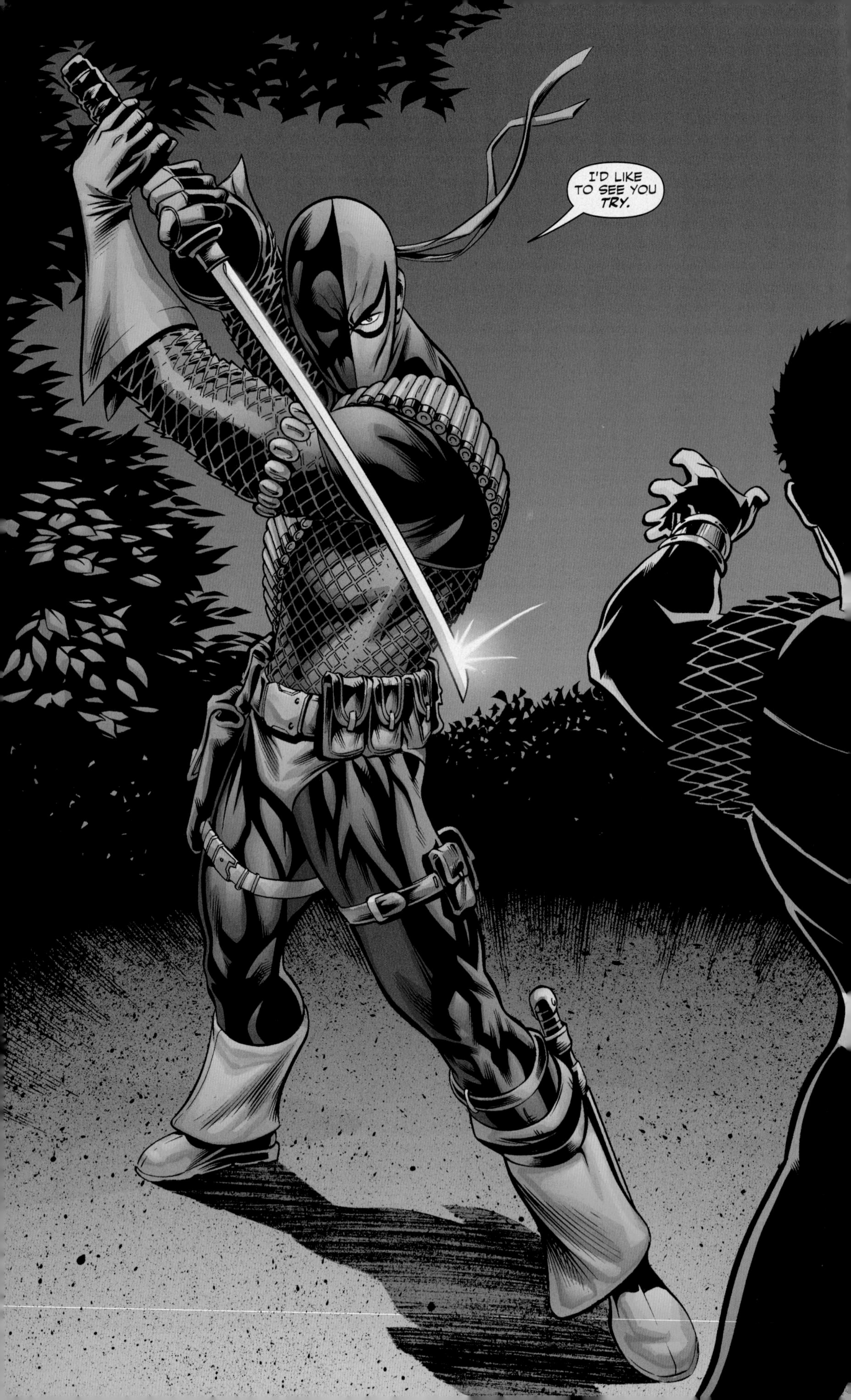
I'D LIKE TO SEE YOU TRY.

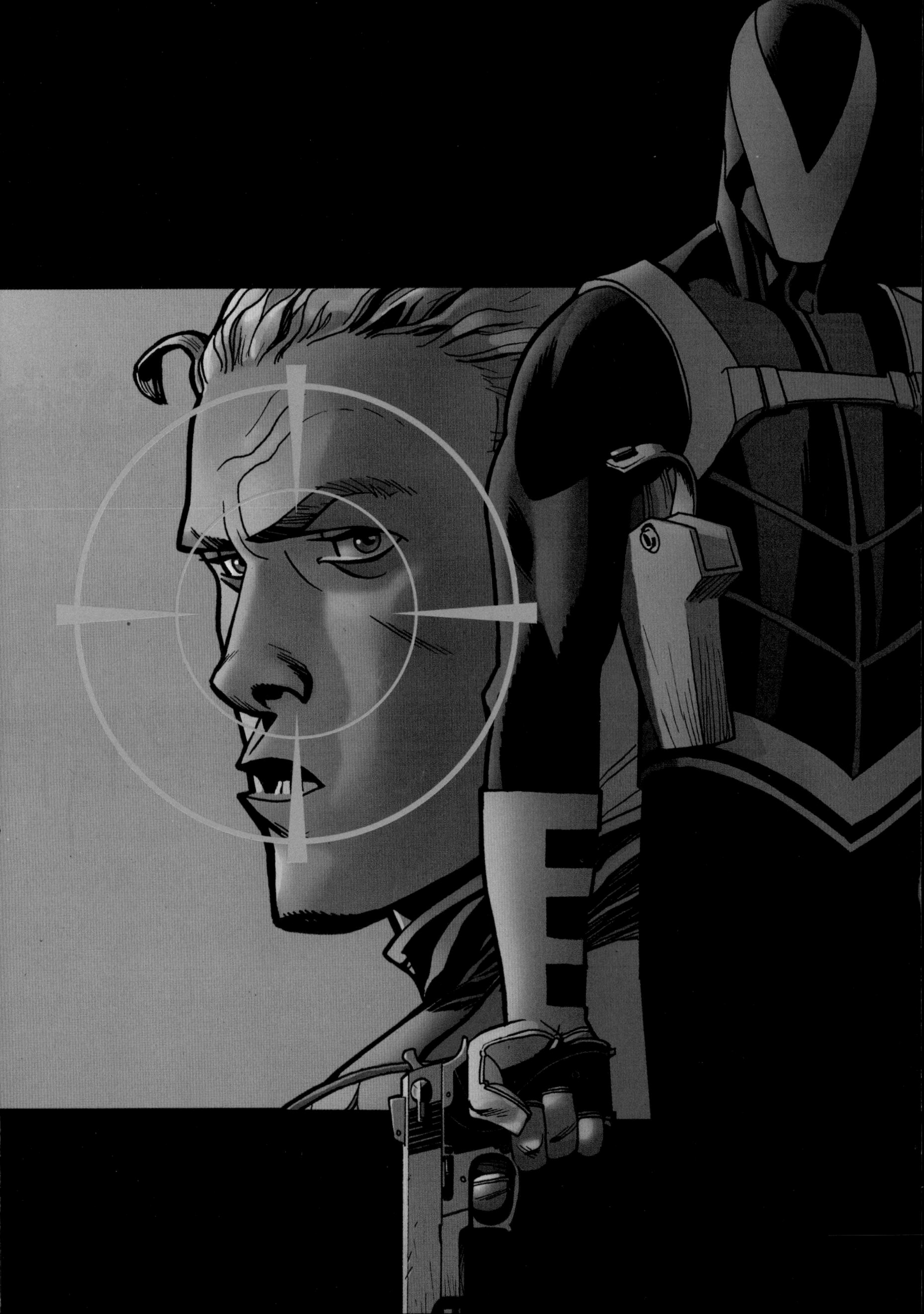

Deathtrap Conclusion: The Eyes of Joseph Wilson

Marv Wolfman
Writer

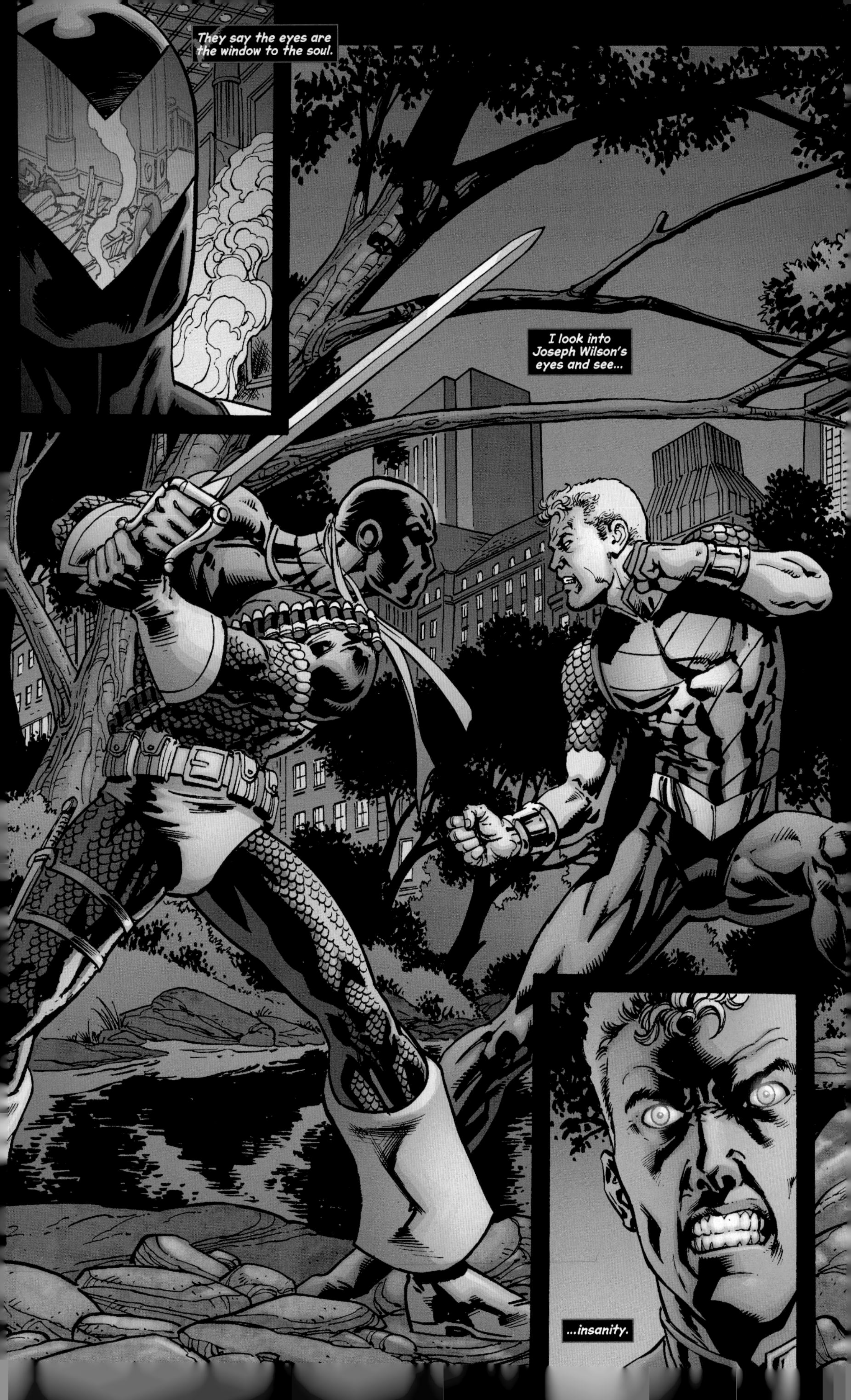
They say the eyes are the window to the soul.
I look into Joseph Wilson's eyes and see...
...insanity.

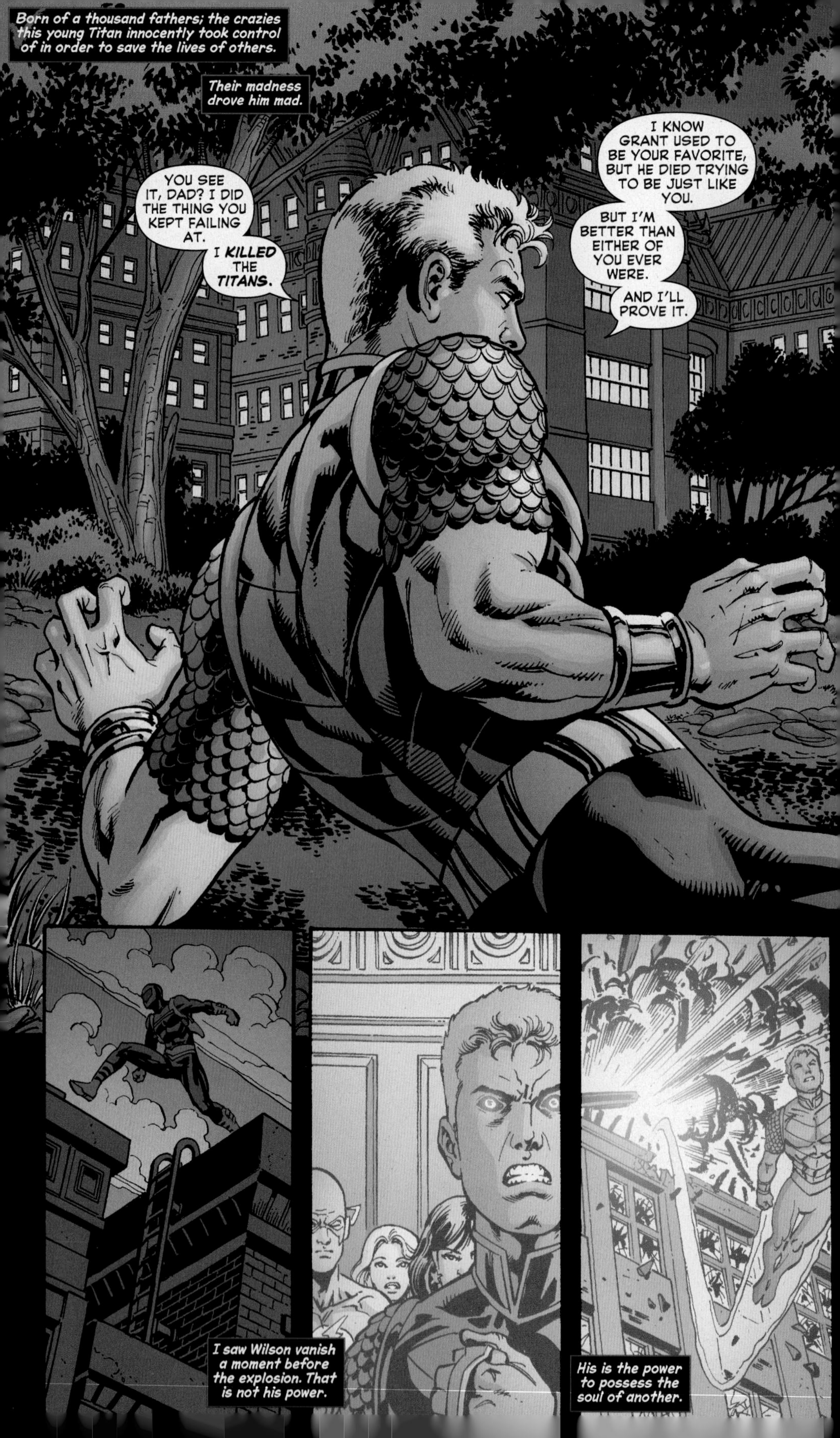
Born of a thousand fathers; the crazies this young Titan innocently took control of in order to save the lives of others.
Their madness drove him mad.
YOU SEE IT, DAD? I DID THE THING YOU KEPT FAILING AT.
I KILLED THE TITANS.
I KNOW GRANT USED TO BE YOUR FAVORITE, BUT HE DIED TRYING TO BE JUST LIKE YOU.
BUT I'M BETTER THAN EITHER OF YOU EVER WERE.
AND I'LL PROVE IT.
I saw Wilson vanish a moment before the explosion. That is not his power.
His is the power to possess the soul of another.

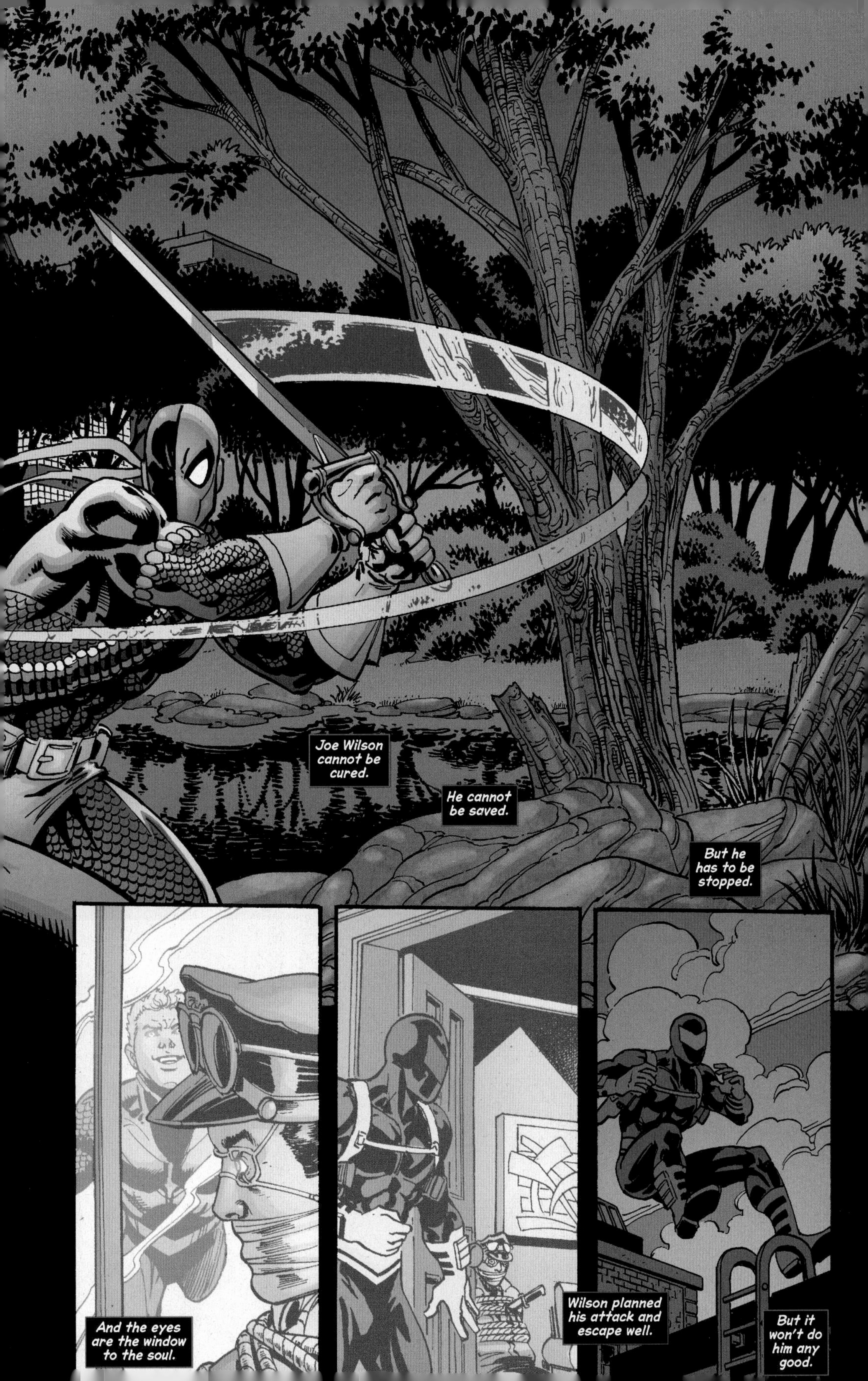
Joe Wilson cannot be cured.
He cannot be saved.
But he has to be stopped.
And the eyes are the window to the soul.
Wilson planned his attack and escape well.
But it won't do him any good.

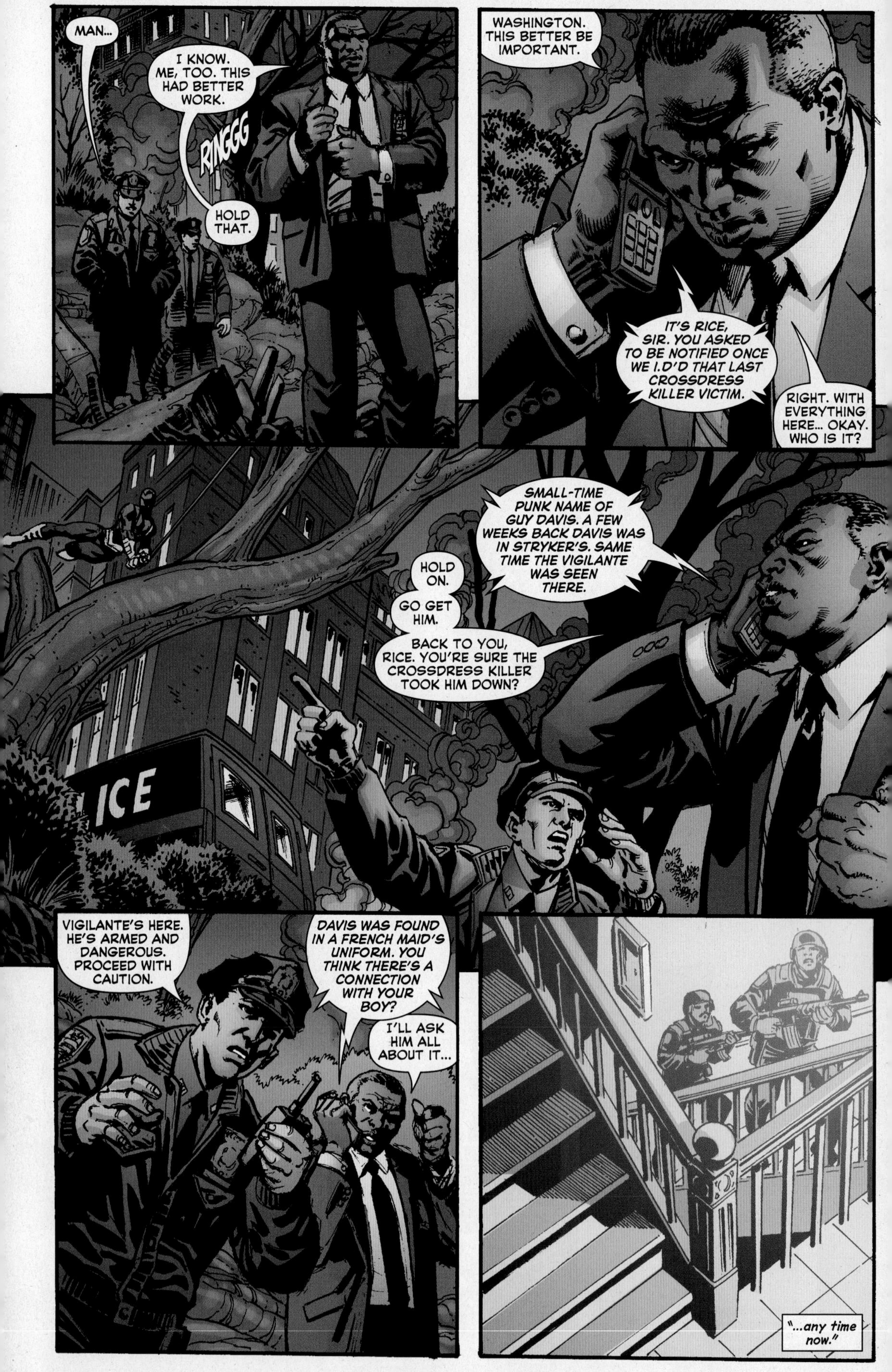
MAN...
I KNOW. ME, TOO. THIS HAD BETTER WORK.
RINGGG
HOLD THAT.
WASHINGTON. THIS BETTER BE IMPORTANT.
IT'S RICE, SIR. YOU ASKED TO BE NOTIFIED ONCE WE I.D'D THAT LAST CROSSDRESS KILLER VICTIM.
RIGHT. WITH EVERYTHING HERE... OKAY. WHO IS IT?
SMALL-TIME PUNK NAME OF GUY DAVIS. A FEW WEEKS BACK DAVIS WAS IN STRYKER'S. SAME TIME THE VIGILANTE WAS SEEN THERE.
HOLD ON.
GO GET HIM.
BACK TO YOU, RICE. YOU'RE SURE THE CROSSDRESS KILLER TOOK HIM DOWN?
ICE
VIGILANTE'S HERE. HE'S ARMED AND DANGEROUS. PROCEED WITH CAUTION.
DAVIS WAS FOUND IN A FRENCH MAID'S UNIFORM. YOU THINK THERE'S A CONNECTION WITH YOUR BOY?
I'LL ASK HIM ALL ABOUT IT...
"...any time now."

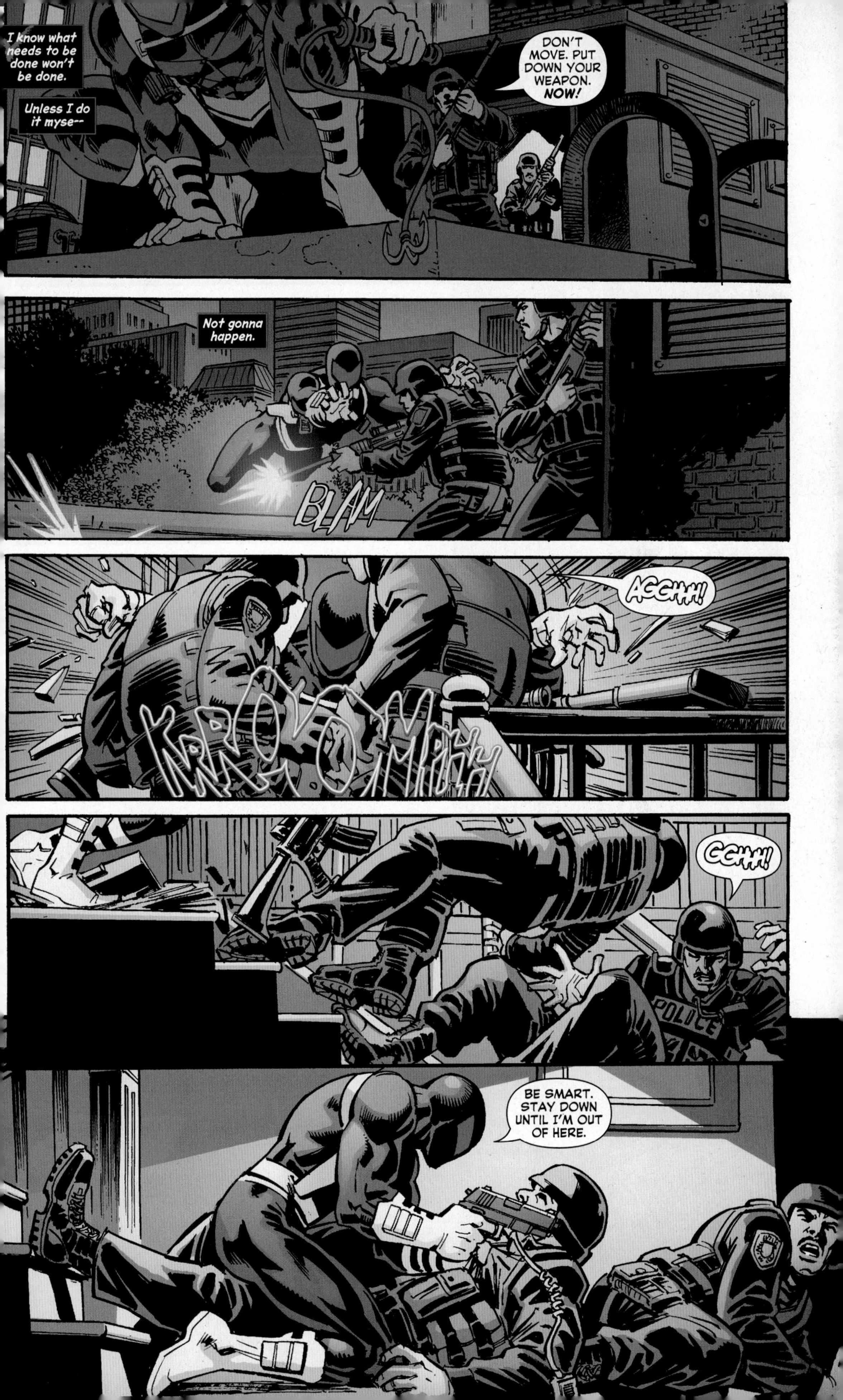
I know what needs to be done won't be done.
Unless I do it myse--
DON'T MOVE. PUT DOWN YOUR WEAPON. NOW!
Not gonna happen.
BLAM
AGGHH!
KRROOOM
GGHH!
POLICE
BE SMART. STAY DOWN UNTIL I'M OUT OF HERE.

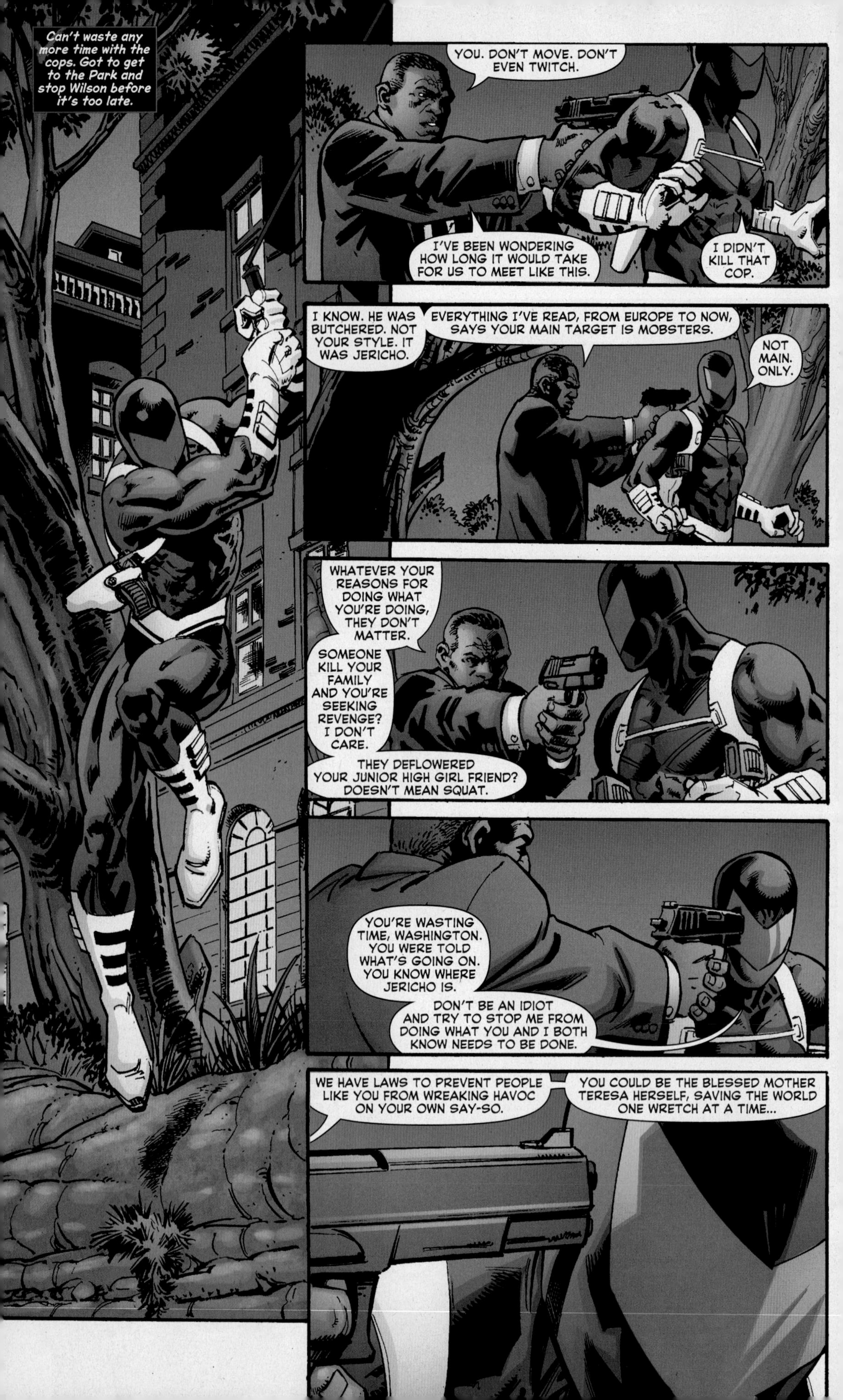
Can't waste any more time with the cops. Got to get to the Park and stop Wilson before it's too late.
YOU. DON'T MOVE. DON'T EVEN TWITCH.
I'VE BEEN WONDERING HOW LONG IT WOULD TAKE FOR US TO MEET LIKE THIS.
I DIDN'T KILL THAT COP.
I KNOW. HE WAS BUTCHERED. NOT YOUR STYLE. IT WAS JERICHO.
EVERYTHING I'VE READ, FROM EUROPE TO NOW, SAYS YOUR MAIN TARGET IS MOBSTERS.
NOT MAIN. ONLY.
WHATEVER YOUR REASONS FOR DOING WHAT YOU'RE DOING, THEY DON'T MATTER.
SOMEONE KILL YOUR FAMILY AND YOU'RE SEEKING REVENGE? I DON'T CARE.
THEY DEFLOWERED YOUR JUNIOR HIGH GIRL FRIEND? DOESN'T MEAN SQUAT.
YOU'RE WASTING TIME, WASHINGTON. YOU WERE TOLD WHAT'S GOING ON. YOU KNOW WHERE JERICHO IS.
DON'T BE AN IDIOT AND TRY TO STOP ME FROM DOING WHAT YOU AND I BOTH KNOW NEEDS TO BE DONE.
WE HAVE LAWS TO PREVENT PEOPLE LIKE YOU FROM WREAKING HAVOC ON YOUR OWN SAY-SO.
YOU COULD BE THE BLESSED MOTHER TERESA HERSELF, SAVING THE WORLD ONE WRETCH AT A TIME...

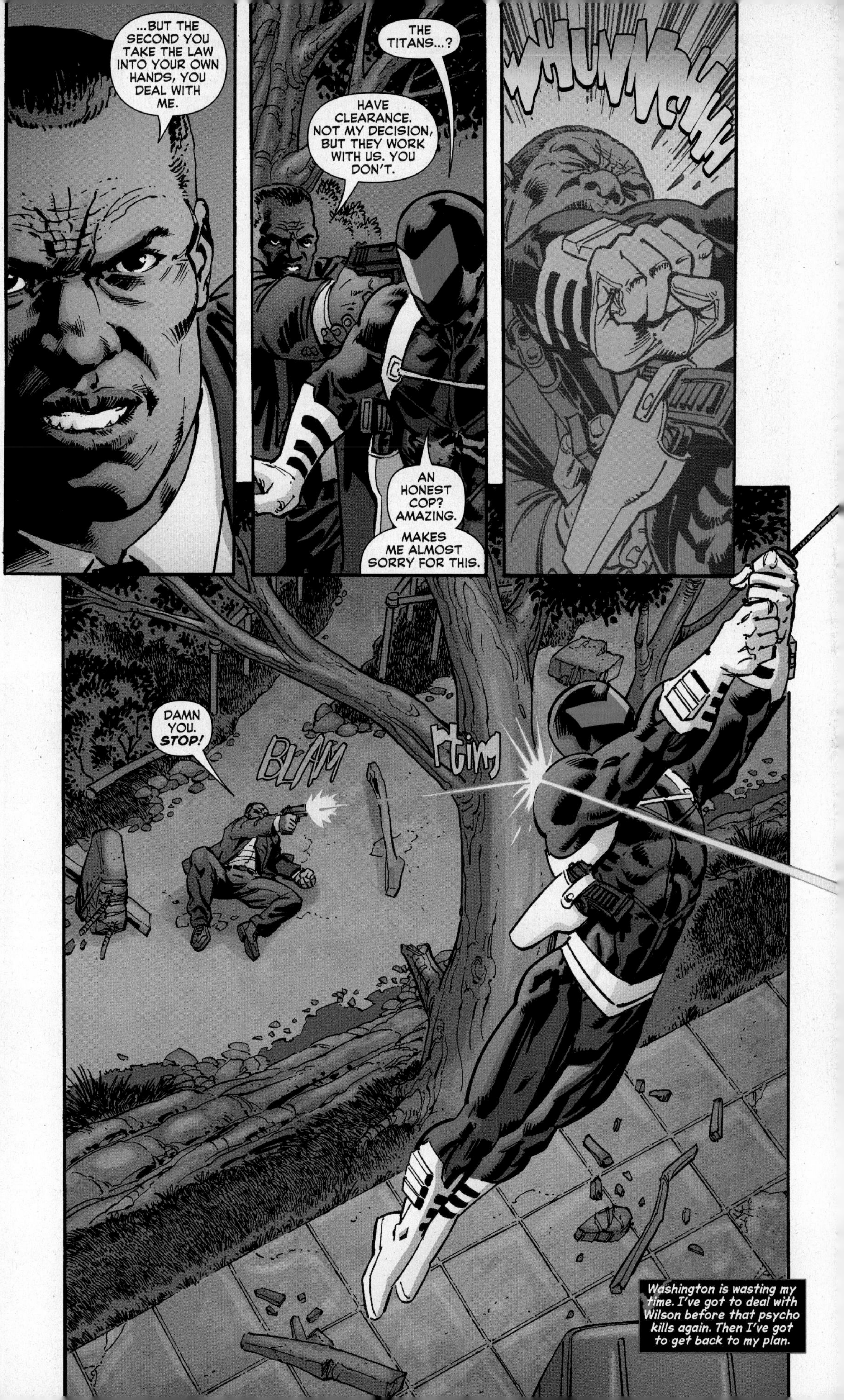
...BUT THE SECOND YOU TAKE THE LAW INTO YOUR OWN HANDS, YOU DEAL WITH ME.
THE TITANS...?
HAVE CLEARANCE. NOT MY DECISION, BUT THEY WORK WITH US. YOU DON'T.
AN HONEST COP? AMAZING.
MAKES ME ALMOST SORRY FOR THIS.
WHUNNCHH
DAMN YOU. STOP!
BLAM
ting
Washington is wasting my time. I've got to deal with Wilson before that psycho kills again. Then I've got to get back to my plan.

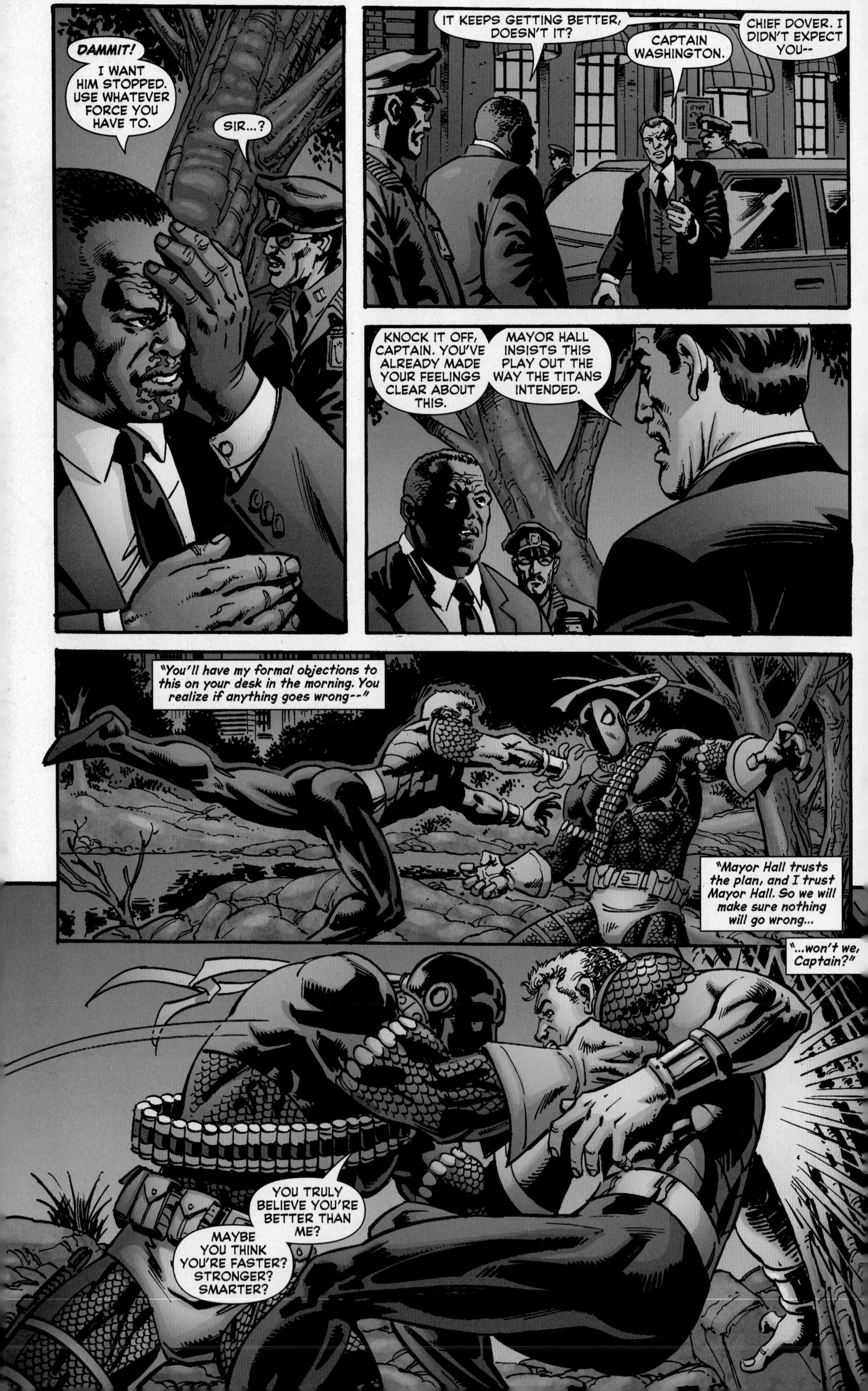
DAMMIT!
I WANT HIM STOPPED. USE WHATEVER FORCE YOU HAVE TO.
SIR...?
IT KEEPS GETTING BETTER, DOESN'T IT?
CAPTAIN WASHINGTON.
CHIEF DOVER. I DIDN'T EXPECT YOU--
KNOCK IT OFF, CAPTAIN. YOU'VE ALREADY MADE YOUR FEELINGS CLEAR ABOUT THIS.
MAYOR HALL INSISTS THIS PLAY OUT THE WAY THE TITANS INTENDED.
"You'll have my formal objections to this on your desk in the morning. You realize if anything goes wrong--"
"Mayor Hall trusts the plan, and I trust Mayor Hall. So we will make sure nothing will go wrong...
"...won't we, Captain?"
YOU TRULY BELIEVE YOU'RE BETTER THAN ME?
MAYBE YOU THINK YOU'RE FASTER? STRONGER? SMARTER?

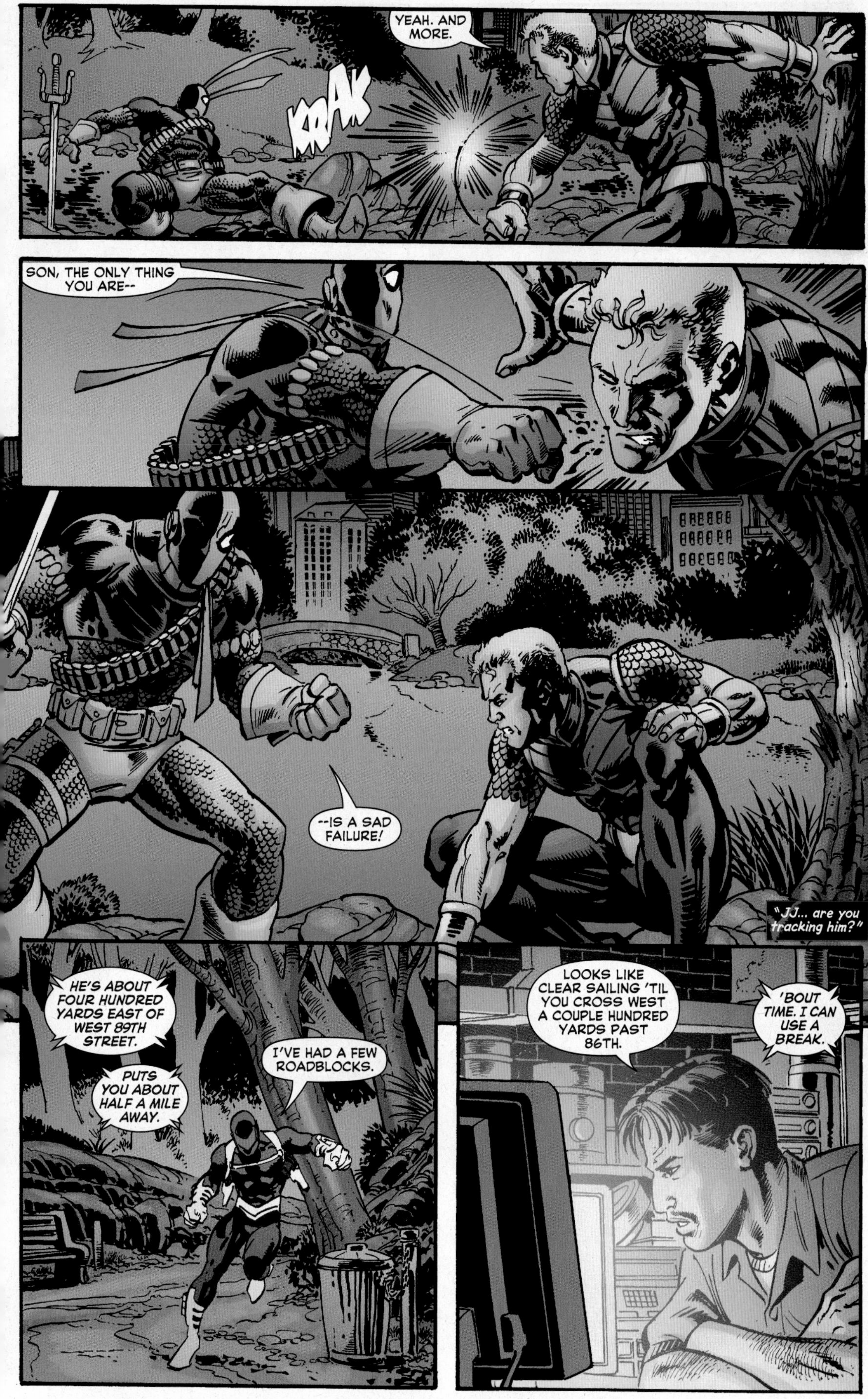
YEAH. AND MORE.
KRAK
SON, THE ONLY THING YOU ARE--
--IS A SAD FAILURE!
"JJ... are you tracking him?"
HE'S ABOUT FOUR HUNDRED YARDS EAST OF WEST 89TH STREET.
PUTS YOU ABOUT HALF A MILE AWAY.
I'VE HAD A FEW ROADBLOCKS.
LOOKS LIKE CLEAR SAILING 'TIL YOU CROSS WEST A COUPLE HUNDRED YARDS PAST 86TH.
'BOUT TIME. I CAN USE A BREAK.

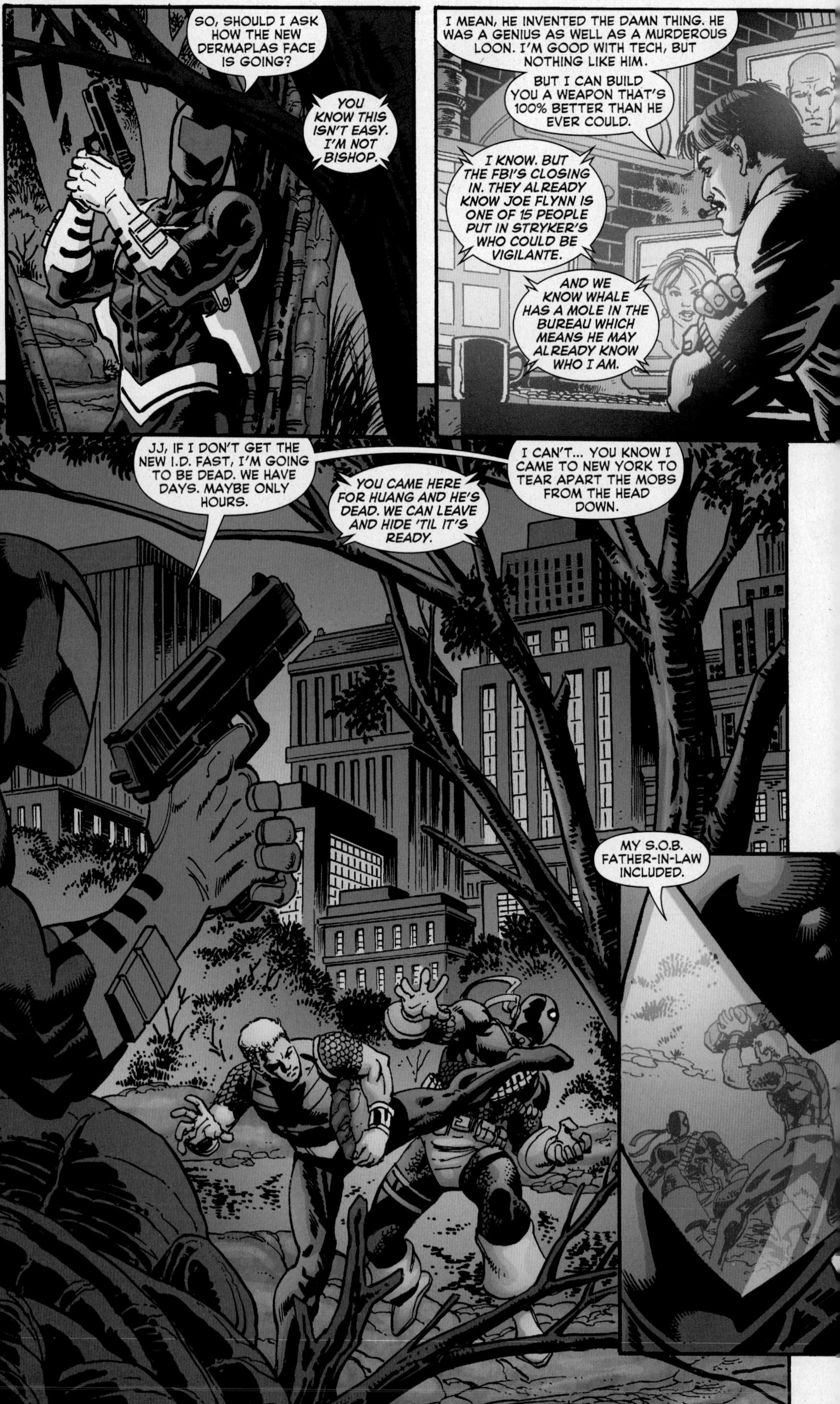
SO, SHOULD I ASK HOW THE NEW DERMAPLAS FACE IS GOING?
YOU KNOW THIS ISN'T EASY. I'M NOT BISHOP.
I MEAN, HE INVENTED THE DAMN THING. HE WAS A GENIUS AS WELL AS A MURDEROUS LOON. I'M GOOD WITH TECH, BUT NOTHING LIKE HIM.
BUT I CAN BUILD YOU A WEAPON THAT'S 100% BETTER THAN HE EVER COULD.
I KNOW. BUT THE FBI'S CLOSING IN. THEY ALREADY KNOW JOE FLYNN IS ONE OF 15 PEOPLE PUT IN STRYKER'S WHO COULD BE VIGILANTE.
AND WE KNOW WHALE HAS A MOLE IN THE BUREAU WHICH MEANS HE MAY ALREADY KNOW WHO I AM.
JJ, IF I DON'T GET THE NEW I.D. FAST, I'M GOING TO BE DEAD. WE HAVE DAYS. MAYBE ONLY HOURS.
YOU CAME HERE FOR HUANG AND HE'S DEAD. WE CAN LEAVE AND HIDE 'TIL IT'S READY.
I CAN'T... YOU KNOW I CAME TO NEW YORK TO TEAR APART THE MOBS FROM THE HEAD DOWN.
MY S.O.B. FATHER-IN-LAW INCLUDED.

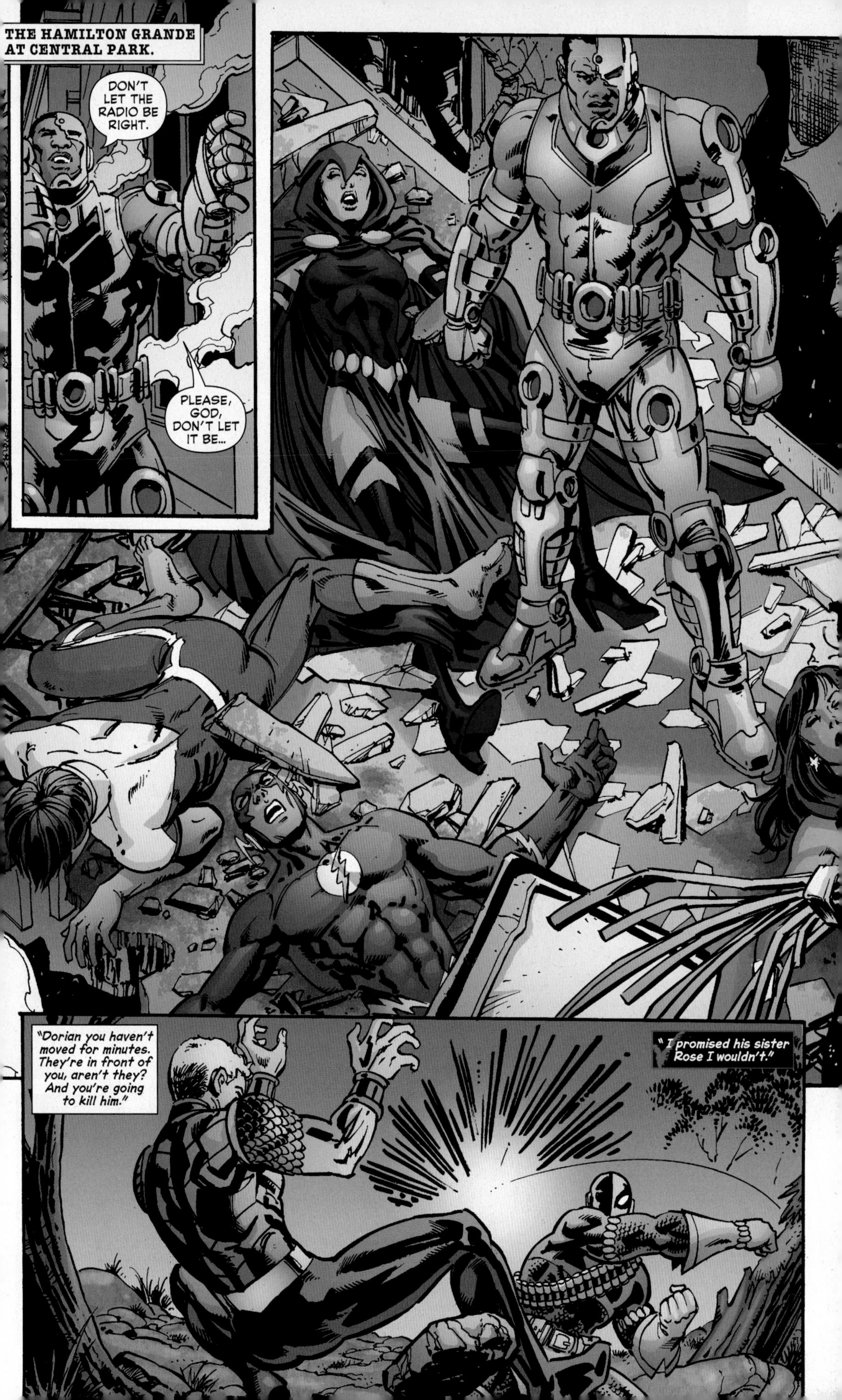
THE HAMILTON GRANDE AT CENTRAL PARK.
DON'T LET THE RADIO BE RIGHT.
PLEASE, GOD, DON'T LET IT BE...
"Dorian you haven't moved for minutes. They're in front of you, aren't they? And you're going to kill him."
"I promised his sister Rose I wouldn't."

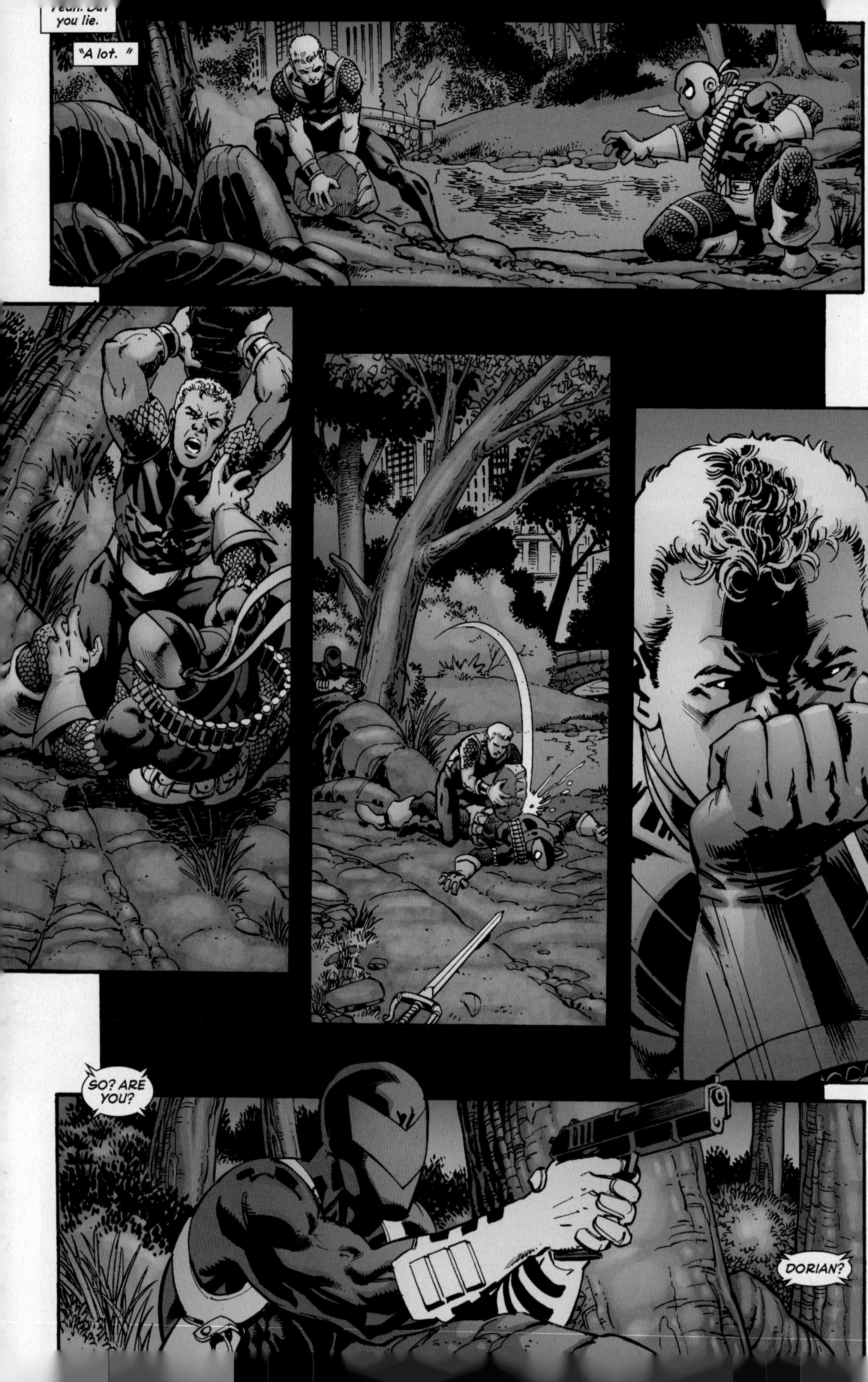

you lie.
"A lot."
SO? ARE YOU?
DORIAN?

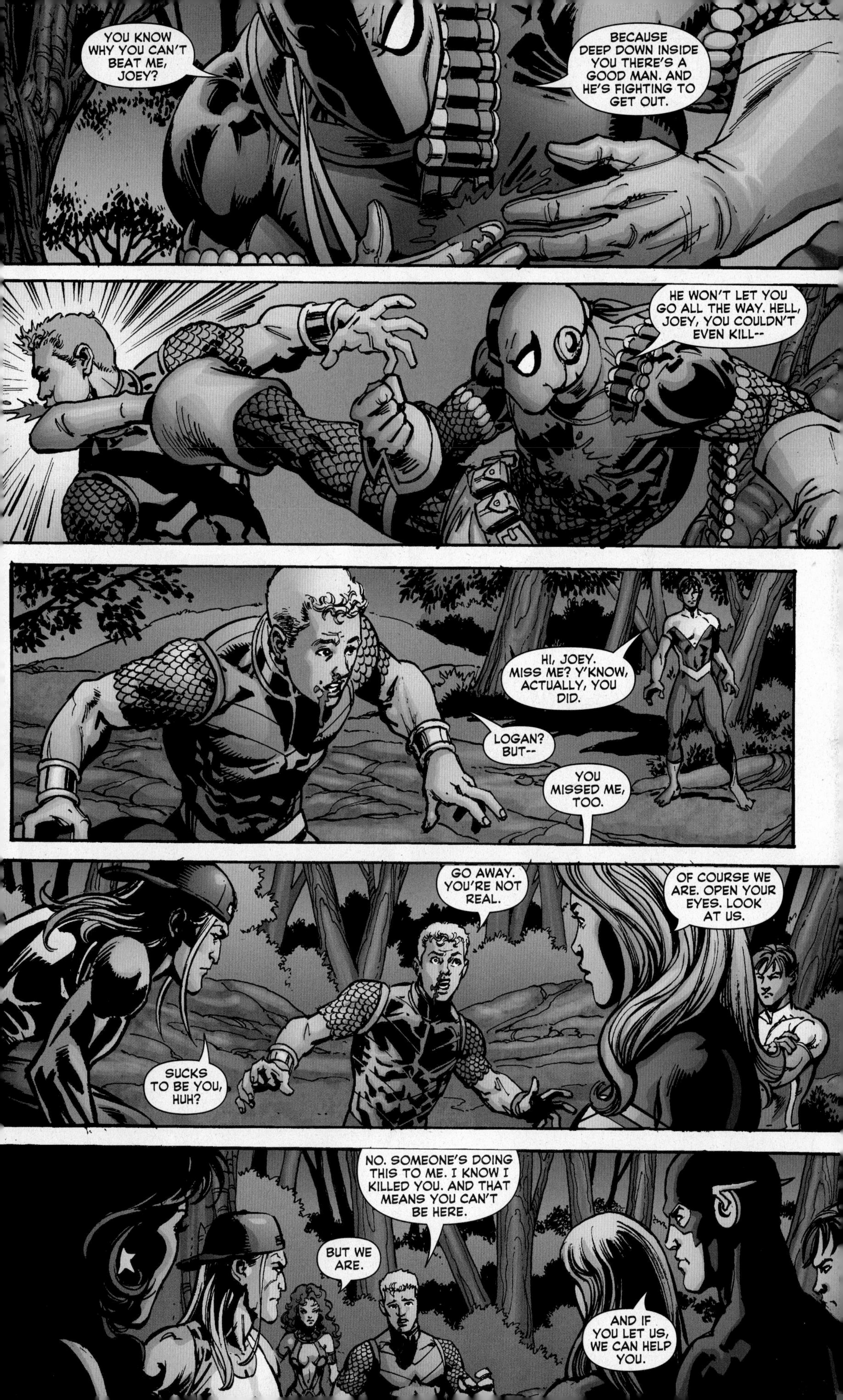
YOU KNOW WHY YOU CAN'T BEAT ME, JOEY?
BECAUSE DEEP DOWN INSIDE YOU THERE'S A GOOD MAN. AND HE'S FIGHTING TO GET OUT.
HE WON'T LET YOU GO ALL THE WAY. HELL, JOEY, YOU COULDN'T EVEN KILL--
HI, JOEY. MISS ME? Y'KNOW, ACTUALLY, YOU DID.
LOGAN? BUT--
YOU MISSED ME, TOO.
GO AWAY. YOU'RE NOT REAL.
OF COURSE WE ARE. OPEN YOUR EYES. LOOK AT US.
SUCKS TO BE YOU, HUH?
NO. SOMEONE'S DOING THIS TO ME. I KNOW I KILLED YOU. AND THAT MEANS YOU CAN'T BE HERE.
BUT WE ARE.
AND IF YOU LET US, WE CAN HELP YOU.

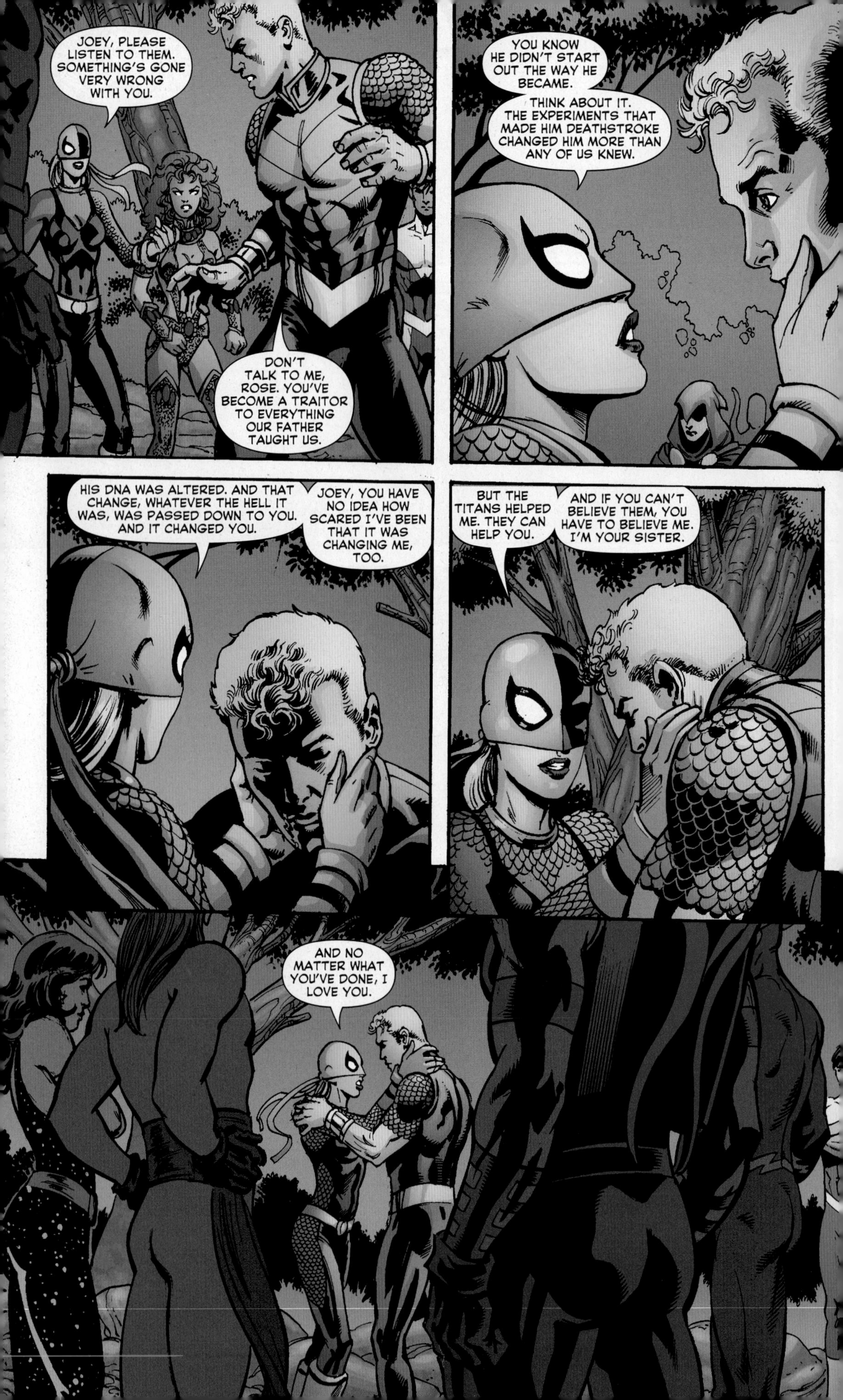
JOEY, PLEASE LISTEN TO THEM. SOMETHING'S GONE VERY WRONG WITH YOU.
DON'T TALK TO ME, ROSE. YOU'VE BECOME A TRAITOR TO EVERYTHING OUR FATHER TAUGHT US.
YOU KNOW HE DIDN'T START OUT THE WAY HE BECAME.
THINK ABOUT IT. THE EXPERIMENTS THAT MADE HIM DEATHSTROKE CHANGED HIM MORE THAN ANY OF US KNEW.
HIS DNA WAS ALTERED. AND THAT CHANGE, WHATEVER THE HELL IT WAS, WAS PASSED DOWN TO YOU. AND IT CHANGED YOU.
JOEY, YOU HAVE NO IDEA HOW SCARED I'VE BEEN THAT IT WAS CHANGING ME, TOO.
BUT THE TITANS HELPED ME. THEY CAN HELP YOU.
AND IF YOU CAN'T BELIEVE THEM, YOU HAVE TO BELIEVE ME. I'M YOUR SISTER.
AND NO MATTER WHAT YOU'VE DONE, I LOVE YOU.

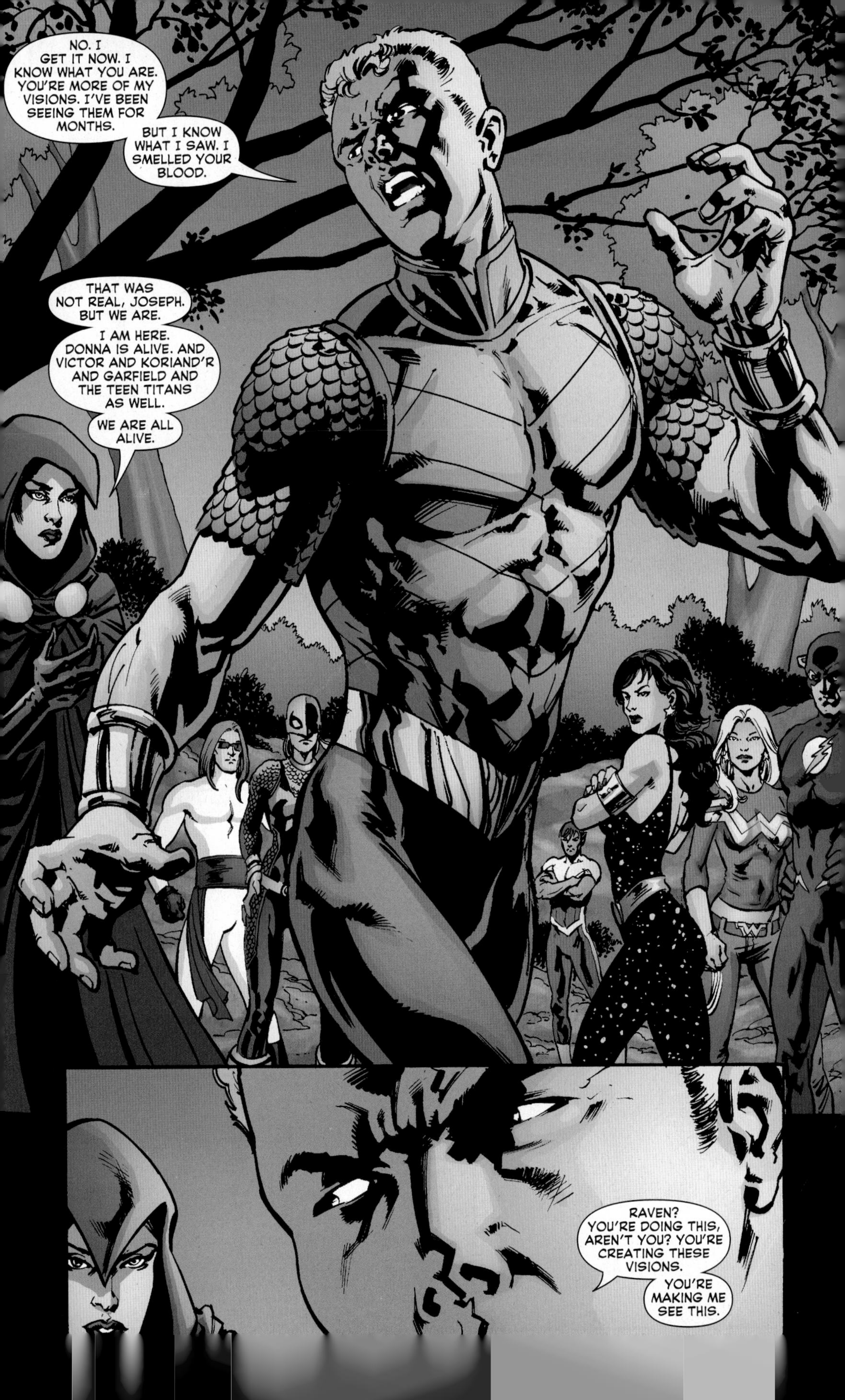
NO. I GET IT NOW. I KNOW WHAT YOU ARE. YOU'RE MORE OF MY VISIONS. I'VE BEEN SEEING THEM FOR MONTHS.
BUT I KNOW WHAT I SAW. I SMELLED YOUR BLOOD.
THAT WAS NOT REAL, JOSEPH. BUT WE ARE.
I AM HERE. DONNA IS ALIVE. AND VICTOR AND KORIAND'R AND GARFIELD AND THE TEEN TITANS AS WELL.
WE ARE ALL ALIVE.
RAVEN? YOU'RE DOING THIS, AREN'T YOU? YOU'RE CREATING THESE VISIONS.
YOU'RE MAKING ME SEE THIS.

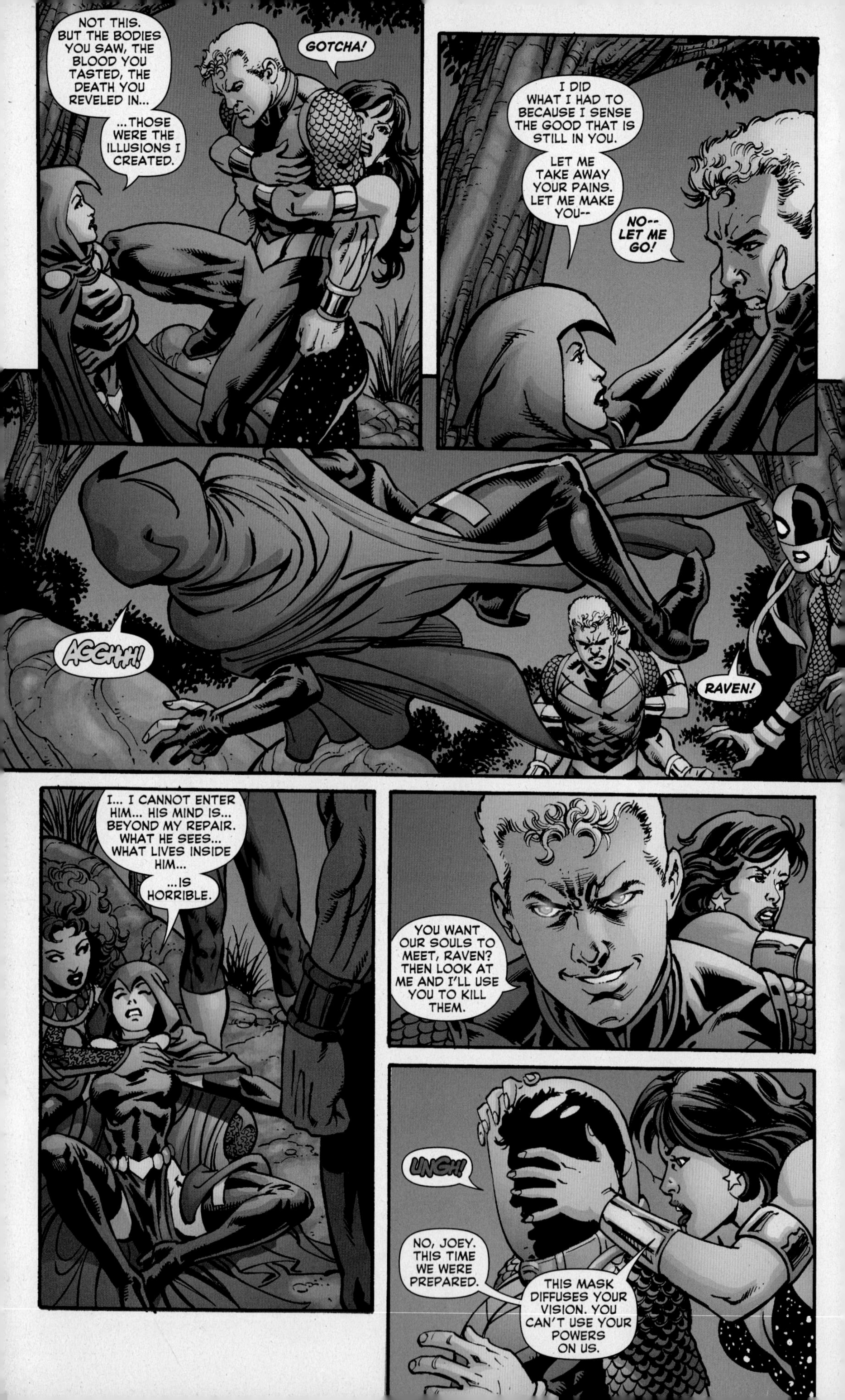
NOT THIS. BUT THE BODIES YOU SAW, THE BLOOD YOU TASTED, THE DEATH YOU REVELED IN...
...THOSE WERE THE ILLUSIONS I CREATED.
GOTCHA!
I DID WHAT I HAD TO BECAUSE I SENSE THE GOOD THAT IS STILL IN YOU.
LET ME TAKE AWAY YOUR PAINS. LET ME MAKE YOU--
NO-- LET ME GO!
AGGHH!
RAVEN!
I... I CANNOT ENTER HIM... HIS MIND IS... BEYOND MY REPAIR. WHAT HE SEES... WHAT LIVES INSIDE HIM...
...IS HORRIBLE.
YOU WANT OUR SOULS TO MEET, RAVEN? THEN LOOK AT ME AND I'LL USE YOU TO KILL THEM.
UNGH!
NO, JOEY. THIS TIME WE WERE PREPARED.
THIS MASK DIFFUSES YOUR VISION. YOU CAN'T USE YOUR POWERS ON US.

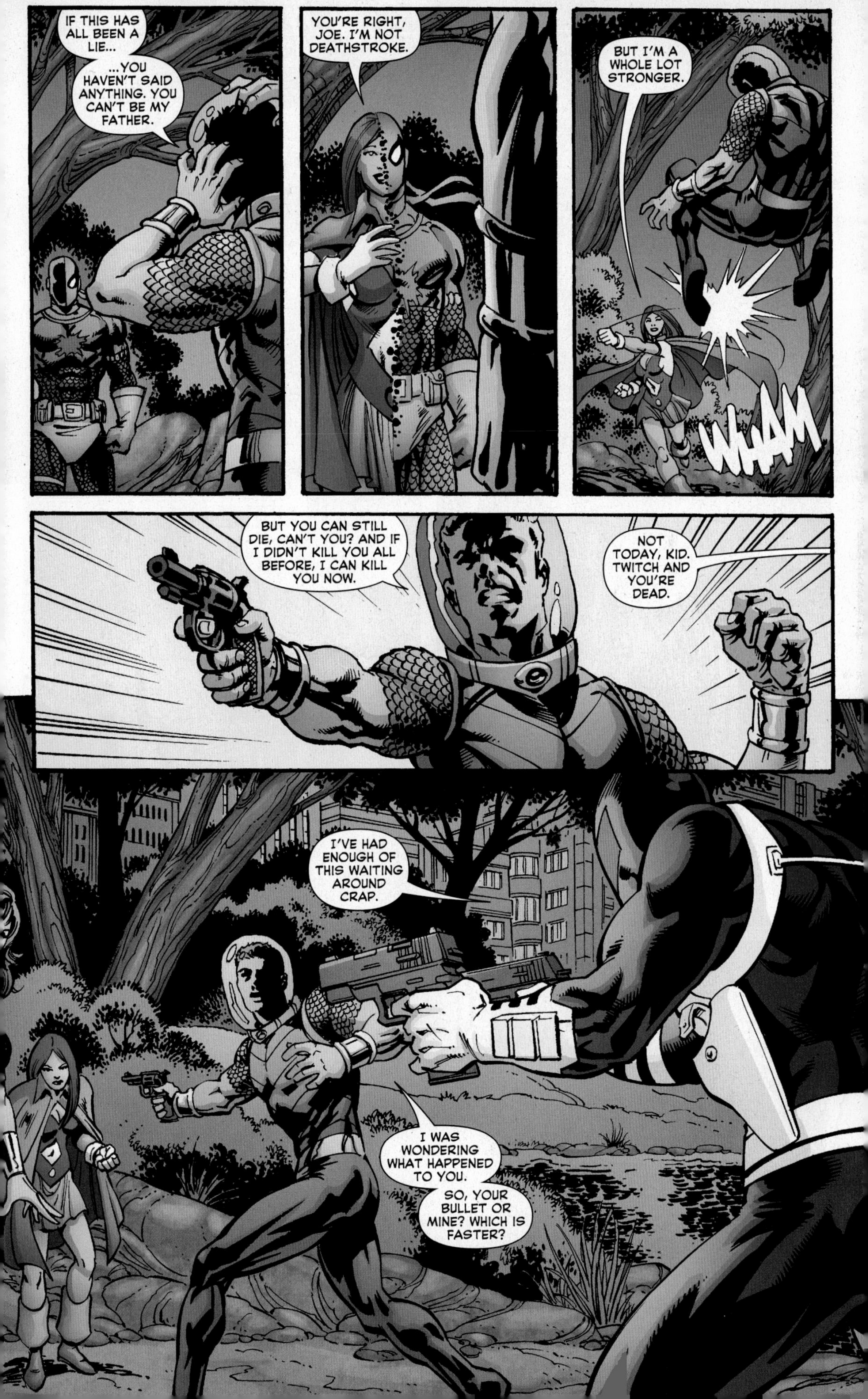
IF THIS HAS ALL BEEN A LIE...
...YOU HAVEN'T SAID ANYTHING. YOU CAN'T BE MY FATHER.
YOU'RE RIGHT, JOE. I'M NOT DEATHSTROKE.
BUT I'M A WHOLE LOT STRONGER.
WHAM
BUT YOU CAN STILL DIE, CAN'T YOU? AND IF I DIDN'T KILL YOU ALL BEFORE, I CAN KILL YOU NOW.
NOT TODAY, KID. TWITCH AND YOU'RE DEAD.
I'VE HAD ENOUGH OF THIS WAITING AROUND CRAP.
I WAS WONDERING WHAT HAPPENED TO YOU.
SO, YOUR BULLET OR MINE? WHICH IS FASTER?

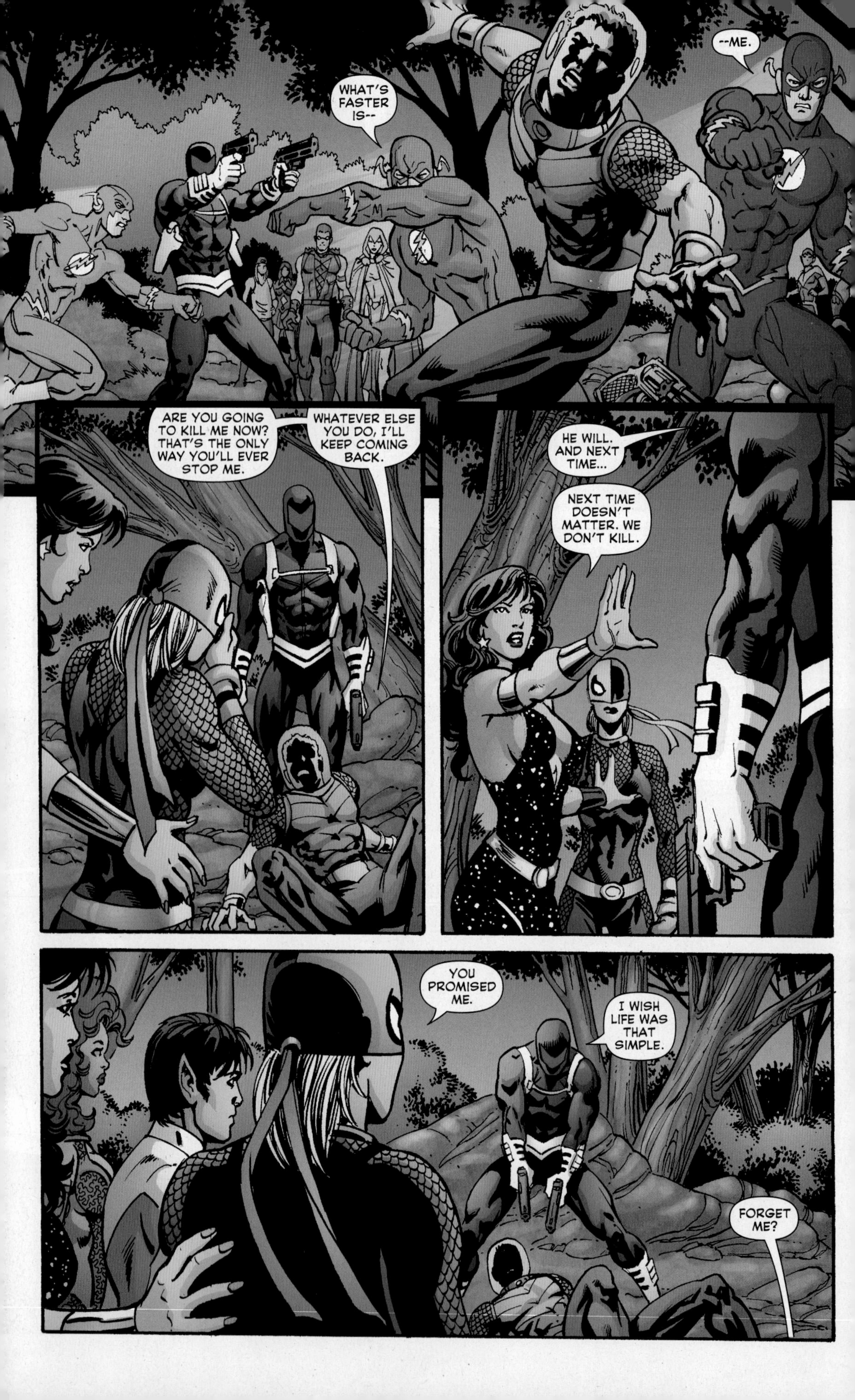
WHAT'S FASTER IS--
--ME.
ARE YOU GOING TO KILL ME NOW? THAT'S THE ONLY WAY YOU'LL EVER STOP ME.
WHATEVER ELSE YOU DO, I'LL KEEP COMING BACK.
HE WILL. AND NEXT TIME...
NEXT TIME DOESN'T MATTER. WE DON'T KILL.
YOU PROMISED ME.
I WISH LIFE WAS THAT SIMPLE.
FORGET ME?

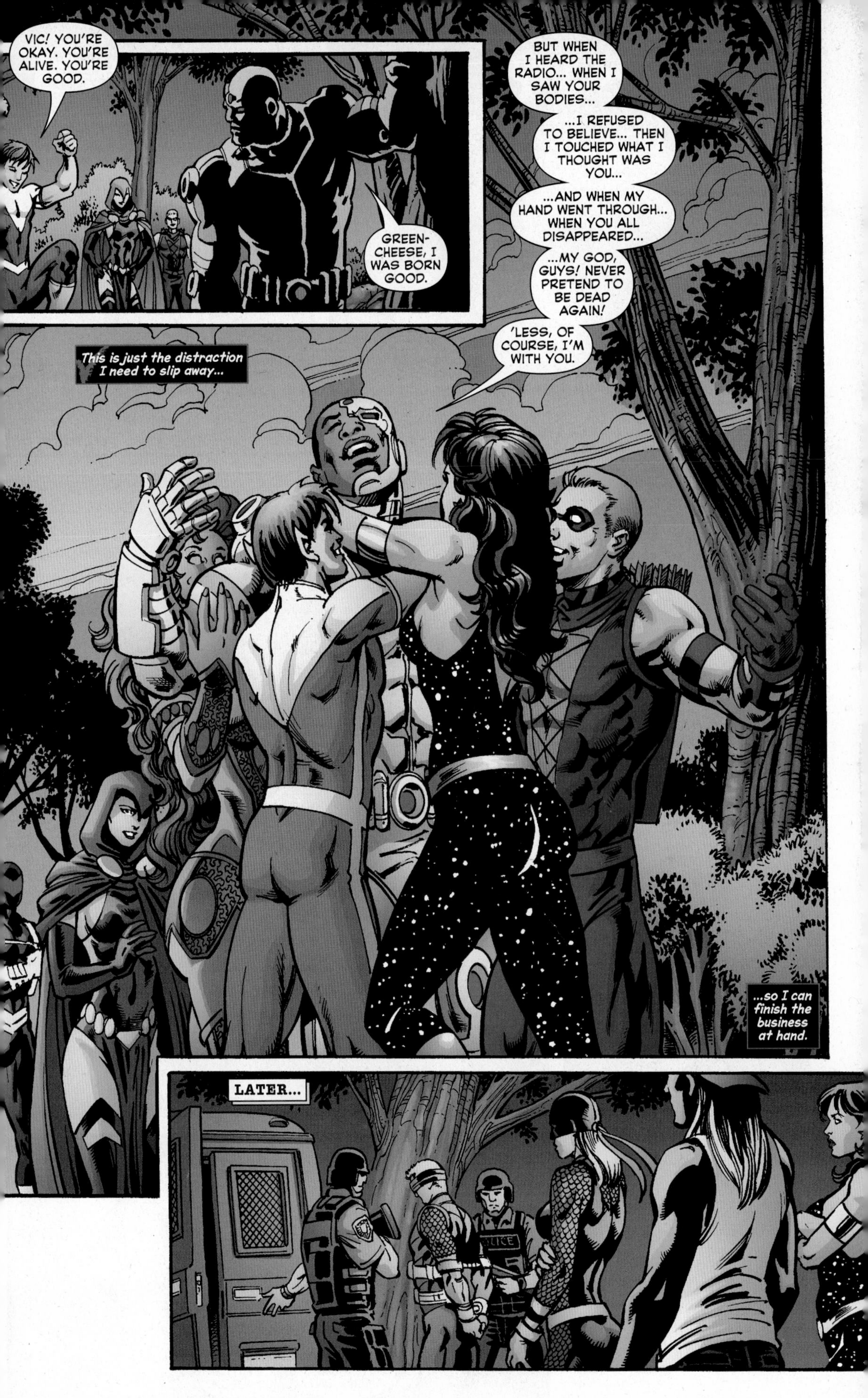

VIC! YOU'RE OKAY. YOU'RE ALIVE. YOU'RE GOOD.
GREEN-CHEESE, I WAS BORN GOOD.
BUT WHEN I HEARD THE RADIO... WHEN I SAW YOUR BODIES...
...I REFUSED TO BELIEVE... THEN I TOUCHED WHAT I THOUGHT WAS YOU...
...AND WHEN MY HAND WENT THROUGH... WHEN YOU ALL DISAPPEARED...
...MY GOD, GUYS! NEVER PRETEND TO BE DEAD AGAIN!
'LESS, OF COURSE, I'M WITH YOU.
This is just the distraction I need to slip away...
...so I can finish the business at hand.
LATER...

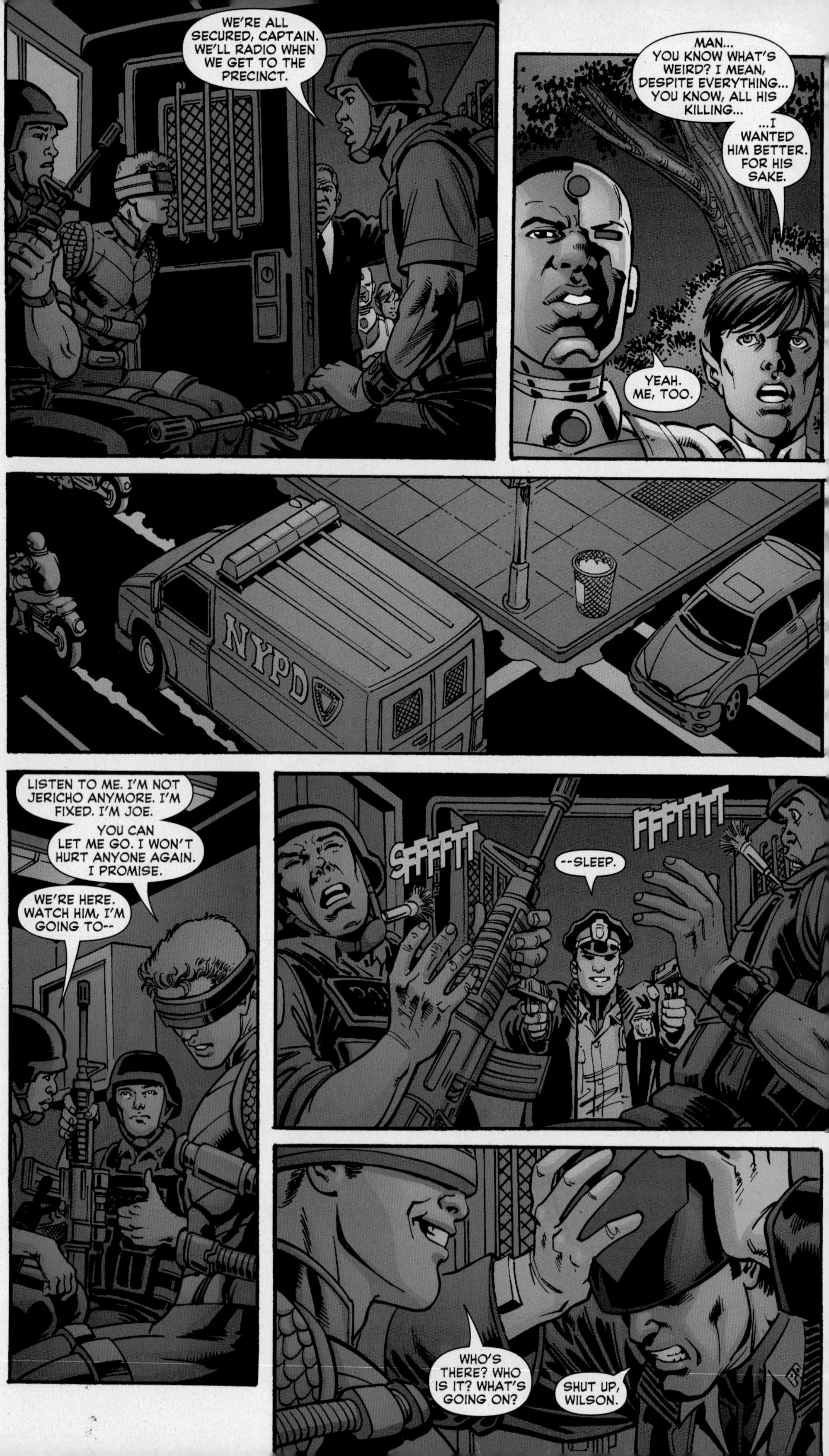

WE'RE ALL SECURED, CAPTAIN. WE'LL RADIO WHEN WE GET TO THE PRECINCT.
MAN... YOU KNOW WHAT'S WEIRD? I MEAN, DESPITE EVERYTHING... YOU KNOW, ALL HIS KILLING...
...I WANTED HIM BETTER. FOR HIS SAKE.
YEAH. ME, TOO.
NYPD
LISTEN TO ME. I'M NOT JERICHO ANYMORE. I'M FIXED. I'M JOE.
YOU CAN LET ME GO. I WON'T HURT ANYONE AGAIN. I PROMISE.
WE'RE HERE. WATCH HIM, I'M GOING TO--
SFFFTT
FFFTTTT
--SLEEP.
WHO'S THERE? WHO IS IT? WHAT'S GOING ON?
SHUT UP, WILSON.

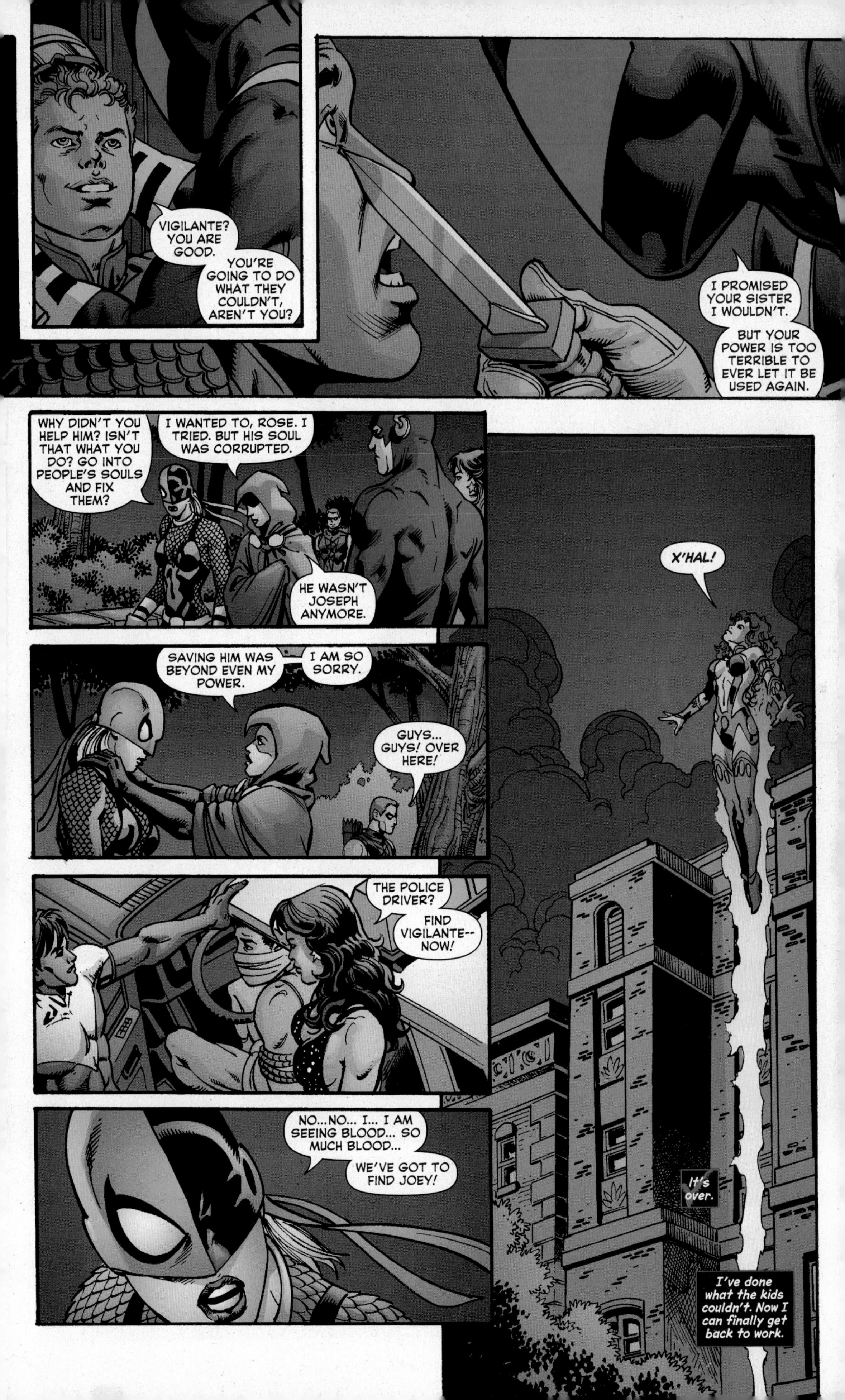
VIGILANTE? YOU ARE GOOD.
YOU'RE GOING TO DO WHAT THEY COULDN'T, AREN'T YOU?
I PROMISED YOUR SISTER I WOULDN'T.
BUT YOUR POWER IS TOO TERRIBLE TO EVER LET IT BE USED AGAIN.
WHY DIDN'T YOU HELP HIM? ISN'T THAT WHAT YOU DO? GO INTO PEOPLE'S SOULS AND FIX THEM?
I WANTED TO, ROSE. I TRIED. BUT HIS SOUL WAS CORRUPTED.
HE WASN'T JOSEPH ANYMORE.
SAVING HIM WAS BEYOND EVEN MY POWER.
I AM SO SORRY.
GUYS... GUYS! OVER HERE!
THE POLICE DRIVER?
FIND VIGILANTE-- NOW!
NO...NO... I... I AM SEEING BLOOD... SO MUCH BLOOD...
WE'VE GOT TO FIND JOEY!
X'HAL!
It's over.
I've done what the kids couldn't. Now I can finally get back to work.

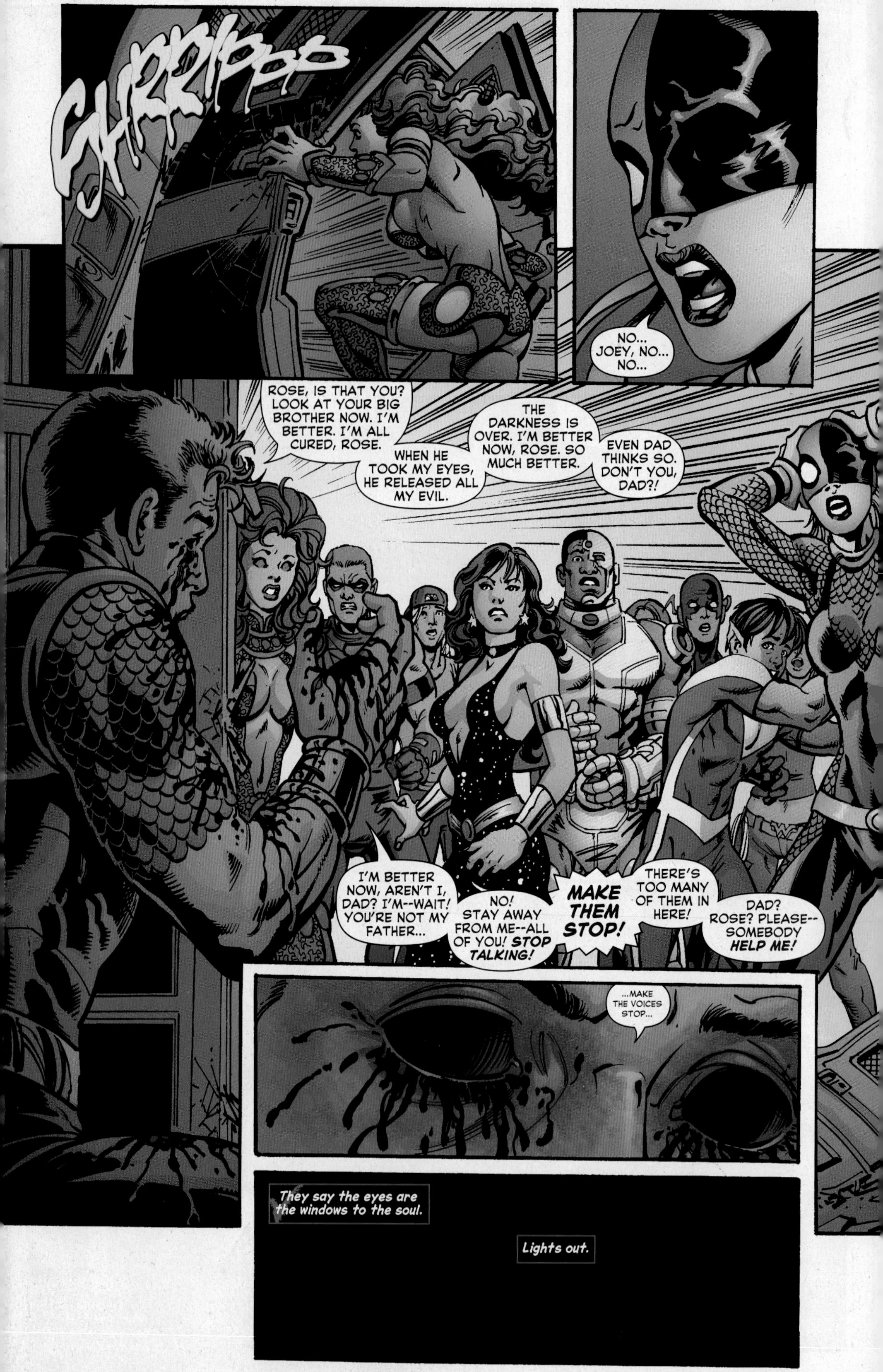
SHRRIPPP
NO... JOEY, NO... NO...
ROSE, IS THAT YOU? LOOK AT YOUR BIG BROTHER NOW. I'M BETTER. I'M ALL CURED, ROSE.
WHEN HE TOOK MY EYES, HE RELEASED ALL MY EVIL.
THE DARKNESS IS OVER. I'M BETTER NOW, ROSE. SO MUCH BETTER.
EVEN DAD THINKS SO. DON'T YOU, DAD?!
I'M BETTER NOW, AREN'T I, DAD? I'M--WAIT! YOU'RE NOT MY FATHER...
NO! STAY AWAY FROM ME--ALL OF YOU! STOP TALKING!
MAKE THEM STOP!
THERE'S TOO MANY OF THEM IN HERE!
DAD? ROSE? PLEASE--SOMEBODY HELP ME!
...MAKE THE VOICES STOP...
They say the eyes are the windows to the soul.
Lights out.

FROM THE WRITER OF
GREEN LANTERN *AND* JSA

GEOFF JOHNS

Witness the gathering of a new team of Teen Titans and their initial battle against an old, familiar foe: the most lethal mercenary on earth, Deathstroke!

with MIKE McKONE

VOL. 1: A KID'S GAME

VOL. 2: FAMILY LOST

VOL. 3: BEAST BOYS AND GIRLS

VOL. 4: THE FUTURE IS NOW

VOL. 5: LIFE AND DEATH

VOL. 6: TITANS AROUND THE WORLD

TEEN TITANS / OUTSIDERS: THE INSIDERS

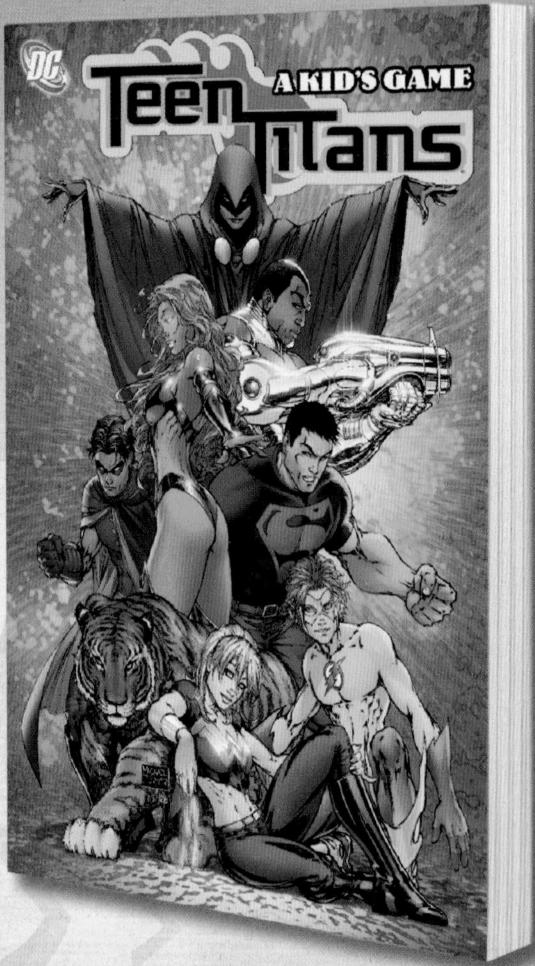
DC
A KID'S GAME
Teen Titans

TEEN TITANS VOL. 2:
FAMILY LOST

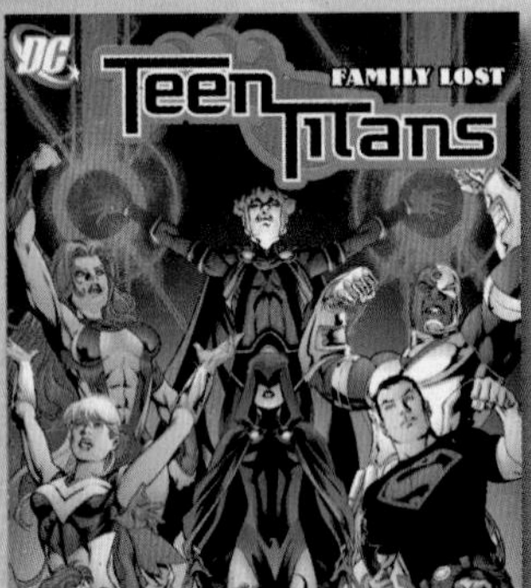
DC
FAMILY LOST
Teen Titans

with
MIKE McKONE

TEEN TITANS VOL. 4:
THE FUTURE IS NOW

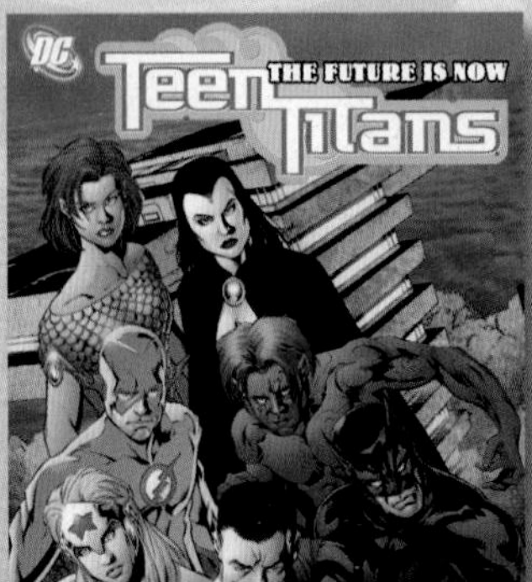
DC
THE FUTURE IS NOW
Teen Titans

with
MIKE McKONE

TEEN TITANS VOL. 5
LIFE AND DEATH

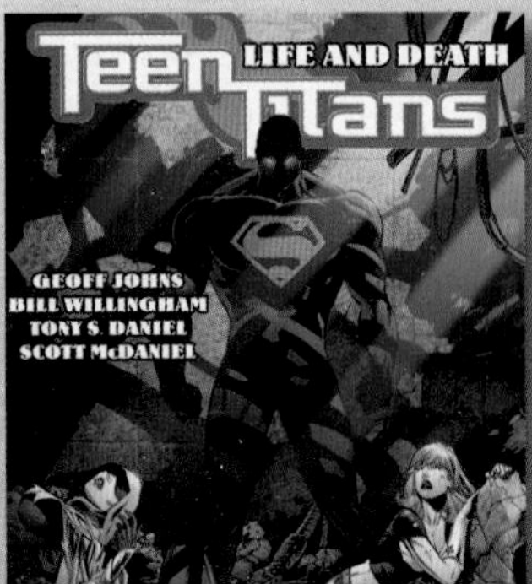
Teen Titans
LIFE AND DEATH
GEOFF JOHNS
BILL WILLINGHAM
TONY S. DANIEL
SCOTT McDANIEL
DC

with
VARIOUS ARTISTS

SEARCH THE GRAPHIC NOVELS SECTION OF
DCCOMICS.COM
FOR ART AND INFORMATION ON ALL OF OUR BOOKS!

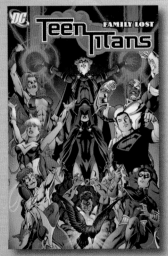

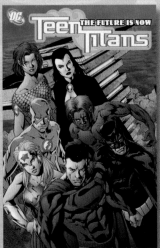

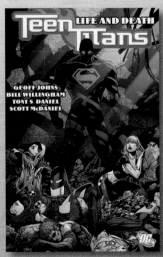